PUBLICATIONS OF THE UNIVERSITY OF MANCHESTER
No. CCLII

HISTORICAL SERIES, No. XXI

# THE PLACE OF THE REIGN OF EDWARD II IN ENGLISH HISTORY

# THE PLACE OF THE REIGN OF EDWARD II IN ENGLISH HISTORY

BASED UPON THE FORD LECTURES DELIVERED IN THE UNIVERSITY OF OXFORD IN 1913

BY

T. F. TOUT, M.A., F.B.A.

*Bishop Fraser Professor of Mediæval and Ecclesiastical History in the University of Manchester*

SECOND EDITION, REVISED THROUGHOUT

BY

HILDA JOHNSTONE, M.A.

*Professor of History in the University of London*

GREENWOOD PRESS, PUBLISHERS
WESTPORT, CONNECTICUT

**Library of Congress Cataloging in Publication Data**

Tout, Thomas Frederick, 1855-1929.
The place of the reign of Edward II in English history.

Reprint of the 1936 ed. published by the University Press, Manchester, which was issued as no. 21 of Historical series and no. 252 of Publications of the University of Manchester.
Bibliography: p.
Includes index.
1. Great Britain--Politics and government--1307-1327. 2. Edward II, King of England, 1284-1327. I. Johnstone, Hilda, 1882-1961. II. Title. III. Series: Victoria University of Manchester. Publications : Historical series ; no. 21. IV. Series : Victoria University of Manchester. Publications ; no. 252.
JN337.T68 1976 942.03'6 76-40284
ISBN 0-8371-9046-0



This edition originally published in 1936 by Manchester University Press

Reprinted with the permission of Manchester University Press

Reprinted in 1976 by Greenwood Press, Inc.

Library of Congress Catalog Card Number 76-40284

ISBN 0-8371-9046-0

Printed in the United States of America

# PREFACE TO THE FIRST EDITION

This book is an expansion and re-arrangement of the Ford Lectures, delivered by me at Oxford in the Hilary term, 1913. It differs, however, considerably from the text of the lectures. This is largely because of my conviction that there is an essential diversity of aim and method between oral discourses and a printed book, which should compel in all cases a certain readjustment of treatment and focus, when the former are made the basis of the latter. I have not indeed scrupled to retain conversational turns of phrase, and other features which suggest the spoken rather than the written word. But in revising the course for the press I have thought it desirable to enter into much greater detail than was possible, or expedient, in a short course of lectures, and to add a large number of notes and two long appendices, which necessarily could not, even in rough outline, be put before the most long-suffering of academic audiences. In both the lectures and the book, a general familiarity has been assumed with the ordinary political and constitutional history of the reign. There has been no need to relate once more a narrative which has been often told already. The last two chapters of the book are essentially an addition, being a free expansion of two or three paragraphs only of the last lecture. In these chapters, notably as regards the dealings of Clement V with Gascony and the whole genesis of the compulsory staple system, the story has been related at some length, because, so far as I know, it has never before been told. Generally however, I have aimed, not so much at narrative, as the setting forth of a special point of view. I give details only when they seem to be directly illustrative of that point of view. This will explain a certain arbitrariness in some of the topics selected for fuller illustration, and the varying scale on which they have been treated.

When asked to deliver the Ford Lectures last year, I was absorbed in a study that has seldom been far away from my thoughts since 1909, though the end of it unfortunately seems hardly in sight. I have been attempting to investigate the extent to which the English king's court and household remained a chief centre of national administration and finance, even after the development of the constitution had brought about the beginnings of the parliamentary system and the consequential separation from the court of the two great administrative departments of state, the exchequer and the chancery, which by that process were tending to become to a considerable extent amenable to aristocratic, if not to parliamentary, control. Under these circumstances, the survival of the quasi-autocratic position of the monarchy in most regions of administration, and even to some extent in finance, seemed to me to require explanation. Accordingly I strove to find that explanation by examining, in such detail as the sources allowed, the history of those branches of the household most concerned in the general work of governing the nation, namely the king's wardrobe and the king's chamber. Closely associated with these was the history of the various "small seals," such as the "privy seal," the "secret seal," the "signet," which were the instruments of these two organs of domestic administration. Their significance had first been suggested to me by M. Déprez's stimulating and interesting introduction to the diplomatic of the small seals.[1] Pursuing these subjects as far as the Revolution

[1] Eugène Déprez, *Etudes de Diplomatique anglaise, 1272–1485. Le sceau privé ; le sceau secret ; le signet.* Paris, 1908. My views on this book have been expressed in *English Historical Review,* xxiii, 556–559. I may take this opportunity of saying that I have now convinced myself that there were "rolls of privy seals," as M. Déprez suggested ; but they were of course not "chancery enrolments," but made in the privy seal

of 1399, I was impressed with the exceptional importance of the reign of Edward II in the history of administrative development in England, and notably as the point in which the marked differentiation of what may roughly be called "court administration" and "national administration," first became accentuated. It seemed to me that this short and turbulent period was the turning-point of the whole process. It was natural, then, when I put aside for a time my chief task, in order to fulfil the pleasant duty which my old University had imposed upon me, that I should willingly embrace the opportunity of studying, alongside with the administrative history of Edward II, such other aspects of his reign as would enable me to ascertain whether my doctrine of a turning-point might not be extended from the administrative to the general history of the period. Fuller investigation has convinced me that this can safely be done. I should add that the material collected for the purpose of the larger book allowed me to anticipate in outline its conclusions when speaking of administrative history. A further amplification and justification of these views will, I trust, in due course appear in the forthcoming work.[1]

How far I have succeeded in establishing my theory of the turning-point, my readers will judge better than I can. I have not, however, gone over the whole vast field with such minuteness as to be in a position to offer more than studies of an avowedly provisional character. I shall be satisfied if I suggest a standpoint which future workers may examine and criticise. When the detailed series of monographs, which, I hope, will soon be devoted to this reign, have seen the light, I shall be equally content, whether further investigation confirms or rejects the very provisional theories I have ventured to put forth. But I sincerely trust that both the

office, and now, I fear, entirely lost. [Conclusive evidence for such enrolment is given by Maxwell-Lyte, *The Great Seal*, p. 26. *Cf.* also Tout, *Chapters*, ii, 80, n. 2.]

[1] [*Chapters in Mediæval Administrative History*. 6 vols. Manchester University Press, 1920–33.]

book and the appendices will be found of some use to future workers on the period.

I have endeavoured to make my book more practical, by indicating, as I go along, what work is, to my knowledge, being done on the reign, and I am glad here to record that a not inconsiderable portion of that work is being undertaken by my colleagues and pupils. If the first results of some of this had not been before me, I should have found my task much harder than it has been. I have mentioned the names of some such workers, as occasion has arisen in the course of my discussions. If I do not set down here their names, or the names of others who have helped me, I am none the less grateful for their assistance and advice. I hope that by making this reign, for the next few years, the centre of the " seminar " studies of my pupils here, we shall some of us have opportunities of testing its soundness.

To many other friends I owe no small measure of thanks, and notably to numerous members of the staff of the Public Record Office, who have never grudged trouble in smoothing my path for me. Here I should wish to express a particular obligation to Mr. C. G. Crump, Mr. Charles Johnson and Mr. Hilary Jenkinson, all of the Public Record Office.

To sound a still more personal note in conclusion, I should like to say—after intimate association with the work of the Publications Committee of the University of Manchester during the ten years the Committee has existed,—how great a pleasure it is to me to issue this book with its imprint. In instituting this Committee in 1904, and providing it with a regular income, the Council of the University made a real contribution to the " endowment of research " in all faculties of the University, notably in the faculty of arts and not least in the department of history. If there is gradually growing up a " Manchester school of history," it is in no small measure due to the wise liberality that has made it possible for twenty-two volumes of an historical series to be printed for the University within the last ten years. Our publications are still in their infancy, and we have still much to learn. Two years ago, however, we had the good fortune to secure the services of Mr. H. M. McKechnie as our secretary. Every author who has published a volume under his auspices knows well the debt under which he lies to Mr. McKechnie's watchfulness and precision in all that relates to seeing his book through the press. But only the Chairman of the Publications Committee is in a position to see in its fulness the secretary's devotion and success, and he would feel that he was neglecting a duty if he omitted to express here his appreciation of Mr. McKechnie's work.

I am indebted for the index to my old pupil and present secretary, Miss Jennie M. Potter, B.A.

T. F. TOUT.

THE UNIVERSITY,
MANCHESTER, 25 *March* 1914.

# PREFACE TO THE SECOND EDITION

In preparing this new edition of my late brother-in-law's book I have been guided by two principles. One was to avoid any pedantic interference with the text, any smoothing away of small roughnesses or enforcement of rigid consistency, such as might destroy the imprint of the writer's personality, so vivid and conspicuous in the original work. The other was to try to put myself within the writer's mind, and in revision make only those additions or alterations which he would have made himself if he had lived. This latter was indeed a bold venture, but undertaken in all humility. I had to help me the notes and queries with which he had covered the margins and fly-leaves of his own copy of the book. I had in some cases his own re-statement of a problem in his *Chapters in Mediæval Administrative History*. Most precious of all, I had the guidance of a familiarity with his methods and opinions gained in an intimacy extending over thirty years, during thirteen of which I was working under his direct inspiration, first as pupil, then as colleague. This helped me to decide how far to incorporate conclusions reached by other workers in the same field since the book first appeared. In the vast majority of cases, he had gladly adjusted his views in the light of new information, and this has been made clear. Where he professed himself to be " quite impenitent " I have left well alone, and thus, for example, his references to " a full parliament of the three estates " remain untouched. I have not felt it to be my duty, either, to try to expand the two concluding chapters, which deal with foreign and imperial policy, the art of war, ecclesiastical, social and economic history. They were put in as an afterthought, made no profession of exhaustive treatment, and aimed merely at exciting interest in the problems involved and suggesting possible lines of research. It is unlikely that in a new edition he would himself have done more than call attention, as I have done, to the response already made to these suggestions. Other investigations in these fields are still in progress, and when completed will require more lengthy treatment than would have been possible here.

A few substantial variations in the text (*e.g.* p. 108, formerly p. 120) are, as it were, by the writer's own hand, since they are taken directly from his notes and as nearly as possible in his own words. All other alterations, whether in text, notes, or appendices, are indicated by square brackets. In these I have tried to bring both the matter and the bibliography up to date, summarising or referring to the work done since 1914 by Mr. Tout himself or by others. To Mr. J. Conway Davies' *Baronial Opposition to Edward II*, in particular, with its appendix of documents, we are indebted for much new material, of which Mr. Tout made use in the relevant section of *Chapters in Mediæval Administrative History*. All the references and quotations, from manuscript or printed sources, have of course been checked. As they number several hundred, it is not surprising that a good many errors and misprints had crept in, and the corrections now made will in some cases also be useful as *corrigenda* for *Chapters*. The details given on p. 318, n. 1, illustrate the sort of difficulties that may occur. The form of reference has been revised in accordance with certain accepted conventions, such as that which distinguishes by the use of roman or italic type between manuscript and printed material, and in the lists of officials the highly abbreviated original references have been expanded into a form easier to use. The citation of public records by their number, applied in the first edition to Issue and Receipt Rolls only, has here been extended to all public records, and in many cases a folio or membrane number has been added where none was given before. It is hoped that the cumulative effect of all these minor readjustments will be helpful to scholars.

The most obvious external contrast between the new edition and its forerunner lies in the arrangement of the lists of officials which fill the last sixty-seven pages. The compilation of these lists was a laborious and valuable part of the original work, and in later years many additions and corrections had accumulated. The way in which the lists were first set out, however, was wasteful of space, and in some cases, notably that of the chancellors and keepers of the great seal, was rather confusing. It seemed worth while, therefore, when revising the contents of the lists, to think out a new method of presentation. I can only hope that readers accustomed to using the lists in their original shape will not resent my intrusion.

The index remains based, as I feel sure Mr. Tout would have wished, upon the work of his former pupil, Miss J. M. Potter, B.A. There have been, however, considerable modifications and additions, and most of the longer entries have been broken up and classified.

When I was invited to prepare this edition by the Manchester University Press and its then Chairman, Professor Tait, to whom I owe so much as teacher and friend, I felt inclined to reply with the alternate deprecation and submission used by William of Newburgh when the Abbot of Rievaulx asked him to write a history of England: *Cum ex illo venerabili filiorum vestrorum collegio plures vobis suppetant, qui hoc opus commodius valeant atque elegantius adimplere, . . . vestrae circa me dignationi tanta sum devotione astrictus ut etiam si fortiora jubeatis non audeam contraire.* It has been a grateful task, and my consolation amid the inevitable imperfections of its performance is the knowledge that the writer himself would have been among the most lenient of my critics. I must thank both the Chairman and the Secretary of the

University Press for much patience, kindness and good advice; I acknowledge gratefully the response given by various friends and pupils of Mr. Tout's to enquiries made from them on special points; and I should like my last word to be one of gratitude to my research secretary, Miss L. M. Midgley, without whose skilful and sympathetic help the work would have been far slower in completion.

HILDA JOHNSTONE.

ROYAL HOLLOWAY COLLEGE,
UNIVERSITY OF LONDON,
*October*, 1936.

# CONTENTS



CHAPTER I



CHAPTER II



CHAPTER III

## Chapter IV



## Chapter V



## Chapter VI



## Chapter VII

## Appendix I



## Appendix II

# ABBREVIATIONS

### i. Manuscript Records

| | |
|---|---|
| A.C. | Ancient Correspondence. |
| Anct. Pet. | Ancient Petitions. |
| Ch. Plea Roll. | Chester Plea Roll. |
| Ch. Enr. | Chester Enrolments (formerly known as Recognizance Rolls). |
| Ch. R. | Charter Roll. |
| Chanc. Warr. | Chancery Warrants for the Great Seal. |
| E.A. | Exchequer, King's Remembrancer, Various Accounts. |
| Enr. Accts. (W. and H.). | Exchequer, Lord Treasurer's Remembrancer, Enrolled Accounts, Wardrobe and Household. |
| G.R. | Gascon Roll. |
| I.R. | Issue Roll. |
| K.R.M.R. | King's Remembrancer, Memoranda Roll. |
| L.T.R.M.R. | Lord Treasurer's Remembrancer, Memoranda Roll. |
| M.A. | Ministers' and Receivers' Accounts, General Series. |
| Misc. Bks. Exch. T.R. | Exchequer, Treasury of Receipt, Miscellaneous Books. |
| R.R. | Receipt Roll. |

### ii. Printed Works.

| | |
|---|---|
| *C.C.R.* | *Calendar of Close Rolls.* |
| *C.Ch.R.*, *C.Chart.R.* | *Calendar of Charter Rolls.* |
| *C.F.R.* | *Calendar of Fine Rolls.* |
| *C.P.R.* | *Calendar of Patent Rolls.* |
| *Cal. Doc. Scot.* | *Calendar of Documents relating to Scotland.* |
| *Cal. Inq.* | *Calendar of Inquisitions post mortem.* |
| *Chapters.* | Tout, *Chapters in Mediæval Administrative History.* |
| *Chron. Ser.* | Dugdale, *Origines Juridiciales, Chronica Series.* |
| Cole's *Records.* | Cole, *Documents illustrative of English History.* |

| | |
|---|---|
| Conway Davies. | Conway Davies, *Baronial Opposition to Edward II.* |
| Dunham. | Dunham, *Radulphi de Hengham Summae.* |
| Foss or Foss, *Biog. Jur.* | Foss, *Biographia Juridica.* |
| *Hist. Doc. Scot.* | Stevenson, *Documents illustrative of the History of Scotland.* |
| Jones. | Jones, *Flintshire Ministers' Accounts.* |
| *Letters of Edw.* | Johnstone, *Letters of Edward, Prince of Wales,* 1304–5. |
| *Lib. Quotid.* | *Liber Quotidianus Contrarotulatoris Garderobae* (1787). |
| Madox. | Madox, *History and Antiquities of the Exchequer of England* (2nd ed., 1769). |
| *Mun. Gild. Lond.* | *Munimenta Gildhallae Londoniensis.* |
| Ormerod. | Ormerod, *History of Cheshire.* |
| *R.G.* | Bémont, *Rôles Gascons.* |
| S.-Brown. | Stewart-Brown, *Cheshire Chamberlains' Accounts,* 1301–60. |
| *Triveti Ann. Cont.* | Hall, *Nicolai Triveti Annalium Continuatio* (1722). |
| Wilkinson. | Wilkinson, *The Chancery under Edward III.* |
| *Y.B.* | *Year Book.* |

## ADDENDUM ET CORRIGENDUM

p. 202, n. 2. *Add* [See Mackenzie, *The Bannockburn Myth* (Edinburgh, 1932) for counter-arguments supported as conclusive by the late Dr. J. E. Morris (*History*, xvii, 40-43)].

p. 283, l. 9 from bottom. *For* Thesaigne *read* Thefaigne.

# THE PLACE OF THE REIGN OF EDWARD II IN ENGLISH HISTORY

## I

## INTRODUCTORY

### (1) Authorities

I have followed the fashion in devoting my chief attention to record sources, none of which, old or new, printed or unprinted, can be regarded as having yielded up all its fruit to the harvester. I have found much that is illuminating, and something that has been disregarded, even in the ancient collections of printed documents, notably in Rymer's *Foedera*,[1] Palgrave's *Parliamentary Writs*,[2] in the Statute Book [3] and the *Rolls of Parliament*,[4] among which latter I must particularly emphasise the extremely valuable and little-known rolls of the parliaments of 1318 and 1319, printed more than sixty years ago by Cole.[5] I also spent much time on the numerous calendars of chancery rolls for which historians are indebted to a former deputy keeper of the records, Sir Henry Maxwell-Lyte. Of these the calendars of patent, close, fine and charter rolls are now complete for the reign, as is the almost equally valuable calendar of inquisitions *post mortem*.[6] From these indispensable calendars we obtain an insight into the methods and working of Edward II's chancery such as was denied to all our predecessors. Moreover, they afford a mass

[1] *Foedera*, vol. ii, pt. i (Record Com., 1818).

[2] *Parliamentary Writs*, vol. ii, pts. i, ii, iii (Record Com., 1830-34).

[3] *Statutes of the Realm*, i, 153-96 (1810).

[4] *Rotuli Parliamentorum*, i, 273-479 (after 1777) and Index (1832).

[5] Henry Cole, *Documents illustrative of English History selected from the Records of the Exchequer*, commonly quoted as Cole's *Records*, especially pp. 1-46 and 47-54 (Record Com., 1844).

[6] *Calendar of the Patent Rolls of Edward II*, 5 vols. (1894-1904); *Calendar of the Close Rolls of Edward II*, 4 vols. (1892-98); *Calendar of the Fine Rolls*, ii and iii (1912); *Calendar of the Charter Rolls*, iii, 107-757 (1908); *Calendar of Inquisitions post mortem*, vols. v and vi (1908, 1910). To these should be added *Calendar of Various Chancery Rolls, 1277-1326* (1912).

of detail, illustrating every aspect of early fourteenth-century history, which has up to now been very little used, but which will enable careful workers to study in detail nearly every branch of the history of the time. No doubt the calendars have their limitations. They have been exposed to much fair and to some unfair criticism, but they are of such enormous value to historical students that their blemishes are but as spots on the sun. Those who criticise the calendars most are those who use them most, and all workers on them who have any sense of proportion will lay little stress on the occasional short-comings of the bold pioneers whose labours have hewn a path, which all may follow, through the tangled underwoods of our ancient chancery records. It is, however, necessary to warn the student of the history of institutions and administration that, especially as regards the earlier published calendars, he can never feel sure that he has collected all the information that they contain until he has worked through the text for himself, since he cannot entirely rely upon the indexes in this relation. The one thing, however, about these publications which is hard to forgive, is the ill-judged parsimony which has printed many of the early volumes of the calendars upon paper of so poor a quality that many pages are already crumbling into yellow dust upon our bookshelves. [A valuable supplement to these chancery calendars is the calendar of all such warrants to chancery under the privy seal as have not left their trace in the enrolments of the chancery itself.] [1] We are still in need of a calendar of the Gascon Rolls, and of the other chancery series which especially illustrate the extra-English activities of the administration of Edward II. The *Rotuli Scotiae* of the Record Commission do something to supply one side of this deficiency,[2] as does the *Calendar of Documents concerning Scotland*, which covers all this reign.[3]

Not less important than the chancery records are the records of the exchequer, among which are also included documents of special importance for us, the remaining archives of the king's wardrobe and the king's chamber. These have no surviving records of their own, but they had to submit their accounts to the exchequer, and the care of exchequer officers has preserved so many of them that we can obtain

[1] [*Calendar of Chancery Warrants, 1244-1326* (1927).]

[2] *Rotuli Scotiae, 1291-1516*, i, 55-205 (Record Com., 1814).

[3] *Calendar of Documents relating to Scotland*, iii, 1-164 (1887).

from the records of the exchequer almost as much insight into the working of the wardrobe and the chamber as we can into the operation of the national treasury itself. Unluckily each student of the exchequer records has still to do his own pioneer work with his own axe, though there is good reason for believing that the authorities of the Public Record Office are now taking in hand the business of calendaring the chief exchequer series of enrolments.[1] Meanwhile, however, the exchequer records are so numerous and diversified, and so bewildering in their variety, that no single individual can hope to do more than sample them for himself. The scholar must here make a selection, and his selection will be determined partly by the probabilities of the particular series yielding him the information that he wants, and partly by the bulk of that series. For my part I must confess that I paid very slight attention to the pipe rolls, the oldest and most famous of exchequer records. This is not because the pipe rolls of the fourteenth century are of little value. I believe that the pipe rolls of the Edwards are quite as important as the pipe rolls of the twelfth century, though few scholars have worked through them and no society has ever been started to set them forth in print. It is rather because their extraordinary bulk has terrified me, and because a series of individual accounts between the king and his numerous sheriffs, bailiffs and ministers, is ill-adapted to give that general conspectus of finance and administration for which I have been seeking. For analogous reasons I have dealt very little with the memoranda rolls, the most puzzling and difficult to study of all the records of the exchequer. I have rather sought for information by working through the more manageable receipt rolls and issue rolls, and I think that my examination of these documents has not been wholly without fruit. These have recently been re-arranged and re-numbered on more scholarly lines than those of the traditional classification, and my references are in each case to the new numbers.[2]

[1] [The deputy keeper of the public records informs me that no printed series is at present (1936) in contemplation. MS. calendars have been made of the *communia* sections of K.R. and L.T.R. memoranda rolls for 1-2 Edw. I and 20 Edw. II—12 Edw. III. Typed transcripts are available in the Literary Search Room at the P.R.O. of L.T.R. miscellaneous rolls 1/3 and 1/4 (memoranda, 1 John and 9-10 John), also of L.T.R. and K.R. memoranda rolls 2-6 Hen. III, and typed abstracts of L.T.R. memoranda rolls 24-37 Hen. III.]

[2] These for Edward II are now Issue Rolls, nos. 141-224; Receipt Rolls, nos. 176-266. Mr. Hilary Jenkinson has given me much help with these.

Existing references to the earlier numeration make it desirable to preserve this also.

I have also gone carefully through a large number of wardrobe and chamber accounts. These are partly to be found in the exchequer enrolments, still appended to the pipe rolls for the greater part of this period, but soon, as the result of one of the administrative reforms of this reign, to be enrolled separately as a new series of "foreign" accounts.[1] The exchequer enrolments of wardrobe accounts are, however, always short and summary. Fuller information as to the doings of wardrobe and chamber is preferentially to be sought in the more elaborate documents which responsible clerks of these departments handed in to the exchequer. These have to be brought together from very different quarters. The great bulk of them are to be found among the records preserved for the exchequer by the king's remembrancer,[2] but some lurk in other collections of the exchequer and chancery and many have perished altogether, while some of the best that survive have escaped from official custody and are to be found in the British Museum, or even further afield. It is from these sources that I have chiefly gathered my material, but I should add to them the very numerous original writs of privy and secret seal still to be found in the archives of the chancery and exchequer, where they have been preserved as warrants or vouchers for the issue of writs from the chancery, or for the delivery of money or money's worth from the exchequer.

The chief chronicles for Edward II's reign are well known, but before briefly dealing with them I should like to remark in passing that on re-reading even the best known chronicles in the light of the study of records, many passages that hitherto had suggested very little become full of meaning. Later on, we shall see in more than one case how an obscure passage in a poor chronicle is of real value in illustrating administrative growth, but to appreciate its importance we

[1] A list of the enrolments under this head can be found in the *List of Enrolled Foreign Accounts*, pp. 102-9 (*P.R.O. Lists and Indexes*, no. xi, 1900).

[2] Those which survive are roughly indicated in *List of Various Accounts*, notably pp. 220-70 (*P.R.O. Lists and Indexes*, no. xxxv, 1912). Modern rearrangements, from the time of Joseph Hunter onwards, have played havoc with the traditional classifications, and greatly add to the difficulties of the modern researcher, who is liable to take the present system for more than it is worth, and who finds, not in this relation only, that the ancient references are now extremely difficult to verify. [These Exch. Accts., K.R., are cited throughout as E.A.]

have to know what roughly were the chief administrative developments of the reign. I have been struck in particular with the interest which the intelligent London annalists show in the working of the machine of government, and the value of their occasional references to it. For the extra-administrative aspects of the reign we could not do without the chroniclers, and we may well be thankful that some of the best of them have been so conveniently brought together in Stubbs' masterly two volumes of the *Chronicles of the Reigns of Edward I and Edward II*. Of these the *Annals of London* are invaluable up to 1317;[1] the trustworthy and detailed *Annals of St. Paul's* cover the whole period;[2] the canon of Bridlington's *Deeds of Edward of Carnarvon*, though compiled more than forty years after Edward's death, are of special importance for the critical events that took place in the north;[3] and the *Life of Edward II*, ascribed on slight evidence to a monk of Malmesbury, is the most human, most coloured, and in some ways the most sympathetic and most critical of a not very strong series of chronicles.[4] We may no longer attribute to Sir Thomas de la More a life of Edward II which even Stubbs was content to accept as so written, but the early sections of Geoffrey le Baker's *Chronicle*, from which the so-called life by More is but an excerpt, have independent value for the last three years of the reign. They can now be read in Sir Edward Maunde Thompson's elaborate edition,[5] and though Baker, the most journalistic and most rabidly patriotic of the Edwardian annalists, is at his worst in dealing with a period somewhat before his own personal memory, we may still find in this history, written after the battle of Poitiers, some touches of sound tradition, some long fragments based, like More's relation of the deposition of Edward II, on trustworthy contemporary documents, which in any other form are never likely to be known to us. Unluckily it is extremely improbable that we shall ever be able to ascertain what measure of truth there is in the moving story of the doing to death of Edward II, by which the early portion of Baker's chronicle will always be best remembered.[6]

[1] *Annales Londonienses* in Stubbs, *Chronicles of the reigns of Edward I and Edward II*, i, 151-241 (R.S., 1882).

[2] *Annales Paulini* in *ibid.*, i, 255-324.

[3] *Gesta Edwardi de Carnarvan* in *ibid.*, ii, 25-95.

[4] *Vita Edward II monachi cujusdam Malmesburiensis* in *ibid.*, ii, 155-289.

[5] *Chronicon Galfridi le Baker de Swynebroke*, pp. 3-34, ed. E. M. Thompson (Oxford, 1889).

[6] [For full discussion of this see Tout, "The Captivity and Death of Edward of Carnarvon," *Coll. Papers*, iii, 145-90.]

The nucleus of Baker's history comes from Adam Murimuth;[1] and Murimuth, with a few personal touches after 1325, is for this period essentially a reproduction of the *Flores Historiarum*, which, so far as this reign is concerned, emanate not from St. Albans, but from Westminster Abbey, [and are usually said to have been] written from 1307 to 1325 by Robert of Reading, one of the monks.[2] Robert's chronicle is valuable as that of a close but bitterly partial observer, the most thoroughgoing and unscrupulous of the literary enemies of Edward II, who hated Templars and Dominicans as profoundly as he disliked the king and his courtiers, and strove to cloak his literary aridity by a pompous and artificial diction that sometimes makes him hard to understand. The Rochester version[3] adds a few and the Tintern version[4] a good many new details to the Westminster narrative, the latter being of special value for the march of Wales, a district seldom happy in possessing anything approaching to a local chronicle.

The true St. Albans chroniclers of Edward II are John Trokelowe, who extends to 1322, and Henry Blaneford, who mainly deals with the year 1323.[5] Both are somewhat meagre, but both, especially Trokelowe, take a more favourable view of Edward and his friends than most of the contemporary annalists. Trokelowe is wanting in chronological precision and method, while Blaneford, in his surviving shape, is but a brief and mutilated fragment. As regards northern affairs, we may add to the annals of Bridlington the chronicle of the Cistercian abbey of Meaux in the East Riding of Yorkshire,[6] and the so-called chronicle of Lanercost, which is [actually a chronicle by two Franciscan writers,

[1] *Chronicon Adae Murimuth,* pp. 11-54, ed. E. M. Thompson (R.S., 1889).

[2] *Flores Historiarum,* iii, 137-232, ed. Luard (R.S., 1890). The Chetham MS., the chief source for this, was started at St. Albans but went to Westminster about 1265 (*ibid.*, i, xiii). [For some objections to the attribution to Robert, at any rate between these dates, see Tout, *Coll. Papers*, ii, 289-304.]

[3] *Flores Hist.*, iii, 327-8.

[4] *Ibid.*, iii, 328-48. This MS., originally at St. Benet's Holme in Norfolk, went about 1304 to Tintern. It is another interesting illustration of the way in which these continuations of Matthew Paris were hawked about (*ibid.*, i, xxii).

[5] *Chronica Monasterii S. Albani. J. de Trokelowe et H. de Blaneford, necnon quorundam anonymorum, Chronica,* ed. H. T. Riley (R.S., 1866); Trokelowe, pp. 63-127; Blaneford, pp. 131-52.

[6] *Chronicon Monasterii de Melsa,* ii, 279-354, ed. E. A. Bond (R.S., 1867).

interpolated, abbreviated, and probably rearranged in part by canons of Lanercost].[1] A few valuable northern details can also be gleaned from the early passages of the *Scalacronica* of Sir Thomas Gray of Heaton, the only lay annalist of this reign.[2] The inaccessibility of the limited editions of these last two writers makes the recent translations of Sir Herbert Maxwell useful, though their scholarship cannot always be implicitly relied upon.[3] A great mass of Scottish detail is in Barbour's *Bruce*,[4] but that epic of Scottish nationality was composed fifty years later, and requires caution in its use, though it should in no wise be wholly rejected, notably as regards the great mass of detail related in it about the fight of Bannockburn. The only other chronicles worth mention are the *Polychronicon* of Higden,[5] the last chapters of Walter of Hemingburgh,[6] and some short passages, of special value to us, in a continuation of Trivet, only published in the first edition of that writer, issued in 1722, and therefore not easily accessible.[7] [A short French chronicle of the reign, as yet unprinted, by an author familiar with official documents, has recently been described by Miss M. V. Clarke.][8]

It would take us too far from our special purpose to dwell upon the mass of ecclesiastical correspondence, such as that contained in the letter books of Christ Church, Canterbury,[9] in the various printed episcopal registers of the reign,[10] or

[1] *Chronicon de Lanercost*, ii, 209-58, ed. Joseph Stevenson (Maitland Club, 1839). [See Dr. A. G. Little's article on "The Authorship of the Lanercost Chronicle," *Eng. Hist. Rev.*, xxxi, 269-79.]

[2] *Scalacronica*, pp. 136-53 (Maitland Club, 1836).

[3] *The Chronicle of Lanercost* (Glasgow, 1913). A discussion of the authorship by Dr. Wilson is on pp. ix-xxxi. *Scalacronica as recorded by Sir Thomas Gray*, pp. 45-76 (Glasgow, 1907).

[4] There are many good editions of Barbour's *Bruce*. The most recent, and one of the most handy and scholarly, is that edited by Mr. W. M. Mackenzie (1909).

[5] *Polychronicon Ranulphi Higden*, viii, 296-323, ed. J. R. Lumby (R.S., 1882).

[6] *Chronicon Walteri de Hemingburgh*, ii, 269-96. This hardly extends to 1315.

[7] *Nicolai Triveti Annalium Continuatio*, ed. Anthony Hall (Oxford, 1722).

[8] [Brit. Mus. Cotton MS. Julius A i, ff. 51-62. See M. V. Clarke, "Committees of estates and the deposition of Edw. II" in *Hist. Essays in honour of James Tait* (1933).]

[9] *Literae Cantuarienses*, i, 32-204, ed. Sheppard (R.S., 1887), of special importance for the last years of the reign.

[10] Among the most useful printed episcopal registers of the reign may be mentioned [the following: for Exeter, that of Walter de Stapeldon, 1307-26, ed. Hingeston-Randolph (1892); for Winchester, those of John de Sandale, 1316-18, and Rigaud de Asserio, 1320-23, ed. Baigent (Hampshire

the large amount of material for the history of the dissolution of the Templars. Still less relevant is the legal material, notable among which are the *Year Books*, published by the Selden Society through the impulse of the late F. W. Maitland.[1] A last word may refer to the municipal material, some of the most important for us being that contained in the *Munimenta Gildhallae Londoniensis*.[2]

## (2) The Personal Aspects of the Reign

The personal aspects of any mediæval period have mainly to be learnt from the chronicles and similar material for narrative history. It is only very occasionally that a record throws a direct light on any problem of personal character, though the abundant details records give us, as to external acts, may often afford new material for the study of motives and therefore for appreciation of character. Nevertheless we have no need to go to unpublished records to ascertain new facts that help us to determine the character of Edward II and his contemporaries.[3] If, then, I begin what I have to say by a few reflections on the personality of the king and of some of his chief agents and enemies, it is not because there is anything very new to offer on this aspect of my theme. There is little fresh to be said as to the personal deficiencies of the unlucky Edward II, that first king after the Norman Conquest, as Stubbs has truly said, who was "not a man of business well acquainted with the routine of government."[4]

Record Soc., 1897); for Bath and Wells, that of John de Drokensford, 1309-29, ed. Hobhouse (Somerset Record Soc., 1887); for Worcester, those of Walter Reynolds, 1308-13, ed. Wilson, and Thomas de Cobham, 1317-27, ed. Pearce (Worc. Hist. Soc., 1927, 1930); and in the publications of the Canterbury and York Society: for Carlisle, that of John de Halton, 1292-1324, ed. Thompson with introduction by Tout (1913); for London, those of Ralph Baldock, 1307-13, Gilbert Segrave, 1314-16, Richard Newport, 1317-18, and Stephen Gravesend, 1318-27, ed. Fowler (1911); for Hereford, those of Richard de Swinfield, 1283-1317, ed. Capes (1908), and Adam de Orleton, 1317-27, ed Bannister (1907); for Rochester, that of Hamo Hethe, 1319-52, ed. Johnson (in preparation; pts. i-iv (1915-31) cover the portion relating to Edward II's reign)]. Of even greater importance is the Record Office *Calendar of Papal Registers, Letters*, ii, 25-253, which covers this reign.

[1] *Year Books of Edward II* (Selden Soc.). [Eighteen] volumes, extending to 1315-16, have already been published, edited by Maitland, Turner, Vernon-Harcourt, Bolland, [Vinogradoff and Ehrlich (1903-28)].

[2] *Munimenta Gildhallae Londoniensis*, ed. H. T. Riley (R.S., 1860), especially vol. ii, the *Liber Custumarum*, compiled at the end of Edward II's reign.

[3] [But see notes 3 and 4, p. 9.]

[4] Stubbs, *Const. Hist.*, ii, 328 (1887).

Chroniclers do not often all agree, but their agreement is absolutely wonderful in dealing with the character of Edward of Carnarvon.[1] They all present the same general picture of that strong, handsome, weak-willed and frivolous king who cared neither for battles nor tournaments, neither politics nor business, and had no other wish than to amuse himself. What contemporaries found hardest to understand was that Edward was not content with seeking his distractions after a royal fashion by participating with his barons in such recognised dissipations as public opinion allowed. He drank and gambled,[2] it is true, and his taste for country pursuits included the traditional delight of his race in hunting, and in the breeding of horses and hounds. As prince he was as well able to cheer his solitude with the company of his high-born nephew, Gilbert of Clare, as with that of Peter of Gaveston, the Gascon adventurer.[3] Yet as king he systematically avoided the society of his nobles for the upstart courtiers who successfully turned his heart from his natural counsellors, the magnates of the land. In the suspected society of his personal favourites about the court, Edward gratified his love of such ignoble sports as racing, rowing, driving, play-acting, farming, smith's work, thatching, digging and similar "mechanic arts," such as no mediæval gentleman had ever affected.[4]

So far all the chroniclers are agreed, though they may vary in tone from bitter malignity to easy-going tolerance or charitable contempt. At one end of the scale is the sympathetic annalist whom we agree without much reason to

[1] The most famous passage in the chronicles on this subject is that in *Polychronicon,* viii, 298-300. This is copied out, word for word, in Knighton, i, 407-8, and with omissions and verbal changes in Canon of Bridlington, p. 91, and *Chron. de Melsa,* ii, 280-1. Other important personal illustrations are in Malmesb., pp. 191-2 ; Lanercost, p. 236 ; *Scalacronica,* p. 136 ; and *Cont. Trivet,* pp. 18-19. There is some risk in arguing what were Edward's personal tastes from records such as the correspondence summarised in *Deputy Keeper of Records, Ninth Report,* App. ii, 246-9, [of which the full text was published by Hilda Johnstone in *Letters of Edward, prince of Wales, 1304-5* (Roxburghe Club, 1931)], or from entries of expenses in wardrobe books, whether of the king or the prince. All great men's households had their minstrels, stud, kennel, etc.

[2] Large sums were handed to him *pro ludo suo* in the first year of his reign (E.A. 373/15, pp. 17, 18). [Similar evidence for earlier dates may be seen in *ibid.*, 363/18, f. 12 (1302-3), and Brit. Mus. Add. MS. 22923, f. 14v (1306-7).]

[3] *Deputy Keeper's Ninth Report,* App. ii, p. 248, [and *Letters of Edw.*, pp. 70, 73].

[4] [For record evidence of this *cf.* H. Johnstone, "The Eccentricities of Edw. II" in *Eng. Hist. Rev.*, xlviii, 264-7.]

call the monk of Malmesbury. This writer finds in the king's backslidings excellent material for gratifying his taste for moralising, but his good wishes culminate only in the pious hope that as the king's best friends get killed off, or are compulsorily relegated to private life, Edward will not do so badly in the future as he had admittedly done in the past.[1] A somewhat more charitable estimate is given by Trokelowe, the St. Albans chronicler. While most writers suggest that Edward was no better than a coward, notably when he fled in a panic from the defeat of Bannockburn, Trokelowe describes in vivid phrase how Edward, roused by the spectacle of his friends' slaughter, rushed, like a lioness bereft of her cubs, on the victorious Scots and drained the life blood of his enemies with his glittering sword, until his escort dragged him against his will to a place of safety.[2] But St. Albans monks thought well of a king who ever loved to visit their house and to propitiate the convent with rich gifts and offerings. In striking contrast to the benevolence of Trokelowe stands the malignity of the Westminster chronicler, Robert of Reading, who resented Edward's aversion to Westminster[3] as bitterly as the barons resented his dislike of their society. But we need not trust too much Robert of Reading, for what are we to think of the fairness of a partisan who believed—I quote his words—that the Dayspring from on High visited Earl Guy of Warwick[4] when that ruffianly partisan, regardless

[1] Malmesb., pp. 237-40. [Two letters written by Bishop Cobham when attending parliament in October 1320 (*Register*, pp. 97, 98), bear personal witness to an improvement at that date. "Rex in instanti parliamento . . . magnifice, prudenter et discrete se gessit, contraque antiquam consuetudinem mane surgens magnum et hillarem prelatis et proceribus vultum fecit," etc. Or again, "Omnes loqui cum racione volentes patienter audivit . . . propter que mirabiliter gens nostra letatur, ad spem magnam morum eius melioracionis adducitur, magis ad vnitatem et concordiam excitatur."]

[2] Trokelowe, p. 86.

[3] In *Flores Hist.*, iii, 169, Reading notes in 1315 how "rex manerium de Insula . . . a conventu Westmonasterii violenter detinuit, nihil solvens pro eodem," and in 1320, records on p. 193, how the king "quoddam tugurrium de patrimonio sancti Petri . . . Burgundia nuncupatum, non sine nota sacrilegii, violenter occupavit." He is equally severe on the division in 1325 of the exchequer at Westminster (p. 232), and the holding of parliaments at Lincoln and elsewhere away from the capital (p. 173). The bad government of the abbey and the total suspension of the rebuilding operations show that Westminster in those days left much to be desired.

[4] *Ibid.*, iii, 151. "A paterno solio respexit afflictum populum *Oriens ex alto*, gratiam infundens in corde militis sui domini Gwidonis de Warewyk," etc. The previous remark, that Pembroke had left Gaveston at Deddington "casui dativo dictum Petrum relinquens, ad ablativum vero in brevi transferendum" is as brutal in idea as it is execrable as a jest.

of the plighted word of the associated earls, sought out and murdered Gaveston in utter defiance of the terms of his capitulation?

It was not so much the king's vices as his idleness and incompetence which his subjects complained of. After all, the business of a mediæval king was to govern, and a monarch who would not take the trouble to do his appointed work had no right to go on reigning at all. We have therefore to make some allowance for the austerity and the grim earnestness of the mediæval mind, which took life and work so seriously, and found so little room for distraction and pleasure in its theory of the universe. Perhaps we more frivolous moderns might judge Edward of Carnarvon less severely than his ascetic contemporaries. If he did not like work, he was not very vicious; he stuck loyally to his friends and was fairly harmless, being nobody's enemy so much as his own. Had the mediæval point of view allowed a lay prince to study at Oxford, and had fourteenth-century Oxford pursued modern sports and pastimes, Edward would perhaps have distinguished himself as a driver of four-in-hands and as an athlete. He would have shown his skill in "mechanic arts" by his knowledge of motor cars and perhaps even have rowed in the University eight. Unluckily his ignorance of Latin would have made it impossible for him ever to have passed Responsions.[1]

Even Edward's friends were not so black as they have been painted. Gaveston himself has been singularly unfortunate in the modern writers who have essayed to depict his character and career.[2] The worst that can be certainly said against him is that he was not a serious politician, that he never aspired to office in the state,[3] that he had too keen

[1] [In 1317 the pope thanked Walter, archbishop of Canterbury, "for having translated his letters to the king into French" (*C. Pap. Lett.*, 1315-42, pp. 430-1).]

[2] These are W. P. Dodge, *Piers Gaveston. A chapter of early constitutional history* (1899), and M. Dimitresco, *Pierre de Gavaston: sa biographie et son rôle* (1898). The former is altogether unsatisfactory, and the latter in no wise represents the school of Paris at its best.

[3] Gaveston is often spoken of as Edward II's chamberlain, but the evidence is more than doubtful. The best comes from *Ann. Paul.*, p. 258, which say that on his accession Edward II "Petrum . . . fecit secretarium et camerarium regni summum," and afterwards earl of Cornwall. This is important, for it is almost inconceivable that Gaveston continued to act as chamberlain after he had become earl of Cornwall. As he became earl on 6 Aug., he could only have been chamberlain for less than a month. Geoffrey le Baker, who wrote after 1356, is the first to suggest (p. 6) that Gaveston remained chamberlain for the whole of his subsequent

an eye to the main chance, that he looked too closely after the financial interests of his Gascon kinsfolk,[1] that his head was so turned by his elevation that he became offensively bumptious, and that he had a pretty but dangerous gift of affixing stinging nicknames alike on his friends and enemies.[2]

career (Hugo Despenser filius fuit ordinatus camerarius regis loco Petri), but Baker is at his worst in dealing with details, as his account of Despenser's appointment, which he puts five years too early, clearly shows. *Ann. Lond.*, p. 151, speak of Peter as "regiam domum tenens," a vague phrase, which might suggest the chamberlainship. I have found no record evidence that Gaveston was ever chamberlain, but that office is so seldom mentioned in the records of the reign that the argument of silence is worthless. The monk of Malmesbury suggests a possible solution when he says, p. 155, that Gaveston was "vivente rege Edwardo sene, juvenis Edwardi . . . camerarius familiarissimus." Unluckily, the extant household accounts of the prince of Wales do not bear this statement out. [They show Peter in 1300-1 (E.A., 360/17) as *puer in custodia;* in 1302-3 (*ibid.*, 363/18, ff. 12, 21v) as *scutifer* and *valletus;* in 1304-5 (*Letters of Edw.*, pp. 70, 73) as one of four *valletz* specially dear to Edward; and in 1306-7 (Brit. Mus. Add. MS. 22923, f. 4) as *miles principis*.] I am inclined to account for all the vague assertions of the chroniclers by the fact that "camerarius" was often still used in a vague sense for any officer of the *camera*, not in the precise sense of king's or prince's chamberlain. I know not the authority for the precise statement in Doyle's *Official Baronage*, i, 438. *Ann. Paul.* suggest the hereditary office.

[1] Conspicuous among these was Bertrand Calhau, his nephew. See Cotton MS. Nero C. viii, f. 88v, a grant to Gaveston of 500 marks "per manus Bertrandi Caillau nepotis sui." This Bertrand was "valettus regis" from at least 1309 (*C.P.R. 1307-13*, p. 159) until the end of 1312, after his uncle's death (*ibid.*, pp. 484, 514). He often received moneys in the wardrobe, negotiated foreign loans, and served on a mission to the papal court. [Many points as to the history of the Calhau family, whose name in its northern form is Caillau, have been noted in an article on "Les institutions municipales de Bordeaux" (*Revue Historique*, cxxiii, 253-93), by M. Bémont, who ranks them with the famous houses of Colom and Delsoler as leaders of civic faction. To one branch, Solerien in sympathy, belonged Peter, mayor of Bordeaux in 1308, and his brother Bertrand, who were sons of Peter Calhau of Rue Neuve (*Rua neva*) and his wife Navarra, daughter of Bertrand de Podensac (Bémont, *op. cit.*, p. 262, and *Rôles Gascons*, iii, no. 3382. By a slip in note on *ibid.*, no. 4469, Miramonde is named as their mother instead of Navarra). In the light of this Mr. Tout rejected his former identification of Gaveston's nephew with this Bertrand, who would be Gaveston's cousin once removed, not his nephew, since his grandmother, Miramonde Calhau, was sister to Gaveston's mother Claramonde, lady of Marsan. To the Colombin branch of the family belonged Arnold Calhau, and possibly also Gaveston's nephew. A Bertrand Calhau came to England with John Colom in 1324 (G.R. 35, m. 13).] Arnold was mayor of Bordeaux (1304), seneschal of Saintonge (1314), keeper of Oléron (1316-23) and played a loyal but somewhat questionable part in Anglo-Gascon history in the later years of the reign. The connexion of Gaveston with both the urban aristocracy of Bordeaux and the territorial houses of Gascony and Béarn is perhaps typical. Materials for working out his family relations could be found in *Rôles Gascons*, *Archives historiques de la Gironde*, and such sources.

[2] The various nicknames given by Gaveston to the magnates are stated in curiously various forms. The strictly contemporary monk of Malmes-

Of the graver charges, which have taken classic shape in Marlowe's powerful but unhistorical tragedy, there is no more evidence than the gossip of several prejudiced chroniclers. I know not whether the saying that the more mud you throw the more is likely to stick goes back, like much of our proverbial philosophy, to the middle ages. In any case it was a principle seldom lost sight of in mediæval controversy. A few years earlier, the men who now voiced the outcry against the Gascon, thought it good policy to strengthen their sound constitutional reasons for driving Walter Langton from the foremost place in Edward I's counsels by accusing him of murder, adultery, simony, pluralism, and intercourse with the devil. The particulars as to the last count are remarkably circumstantial. The bishop of Lichfield had not only had many conversations

bury, p. 161, speaks of his habit of affixing "turpia cognomina" to earls and barons. Warwick's description as "black dog of Arden" has the contemporary authority of *Flores Hist.*, iii, 152, and the somewhat later testimony of the *Lanercost Chron.*, p. 216, which says that Gaveston gave other nicknames, though it specifies none of them. The earliest sources for the other names date from the reign of Edward III, and include the French and English "Brute" chronicles, which, up to 1333, were written not long after that date, and so are nearly as contemporary as Reading himself. *The English Brute* (*The Brut or the Chronicles of England*, ed. F. W. D. Brie, Early Eng. Text Soc., 1906, p. 207) calls Gloucester "horessone," Lincoln "broste bely," Warwick "blanke hounde of Arderne" [or preferably in the reading of two other MSS., "blac" or "blake"] and Lancaster "cherl." The even earlier *French Brute*, quoted by Sir E. Maunde Thompson on p. 184 of his edition of Geoffrey le Baker, gives these in French as "filz a puteyne," "boele crevee," "noir chien de Ardene" and "vielers," *i.e.*, "fiddler" not "churl." Next comes William of Pakington's French Chronicle, which was written before 1376, for it is dedicated to the Black Prince, whose treasurer Pakington (d. 1390) had been. It is only known from the summary in Leland's *Collectanea*, ii, 461 (1770). It agrees with the *French Brute*, but it translates the harsh reflection on Gloucester's mother as "cocolds byrde" and explains "vielers" as "porceo quil est greles et de bel entaile," *i.e.*, "slim and tall." Walsingham, *Hist. Angl.*, i, 115, here based upon the King's Library MS., not much later than 1392, agrees in calling Warwick "black dog," but styles Lancaster "the player" and Pembroke "Joseph the Jew" "eo quod pallidus esset et longus." This latter now appears for the first time. It looks as if Gaveston varied his nicknames on occasion, but there seems plenty of good evidence for his foolish habit. The *English Brute* suggests that he was not consistent in his insults. "And meny othere shames and scorn ham saide." No wonder the magnates were "ful angri and sore annoiede." Gaveston's attack on Joan of Acre, doubtless a malicious reference to her *mésalliance* with Ralph of Monthermer, was particularly outrageous, as she was the king's sister, and the mother of his own wife. Gaveston's wife's brother, Gilbert of Gloucester, was, moreover, the last of the magnates to give up his Puckish brother-in-law. For the date and sources of the *English Brute* see Brie's *Geschichte und Quellen der mittelenglischen Prosachronik, the Brute of England* (1905). For the whole question see Sir E. M. Thompson's excellent note to Baker, pp. 183-4.

with the evil one, he had done homage to him as vassal to lord, and had ratified his submission with a kiss.[1] Still more to the point were the accusations of depravity which at the very moment of Gaveston's fall were being brought against the unlucky Templars, both in France and England.[2] It is impossible to take these vague charges seriously.

The barons were on safer though narrower ground when they accused Gaveston of being a foreigner. Yet even here the barons' definition of an alien was that of particularists of the narrowest sort. Such an accusation has little weight when directed against a Béarnais who was the son of a father who had grown grey and endured prison [3] in the service of Edward I, and was not only a natural born liegeman of the king, but brought up as a ward in custody in the household of the king's eldest son. Such a household we may regard as the fourteenth-century equivalent to a very select and exclusive Eton and Sandhurst combined for the young aristocrats of that period. The charge of being an upstart is easy to make and hard to refute. Yet Gaveston's family, if not of the first rank, belonged to the higher territorial and civic aristocracy of Gascony.[4] Perhaps the shrewd monk of Malmesbury got as near as any one to the root of the matter when he declared his conviction that, if Peter had from the beginning behaved prudently and humbly before the English magnates, he would never have had any of them opposed to him.[5] It was as the enemy of baronial pretensions, rather than as the royal minion or the upstart, that the magnates pronounced the doom of Gaveston.

[1] See for these charges, *Foedera*, i, 956-7; *C. Pap. Lett.*, i, 607; *Flores Hist.*, iii, 305-6.

[2] For the charges against the Templars see *Ann. Lond.*, pp. 176-98. The allegations of the French against Boniface VIII were equally gross, and so were the accusations brought against Guichard of Troyes. See Rigault, *Le Procès de Guichard, évêque de Troyes* (1897).

[3] *R.G.*, iii, no. 4472.

[4] See above, p. 12. The paternal stock came from Gabaston, in Béarn, cant. Morlaas, arr. Pau, dep. Basses Pyrénées.

[5] Malmesb., p. 168. It is some confirmation of this point of view that seven earls witnessed the charter of 6 Aug. 1307 (*Foedera*, ii, 2), by which Edward made Gaveston earl of Cornwall at Dumfries. These were Henry of Lincoln, Edmund of Arundel, John of Richmond, and Aymer of Pembroke among the more "royalist" earls. The others were Thomas of Lancaster, John of Surrey, and Humphrey of Hereford, all soon to be his bitter enemies. It is sometimes said that witnessing a charter at this date was a formal act, and did not involve personal presence or consent. Without stressing the point, it is hard to believe that the chancery would have dared to put down as "witnesses" men opposed to Gaveston's advancement.

There is more to be said for the younger Hugh le Despenser than there is for Gaveston. Indeed it is hard to see how this son of the mighty baron, who had devoted his life to the service of the great Edward, was in any invidious sense a favourite at all. At least he was not so till the year 1321. He was doubtless greedy and ambitious, but he had brains enough to formulate something like a theory of constitutional law,[1] as well as his personal policy of using his share of the Gloucester inheritance to make himself the autocrat of south Wales. He showed, too, prudence enough, after his return from banishment in 1322, to abandon a line of action which, much more than his personal relations with the king, had brought about his temporary downfall. Starting from ancestral traditions that inclined him naturally to the cause of Thomas of Lancaster and the stalwarts of the opposition, Despenser's political affinities, before his too complete triumph in 1322, were much more with the earl of Pembroke and the "middle party" than with the mere courtiers. It was only after that date that he definitely turned his back on his early career by falling back into curialist ways. Subsequently, when brought face to face with the responsibilities of power, Despenser failed as utterly as any of his predecessors. Yet even then Despenser deserves some commendation for remaining a reformer to the last, and perhaps also for the self-restraint which allowed him to pass through the five years of his triumph from 1322 to 1326 without so much as taking to himself the coveted title of earl of Gloucester. Unluckily for him, he indulged in wanton acts of tyranny and oppression which belied his grand theories and involved him in sudden and irremediable ruin. Here again, however, he was done to death by rivals who grudged his supremacy in the march of Wales quite as much as they disliked the unpopular minister. The opposition under Edward II had an unhappy knack of exciting sympathy for all who came under its ban.

Edward of Carnarvon and his intimates, then, have been on the whole rather too severely judged at the bar of history. Yet the most friendly eye can see little to praise in any of the three, though it may be admitted that they have at least as much human nature in them as the singularly unattractive leaders of the baronial opposition. Five earldoms[2] and

[1] See below, p. 130.

[2] Thomas was earl of Lancaster, Leicester and Derby by succession from his father, earl Edmund of Lancaster. With the Leicester earldom

close kinship with the two greatest monarchs in the west [1] gave neither dignity, policy, patriotism nor common sense to that most impossible of all mediæval politicians, earl Thomas of Lancaster. Sulky, vindictive, self-seeking, brutal and vicious, he had just enough sense to realise that the duty of an opposition is to oppose, but he had not application or intelligence enough to understand that, when the opposition leader gets the reins of power into his own hands, his business is to govern the state, not to thwart his personal enemies. His treatment of Gaveston was dishonourable to the last degree, and his intrigues with the Scots a public scandal of the worst type. The "good cause" for which he is supposed to have fought must have been an exceptionally good cause to profit by the advocacy of so incompetent and stupid a personage. Yet almost as unlovely as Lancaster was his fellow-worker in the tragedy of Blacklow Hill, Guy Beauchamp, earl of Warwick. Of Warwick, the actual perpetrator of the outrage at Deddington, all that we can say in favour is that the wise old earl of Lincoln had so high an opinion of him that he advised his son-in-law, earl Thomas, to be directed by his counsels.[2] The chroniclers also claim for him a knowledge of literature seldom found in the higher nobility of his age.[3] This aspect of Guy of Warwick, combined with his treachery, reminds us of the cultivated aristocratic ruffians of the Renascence.

Of the other earls it can be only said that they are as like each other as a series of peas, and that it needs a very vivid historical imagination to assign to most of them any distinct

went the hereditary stewardship of England. As the holder of the forfeited earldoms of Simon of Montfort and Robert of Ferrers, Thomas was doubly pledged to the constitutional tradition. From his wife, Alice Lacy, came Henry Lacy's two earldoms of Lincoln and Salisbury.

[1] Edward II was his first cousin. His half-sister, Joan, daughter of his mother, Blanche of Artois, queen of Navarre and countess of Champagne, was the wife of Philip IV. Philip IV was, therefore, his brother-in-law, and Louis X, Philip V, and Charles IV were his nephews.

[2] Trokelowe's (pp. 72-3) long deathbed harangue of the old earl of Lincoln is certainly not historical in form. The good advice includes the protection of the Church from the Romans and the crown, the maintenance of Magna Carta, deference to the advice of Winchelsea and the clergy, and the selection of Englishmen for his household offices and the wise direction of his "familia." In matters of politics he is to follow Warwick, "qui prae caeteris paribus sano consilio et maturitate pollet." It is more like a programme of the ordainers' policy than the personal views of a loyal servant of Edward I.

[3] "Virum sapientem et probum" (Lanercost, p. 216); "homo discretus et bene litteratus, per quem totum regnum Angliae sapientia praefulgebat" (*Ann. Lond.*, p. 236; *cf.* Malmesb., p. 212).

individuality. A good scholar, trained in the schools of Paris, has recently written at length the biography of John of Brittany, earl of Richmond, but she has been quite unable to tell us what manner of man he was.[1] Perhaps the only two remaining earls whose personality can be outlined with any clearness are John of Warenne, earl of Surrey, the most brutal and disreputable, and Aymer of Valence, earl of Pembroke, the most intelligent of the higher nobles. Of Warenne's demerits I have spoken at length in the *Dictionary of National Biography*, and there is no need to say anything now, but Pembroke is, I think, the most neglected character of the reign, and in many ways the most interesting and attractive of the lay nobles. If we are to make a hero in the reign at all, earl Aymer of Pembroke has surely the best claim to that distinction. In one generation this son of Henry III's hated Poitevin half-brother had acquired with his mother's inheritance of the Welsh palatinate of the Marshals some portion of the great Marshal tradition of efficiency, patriotism, and loyalty. Pembroke, the hero of the rout of Methven of 1306, one of the few leaders at Bannockburn who lost none of his honour on that fatal field, and in the worst times that followed ever a strenuous defender of northern England against the Scots, remained a vigorous member of the baronial opposition so long as the policy of the ordainers meant the reform of the administration and the cleansing of the Augean stables of the court. His alliance with earl Thomas, shattered when the great man backed up Guy of Warwick in his disregard of earl Aymer's plighted faith to Gaveston, was practically never renewed. Driven to association with the king by the treachery of his baronial allies, Aymer remained indefatigable as a mediator and a peacemaker. Almost completely effaced when in 1316 the parliament of Lincoln chose earl Thomas as the chief counsellor of the king, his chance came again when Lancaster still continued, as head of the executive, that policy of sulking and abstention which had characterised him as leader of the opposition. Lancaster's failure enabled Pembroke to bring about a solid coalition between the more reputable curialists and his own associates of the so-called middle party, and of this liberal royalist party he was the soul. From the treaty of Leake, in August 1318, until the return of the Despensers,

[1] Inna Lubimenko, *Jean de Bretagne, comte de Richmond* (Paris, 1908).

in February, 1322, Pembroke exercised the preponderating influence, and his authority remained strong until the conclusion of the long truce with the Scots in June, 1323. I shall later take opportunity to treat in more detail of the policy pursued by Pembroke during these years, but even at this stage I should like to claim for him the chief part in bringing about comparative peace and prosperity and the large measures of reform which mark this period.[1] A study of the exchequer and wardrobe records for this period has convinced me not only that Pembroke was the chief directive agent of the prevailing policy, but that he was the only one of the great magnates who worked hard in the daily routine of politics, the two Despensers themselves not excepted. His last act of authority in domestic affairs was the insistence in 1321 on the banishment of the Despensers, and here we shall not be wronging him if we assume that the danger to his Welsh earldom's independence, that necessarily followed from the younger Hugh's schemes of south Welsh domination, had something to do with bringing him to a clear decision. In the troubles that ensued Pembroke, perhaps because he had become so habituated to posing as a mediator, did not take a sufficiently strong line. His position was of course singularly difficult, balanced between the Scylla of the Lancastrians and the Charybdis of the courtier faction. The result was that when the Despensers came back and the militant opposition met its doom at Boroughbridge, he is open to the suspicion of being hardly firm enough to outwit the king and his favourites. Yet it was not until his premature death in 1324 that the situation became hopeless, and that there began that renewed period of complete curialist control which in three years brought about the collapse of the king and his friends in the final tragedy of the reign. With base ingratitude, Hugh le Despenser and Robert Baldock withheld from the widowed countess, a young bride of less than two years before, some of the dower lands to which she

[1] In his excellent summary of the political parties in the critical years of the reign, in the introduction to his *Chronicles of Edward I and Edward II*, Stubbs calls Pembroke the king's wisest and truest friend (ii, lxxix); yet elsewhere he hardly seems to me quite fair to Pembroke and the "politiques" of the middle party. He is too convinced that Lancaster's was the "party of freedom," and that Pembroke and his followers were "without any affection for the king or any aspirations for freedom" (*ibid.*, i, cxiv). But was Lancaster in any sense a champion of freedom, and were there three parties "throughout the reign"? The point of view is too general, and a thought too modern.

was entitled.[1] It is clear that when the earl was removed not even a pretence was made of showing any respect for his memory. So hard is it to form a picture even of Pembroke's personality that we welcome even Gaveston's derisive nickname "Joseph the Jew," the more so since we are told that he was so described because he was "pale and tall." [2]

It would be easy to go on with the personal aspects of the reign, and in particular to extend our survey to the chief ecclesiastics of the period. Of these, however, two only can be clearly recognised as possessing a strong personality of their own, and these two had already done their best work when Edward of Carnarvon mounted the throne. These were of course Thomas Winchelsea, archbishop of Canterbury, the old king's chief foe, and Walter Langton, bishop of Lichfield, the chief minister of Edward I's latter years. Of these archbishop Winchelsea was at once brought back by the new king from his long exile, but the stubborn prelate forthwith took up his former attitude of opposition to the crown, and usefully employed his declining years in providing the lords ordainers with brains and a policy. While bringing the archbishop home to his province, Edward II paid off old scores by putting Langton in prison and exposing him to the bitterest persecution. Though the astute courtier soon wriggled his way back into some show of favour, he was too unpopular to be made an effective instrument, and too uncertain of his line of action to be really trusted. Though he survived until 1321, it would have been better for his fame had he died earlier, so numerous and so unworthy were the later vicissitudes of his strangely chequered career. I have no need to speak at length of the younger generation of political bishops, whose meanness and self-seeking have been scarcely too severely castigated by Stubbs. These latter, the Reynolds, the Orletons, the Hothams, the Stratfords, the Airmyns and the Stapledons at least had their full share both in determining

[1] *C.P.R. 1364-67*, pp. 275-6, summarises an exemplification of a petition of Mary, widow of earl Aymer, that Baldock, "sometime chancellor," had refused her dower in Pembroke's Monmouth lands, and that Hugh le Despenser refused to allow the escheator to make return of her dower lands in Hertford and Haverfordwest "because he coveted them." Mary of Saint-Pol, Countess of Pembroke, long survived her husband, and died about 1376. See later, p. 216, for her foundation of Valence Mary, or Pembroke College, Cambridge, in his memory in 1347 (*ibid.*, 1345-48, p. 444). [For a detailed study of her life, with appended documents, see Mr. Hilary Jenkinson in *Archæologia*, lxvi, 401-46 (1914).]

[2] Walsingham, *Hist. Angl.*, i, 115. See also note 2, above, p. 13.

policy and in working out its details. If their general record be a chequered one, some of these men anyhow had their more attractive aspects. Orleton and Stratford were scholars of repute.[1] Robert Baldock, even, was a doctor of civil law.[2] These are early instances of the way in which fourteenth-century Oxford began to make its way into the public service. To bishop Hotham we are indebted for the glorious octagon and retrochoir of Ely. We owe to Stapeldon a large part of both nave and choir of Exeter cathedral, and Oxford, at least, must not forget that he was the founder of Exeter College. Politically, also, he was not afraid to assert constitutional principles. Thus when asked in January, 1322, to endorse in writing the advice given by the provincial council held at London in the previous December, from which he had been absent, as to the reversal of the exile of the Despensers, he boldly stated his view that a sentence originally passed by parliament ought to be revoked by a similar assembly.[3] It should also be remembered that at least one prelate of the official class preserved his reputation unblemished throughout a long life. Many years of court service did not corrupt the fidelity or diminish the piety and charity of archbishop Melton of York.[4]

However much they differed in personal character, not one of these bishops soared conspicuously above his fellows. After all, they were simply the most successful members of the large class from which they were drawn, the great body of king's clerks who constituted what in modern phrase we may call the permanent civil service of the period. The permanent staffs of the great offices of the court and state bulked as little in the chronicles of the fourteenth century as do their modern counterparts in the newspapers of our own day. However,

[1] Blaneford, pp. 140-1 (*apud* Trokelowe, Rolls Series), calls Orleton "vir maturus et litterali scientia excellenter ornatus," and Stratford, "juris civilis doctor eximius," who "in artibus inter omnes clericos hujus facultatis regni Anglicani reputaretur . . . excellentissimus" (*ibid.*, p. 147). Orleton was a doctor of canon law (*Foedera*, ii, 162). Canon A. T. Bannister, in his *Introduction to Orleton's Register* (Cant. and York Soc., 1908), makes the best case he can for Orleton's character, but is more successful in demonstrating his ability than his morality.

[2] *Drokensford's Register*, p. 215 (Somerset Record Soc.).

[3] "Quia, tamen, dicta consideracio tempore parliamenti facta fuit, videtur nobis . . . quod revocacio predicte consideracionis honorificencius, utilius, et securius fieri poterit in parliamento quam alibi" (*Register*, p. 442).

[4] Malmesb., p. 283, "Et quamvis inter curiales diu conversatus, mores tamen a convictu non traxit, sed, obviata Anglorum cupiditate, per Dei gratiam impollutus semper permansit."

all these, so far as they come within our purview, will have their place later on.

Stubbs' survey of the chief actors of the reign of Edward II led him to point the obvious moral of their inferiority to the men of preceding generations, and to draw eloquent generalisations as to the falling off of the incoming fourteenth century in character and ideals from the thirteenth century, the golden period of mediæval civilisation. It is difficult to cavil at anything that he says, and yet one cannot feel over sure that his conclusions are altogether in accordance with one's impressions of the time. The more one works at history the less one feels satisfied with any broad statements as to the general character of any age. And I think the decadence of the age of Edward II is in no wise so clear as it would seem at first sight. Let it be admitted that the leaders were markedly inferior. Rather let it be at once said that there were few leaders who really led. Yet with all his caution and all his wisdom, Stubbs goes too far when he teaches that the barons and bishops of the early fourteenth century were cast in a meaner mould than the heroes of Runnymede, or of the age of Simon de Montfort, or even of the opposition to the declining years of Edward I. As far as the rank and file goes, both the barons who won the Great Charter, and their grandsons who laid low the power of the crown in the Mad Parliament, were every whit as stupid and as greedy, as narrow and as self-seeking, as were the mass of the lords ordainers. Yet we must not on that account regard them as negligible quantities in history. Their work was a great work in its results if not in its motives, and we must not neglect to appraise it from that standpoint. On the wider question I do not in the least believe that the fourteenth century was any worse than the thirteenth. On the contrary, it was on the whole a better, and certainly a more pleasant, time to live in. It is one of the comforting lessons of history that the dull reigns of the indifferent kings are as worthy of study as the most famous and splendid periods. Neither the state nor society ceased to function because the king's weakness made the state a little more ineffective, and the barons' turbulence made social conditions a little more disorderly, than the normal ineffectiveness and disorder of the slack, easy-going times which we call the middle ages. We exaggerate, moreover, the part played by the state and statesmen in moulding mediæval conditions.

Neither the wisdom of Edward I nor the folly of Edward II could do very much to alter the general stream of tendency. Ordinary men lived their lives under the weak Edward of Carnarvon very much as they lived their lives under the "greatest of the Plantagenets." Our period is no mere blank page between two glorious chapters. Even the reign of Edward II has its contribution, if it be a modest one, to the almost unbroken story of the development of English society, politics and institutions.

I have already stressed the dearth of great men, the lack of strong leaders, in the reign of Edward II. From the impersonality of the reign follow some not unimportant results. No historian now is a whole-hearted follower of Carlyle and Froude. But we need not be of the school of hero-worshippers to recognise that sometimes a great personality may deflect to some extent the general character of his time. There was no such force at work in the England of Edward II. On the contrary, the absence of such disturbing elements enabled the ordinary man to work out his career the more easily and comfortably. You can see machinery, already set up by the master engineer, going on by itself, so to say. The complicated engines of state, the much more intricate mechanism of society, have to do their work as best they may, untended save by the ordinary craftsman who lubricates the bearings and touches the handles which start or stop them. More than this, the artisans who drive the machines have been trained in a good school. They may not always be the most estimable of men. They may be self-seeking, venal, deferential, brutal, slack or cruel, as it suits their turn. But they have gone through their apprenticeship in their craft. If they seek their own interests and their own distractions, they discharge their daily task. They do not get drunk while they are driving their engine. And so the machines keep on revolving, despite wars and rumours of war. And I may say in parenthesis that, except in the north, there were more rumours of war than wars all through the reign.

It follows that the real work of ruling England under Edward II fell not on the king and the earls, not on the leading prelates or the few prominent statesmen, but rather on the rank and file, who guided the administrative machinery. Great changes, great reforms are not to be expected under such circumstances. But the clever craftsman who tends the machine is just the sort of person to devise some little improvements of its mechanism, those simple inventions which enable the machine to do its work better and more economically. Let us, however, drop a metaphor which suggests a merely mechanical theory of the state, and follow rather the sounder doctrine that the state is an organism. From this point of view we may say that the growth of the state and society goes on the more readily, and perhaps after a more wholesome fashion, when the ordinary operations of the seasons are disturbed by no alternating periods of excessive heat or cold, by none of those great natural convulsions which baffle all calculation. The importance of the reign, then, is that it shows us how late mediæval administration, and late mediæval society, went on when left to themselves.

## (3) The General Scope of the Work

During the last twenty-five years I have often had occasion to study some one point, aspect or personality of Edward II's reign, and on two occasions I have attempted a general survey of it so far as that could be done in the light of the printed authorities. The results of these two examinations have been printed in my life of Edward II in the *Dictionary of National Biography*, and in the chapters devoted to that reign in the third volume of Longmans' *Political History of England*. But in neither of these studies did I find much occasion to depart from the traditional and conservative view of these twenty years of English history. Since then my investigations into certain aspects of administrative history of the fourteenth century have forced me to study with more particularity than before some sides of Edward II's reign. In particular I have gone through such records as I could find to illustrate the machinery through which the king's court and household were enabled to extend their sphere of operations from the government of the monarch's domestic establishment to the administration of the realm. I do not profess to have made more than a cursory examination of the immense mass of record and manuscript material that still exists for the study of the administrative aspects of this reign. But I had not gone very far with my study before I became convinced that all the earlier work on the reign has been based upon such imperfect appreciation of the evidence available that it cannot be regarded as in any sense final.

I cannot even except from this judgment the great work of Stubbs, though that must always remain the starting-point for new investigations of the period. It is not too much to say that Stubbs has done more for the history of Edward II than any other scholar that has ever lived. He has not only given a wonderfully sure survey in his *Constitutional History*, but in his admirable edition of the *Chronicles of Edward I and Edward II* he has provided new material for its study, illuminated by his own clear and searching commentaries. Yet save for these chronicles Stubbs limited himself to printed material, and his absorption in the parliamentary struggle of the time rendered him indifferent to certain aspects of its history. He certainly never appreciated the real importance of the reign as the turning-point in our later administrative history. Even to Stubbs, then, the real perspective of the period was not fully revealed, and those of us who have followed in his footsteps have been equally blind to it.

I do not claim to have had any new revelation. On the contrary, I strongly hold the view that it is not possible to come to any definite judgment on the reign until it has been re-written on a larger and more comprehensive scale than has hitherto been attempted. Such a history must be composed in the light of the whole material, record and narrative, printed and unprinted, that is available. Of no aspect of the reign can it be at present said that there is an exhaustive study in existence. It is not the case even with regard to those sides which are most familiar to us, such as the narrative, political, parliamentary and ecclesiastical history. Other aspects of the reign have hardly been considered seriously at all, and we have still to seek for even summary treatment, with adequate scholarship, of its economic, social, and, what is more important for my purpose, its administrative history. Unluckily elaborate and detailed narrative histories of a short period are now somewhat out of fashion, and the more austere type of modern scholar tends to depreciate their importance and value. I do not say that they are the most alluring type of historical composition, but I do say that there is a danger in our modern habit of splitting up knowledge in specialised monographs. The conditions precedent of a definitive study of any particular branch of history are surely the adequate statement of the ordinary narrative history on a large and adequate scale. We want for the reign of

Edward II such detailed treatment as Freeman strove to give to the reigns of William I and William II, or such as Mr. Wylie has given to the reign of Henry IV, or, to take a modern instance, such as Gardiner began and Sir Charles Firth is carrying on for the first half of the seventeenth century, or, to finish with a foreign example, such a study as M. Delachenal is now making of the reign of Charles V of France.[1] Such a presentation of the reign must be based upon real insight into social, administrative, economic and ecclesiastical conditions. Imperfect acquaintance with the institutions and atmosphere of the time is the rock on which most of the old-fashioned narratives of "civil and military" transactions have split. Luckily we have an admirable example of how such reconstructive work should be performed in the few illuminating pages in which Stubbs has elucidated some of the later crises of Edward of Carnarvon's history in his introduction to the *Chronicles of Edward I and Edward II.*

My own task in reference to this reign is a much humbler one. It would be courting certain failure to attempt to write consecutive narrative history in a few short chapters, though I have, rather sporadically it is true, made an effort to tell some aspects of the story which I do not think have been adequately emphasised. But I am impelled to do so since with this study I shall be compelled to bid a final adieu to the general history of the reign. I am, however, happy to think that we shall not have to wait indefinitely for a detailed history of Edward II.[2] What I shall aim at will be not so much narrative as description, criticism, and the statement of a point of view that I venture to hope will not be found absolutely a stale one. I do not think that the existing narratives will have to be re-written, though of course they will have to be corrected, as all historical work has to be. Correction of detail is, however, never a very important thing. It only becomes important when we are dealing

[1] [Now complete, in five volumes. Paris, 1909-31.]

[2] My former pupil and colleague, Miss Hilda Johnstone, now Reader in History in the University of London, has already made progress in collecting material with a view to attempting a complete study of the reign. [*Cf.* Hilda Johnstone, 'England; Edward I and Edward II' in *Camb. Med. Hist.*, vii, 393-433. A more complete study of Edward II's reign is in preparation, but has hitherto been delayed, perhaps with some slight excuse in view of four years spent in war work and new responsibilities assumed in 1922 as professor of history.]

with books so weak in their general scholarship that they themselves are utterly unimportant. Yet the simple truth is that "discoveries" in history are for the most part discoveries of detail. They only become of value when treated in the mass, and when they enable us to construct some general picture, solve some real problem, or build up some new generalisation. In this instance I do not aspire to paint a new picture, but rather to build a somewhat larger and more appropriate frame for the old one. At the most I should wish to sketch in a new background to the stage on which the old figures may re-enact their ancient parts.

I have already explained that I approached this reign from the standpoint of its unwritten administrative history. Applying the ideas which I had derived from the study of that aspect of the reign to other points of view, I had the conviction forced on me that here also the importance of the reign had not been properly appreciated. The result was that my studies soon went far beyond the administrative field. No doubt in the attempt to cover the wider ground a good deal has been lost in thoroughness. I am well aware, however, that I am only at the beginning of the subject. I only aim at indicating the general lines upon which such a detailed history as seems desirable ought to be written. It is an attempt to suggest a point of view for future workers. What this standpoint is must now in some fashion be explained. How far it is a true one, the future historians of the reign must decide.

The reign of Edward II is generally regarded as a series of rather futile revolutions, each involving a change of government which was to a very partial extent a change for the better. It is true that there was some revolutionary legislation, but it is one thing to pass a revolutionary law, and another thing to execute it. The chief innovations of the reign, the ordinances of 1311, were often re-enacted, but never were fully carried out, and were repealed eleven years later. Only for one brief period, between 1318 and 1322, were they within a measurable distance of being observed, and their execution during these years was due to a compromise between the better elements in both court and opposition, which necessitated their being carried out in a spirit that was charitable both to vested interests and to the personal susceptibilities of the king and his friends. The result of all this was that there was a striking continuity in the administrative personnel all through the reign. A favourite might be dismissed; a magnate might retire from court in a huff: but the everyday workers who governed the country went on, despite all threatenings, from 1307 to 1318, and if the worst, or the least prudent, were dislodged between 1318 and 1321, the old gang was back again by 1322, and continued to control affairs until the final *débâcle* of 1326. And this is true despite the fact that the ordinances, formulated in 1310 and 1311, demanded a thorough clean sweep of the administration, and that these ordinances remained the law until 1322. The explanation is that, like most mediæval legislation, the ordinances expressed an ideal of reformation working in men's brains rather than a new act of parliament which it was intended to carry out. That Edward II of all people was able to resist in fact what he accepted in name needs, however, further explanation, and that explanation is based upon the fact that the king's court was not a mere fortuitous aggregation of disconnected and incompetent courtiers, but a solidly organised institution, with traditions of government and influence. These were but little disturbed when an unpopular favourite whose enormities loomed large in the public eye, a Gaveston or a Despenser, was hurled overboard to lighten the ship of state, when thrown on its beam ends by a tempest of public opinion. Stubbs has taught us to speak of the court party as a continuous element in fourteenth century politics, but it does not seem that he ever fully realised what a solidly organised institution the court was, and how it had under its control resources of administration that enabled it to direct every department of the state. To explain this we shall have to go at some length into the system of administration which Edward II inherited from Edward I, the part which the organised court took in the government, and the extent to which it enabled the king to evade his obligations to parliament, and entrench himself against the nation in a household manned by his own personal dependents. By these days the great departments of state, the exchequer and the chancery, that is to say, the department of finance and the department of administration and secretarial work, though originating from the king's household, had become self-contained, independent, definite offices of government, each with a personnel and a tradition of its own, so well defined that it was easy for a parliament which insisted on the appointment of the responsible minister who directed it, the treasurer or the chancellor, to obtain the control of the whole department. But, although chancery and exchequer had branched out of the ancient court system, the *curia regis* still remained much as it had been before, and in the course of the thirteenth century administrative convenience rather than political design had supplemented the official secretarial and financial departments by a court office which, retaining its primitive undifferentiated character, was at once the court department of finance and of administration. This was the office of the wardrobe. We shall never understand the fourteenth century aright unless we grasp the importance of the wardrobe as well as of the chancery and the exchequer. It was to the almost permanent officials who staffed these three departments that the remarkable administrative reforms were due all through the reign. They were few in the earlier, more confused and conservative period, which ranges from 1307 to 1318. Between 1318 and 1323 they were exceedingly numerous and important.

In subsequent chapters I shall have occasion to explain in some detail the nature of these administrative reforms which, I venture to think, give the reign of Edward II a place of its own in English history. Some of them are fairly well known and generally recognised, notably the reforms of the exchequer, begun by the treasurer Stapeldon about the year 1323. Very little attention, however, has been paid to the reforms of the household, which resulted from the household ordinance of York of 1318. I do not think that anyone has recognised how many significant and permanent changes in household economy arose, quite early in the reign, from the defensive measures taken by Edward II and his courtiers to protect themselves from the efforts of the ordainers to include the offices of the court, as well as the great offices of the state, within the sphere of their influence. Though the chancery was less affected by the practical reforming spirit than either the exchequer or the household offices, this period witnessed some striking changes in it, and in particular the last stages of its differentiation from the household. Equally important with the reforms of the old offices was the settlement of their relations with each other. The result of this was that the sphere of each department of state was more rigidly and clearly defined. Moreover, the increasing complexity of administration involved not only the strengthening of the old offices, but the virtual erection of new ones. In particular the household administrative system threw off vigorous offshoots which gradually became new offices of state on their own account. Even the traditional local administration was influenced by the practical reforming spirit. The sheriffs were at last chosen from the gentlemen of their own shire, obtained their appointment from the chancery, and were limited to a short period of office. The two great escheatorships were broken up into local escheatorships, each of which was confined to three or four adjoining counties.

The importance of the reign of Edward II does not entirely depend upon its place in administrative history. Though the administrative aspect of affairs will never be far from my thoughts, I must also speak of other features of the reign which are only less significant. Here, as when dealing with administration, we may split up the reign into two periods, the dividing line between which runs somewhere near 1318. In the earlier period an effort is made to carry on the government on the lines laid down by Edward I. But the policy of Edward I was, as I shall try to show in the next chapter, on the verge of collapse at the moment of the great king's death. We are accustomed to glorify Edward I as the "greatest of the Plantagenets" and the founder and organiser of our free constitution. That Edward established constitutional government in England was the result of historical accident much more than deliberate design. Certain it is that Edward I had, no more than Philip the Fair, any conscious intention of taking the people into partnership with him or of promoting any sort of constitutional freedom. All that the old king sought was to get the help of the lower estates, the country gentry and the merchants of the towns, in his inevitable struggle against the privileged baronage and episcopate, which loudly demanded that they alone should help the king in the rule of the land, but made it the condition of their help that the king should frame his policy in accordance with their ideals. When Edward I died that struggle of king and baronage was still fiercely being fought. But Edward had made great progress after his humiliations between 1295 and 1300. He had divided the baronial leaders; he had seized upon the Bigod inheritance and bridled the Clares and the Bohuns; he had driven Winchelsea and Bek into exile; he had evaded his obligations to the estates; and he had managed to strengthen his hold over Scotland despite the unwillingness of the magnates to second his wishes. Had he been a younger man, had he had ten years more of life, he might have combined the humiliation of baronage and episcopate with the real subjection of the Scots. In that case who can doubt but that he would have dealt as roughly with constitutional freedom as ever French autocrat had done? It is easy to imagine a history of England in which Edward I appears as the English Philip the Fair, as the organiser of despotism, not as the pioneer of constitutionalism. That such was not the case in English history is, I think, largely due to the reign of Edward II.

The ineffectiveness of Edward II's reign made permanent the constitutional machinery of the reign of Edward I, and so began that differentiation between English and French history which certainly did not exist under Edward I, but was clearly evident under Edward III. Looked at from this point of view Edward II's reign has its constitutional as well as its administrative importance. A strong successor to Edward I might have made England a despotism; his weak and feckless son secured the permanence of Edwardian constitutionalism. It is inevitable under such circumstances that the constitutional movement of the reign should assume something of an oligarchical and reactionary character. Yet we must not overstress the current view that the work of Edward I had counted for nothing, and that the barons of 1311 were just in the same position as the barons of 1258. It is true that the twofold claim of the ordainers to appoint ministers of state and to include within that category the chief household officers had been formulated as clearly in 1258 as in 1311. Yet we shall see later that the parliamentary history of Edward II's reign shows a steady undercurrent towards the increasing participation of the commons in deliberations of state. In the twenty years of the reign the commons were summoned by writ to parliaments no less than twenty-five times,[1] though the actual proceedings of these disorderly gatherings, where the magnates with their armed followers had the last and the first word in each discussion, had no doubt more affinities to those of a Polish Diet than to those of the orderly parliaments of more modern

[1] [Mr. Tout noted here "But *cf. Mirror of Justices* (Selden Soc.), p. 8, for a view of parliament." I judge his reference is to that treatise's romantic description of how King Alfred "ordena pur usage perpetuele qe a ij fois par an ou plus sovent pur mestier en tens de pees sassemblerent a Londres pur parlementer sur le guiement de poeple," etc.]

date. Yet there was, notably in the policy of the Despensers and the acts of the parliament of York of 1322, a real tendency towards the development of constitutional theory, as well as towards the amplification of constitutional practice. The conditions of fourteenth-century society, which remained essentially aristocratic, necessarily prevented either of these tendencies going very far. Yet enough remains to show that the reign of Edward II was in constitutional as well as in administrative history a real turning-point in the history of England. The constitutional position I shall strive to work out, as I dwell in my third and fourth chapters on the general political and administrative history of the reign. Administrative reforms I shall consider in the fifth.

In my last two chapters I shall pass in inadequate review certain miscellaneous aspects of the reign, which are more conveniently treated apart from the general currents of political and constitutional history and of administrative reform. Here also I shall endeavour to suggest the extent to which the reign forms a turning-point in our history. In what we may by anticipation call imperial history this certainly was the case. The reign saw the establishment of the political independence of Scotland, the reduction of the English power in Ireland to that extreme weakness in which it lay until the days of the later Tudors, and a new stage in the decline of the power of the English dukes of Gascony. But as some compensation to this reaction from the imperialistic visions of an Edward I, we see in the Welsh and Marcher history of the reign real anticipations of Tudor policy. We must not regard as unimportant even the foreign and military history. The insignificant foreign policy of Edward II has its prophetic note in its anticipations of the Anglo-French relations of the period of the Hundred Years War, just as the array of Bannockburn and Myton, and still more the adoption of Scottish tactics by the borderers who won the battle of Boroughbridge, afford a real anticipation of the methods of English warfare that astonished all Europe when exhibited on a great scale at Crécy and Poitiers. In ecclesiastical history, also, the reign which first saw the suppression of a great order by the ecclesiastical power, the frank seizure of the alien priories by the state, and the systematisation of papal appointment to English bishoprics, has also its contrasts to offer. Lastly, the social and economic aspects of the reign have their lessons. The slackness of government and the constant threatenings, and occasional happenings, of war did not prevent the later part of the reign witnessing a certain restoration of order and material prosperity. Thus it is that the period was marked by strong tendencies in the direction of the organisation of trade on national lines and the growth of English economic self-sufficiency, such as are currently thought only to have begun under Edward III. This is notably the case with regard to the development of the English staple system, every important feature of which was established before the fall of Edward II. I have, therefore, not thought it out of place to deal at some length with the origins of this characteristic feature of our mediæval commercial policy.

## II

# THE INHERITANCE OF EDWARD II

## (I) Policy and Administration in General

Edward of Carnarvon inherited from his father a splendid tradition and an admirable system of organisation and administration. He has often been reproached with being an unworthy heir of his father's greatness, and essentially the reproach cannot be gainsaid. It can, however, be pleaded in extenuation of his shortcomings that he inherited, along with the institutions which his father had so meticulously defined and carefully developed, the obligation to carry on his father's policy. This involved a burden so overwhelming that it nearly had broken the back of his great father, and proved all too heavy for the degenerate son. It was perhaps an easy task to walk in the footsteps of Edward I as regards carrying on his methods of government and administration. But Edward I had stretched to the uttermost the institutions which he had fashioned in the hope of being able to perform a task for which his resources were absolutely inadequate. And, whether Edward of Carnarvon liked it or not, circumstances more powerful than his own volition compelled him to take up and bear with him his father's burden.

Accustomed to revere in Edward I the greatest of the Plantagenets, we do not always sufficiently appreciate how complete was the failure of that king's declining years. He was pledged to conquer Scotland and hold it in subjection. He was forced to constant vigilance to keep down the Welsh and uphold the declining fortunes of the Anglo-Norman colony in Ireland. Moreover, there was the double obligation of maintaining the political and economic interests of England and its king in Gascony and Flanders, and the inevitable cleavage of interest between France and England which that policy involved, however much the divergence of standpoint might be cloaked over by marriages and treaties. In addition to the burden of these national and feudal obligations there was also the chronic difficulty with the church, recently emphasised by the breach between Edward I and Winchelsea, and but partially mitigated by the comparative complaisance of a pope from the Bordelais. But worst of all was the discord between Edward and his own barons, accentuated by the ruthless persistence with which he evaded the hated concessions extorted from him in the hour of his worst need, and by the greediness with which the spoils of the escheated earldoms and baronies were gathered in. Equally grave was the collapse of the national finances under the strain which Edward had put upon them. Constant wars and a divided nation involved a financial burden which Edward was quite unable to sustain. The once order-loving monarch had ceased to balance his income and expenditure. The wardrobe accounts, which best show Edward I's war budgets, testify year after year to a large deficit on the income side,[1] and for the last years of the reign were rarely made up and never enrolled.[2] The receipt rolls of the exchequer show in their scanty totals how much less taxes now yielded than they had done in the great days of the reign. Though the utmost pressure was brought to bear on the taxpayer, the sulkiness of the barons, the exhaustion of the cultivator, the demoralisation of the executive, all combined to make inadequate the yield that resulted from the strenuous efforts of the king and his ministers. The result was that the old king, despairing of his own people, fell back on the foreigner, on the alien merchants, whom he had bribed to grant him new customs, and on the Italian bankers, who made him the temporary advances by which alone he could stave off bankruptcy, and keep alive his starving soldiers and debt-burdened ministers, who had long ceased to expect to be paid the king's wages. At last the Frescobaldi would only continue their loans if they were permitted to keep in their hands the collection of the customs. This great source of revenue was accordingly handed over to them, much as a spendthrift oriental potentate or a bankrupt South American republic has nowadays

[1] For every year of Langton's keepership of the wardrobe, 1290-95, the wardrobe spent more than it received (Pipe Roll 138, mm. 25, 26; *ibid.* 139, m. 6; *ibid.* 144, m. 20. [See for full discussion of whole question *Chapters*, ii, 90-4.]

[2] For instance, Langton's wardrobe accounts for the period before he became treasurer of the exchequer were not rendered until 1300. No wardrobe accounts were enrolled between 26 E. I and 1 E. II (*P.R.O. Lists and Indexes*, no. xi, *Enrolled Foreign Accounts*, p. 102).

to abandon to European creditors the administration of the local revenue. And in the midst of all this financial anxiety came all the unexpected troubles which followed from the brilliantly successful revolt of Robert Bruce. Most admirable is the stern energy and ruthless eagerness with which the old king stuck to his task to the end. He would not give up Langton, however fiercely the barons attacked the faithful minister. He paid no heed to the threatenings of old age. He disregarded his broken health, his disobedient heir, the rebellious archbishop and the sullen baronage. He went on steadily with his work until death came upon him on the eve of the projected Scots invasion. He had overborne the worst of the opposition, and was on the high road towards making himself an autocrat. But he paid a heavy penalty for his hard won and precarious triumph. Probably no mediæval king left his finances in a more hopeless confusion than did the great Edward. Certainly none of them ever handed to his successor so heavy a task with such inadequate means to discharge it.

So much for the bad side of the young king's inheritance. Let us now turn to what we may call the good side, the inheritance of the Edwardian constitution.

With regard to Edward I's parliamentary and constitutional policy I have absolutely nothing to say, save to reiterate the suggestion that I have thrown out earlier that we read the history of the king's long reign through very modern spectacles if we regard him as the conscious founder of a free constitutional system. Edward I had not a much clearer vision of the future history of England than had the barons of Runnymede, whose shortsightedness and narrow sense of self-interest have been recognised, perhaps almost too much emphasised, by most recent scholars. Edward sought to establish the royal power, the barons to consolidate aristocratic privilege. But we must at least admit that as a result both the one and the others did bear their part in building up a system which went far beyond their imaginations. From this point of view it is, I think, a mistake to allow certain superficial resemblances between the reigns of Henry III and Edward II to blind us to the fact that there was a deep gulf between them. Now that gulf was dug by the Edwardian definition of the constitution. What was the legislative, deliberative and taxative system, which Edward II inherited from his father, is written for all time in Stubbs' *Constitutional History*.

That system was still, however, in the making, still perhaps much more fluid than Stubbs' doctrine of definition will allow. It was, I think, still uncertain whether the Edwardian system would result in a limited monarchy, tempered by aristocratic and some measure of popular control, or in an autocracy of the type established by Philip the Fair, and I have already claimed that it was only as a result of the reign of Edward II that the institutions of his father assumed the form in which they became permanent in history. Unluckily an unconfessed, and perhaps half-unconscious, change of plan prevented Stubbs from dealing with the machinery of English administration under Edward I with the same masterly thoroughness that he showed in describing the administrative system of the early Angevins. So far as the change was conscious, it was due to his rather too exclusive preoccupation with the origins of our modern constitution, and in particular with the origins of our parliamentary institutions. The shire moot and the hundred moot, the circuits of the royal justices, and the juries with whom they dealt, were important to Stubbs, because in the local representative system of the Angevins he saw the beginnings of the representative parliaments, and all that gave the later English constitution its special character. When the shire moots and the juries had done their work, and had produced what we may by anticipation call the House of Commons, the local courts and their sworn committees had no longer any special interest for the "constitutional" historian. They became mere antiquities without any clear practical value and, therefore, might be safely relegated to the background. As a result of this presupposition we have in Stubbs much about the exchequer of the Angevins, but very little about the exchequer of the Edwards, nothing more than a few pregnant suggestions as to the Edwardian chancery, and not so much as a casual hint as to the importance of the wardrobe. One reason for this was doubtless the fact that Stubbs was seldom a haunter of the Public Record Office, and it was there and only there that the materials could have been found for an adequate study of these subjects. Accordingly the administrative machinery through which our fourteenth-century kings ruled England is still very imperfectly known.

In respect to the history of administration English scholars have done much less for their own country than have the scholars of France for the administrative institutions of their land during the later middle ages. Let us, for a moment, compare the scope and treatment of constitutional history in Stubbs' great work with the scope and treatment of the corresponding matter in the book that most nearly corresponds to the *Constitutional History* in French historical literature, I mean M. Paul Viollet's three volumes on the *Histoire des Institutions Politiques et Administratives de la France* during the middle ages. The one is "constitutional," the other "institutional" history. With one writer, administration recedes to the background after the twelfth century, and narrative political history is never lost sight of. With the other, administration is from first to last the root of the matter. It is no longer possible to maintain with the last generation that this difference is due to the difference of the historical development of the two countries. There was as good an administrative system in fourteenth-century England as there was in fourteenth-century France, only we have not taken the trouble to study it. We have nothing dealing with English administration to correspond to such treatises as M. Morel's *Grande Chancellerie Royale*, or M. Borelli de Serres' *Recherches sur Quelques Services Publiques*, two books which I mention *exempli gratia* rather than because they alone cover the field. It is not that our English archives have not material for such studies. On the contrary, the English records are more abundant than the French. The reason for our ignorance is simply that we have shamefully neglected our opportunities and that English scholars have not perceived the necessity of devoting their attention to problems of mediæval administration. Among more recent writers, Maitland fully appreciated the importance of this subject, and has suggested some of the main principles on which it should be treated in more than one of his works, notably in his remarkable introduction to the *Memoranda de Parliamento*, the roll of the parliament of 1305. He has, however, never worked out the problem in detail, and some of his most stimulating suggestions may perhaps not be sustained when we get face to face with the detailed facts. However, both Stubbs and Maitland, though they did not take us very far, put us on the right line. They knew that the chancery was, in Stubbs' phrase, the "secretariat of state for all departments," and that the exchequer was primarily a financial organisation. They were quite guiltless of any share in the improbable doctrine, which can be read in some places, that there was a time when the exchequer was the chief administrative department, and that it was only in the early fourteenth century, perhaps under Edward II, that the chancery established its superiority over it and limited it to matters of finance.[1] However, neither Stubbs nor Maitland realised that, constantly overlapping both chancery and exchequer, the king's wardrobe habitually performed the essential functions of both, and set up a dual system of government which almost reminds us of the "double cabinet" of George III, which Burke spent all his eloquence in denouncing.

To describe at length the institutions by which, under Edward I, the central authority of the crown was exercised in the everyday work of governing the country, is much too elaborate and intricate a task to be attempted here. I must, however, attempt to suggest what seem to me to be the essential outlines of this subject, for, unless we grasp how Edward I governed England, we read awry all the history of the fourteenth century. Indeed, it is not too much to say that, without a proper appreciation of the administrative machine and of its functions, our wonderful collection of fourteenth-century records lose half their meaning, and more than half their coherence. We may calendar our chancery rolls, and classify and study the forms of every type of mediæval document. We may pore over mediæval handwritings until fourteenth-century documents become almost as easy to read, sometimes much easier to read, than our private correspondence. Nevertheless the work of calendaring and indexing, essential though it be, the study of diplomatic forms and palæography, excellent though they are, will profit us little, unless we also realise that these auxiliary sciences will only yield their full results to scholars versed in the details of mediæval administration. I emphasise this point because in my judgment the work that it is most important to do in late mediæval English history is to re-construct the system of everyday administration through which our kings and ministers governed the country. Not very much has as yet been published on this subject, but I am glad to know that earnest efforts are now being made to break

[1] This heresy is strongly expressed in the suggestive paper of that excellent scholar, the late Mr. Arthur Hughes, on "the Parliament of Lincoln of 1316," *Trans. Roy. Hist. Soc.*, New Series, x, 41-58 (1896). See below, p. 165 and n.

up the ground in some of the more fruitful portions of this vast and unexplored field. I know that on both sides of the Atlantic very serious attempts have been made to grapple with the fourteenth-century exchequer, which is quite as important, though much less known, than the exchequer of the Angevins.[1] I know that there has just been published an elaborate and systematic study of the king's council in the later middle ages, the work of an American scholar.[2] Nearer home I am glad to announce that a young mediævalist has made good progress in an effort to unravel the intricacies of the organisation of the chancery up to the end of the fourteenth century.[3] And I hope it will not be thought egotistical if I repeat that I hope myself to publish before long an attempt to appreciate the part played by the curialist administrative system, the wardrobe and the chamber, in thirteenth and fourteenth century history.[4] The ground which we all have to cover is vast, and none of us can hope to present anything more than tentative and preliminary studies. We shall be quite content if we do something to clear the ground, and encourage another generation of scholars

[1] I may particularly refer to the work of Mr. Hilary Jenkinson, of the Public Record Office, on the exchequer. Some of his conclusions are set forth in his remarkable papers on "Exchequer Tallies" in *Archæologia*, lxii, 367-80 (1911), [and "Medieval Tallies, public and private" in *ibid.*, lxxiv, 289-351 (1925)]. Important results to general exchequer problems may also be expected from the study of taxation on moveables, by Professor J. F. Willard, of the University of Colorado, which, Mr. Willard informs me, will soon be completed. [His *Parliamentary Taxes on personal property: a study of mediæval English financial administration*, was published by the Mediæval Academy of America in 1934. Among his numerous previous studies in this field special attention may be drawn to three articles on taxation on moveables in the reigns of Edw. I, Edw. II and Edw. III in *Eng. Hist. Rev.*, vols. xxviii, xxix, xxx, and to his work on "The memoranda rolls and the remembrancers" in *Essays presented to T. F. Tout*, pp. 215-29 (1925). Of recent years much addition to our knowledge of the exchequer has been made by Miss Mabel H. Mills, notably in her introduction to the Pipe roll for 1295, Surrey membrane (Surrey Record Soc., xxi, 1924).]

[2] The monograph by Professor J. F. Baldwin, of Vassar College, on the *King's Council in the Middle Ages*, was published in the autumn of 1913 by the Clarendon Press. Some of its conclusions have been foreshadowed in Mr. Baldwin's valuable articles in the *English* and *American Historical Review*.

[3] My former pupil and colleague, Miss L. B. Dibben, has written two important papers in the *English Historical Review* on "Secretaries in the thirteenth and fourteenth centuries" (xxv, 430-44) and "Chancellor and Keeper of the Seal under Henry III" (xxvii, 39-51). [In 1929 Dr. B. Wilkinson, another pupil, published his book on the *Chancery under Edw. III*.]

[4] [This took shape in the six volumes of his *Chapters in Mediaeval Administrative History*, published 1920-33.]

to pursue still further these fascinating lines of study, which are crying aloud for further investigation.

## (2) The Exchequer under Edward I

It is well known that all the administrative machinery by which the princes of mediæval Europe sought to rule their dominions was based upon the organisation of their domestic households.[1] Absolutely no distinction existed in those primitive times between the sovereign in his private capacity as owner of a great estate and master of an extensive domestic establishment, and the sovereign in his public capacity as the political ruler of a nation. Those who clearly grasp this fundamental point will, I may say in passing, appreciate at once the essential unsoundness of the old-fashioned doctrine which distinguished, even in the eleventh century, between the king's domain, the king's personal property, and "folkland," then erroneously regarded as the national estate of which the king had only the administration.

The first faint beginnings of an orderly system of administration and finance arise from the king's chamber, which was, in the days of Edward the Confessor, when we can first see it at work, literally the king's bedroom. We see what this archaic state of things meant in the well-known story how Edward the Confessor kept his treasure in his bedroom, so that the thief who aspired to rob the national treasury had to wait until the king took an after-dinner nap before he could venture to steal into the royal chamber, and extract from the king's treasure chest some portion of its precious contents.[2] After the Norman conquest this primitive arrangement became ancient history. Stubbs has shown us how under Henry I and Henry II the Angevin monarchy exercised its authority through two great organisations, the *curia regis* and the exchequer. Of these the exchequer had

[1] In the description of the exchequer which follows I shall limit myself to a few general references. I have based my account on Madox's *History of the Exchequer* (1769) supplemented by more recent work, such as that of Mr. J. H. Round, Mr. H. Hall and Mr. R. L. Poole. An excellent short account of the exchequer by Mr. Charles Johnson is in *Encyclopædia Britannica*, eleventh edition, x, 54-6. My own studies of exchequer records, notably the receipt and issue rolls, have enabled me to add a few points.

[2] See the passage in the metrical life of Edward in Luard's *Lives of Edward the Confessor* (R.S.), p. 53. Compare J. H. Round, *The King's Serjeants*, p. 121.

by the reign of Henry II almost entirely separated itself from the perambulating king's court. It had settled down in a home of its own at Westminster. It had officers of its own, who still combined their exchequer function with other employments in the *curia regis*, but gradually, as exchequer work grew, became more and more tied down to their own department. Even under Henry II, placemen whose primary business was not with finance felt themselves uncomfortable when tradition required their attendance at the exchequer. Thus the chancellor was so seldom present at its sessions that, in the absence of his seal, it was already found necessary by the days of the *Dialogus* that the exchequer should have a seal of its own. This exchequer seal was probably in its origin a mere duplicate of the chancellor's seal, but it soon became a true departmental seal with a keeper of its own, the chancellor of the exchequer, and this officer soon ceased, even in name, to be the true chancellor's deputy. This exchequer seal is, I am convinced, the first departmental seal, apart from the general royal seal, to come into existence in any country in western Europe.

A great expert has studied so recently the twelfth-century exchequer, that there is no need for me to say any more about it.[1] I only want to insist that the exchequer organisation went on quite continuously through the thirteenth to the fourteenth century. It was still, when our reign began, the department of state which was most clearly differentiated from the other political offices. It had the longest history, the most glorious traditions, and its staff possessed the keenest sense of the supreme value of its constituted usage. Though its origin went back to a time when only ecclesiastics were expected to have the knowledge of business involved in an acquaintance with reading, writing and arithmetic, the exchequer had always been partially officered by laymen. Accordingly its staff remained divided between the layman and the clerk. This was for our period equally the case as regards each of the two branches into which the exchequer had long been divided. These were the "lower exchequer" or "exchequer of receipt," and the "upper exchequer" or

[1] See R. L. Poole's *The Exchequer in the Twelfth Century* (Oxford, 1912). Mr. Hilary Jenkinson's interesting article on "William Cade, a Financier of the Twelfth Century," *Eng. Hist. Rev.*, xxviii, 209-27, and the discussion which it originated in the same periodical, have more recently illustrated another aspect of this subject.

"exchequer of account." This distinction, of great importance from some points of view, is for our present purposes not very vital, save that the natural place for the greater dignitaries was the more important exchequer of account, so that they were often content to be represented by deputies and clerks at the "receipt." The head of the exchequer, the treasurer, was a great officer of state, generally second only to the chancellor, though, if endowed with greater capacity or more fully possessed of his sovereign's confidence, he might easily become the *de facto* chief minister, as was emphatically the case with Walter Langton, bishop of Lichfield, the treasurer from 1295 to 1307. The treasurer was practically always an ecclesiastic, but there was no impropriety in a lay baron undertaking the treasurer's duties, if accident or affairs took him away from his post. Next to the treasurer came the two chamberlains, whose name takes us back to the eleventh century, before the exchequer had been differentiated from the royal chamber. Originally they represented the lay element in the exchequer. They were under the Angevins unlearned knights who could not calculate on parchment, or indite rolls and accounts in Latin. The tally system, if not devised for their convenience, was doubtless easier for them to understand. But by the fourteenth century the *miles litteratus* had ceased to be a rare phenomenon, and there was no longer any need for drawing so hard and fast a line between clerk and layman. One result of this is that we find clerical chamberlains of the exchequer, as for instance the notorious Adam of Stratton. Under Edward II the clerical chamberlain is the rule, not the exception.

The extension of education to laymen broke down the ancient distinction between the clerical officers of the exchequer, dependent on the treasurer, and the lay "sergeants," dependent on the chamberlains. With it went one good reason for separating the "receipt," controlled by the chamberlains, from the "exchequer of account," directed by the treasurer. The "receipt" now had, in the issue and receipt rolls, records of its own which required clerkly skill to manipulate. Also the exchequer tallies were no longer rude devices to enable unlettered laymen to keep accounts, but either were checks upon the written records or an elaborate instrument of credit that anticipates the modern cheque, note and exchequer bond or bill. Again, the four or five barons of the exchequer, whose existence as a special class of officers only begins after the majority of Henry III, were indifferently clerks or laymen.[1] Despite this fact, their natural sphere was the exchequer of account; so much so that it became customary for writs addressed to this department to be addressed "to the treasurer and barons of the exchequer," just as writs destined for the "receipt" were addressed "to the treasurer and chamberlains."

Some exchequer offices, however, remained clerical. The chancellor of the exchequer, keeper of the exchequer seal, was still always a clerk, though he was now a purely exchequer officer. He was equal in rank and salary to the barons. There were also the two "remembrancers" of the exchequer, clerks always, because especially charged with the *memoranda* which concerned the interests of the department, and therefore with the composition of the *memoranda* rolls. The origin of the officers is not yet clear, but originally they were two persons keeping almost duplicate rolls for precaution's sake. Already under Edward I one was called occasionally "king's remembrancer" and the other "treasurer's remembrancer."[2] There was also the clerk who kept the issue and receipt rolls of the lower exchequer, the later "clerk of the pells." A treasurer's clerk was also specially appointed to "sit at the receipt," that is to take and issue moneys during the short vacations when the exchequer was technically closed. There is no need to dwell upon the remaining clerks, ushers and other subordinate officers. The issue rolls show that wages were commonly paid to the following officers of the receipt: two chamberlains at 8d. a day, three scribes at 5d., a porter at 5d., a weigher at 12d., three tellers at 3d., and an officer responsible for watch and lights who received only 1½d.

Essentially the exchequer staff had become by this time a staff of experts, of professional men whose lives were devoted to exchequer work, and who were as much permanent civil servants as the clerks of our present-day treasury.[3] This fact is the more remarkable since all the lay offices of long standing in the exchequer were "in fee," or "held by

[1] See for this App. II, pp. 298-302.

[2] [For the new division of duties between these officers, and the differences between their rolls which resulted, in the reign of Edward II, see Prof. J. F. Willard, "The Memoranda Rolls and the Remembrancers, 1282-1350," in *Essays . . . presented to T. F. Tout*, pp. 215-29.]

[3] In 1231 Peter des Roches invited to Winchester for Christmas "regem, justiciarium et episcopos et comites et barones et clericos de scaccario et alios nobiliores quotquot habere potuit" (*Ann. Dunstable* in *Ann. Mon.* (R.S.), iii, 127).

serjeantry," that is to say, were hereditary pieces of property, and quite outside the control of the crown. But the greater of these hereditary royal officers, notably the "chamberlains in fee," were magnates too distinguished to do the work themselves. Accordingly they acquired the habit of nominating some one to act on their behalf. As a rule these nominees fell easily into line with the king's chosen servants, and were quite their equals in professional zeal and devotion to the interests of the crown. Though there was occasionally friction between the hereditary household officers and the king as regards the appointment of the actual men to do the work, I have found nothing to correspond affecting the relations of the actual and nominal officers of the exchequer. Perhaps the fact that the right of the hereditary official to appoint was uncontested made matters easier in practice.

This was notably the case with the chamberlainships. The two hereditary chamberlainships, which went back to the twelfth century, passed from the houses of Malduit and Fitzgerald[1] to the Beauchamp earls of Warwick and the Redvers earls of Devon. When the Redvers lands reverted to the crown, Edward I and his successors kept permanently the right of appointing one of the "chamberlains of the receipt," who discharged the duties of this hereditary chamberlain.[2] But the earl of Warwick still nominated the second chamberlain of the receipt, and under Edward II we have the curious spectacle of a truculent opposition leader choosing of his own free will the joint holder of the second office, in point of dignity, in the finance ministry of the crown.[3] The accident which, after earl Guy's death, put his inheritance

[1] For their early history see Round, *Commune of London*, pp. 83-5.

[2] Up to Edward I's time there were different deputies appointed to the "upper" and "lower" exchequers; see Madox, ii, 297, for an instance. But under Edward II we find scanty mention of a separate chamberlain of the upper exchequer. The "chamberlain of the receipt" is often called simply "chamberlain of the exchequer."

[3] Guy nominated not only the chamberlain of the receipt but the usher of the receipt and the keeper of the tallies. See I.R. 177, m. 1. "Cum loco magistri Johannis Golafre, nuper unus camerariorum scaccarii nostri de recepta, per bone memorie Guidonem de Bello Campo, nuper comitem Warewyk, defunctum, qui de nobis tenuit in capite, deputati, quod quidem officium per mortem eiusdem comitis in manu nostra existit," the king has appointed Mr. William of Maldon by patent of 1 Sept. 1315. Compare *C.P.R. 1313-17*, p. 345; and pp. 357, 637, for the keepership of the tallies. The social position of some of Edward II's chamberlains was considerable. The office was successively held by a Percy, by the brother of John Cromwell, steward and banneret, and by one of Edward II's Spanish kinsfolk. The marshal of the exchequer was similarly the deputy of the earl marshal (Madox, ii, 284-90).

into the hands of a boy two years old, left the king free from 1315 to 1326 to appoint his own men to both chamberlainships.

Even the weighers, the melters, the ushers, and their like held their offices as hereditary serjeantries.[1] Perhaps the steady tendency to appoint clerks to do chamberlain's work, indeed the general preference for clerical ministers, may have had still one root in the feeling that a clerical office could not become an hereditary one. More certainly the steady rise in importance of the barons, who were appointed by the king, may be explained by the fact that they represented the ruler's free choice. The barons were now indifferently clerks or laymen, and were either promoted exchequer or wardrobe officers, or sometimes appointed from the outside. The barons were still revenue officers, not as yet judges. Yet the striking career of Hervey of Staunton shows that lawyers were already wanted for exchequer work. Staunton was a clerk in priest's orders and the son of a prosperous Midland knight. His official career was divided between the exchequer, of which he was a baron and chancellor, and the two benches of the common law, of each of which he was in turn justice and chief justice. And already instances had occurred of distinguished pleaders in the common law courts, successful "king's serjeants," leading barristers, as later ages would have called them, being made barons of the exchequer because of their success at the bar.[2]

The treasurer was nearly always appointed from outside the exchequer staff. It was, both under Edward I and later, very common for the treasurer to be transferred from one of the great wardrobe offices. Yet there is in our period one important case of promotion within the department. This is that of the energetic exchequer officer, Sir Walter of Norwich, a clerk in early life, who renounced his clergy and became a baron of the exchequer and treasurer more than once, and that though he was a knight and a married man. He is one of the numerous instances of men of this age who started life as clerks and abandoned their clergy to found a family and adopt the knightly career.[3] An even more *bona fide* lay

[1] See, for instance, J. H. Round on "The Weigher of the Exchequer" in *Eng. Hist. Rev.*, xxvi, 724-7, and in the *King's Serjeants*, p. 121.

[2] See App. II, pp. 301-2.

[3] Other examples are Hamo of Chigwell, clerk, who became fishmonger and mayor of London, and John of Benstead, clerk, keeper of the wardrobe and chancellor of the exchequer, who became a judge, a knight, and a married man. [See "John de Benstede and his missions," by C. L. Kingsford, in *Essays . . . presented to R. L. Poole*, pp. 332-44 (1927).]

keeper of the treasury was Sir Roger Bellers, also a baron of the exchequer, of whom we shall hear more later. Normally, however, the treasurership was still a strictly ecclesiastical office.

I have sometimes been tempted to imagine that the fact that a certain proportion of the exchequer officers owed their places to hereditary right, or baronial nomination, may partially account for the singularly detached and independent standpoint which the exchequer, like the hereditary parliament of Paris in a later age, not seldom maintained against the crown. It may, moreover, be suggested that the full recognition which the baronage always gave to the rights of the exchequer in our period is due, not only to the innate conservatism of the English radical opposition, but also to their appreciation of the fact that they had other ways of bringing pressure to bear on the crown than by open coercion, as for instance by providing men of their own way of thinking with places in the exchequer. Anyhow any possible alternative to the exchequer was exceedingly distasteful to the baronial opposition. Accordingly every fresh vindication of constitutional liberty, from the Provisions of Oxford to the *Articuli super Cartas*, from the *Articuli super Cartas* to the Ordinances of 1311, insisted as a cardinal principle of reformation that the "issues of the land" should be paid into the exchequer, and accounted for there at the proper time by the proper persons.

It was a far cry in the fourteenth century between passing a law and carrying it out in practice. Nevertheless Edward I and Langton found it convenient to yield, in form at least, to the baronial demand that the issues of the land should be paid into the exchequer. Under Henry III and in the early years of Edward I revenue flowed indifferently into either the exchequer or the wardrobe. After 1295, when Langton became treasurer, the accounts show that it became usual for the wardrobe to receive its chief supplies through the exchequer, and to depend but to a trifling extent on its "foreign receipt," as that portion of the wardrobe revenue was called which did not go through the books of the exchequer.[1] The change was more apparent than real, and was in practice largely a matter of book-keeping. Its effect was, however, to make the exchequer the direct office of account for all national revenue. As a matter of fact a mere

[1] [For figures see *Chapters*, ii, 89-90.]

trifle of the sums accounted for was really paid over by the tax collectors in hard cash into the exchequer, though by ingenious devices all revenue was made to pass through some exchequer account. What happened was that, when the great spending departments, chiefest among which was the wardrobe, went to the exchequer for further supplies, they took away with them for the most part, not money, but dated tallies. These tallies were in form exchequer receipts drawn out in favour of the sheriffs, and other tax collecting ministers of the crown, for sums known to be due from them to the exchequer, but not yet paid.[1] Armed with these tallies, the officers of the wardrobe could go to the sheriffs, take from them any money or supplies that they happened to have collected, and transfer to them their own tallies to an amount corresponding to the sums which they had received. These tallies the sheriffs in due course produced at the exchequer as vouchers that they had paid already the amounts recorded on them. The sums thus accounted for, though never seen in the exchequer at all, were duly entered upon the exchequer rolls. Thus by an ingenious fiction the magnates' claim was vindicated. The issues of the land, at least, *appeared* to pass through the exchequer. In practice, however, the king still received in his wardrobe a large share of the taxes direct from the collectors, without the vexatious delays involved in these sums passing through the intermediate channel of the exchequer. An indirect result was that exchequer tallies became instruments of credit, and helped to make more subtle the financial and credit system of the English executive. A further consequence of the practice was that the receipt and issue rolls by no means always present a satisfactory indication of the actual sums received and expended by the crown. The neglect of this fact has diminished the value of some modern attempts to calculate the royal revenue.

It is a curious commentary on the view sometimes held that in the later years of Edward I the exchequer overtopped the chancery, when we discover that the issue rolls of this period testify, on the whole, to the inactivity of the great revenue department. These issue rolls, one for each of the two exchequer terms of the regnal year, are clumsy documents in two columns. On the right-hand side are entered what may be called the departmental expenses,

[1] Much new light is thrown on this subject by Mr. Hilary Jenkinson's article on "Exchequer Tallies," already referred to above, p. 39, n. 1.

the wages of the officers of the exchequer, the cost of parchment, ink, green wax, baskets, chests and other apparatus for storage and safe keeping. With these go a few pensions, grants and other casual payments made directly out of the exchequer. On the left-hand side is a sort of current account with the heads of the great spending departments, the keeper of the wardrobe specially, and also a few other officials such as the constable of Bordeaux, who was finance minister for Gascony, and the chamberlain of Scotland, who acted in the same capacity for such parts of the northern kingdom as were from time to time effectively administered by the English kings. But by far the largest payments went to the wardrobe. These were authorised by huge block writs of *liberate*, amounting often to sums such as £10,000 or £20,000, by virtue of which the wardrobe officers got what tallies they needed in constant driblets. The gradual paying off of these lump sums by a series of petty disbursements is recorded in detail. This fashion involved entries so numerous that their running account often overflows into the blank spaces of the properly departmental or right-hand column of the roll. The result was a limitation of exchequer business in its financial side to accounting, which left the exchequer officers with plenty of leisure to hold pleas, draft correspondence under the exchequer seal, and turn their hands to any business of the king that happened to be in need of trained workers for its execution. Even with the more strictly differentiated government offices of modern times, it is not unusual for a hard-pressed department to borrow clerks from a more leisurely or longer established office. I am told that the new commission for administering the National Insurance Act has to some extent depended upon such labour.

Another point also should not be forgotten. Alone of the early fourteenth-century offices of state, the exchequer possessed permanent, roomy and convenient buildings of its own at Westminster. If the law courts, and notably the common bench, had already begun to follow the exchequer's example, the remaining offices of state, the chancery and the wardrobe, still followed the crown, or at least tried to do so. But the occasional migrations of the exchequer at this time were always to some other fixed spot. In the days of Edward I's troubles with Wales, that place was always Shrewsbury. Later, when politics made it convenient to locate the seat of government near the Scottish border, and near—I may add—the headquarters of the most turbulent of the baronial opposition, the spot chosen was generally York. The migrations of the exchequer from Westminster to Shrewsbury and York were such noteworthy events that they are duly recorded not only in the departmental archives but in the chronicles, notably in those of London and Westminster.[1] There we can read of the long train of waggons that conveyed to the north the records and rolls of the exchequer, among which Domesday book was still of such practical importance that it was never left behind. We can trace in the tone with which London chroniclers deplore these migrations, and welcome back the exchequer to its natural home, the beginnings of the proud consciousness of the dwellers on Thames side that London was the natural centre of all these state activities, and that there was something amiss when they were removed from their accustomed haunts. The "metropolis" began to patronise the "provinces"; but under Edward II the north country had it all its own way.[2]

Those too faithful disciples of Madox, who see the exchequer in all things, have somewhat disturbed the stream of administrative history by their conviction that, before what Madox calls the "declensions of the exchequer from its ancient grandeur" in the thirteenth century, the council and the chancery were often held "in the exchequer," and that the exchequer was already as a law court the rival of the two benches, and had even begun to be a court of appeal. I fail to see that after the death of John the exchequer really fell away from its former importance. On the contrary the early thirteenth century saw new developments of exchequer machinery and the growth of new exchequer offices to an extent quite incompatible with a restriction of its influence. It was under John and the minority of his son that fresh series of exchequer records are first known to have existed in the issue rolls, the receipt rolls and the memoranda rolls,[3]

[1] See for Shrewsbury *Flores Hist.*, iii, 48, 56. For York, see *Ann. Paul.*, pp. 286, 303, 305.

[2] [See D. M. Broome, "Exchequer Migrations to York" in *Essays . . . presented to T. F. Tout*, pp. 291-300.]

[3] The continuous succession of issue rolls begins in 5 Henry III, that of receipt rolls in 14 John, and that of both series of memoranda rolls in 2 Henry III. Mr. H. Hall has, however, published a fragmentary receipt roll of 1185, and there was something called a memoranda roll under John. Of course, these early rolls were not drafted with the technique of the developed rolls. Messrs. Crump and Johnson inform me that a clear differentiation between the rolls of the king's and the treasurer's remembrancers was already marked by 53 Henry III; and probably earlier.

4

and the first third of the thirteenth century was the time of the clear differentiation of such exchequer ministers as the chancellor and the remembrancers, and the beginnings of the transference of the designation baron of the exchequer, applied at first to all royal ministers who had a seat at the national board of finance, to a special class of dignified officers, with a definite status, function and salary. All that we can safely say is that after the reign of John the exchequer was less solitary in its grandeur than it had been in the twelfth century. In the thirteenth and fourteenth centuries, as earlier, it still, primarily and essentially, remained an office of finance. This remained the contemporary view of its functions up to our period. The same constitutional documents of Edward I and Edward II which insisted on the right of the exchequer to receive and control the issues of the realm, prohibited the exchequer from hearing pleas in which the king's revenue was not concerned.[1] The insignificance of the judicial business of the exchequer, even under Edward II,[2] shows that this prohibition was at least respected to the extent that exchequer judicial business did not materially increase before the reforms of the end of that reign had become effective. Just as they restrained its jurisdiction, so did the barons of Edward I restrict its administrative work to matters directly associated with its proper sphere. They limited the use of the exchequer seal and of exchequer writs to strictly departmental correspondence. Thus the ordinances of 1311 prohibited the appointment of a sheriff under the exchequer seal, a common practice of Edward II in his youth, because this involved a usurpation of the essential function of the office of state, the chancery. This veto was repeated by the parliament of Lincoln of 1316, and, when in 1322 the ordinances were repealed, this provision and this provision only was still continued at law. Thus, the magnates,

[1] See, for instance, *Articuli super Cartas*, § 4, " Estre ceo, nul commun plai ne seit desoremes tenu a l'escheqer countre la fourme de la grant chartre " (Bémont, *Chartes des libertés anglaises*, p. 104). The series of exchequer plea rolls begins in 20-21 Henry III, and is practically continuous after 51-52 Henry III (*P.R.O. Lists and Indexes*, no. iv, *Plea Rolls*, p. 66).

[2] See Mr. G. J. Turner's Introduction to *Year Books of Edward II*, iv, xxi-xxii. " The rolls (of exchequer pleadings) of the four terms of 4 Edw. II are sewn together in a single file and number no more than fifty-three, whereas there are as many as five hundred and nineteen rolls of the common bench for Michaelmas term alone." Mr. Turner also points out that " so far our Year Books have contained no reports from the exchequer."

who were so strong on the constitutional rights of the exchequer, were equally insistent that it should limit itself to its own proper functions.

Conjectures are always hazardous, but in the light of these facts I am inclined to suggest, with all reserve, that we may find at least a partial explanation of many of the extra-financial acts often described as done "in the exchequer," and sometimes imagined to be done by the exchequer, by the circumstances that departments, less well off than the exchequer in the matter of housing, found it convenient to do their work on exchequer premises, lent to them for the purpose.[1] Thus when the chancery holds upon occasion a sitting in the exchequer, we are not to imagine that there is some subtle inter-relation between the two departments. We have simply an instance of the officials of an office with no home of its own meeting in the office of another department better provided with house-room. We can explain in the same fashion the instances given by Madox of the king's council sitting in the exchequer.[2] They are so numerous that, as Mr. Charles Johnson has shown,[3] there was by 1324 a "place within the exchequer customarily used for holding councils." And in this council chamber within the exchequer we can

[1] The baronial view was that chancery and the king's bench ought to "follow the king," a view incompatible with any fixed headquarters. See, for instance, *Articuli super Cartas*, § 5, "D'autre part le roi voet qe la chauncelerie et les justices de soen banc lui suient, issint q'il eit touz jours pres de lui ascuns sages de la lei," etc. (Bémont, *u.s.*, p. 104).

[2] Madox, ii, 26-32.

[3] *Eng. Hist. Rev.*, xxi, 726-7, "The Exchequer Chamber under Edward II." Mr. Johnson here prints a letter written by the most prominent chancery clerk, William of Airmyn, to the chancellor, reporting how he had held conference with the chief justices of the two benches, a baron of the exchequer and a justice of the common bench, assembled "in loco de scaccario pro consiliis habendis consueto." The report is written "in dicto loco scaccarii." See also particulars in *Cal. Inq. Misc.*, ii, 176. Similarly, in a document published by Mr. Salisbury in *Eng. Hist. Rev.*, xxxiii, 81, the archbishops of Canterbury and Dublin, the earls of Pembroke and Hereford, and other great persons, are shown in June, 1318, meeting the king's council "a Westmouster *al petit Escheqer* pur conseiller . . . nostre seignur le Roi" concerning the Scottish invasion. The words italicised are in the original underlined for deletion. Other instances of councils held on exchequer premises under Edward II can be found in *Ann. Lond.*, p. 217, "Tunc die statuto (21 Sept. 1312) venit major cum aldermannis ad scaccarium coram consiliariis regis." The Londoners already presented their sheriffs "coram baronibus scaccarii et consilio domini regis apud Westmonasterium" (*ibid.*, p. 218). [The queen's exchequer was similarly utilised. In 1342-43 a payment "de curialitate" to the ushers of the king's exchequer was made "per consensum tocius consilii regine tunc sedentis in scaccario eiusdem regine" (M.A. 1091/9, m. 7).]

easily understand select judges from the two benches joining with chancery and exchequer officers to discuss knotty points of law. This furthered the judicial side of the work of the court, and helps to explain why it was found useful to import into the exchequer, as barons, both successful pleaders in large practice and lawyers with wide judicial experience, like Hervey of Staunton, the principal judge of the great eyre of Kent in 1313-14, but afterwards in succession baron and chancellor of the exchequer. From such meetings it is easy to see that there arose gradually that "exchequer chamber," which the legislation of later periods erected as a formal court of appeal. It is very likely that this council chamber of the exchequer was, as Mr. Johnson suggests, the *thalamus secretorum*, hard by the house where the exchequer sat, to which in the reign of Henry II the barons retired when they wished to discuss secrets, or to deliberate, without disturbing the calculations of the officials busily engaged on the accounts in the adjoining exchequer house.[1] But by the reigns of Edward I and Edward II the exchequer premises contained, I imagine, more than one private room, so that we must not be too certain as to the identification of localities until definite evidence happens to crop up.

## (3) The Chancery under Edward I

I have lingered longer than I should have wished over the exchequer, and shall have the less space to discuss the chancery.[2] The chancery was, of course, the great secretarial department, the office of state, and its head, the chancellor, was not merely a supreme judge, like the modern lord chancellor, but the king's natural prime minister, like the *Reichskanzler* of the modern German empire or the secretary of state of the United States. From the twelfth century onwards it was the essence of the function of a chancellor that he kept his master's seal, and the keeping of the seal involved the drafting of the state documents to which the king's seal was affixed. Also the composition of the letters in its turn involved a leading share in the determination of the policy

[1] *Dialogus de Scac.* I, vii, E (Oxford ed., p. 92).

[2] In writing this short account of the chancery I must particularly acknowledge my debt to Miss L. B. Dibben, who has kindly given me access to her manuscript collections for the history of this office. The results of her working through the hanaper accounts are of special interest and importance.

expressed in them. It was the very intimacy involved in these delicate functions which kept the chancellor near the court, so that the chancery did not become an office of state, separate from the court, until a good century after the complete differentiation of the exchequer from the *curia regis*. Even the immense increase of chancery business involved by the institution of the system of chancery enrolments, which goes back, as we know, to at least the early years of John, did not do much to separate the chancery from the *curia*.

The first steps towards separation were not due to the increasing importance of the work done by the chancery. They rather flowed from the overweening sense of their own importance felt by the mighty chancellors of the early thirteenth century who, buying their office for life from impecunious kings, administered it and its revenues for their own profit and glory. These " baronial " chancellors came to an end through the jealous desire of Henry III to rule through clerks and subordinates directly dependent on himself. After 1238 Henry " took the chancery into his own hands," brought the chancellors back to court, and assimilated them and their office in all ways to the domestic offices of the king's household.[1] In opposition to the king's policy of domestic chancellors, the barons demanded a chancellor of independent position nominated by themselves. Neither party altogether prevailed. These antagonistic points of view became less important, since after their triumph, the barons showed such jealousy of each other that they had no mind to restore the old-fashioned chancellor for life, who might well prove as dangerous to the aristocracy as he had threatened to be overmighty for the crown. Accordingly the barons of 1258 soon accepted the new arrangements which Henry III had made for keeping the chancery under his own control. These arrangements included the retention in the hands of the government of the profits of the seal, and their administration by the " hanaper " department, which, for a century after its institution, remained a loosely attached dependency of the wardrobe to which it accounted for the issues of the seal. On the other hand, the chancellor was compensated for losing his best chances of exploiting his office in his own interests

[1] [Dr. Wilkinson questions this view, preferring the theory of Stubbs, that Henry temporarily suspended the chancellorship, while the seal was kept by subordinate officials. For full discussion see his *Chancery under Edward III*, App. II, pp. 194-8.]

by receiving a "chancellor's fee," ultimately fixed at £500 a year, and by having put under him a special group of king's clerks, the clerks of the chancery, for whose maintenance he was responsible, and with whose help he discharged the secretarial duties of his office.[1]

The result of this process was that at the end of Henry III's time the chancellor, though still a court official following the king, had a staff of his own, entirely separate from the chaplains and clerks of the household. The clerks of the chancery soon developed a departmental tradition and *esprit de corps* that began to rival the strong corporate feeling of the exchequer officials. The conservative, not to say the reactionary, policy of Edward I, put back into the hands of his great chancellor, bishop Burnell, the administration of the chancery on the lines followed by the baronial chancellors of fifty years earlier. The close union of policy and the personal intimacy existing between Edward and his minister prevented much harm arising from the independence allowed to Burnell. After his friend's death, however, Edward took care not to repeat this experiment again. The king's next chancellor, John Langton,[2] was a good official of no personal distinction, who had spent his life as a chancery clerk in performing the routine business of the office over which he was now called upon to preside. Unlike Burnell, he was not allowed to make his profit out of his office, but immediately on his appointment the "chancellor's fee," for the support of himself and his clerks, was revived, and was thenceforth practically permanent. Langton's successors were men of the same type, who play a very insignificant part in history as compared with the masterful treasurer of those years, Walter Langton. Perhaps the obscurity of Edward's later chancellors hastened the development of the office of the chancery on purely business lines. Certainly the tendency for the chancellor and his clerks to go "out of the household," and build up a separate department of state of their own, now went on apace.

When Edward of Carnarvon became king, the chancellor and chancery were rather nominally than really part of the

[1] Miss Dibben has worked out the position of the chancery under Henry III in her article on "Chancellor and Keeper of the Seal under Henry III," in *Eng. Hist. Rev.*, xxvii, 39-51.

[2] "Et successit ei (*i.e.* to Burnell) in cancellaria Johannes de Langethone, ad tunc clericus simplex de predicta cancellaria" (*Ann. Dunstable* in *Ann. Mon.* (R.S.), iii, 373).

household.[1] The chancellor and his clerks were often separated from the king for long periods of time. There was no longer any need for them to be always in attendance at the court, since there had grown up a household secretariat, whose instrument, the privy seal, was quite adequate for the king's personal correspondence, and was particularly useful to him as an easy means of carrying on written communications with his chancellor. In the law book called Fleta, by an anonymous writer who wrote about the time of Burnell's death, *cancellaria* and *hospicium* are contrasted with each other.[2] His descriptions make it clear how different were the clerks of the chancery from the clerks of the wardrobe. He emphasises the fact that the keeper of the privy seal, who was a wardrobe clerk, was the only keeper of a royal seal in England who was absolutely independent of the chancellor.

As the chancery ceased to follow the king, it began to realise the convenience of having fixed quarters of its own. So early as 1280 Burnell, leaving the king to hunt in the New Forest, betook himself to London, "as if to a fixed place where all seeking writs and prosecuting their rights could find the appropriate remedy." [3] It must not be imagined from this that the chancery was becoming a law court or going to settle down in London. Evidently, however, there was already a tendency in both directions. It is a sign of the times, therefore, that while, as we have seen, the conservative barons stipulated in 1300 in the *Articuli super Cartas* that the chancery and the king's bench should, after ancient fashion, still follow the king, the more radical king took up an exactly contrary line and ordered the chancery as well as the exchequer to remain at Westminster during his last expedition to Scotland in 1306.[4] And even the barons

[1] [But the clerks were not, as stated in 1st edn., "living with their chief a self-contained and semi-independent collegiate life in the household of the chancery." Mr. Tout revised this view in the light of the discoveries made by Dr. B. Wilkinson and Dr. G. O. Sayles. For details see Tout, *Chapters*, iii, 210, n. 3, and "The household of the chancery and its disintegration," reprinted with some additional notes by Dr. Wilkinson in *Collected Papers*, ii, 143-71. *Cf.* also Dr. Wilkinson's *Chancery under Edward III*.]

[2] Fleta, *Commentarius Juris Anglicani* (1647), pp. 75-8, describes the chancery, and then, pp. 78-9, goes on to the *hospicium*.

[3] *Ann. Waverley* in *Ann. Mon.*, ii, 393.

[4] *C.C.R. 1302-7*, p. 455. Edward soon found this policy inconvenient, for, before the parliament of Carlisle of Jan. 1307, we find the chancellor and some of his clerks lodged at Carlisle in close attendance on the king (*ibid.*, p. 529).

of 1300 regarded chancery clerks as lawyers by training if not by function, coupling them with the judges of the bench as men "learned in the law." The process that made the chancery a law court was, however, hardly in its infancy. Accordingly we need have no hesitation in saying that part of the inheritance which Edward II received from his father was a well-ordered and efficient chancery, sufficiently dependent on the crown to do the royal will, but having already acquired an essential life of its own apart from the royal household,[1] and capable upon occasions of setting up the traditions of the chancery as its protection from arbitrary caprice, just as the author of the *Dialogus* could balance the customs of the exchequer against the interests of a king so strong as Henry II.[2] Unlike the exchequer the chancery was purely served by clerks. Distinctions were already beginning to be made between clerks of various degrees, but we must not yet call the highest clerks of chancery by the name masters of chancery, which became their appropriate title a generation or two later. At all times the household of the chancery included clerks of great ability and the highest education. The chancery office afforded an admirable career to the ambitious young civilian or canonist from the universities. Many such chancery clerks attained great eminence, such as the brothers Airmyn, and the higher subordinate posts, under the chancellor, notably the keepership of the rolls of the chancery, were already offices of dignity and influence. Moreover, other chancery clerks, who failed to reach the highest rank, secured a very comfortable and dignified position, such as, for instance, the chancery clerk of Edward II, Adam of Brome, the founder of Oriel College. In all essentials the chancery had become a national office of state, like the exchequer itself.

## (4) The Wardrobe under Edward I

There remains a third branch of the royal service which I dare not call a department of state, for its essence was that it was still only a department of the household. The

[1] Yet the old tradition died slowly. So late as 1314 the chancery clerk, Adam of Osgodby, then keeper of the *domus conversorum*, is called in a patent a member of the royal household (*C.P.R. 1313-17*, p. 170).

[2] *Dialogus*, I, iiij A (Oxford ed., p. 66) defines the function of the exchequer officials to be "ut regis utilitati prospiciant, salua tamen equitate, secundum constitutas leges scaccarii."

king's wardrobe [1] was, speaking roughly, the financial and secretarial department of the king's household, the domestic and semi-private exchequer and chancery of the king, hopelessly overlapping the national exchequer and chancery in all its functions. Its possession of an authority concurrent with the national departments of state immensely added to the confusion and complication of the English administrative system. With all its love of system making, the mediæval mind was in its practical aspects hopelessly unsystematic. To assign two persons, or two organisations, to do the same work seemed to the mediæval man the most natural thing in the world, and it never occurred to him to get rid of anything because it had ceased to meet any intelligible want. It is to this habit, looked at in its widest light, that we must assign the fact that the dying middle ages left early modern society strewn with wrecks of derelict mediæval institutions, which long continued in existence out of mere traditionalism, after the middle ages are supposed to have ended. In quite modern times great cataclysms, like the French Revolution, and new developments, like the movement towards national states, have decently interred many of these relics of the past. But every would-be reformer knows that plenty of them still cumber the ground, and remain so solidly compact that they defy all his efforts to clear them out of the path of progress. In the middle ages themselves, the survival of the old, which ought to have been, but was not, supplanted by the new, is the commonest thing in the world. We have the empire and feudalism surviving national monarchy, and we have baronial parliaments co-existing side by side with the parliaments of the three estates which should have taken their place.

It was in the same spirit that the primitive, undifferentiated household organisation of earlier times still continued its existence after the two great departments of state, the exchequer and the chancery, had grown out of it. Thus when in the early twelfth century the exchequer differentiated itself from the king's court, there still remained a household department of finance, the *camera curie*, whose operations we can obscurely trace from the pipe rolls of the Angevin period, and which still discharged, on a more modest scale, the

[1] The following pages contain some of the leading conclusions which are developed at greater length in [*Chapters*, ii, 1-163. The authorities on which they are based are there given.]

financial functions which an age of pure reason would have relegated entirely to its mighty offspring, the king's exchequer. Similarly, at the turn of the twelfth and thirteenth centuries, we discover that, as soon as the chancery began to separate itself from the court, there remained a court secretarial and administrative department, whose instrument was the privy seal, and whose direction seems to have been entrusted to that same "chamber of the court" which administered domestic finance.

In the very first years of the thirteenth century things are further complicated by the king's wardrobe appearing in close relation to the king's chamber, though already clearly possessing a separate existence of its own. Now the king's chamber and wardrobe mean, of course, the place where the king slept, and the adjacent ante-room where he hung up his clothes. In our records, however, the expressions mean a great deal more than this. They suggest organised household offices with trained staffs which, if originally set up at court to wait upon the king in the most private aspects of his life, were soon called upon to justify the confidence which these intimate relations with the monarch had created, by aiding the king to discharge his general functions in an age when no distinction was made or thought of between the private and the public aspects of sovereignty. The result was naturally that the domestic departments were not content to limit themselves to the work of governing the king's household. They were equally the king's helpers in the general administration of his realm. The twelfth and thirteenth centuries saw the erection of the chancery and exchequer as offices of national administration. But no one dreamt in the thirteenth century of making a distinction between the ruling of the court and the ruling of the nation. The wardrobe and chamber therefore went on just as they had done before. Accordingly the court offices continued to overlap with the chancery and the exchequer, which had arisen from them. They shared with them the administration of the kingdom, while discharging their fundamental duty of ordering the royal household. Of these domestic departments the chamber soon sank into the background, though it continued an obscure and domestic existence and was revived, as we shall see, under Edward II. It is a peculiarity of English history that the cameral department of the household largely gave way before the growing importance of the wardrobe. This process was completed within a few years of the end of the minority of Henry III, and from that time we hear comparatively little of the chamber, but more and more of the king's wardrobe.

During the second half of the thirteenth century the wardrobe took definite shape as the financial and administrative department of the king's household. It was officered entirely by clerks,[1] though only a few of the many clerks attached to the household had the right to share in the delicate and confidential functions of *garderobarii*, the clerks of the king's wardrobe. The chief clerk, the head of the establishment, was called sometimes the keeper of the wardrobe, and sometimes the treasurer of the wardrobe. As he is often, especially in the thirteenth century, simply called the king's treasurer, it is easy to see why holders of the office have often been confused by historians with the treasurer of the exchequer. Under the keeper or treasurer was a controller, who kept a counter-roll of the household accounts by which the keeper's returns could be checked. By Edward I's time, the controller was also the keeper of the privy seal, an instrument which was already in existence at the beginning of the reign of John, originally as the seal of the chamber and ultimately, in the course of Henry III's reign, as the seal of the wardrobe. Accordingly the controller was practically the head of the king's domestic chancery, just as the keeper was the chief of the domestic treasury. Gradually other clerks group round these two, such as the cofferer, who looked after the details of the accounts, and kept the cash box, the *ostiarius*, whose most important work was perhaps to direct the ceaseless wanderings of the department, the *sub-ostiarius*, who assisted the *ostiarius*, and a few others. But the wardrobe staff was never large and often had to be supplemented at times of crisis by clerks borrowed from other departments. It was perhaps because its numbers were so restricted that the wardrobe opened a career to talent and ambition far wider and more adventurous than the chancery itself. The chancery clerks were better paid, more highly educated and had a more certain career. As a compensation they attracted little the attention of the king, and still less that of the public. Accordingly their prospects were the limited circumscribed chances of an honourable official career. The wardrobe clerks, on the other hand, enjoyed the constant personal intercourse

[1] "Habet etiam rex alios clericos in hospitio suo, ut thesaurarium garderobae suae, quae est locus clericis tantum assignatus" (Fleta, p. 78).

with the sovereign which their life at court involved. Besides this, the offices of state always tended to be trammelled by rules and traditions. The court offices were free to carry out the king's wishes in any way that they liked and easily able to make precedents and attract business to themselves by any means in their power. This was pre-eminently the career open to talent. Unscrupulous, illiterate, greedy and pushing as they often were, the wardrobe clerks had a chance to show their brains, their courage, their character and their energy. If some of them had the academic training and the legal lore of the chancery clerk, they were probably converts from the diplomatic side of the king's household clerks. It is no wonder that nearly all the most notable clerical ministers of the reigns of the Edwards began their career in the wardrobe, and made their way through the wardrobe to the highest offices of church and state. Famous instances of this were Edward I's two strongest ministers, Robert Burnell and Walter Langton.

Though the wardrobe was, in Fleta's phrase, *camera clericorum*, an office staffed with clerks, there was an obvious need for constant co-operation between the leading clerks of the wardrobe and the chief lay officers of the household, especially the knights, or bannerets, who held such offices as those of steward, chamberlain and marshal of the household. These offices were doubtless the same in origin as the hereditary dignities of steward, chamberlain and marshal, which had long been annexed to three of the greatest earldoms. But by the thirteenth century a clear distinction had arisen between the hereditary and the working court offices, bearing the same names, and in origin not distinguishable from them. Under Henry III the holders of the former posts, the earls of Leicester, Oxford and Norfolk were glorified with the style of steward, chamberlain and marshal " of England," [1] while their namesakes were simply the " king's chamberlain," and the steward and marshal " of the household." But it is significant that kings who suffered hereditary offices in the exchequer, and even allowed the keepership of their palace to descend by hereditary right,[2] would not permit that the two chief knightly

[1] For this see the late L. W. Vernon Harcourt's *His Grace the Steward and Trial by Peers*, especially pp. 121-2. Simon de Montfort called himself " senescallus Angliae " in 1255. Yet in 1221 the hereditary stewardship is called " senescalcia hospitii domini regis " (*ibid.*, p. 77).

[2] The well-known robbery of the " treasury " at Westminster in 1303 was facilitated by the carelessness of John Schenche, keeper of West-

offices of the household should be disposed of by other hands than their own. Though the household steward and chamberlain were nothing more in origin than lieutenants of the corresponding hereditary magnates, their independence was already secured by the fact that they were appointed by the king. Though the earl marshal had still a little authority at court, it was thought an unheard of presumption when Thomas of Lancaster, as inheritor of the hereditary stewardship, claimed the right of nominating the household steward as his deputy.[1] Yet Thomas' political associate, Guy of Warwick, was suffered all his life to nominate a chief officer of the exchequer.

Taken together, the chief clerks and knights of the king's *familia* were jointly the king's *secretarii*, his confidants and intimates, the natural official ring of inner advisers of the crown. They were not as yet "secretaries" in the modern official sense, though such a secretariat was in process of development, and was to be made permanent before the fourteenth century had run half its course.[2] Of the clerical *secretarii* I have spoken already; of the lay ones, we have chiefly to emphasise the important position of the steward, the knightly counterpart of the keeper of the wardrobe and for all practical purposes the lay head of the royal household. In much of the domestic administration of the court, the steward acted jointly with the keeper of the wardrobe, the clerical head of the household, and his essential equal in rank, privileges and emoluments. The marshal was less prominent, and the chamberlain, though important enough in his own sphere, as the "keeper of the king's head," to use the curious phrase of an early fourteenth-century monk,[3] was separated from his household colleagues by being the head of the semi-independent branch called the king's chamber, of which we shall have more to say anon. But the larger household organisation embraced all these officers, as well as many

minster Palace, by reason of his wife's hereditary fee. Nevertheless, he was in due course restored to his office (*C.C.R. 1302-7*, p. 244). [On this see Tout, "A Mediæval Burglary" (*Coll. Papers*, iii, 93-115). But Mr. Charles Clay has pointed out that the disorder at the palace was due not to Schenche himself but to an ill-chosen deputy (*ibid.*, p. 98, n. 2).]

[1] See later pp. 114-5, 119-120. For the Marshal's authority see App. I, pp. 253-4, 279; *C.P.R. 1330-34*, pp. 40, 179; [and *Chapters*, ii, 252-3].

[2] For this subject see Miss L. B. Dibben's "Secretaries in the Thirteenth and Fourteenth Centuries" in *Eng. Hist. Rev.*, xxv, 430-44. Miss Dibben emphasises the official side as far as her authorities allow.

[3] "Custos capitis regis" (*Flores Hist.*, iii, 194).

others, and also the wardrobe clerks and the other household clerks, the "clerks of offices," as the secretaries of the kitchen, stables, and similar purely domestic departments were called, and their like. It is because, underlying the apparent confusion of the disorderly royal household, there was a very solid, active and continuous organisation that court influence was always so large a factor in the political life of the whole fourteenth century. It went on whether the king was weak or strong, whether the favourites and high officials were competent or incapable. It was not so much a personal as an organic influence on our national life. To appreciate it is to get at the secret of fourteenth-century political history.

Within the wider body called the household lay the narrower and closer organisation of the wardrobe, and it was the lesser body which gave coherence, direction and system to court policy. Under Henry III the wardrobe was chiefly favoured in those periods when the national offices were falling under baronial control. When free to act as he wished, Henry III had no desire to set up court officers against national ministers. His aim was rather to treat every branch of his service as an office of the court, and to deal with the chancery and the exchequer on the same lines as the wardrobe. Edward I in most respects carried on his father's policy in this matter, and for the greater part of the reign he used, as his favourite executive instrument, the wardrobe rather than the chancery and the exchequer, because it was more elastic, more dependent, less trammelled by routine, and above all constantly at his side. Accordingly he continued a policy, already initiated under his father, of treating the wardrobe as the great spending department, the war office and the naval office in times of trouble, the centre of secret diplomacy and confidential action at all times. The result is that the wardrobe, though including all household work within its sphere, was only technically a department of the household. The king's court was regarded as coextensive with the nation; the king's knights and guards, afforced by the national and feudal levies, became the national army; the king's ships the basis of the national navy. No line was drawn between the domestic service of the court and the public service of the state. The wardrobe clerk, after a busy day of inspecting the meat, sampling the beer, listing the jewels and precious furs, paying, punishing, promoting the king's cooks, valets, ushers, grooms and other domestic servants, went straight to occupy himself in the political and military administration of the kingdom.

The wardrobe was financed under Edward I by a large proportion of the national revenue being paid directly into it, without going through the exchequer at all. Thus in the two years of the great Welsh war, 1282–84, over £200,000 passed through the coffers of the wardrobe, while the receipts of the exchequer, so far as they are known, seem to have been quite insignificant. In doing this, Edward had, I imagine, no other motive than administrative convenience, but when a few years later he had, like his father, to face a powerful, unscrupulous and united baronial opposition, he continued from policy what he had perhaps begun from practical considerations of utility. The result is seen in the emphatic way in which the barons of the last ten or twelve years of Edward I's reign try to strengthen the chancery and the exchequer at the expense of the wardrobe. It was to conciliate them, as we have seen, that Edward or Langton invented the ingenious device by which the revenue seemed to flow into the exchequer, while it really continued to pursue the channels preferred by the court. It may be doubted whether Bohun, Bigod and Winchelsea were taken in by such transparent devices. Anyhow they did not relax their watchfulness, and they still turned their direct attention to the court offices, as the source of all the national troubles. We can illustrate this by the new demands, first voiced in 1300 in the *Articuli super Cartas*, that the small seal, that is the privy seal of the wardrobe, was not to be used so as to deprive men of their legal rights. Against this was provided the remedy of insisting on the continued itinerancy of the chancery and great seal with the court. Thus the domestic secretariat fell under the same suspicions that had already been excited by the domestic treasury. In the same spirit, prises and purveyances for the wardrobe were rigidly limited and carefully checked. It was because the *Articuli super Cartas* so largely concerned themselves with restricting the sphere of his household organisations that Edward I bitterly resisted them. Even more than the forests, the household was the special region of royal autocracy. We are now on the threshold of a constitutional conflict, in which the royal attempt to intrench itself in the court organisation is answered by the effort of the baronage to appropriate to their own use the machinery of the court as well as the machinery of the state.

It is this conflict which gives the reign of Edward II a special importance for us. But it is significant that the first rumblings of the storm began during the declining years of the old king.

I must not, however, deviate too far from my present purpose. All that I want to suggest is that by the reign of Edward I the king's wardrobe, with its instrument the privy seal, was from the king's point of view a third great department of government, which had for him the supreme advantage of being entirely at his own disposal, and yet was quite as well manned, financed, and organised as the two great departments of state. How many-sided the activity of the wardrobe had now become may be additionally illustrated by the fact that it had itself begun to split up into sub-departments. I have already mentioned one of these in the *hanaper* department, which under the clerk of the hanaper administered and accounted for the profits of the great seal. This, until 1324, was strictly a department of the wardrobe, though its business had become altogether out of relation to household needs. A second branch of the wardrobe, which also arose in the middle part of Henry III's reign, was the *great wardrobe*,[1] so-called not because of its importance, but because it dealt with bulky commodities. As the organisation for the purchasing, manufacturing and storing of cloth, furs, spices, groceries, delicacies and luxuries of all sorts, and of other storable articles needed for the court, the great wardrobe is of all branches of the wardrobe the least interesting to the constitutional historian. Nevertheless in times of war it at once became the army clothing department, and a factory and store-house for armour and arms. Early in the fourteenth century the office for cloth and the office for arms and armour were separated, and the latter became a new wardrobe office which soon got the name of the king's *privy wardrobe in the Tower of London*.[2] It is only when the Hundred Years' War begins that this privy wardrobe has any importance, but I mention it here to complete the list of wardrobe departments in existence when our reign began. Each was under its responsible head or clerk, and had a certain amount of local autonomy, but each was a mere branch or dependency of the parent institution, to which it tendered its accounts and to which it was responsible.

The wardrobe system was not peculiar to the king's household. Every earl and baron had a *familia*, a household,

[1] [Fully treated in *Chapters*, iv, 349-437.] [2] [*Ibid.*, pp. 439-40.]

which followed pretty closely the lines of the *domus regis*,[1] in proportion to the lord's resources, and in each of these baronial establishments the wardrobe clerks were the directive and organising force.[2] [Prof. J. F. Baldwin has described in detail the household administration of Henry Lacy and] Thomas of Lancaster,[3] whose household, council, clerks, knights, counsellors and retainers loom so largely in the annals of the time.[4] We are fortunate also in still possessing records of the wardrobes of the queen,[5] and the king's sons. In particular there survive several instructive account books of the wardrobe of Edward of Carnarvon, when prince of Wales, which enable us to study his early life and the organisation and personnel of his household in a detail such as is impossible for any earlier king's son in our history. The queen's wardrobe and the prince's wardrobe were organised on exactly the same lines as the king's wardrobe, but, like the great wardrobe and the privy wardrobe, were looked upon as dependent branches of it. In the case of Edward of Carnarvon we feel pretty sure that his wardrobe officers were appointed, and strictly controlled, by the old king. It is nevertheless of great importance to realise that the household officers of the younger Edward, when he was prince, formed a well-organised body of intimate friends and congenial companions, to whom the young ruler was already closely attached. If we turn over surviving wardrobe accounts of the prince of Wales, we shall find among the inmates of his household nearly all the names of those persons most intimately associated with Edward during his reign.[6] Among the prince's officers for the last year of the old king's life we find that Walter Reynolds was his treasurer and William Melton his controller. William of Boudon, the future treasurer of queen Isabella, was his usher. Ingelard of Warley and Nicholas of

[1] Each baron had his *concilium* as well as his *familia*. It was through the help of a member of his *concilium* that Roger Mortimer of Wigmore escaped in 1324 from the Tower. Two other councillors met the fugitive with a boat (Blaneford, *apud* Trokelowe, p. 146).

[2] [On the household of the lord and lady of Eresby see *Chapters*, ii, 182-3.]

[3] [*Eng. Hist. Rev.*, xlii, 180-200.]

[4] Higden (*Polychronicon*, viii, 314) says that Thomas left "cuncta agenda sua ad nutum unius hominis secretarii sui." [This was probably Robert Holland, his receiver. For information on him and other of Lancaster's knightly *familiares* see *Chapters*, ii, 185-7.]

[5] [Treated in detail in *Chapters*, v, 231-89.]

[6] [For details see *Chapters*, ii, 166-81, and Johnstone, *Letters of Edw.*, pp. xi-xxix, xxxv-xliv.]

Huggate were among his clerks. Among the laymen were Robert Haustede, his steward, Guy Ferre, Oliver of Bordeaux, one of his esquires, and John Charlton, an esquire of his chamber recently advanced to knighthood. In short we find that only one name is wanting among those most closely associated with Edward's policy as king. This is the name of Peter Gaveston. Firstly as a ward in custody, then as a squire and knight of the prince's household, Gaveston had figured largely in previous rolls. More recently, however, the old king, coming to the conclusion that his influence was a bad one, had tried to mend his son's ways by driving his most intimate friend into banishment. The result was that the friction, already felt between the king and his heir, became acute and naturally extended down from the two chief personages concerned to their respective followers. We shall see in the next chapter the importance of this. We shall find that the accession of Edward II is found to involve not only a change of monarch, but the transference of the chief direction of affairs from the household of the old king to the household of his unworthy heir.

## III

## THE STRUGGLE FOR THE ORDINANCES

### (1) The Three Periods of the Reign

The history of the reign of Edward II divides itself into three periods, and these periods are not the less well marked because there is some difficulty in drawing the exact lines that separate them from one another. The first and longest runs from the king's accession to about 1318, by which time the failure of Thomas of Lancaster to carry into effect the policy of the ordinances was absolutely made patent to all England. It was, administratively, a period in which the system of Edward I, severely strained during the last years of the old king's reign, utterly broke down. Bannockburn showed the futility of the attempt to uphold the English king's authority in the north, while the baronial effort to revive aristocratic control, by recurring to the traditions of the reign of Henry III, was more successful in its negative side of ruining the royal autocracy, than in its positive side of supplying an alternative system of efficient government. This period attains its culminating point in 1316, when earl Thomas was made the king's chief counsellor by the parliament of Lincoln, and ends when he was deprived of that position, two years later. But underlying the troubles that filled those years, there were the beginnings of that readjustment of parties by which subsequent progress was to come. As this new balance of political forces established itself, we get gradually into more stormy but more interesting times. Thus the second great period of the reign, the years of crisis and of reconstruction, began in 1318, when the new middle party of Pembroke seized possession of the state, and upheld a definite policy of constructive reform which, however hampered in its execution, brought with it at least the promise of better things. The critical central period went on from the treaty of Leake in 1318 to the parliament of York in 1322, which consummated the triumph of the Pembrokians, allied with the courtiers, over the remnants of the discredited faction of the ordainers. But the fruits of that triumph went not to Pembroke and his friends, but to the king and the Despensers. Reaction followed in the wake of the royalist-Pembrokian coalition. The reaction had all its own way during the third period of the reign from 1322 to 1326, and then collapsed suddenly in the dramatic fall of the king and his favourites.

At every period of the reign the personnel of the administration seems to me to be of great importance. I shall, therefore, feel obliged to direct special attention to the somewhat neglected subject of the tenure of the chief offices of state during the reign. But the details of the fluctuations of Edward II's official advisers are too dull, and their significance too uncertain, for it to be possible to do more here than to dwell upon the more significant ministerial changes. Which of such changes are significant is, however, by no means an easy matter to decide. With the object of affording materials for the examination of this question, I have been at some pains to draw up and print in an appendix, as complete a list as I could make, of all the leading officials of the reign.[1] Some of the lists were easy enough to compile; but others present great difficulties and I cannot pretend to have done more than make the way easier for my successor. If the majority of these lists of unknown worthies do not seem to suggest very much, they will at least afford a basis for a more accurate and detailed study of the reign. What the study of English mediæval history wants, if it is to be kept up as a living thing, is more technical and detailed cataloguing and systematising of the dry facts. It is only when the spadework of history has been done that we may hope to come to any authoritative generalisations. And until substantial progress has been made in this direction, we must renounce any hope of solving the problems of the period.

I must frankly confess that I am by no means clear as to the significance of a large number of the personal changes in the rulers of England at this period as tabulated in these lists. We must not expect consistent politicians in the fourteenth century; we must not even expect consistent policies in parties. Yet political parties, if not already made, were in the making, and if there were more vicars of Bray than there were officials willing to sacrifice themselves for

[1] See below App. II, pp. 285-352.

their principles, the strong personal ties, which bound vassal to lord, pupil to master, and follower to leader, did largely help to keep up a near approach to consistency among the rank and file. It was something gained, if large classes of officials recognised a simple principle of policy in the natural one of obedience to command.

In approaching the personal changes in the offices of state during the earlier half of the reign, I have already emphasised the point that the reign is, as a whole, remarkable for the continuity of the administrative personnel. There were many changes when the king came to the throne. In accepting his father's policy, Edward II did not accept his father's ministers. But after these critical changes, there are remarkably few that can be set down to conscious changes for political reasons. The ordinances required the appointment of ministers in parliament. Some changes accordingly took place in 1311, and more in 1314, in obedience to the barons' demand. But in 1316 the reorganisation of the *familia regis*, for which the ordainers had clamoured, was still unfulfilled. The result was that in 1318, eight years after the passing of the ordinances, the ordainers had not succeeded in making a radical reform of the king's unsatisfactory household.

### (2) The Changes after Edward II's Accession

Let us begin with the changes which followed immediately upon Edward of Carnarvon's succession. To understand these we must know what were the ministers he displaced in favour of his own friends.

When Edward I died Walter Langton, bishop of Lichfield, the treasurer, was by a long way the most trusted and forcible of the king's ministers. Compared with Langton, Ralph Baldock, bishop of London, the chancellor, was a man of very secondary importance. After Langton the men who really counted were the two chief clerks of the wardrobe, John of Drokensford, or Droxford,[1] keeper of the wardrobe, and John of Benstead, or Binsted,[2] recently controller of the wardrobe.

[1] Drokensford is always so styled in contemporary records, but Droxford is the modern form of the Hampshire village from which he derived his surname.

[2] The "Benstede" of contemporaries is, I suspect, Binsted, near Alton, Hampshire, where John held property at the time of his death (*Cal. Inq.*, vi, 285). It may, however, have been Banstead in Surrey, or one of the several Binsteads. In the face of this doubt, I have preserved

Droxford, an intimate ally of Langton's, seems to have been mainly charged with the financial side of the wardrobe, while Benstead, after the fashion of Edward I's reign, was, as controller, keeper of the privy seal.[1] He was therefore responsible for the administrative side of the wardrobe, and for that reason is called with special appropriateness "the king's secretary." It followed that the old king's chief confidence was given to the former *garderobarius*, Langton, and to the two leading wardrobe officers at the moment.

Drastic ministerial changes followed Edward I's death, but they were neither so sudden nor so complete as some of the chroniclers suggest.[2] It was only after the lapse of some months that even the head officials were changed.[3] And as regards minor functionaries, the insistence that all should receive a new commission from the new king blinded the chroniclers to the undoubted fact that many of the newly empowered officers in the exchequer, the two benches and other semi-political and judicial posts, were the same individuals who had already been acting during the old king's last years. However, almost a clean sweep was made of the leading men, and the chroniclers had some reason for affirming that their successors were men of an altogether lower stamp. Within a few weeks of his accession the new king drove Langton from office, threw him into prison, and seized all his property. Bishop Baldock also was relieved of his post, while Droxford was transferred to the comparatively subordinate office of chancellor of the exchequer. Of the old king's four chief advisers, only one, Benstead, received promotion, being put in Droxford's post as keeper of the wardrobe. Edward II chose as his chancellor that trusted old official of his father, John Langton, bishop of Chichester, who had already been chancellor between 1292 and 1302.

the contemporary "e," and called him Benstead, though my general rule is to write place names in their modern form, even when used as surnames. [*C.C.R.* 1339-41, p. 631, is decisive in favour of Binsted.]

[1] It is certain, from Add. MS. 7965, m. 29, and *Lib. Quotid. Garderobe anno regis Edwardi primi xxviii*° (Soc. Antiquaries, 1787), pp. 75, 313, and 326, that Benstead was keeping the privy seal as early as 1296-1300, being already controller of the wardrobe. In the light of this fact, Maitland's conjecture that John Berwick was possibly keeper of the privy seal in 1305 can be readily dismissed (*Memoranda de Parliamento*, p. cix).

[2] For instance, *Ann. Paul.*, p. 257; *Lanercost*, p. 210.

[3] [This needs some modification. Edward I died on 7 July; Reynolds was made treasurer on 22 August; John Langton was already acting as chancellor on 18 August; the new keeper and controller of the wardrobe were in office from 8 July.]

Neither Benstead nor John Langton held these offices for long. The keeper of the wardrobe was removed after a year and was succeeded by Droxford, who also kept this post for a year only. The chancellor, an old man, and not a pronounced politician, remained in custody of the seal for nearly three years. It is unlikely that any of these three had any large share of the new king's confidence. That of course went mainly to Peter Gaveston. I cannot accept the statement of several chroniclers that Gaveston was the new king's chamberlain.[1] In any case, however, Gaveston's influence was not due to office, but to his personal intimacy with the king. Undoubtedly he controlled the household, though we cannot but be sceptical as to his holding a specific post in it.

It is of some significance that the official representatives of the new king's personal policy were the two chief officers of his wardrobe as prince of Wales. These were Walter Reynolds, the former keeper of the prince's wardrobe, and William Melton, its former controller. Both had begun their official career as king's clerks, and doubtless owed their appointment as chiefs of the prince's wardrobe to the old king. At the best of times Edward I had been singularly indifferent as to the personal character of his ministers, and it is only fair that he should share in the discredit which history has meted out to his son for his patronage of the unworthy and incompetent Reynolds. Perhaps Edward II ought also to take his part in the merit of being equally loyal to the high-minded and competent Melton.[2] Even of Reynolds it is right to say that though he may have strengthened his hold on the young prince's favour, as chroniclers tell us, by his consummate gifts as a manager of theatricals[3] he had

[1] See earlier, p. 11, note 3.

[2] Melton, previously a clerk in queen Margaret's wardrobe, [and her cofferer in 1299-1300 (*Lib. quotid.*, p. 357)] had been in Edward of Carnarvon's service ever since his appointment as prince of Wales in 1301; from 1301-4 as chamberlain of Chester (A. Jones, *Flintshire Ministers Accounts*, Flintshire Hist. Soc., 1913, pp. 1-48). [His earliest account, 7 Feb. to 29 Sept., 1301, survived in private custody, and in 1934 was deposited in the Nat. Library of Wales (Wynnstay MS. 86). See below p. 333, n.] From 1304 to 1307 he was controller.

[3] Malmesb., p. 197, describes Reynolds as "simplex clericus et minus competenter litteratus sed in ludis theatralibus principatum tenuit et per hoc regis favorem optinuit." But can we trust a writer who ignores Reynolds' early official career and Edward I's responsibility for his choice? In 1299-1300 Reynolds was "clericus magne garderobe Edwardi filii regis" (*Lib. quotid.*, p. 56). He had been the prince's "treasurer," *i.e.*, keeper of his wardrobe, since 1301 (R. Stewart-Brown, *Cheshire Chamberlains' Accounts, 1301-60*, Lancashire and Cheshire Record Soc., 1910, p. 12).

for years held the responsible post of head of his household, and manager of his finances, to the satisfaction of Edward I, and was therefore not likely to be a mere purveyor to the young man's pleasures. Reynolds now succeeded Walter Langton as treasurer, remaining at that office until 1310. In May of that year John Langton was, as the chronicler says, deposed to his own honour from the chancery by the king.[1] Thereupon Reynolds stepped into his place. He was already bishop of Worcester and before long, by a scandalous transaction between Edward II and Clement V, became the unworthy successor of Winchelsea as archbishop of Canterbury. It is perhaps further evidence of Reynolds' easy-going ways that, both as treasurer and as chancellor, he seldom acted in person, some exchequer or chancery clerk frequently serving as his deputy.[2] The less pushing and showy Melton became the controller of Edward II's wardrobe, and keeper of his privy seal. Melton retained this office for seven years under three different keepers, and between 1314 and 1316 held the higher dignity of keeper of the wardrobe, occupying this post until the royal favour made him in 1317 archbishop of York. Thus the two chiefs of the prince's wardrobe attained the two archbishoprics of the English church. We shall hear something of them again, of Reynolds for evil, and of Melton for good, for the whole of the rest of our period.

The promotion of Reynolds and Melton did not stand alone. A comparison of the last wardrobe accounts of Edward as prince with his later wardrobe accounts as king shows that substantially the whole household staff of the prince of Wales was transferred to the household of the new king. This was equally the case as regards the lay and the clerical staffs of the prince's household. With reference to the former we may add to the names mentioned in the last chapter that of Gaveston, now earl of Cornwall, and husband of the king's niece, Margaret of Clare, and that of his brother-in-law, the king's nephew, Gilbert of Clare, who soon became old enough to take up the personal management of his earldom of

[1] "Depositus per regem ad honorem suum" (*Ann. Paul.*, p. 268). Reynolds became his successor, "communitate tamen Angliae non consentiente" (*ibid.*, p. 269). The Receipt Roll of the Exchequer carefully notes that Langton left the treasury "non amotus pro transgressione, sed sponte et de licencia et bona voluntate regis" (R.R. 188, m. 1).

[2] He had only acted in person for a few months. His successor as treasurer, John Sandall, had been his *locum tenens*. Sandall was not, as Stubbs says, a "protégé of Winchelsea" (*Const. Hist.*, ii, 354). He had no leanings to the clerical party, but was a moderate and colourless official.

Gloucester. Great earls, whether of Gloucester or of Cornwall, were too magnificent personages to remain household officials even of a king, but the policy of earl Gilbert was always strongly influenced by his personal associations in youth. Edward immediately made steward of his household, Miles Stapleton, recently his steward as prince. More permanently associated with Edward II's household was the pushing Shropshire squire, John Charlton, who, already a knight of the prince's household, retained his post when his master became king and by 1310 or 1311 had become the court chamberlain of Edward II. Charlton showed great dexterity in using the royal favour to establish himself as lord of Upper Powys, a district to which he had some claim as the husband of the great Welsh heiress, Hawise Gadarn, who represented the ancient line of the princes of Powys. Besides knights, the members of the prince's household remaining in his service as king included nearly all the prominent wardrobe clerks of the reign.[1] Among them we may specially mention the hated Ingelard of Warley, who succeeded Droxford as keeper in 1309, and whose removal from court, demanded by the ordainers, was successfully resisted till the end of 1314.[2]

Long before all these changes had been carried out, Edward II's policy had hopelessly broken down. It seems a paradox to say that the young king's political objects were the same as those of Edward I, just as it once seemed a paradox to say that the policy of James I was to continue on the lines of queen Elizabeth. Nevertheless I am quite sure that this statement is true. Edward has often been reproached with giving up voluntarily the conquest of Scotland. He cannot be severely censured for breaking off the campaign of 1307 to secure possession of the throne. That his subsequent efforts to come to close quarters with Robert Bruce were failures is partly, but only partly, to be ascribed to his frivolity and want of enterprise. If Gaveston is to be condemned for most of his master's errors, he certainly is not to be blamed for this, for when serious hostilities were renewed, the most hostile chroniclers admit that the favourite comported himself against the Scots like a gallant warrior.[3]

The blame for neglecting to recognise the seriousness of

[1] All this illustrates *Ann. Paul.*, p. 257: "adhaesit consilio juvenum, qui secum ab adolescentia fuerant conversati."

[2] [Though Peter of Collingbourn was in office for a short time in Jan. and Feb. 1312; see App. II.]

[3] *Ann. Lond.*, p. 174; Hemingburgh, ii, 278; Baker, p. 4.

the Scots revolt fell much more heavily on the earls and barons of the opposition. The weakness of the English defence was, however, most of all due to the utter disorder of the royal finances, for which the old king must bear nine-tenths of the responsibility. We have only to turn over the issue rolls of the exchequer, and such wardrobe accounts as survive of the early years of Edward II's reign,[1] to see into what desperate straits the king's revenues had fallen. All the revenues of the exchequer went to the wardrobe or to the English chamberlains of Scotland, who financed what remained of the English army and administration in Scotland. The supplies thus available were but a drop in the bucket of expenses. New taxes were tried but found unproductive. One keeper of the wardrobe after another gave up his task in despair. Not one of them was able to put his accounts together in a shape which would pass muster with the exchequer officials. Years after they had left office, the keepers of the wardrobe were still receiving monies from the exchequer and endeavouring to pay off their debts. The issue rolls for these years present a curious spectacle. The accounts with the keepers of Edward I's latter years and those of the new king's reign were still kept open. We find at the same time Droxford receiving and paying monies as keeper of Edward I and as keeper for the second year of Edward II. Benstead's accounts as keeper for the first year of Edward II still remained open, and were only finally passed by the exchequer in time to be enrolled in the Pipe Rolls of 16 Edward II, sixteen years after Benstead had gone out of office, and after his death.[2] Droxford's accounts for 2 Edward II and Warley's accounts between 1309 and 1314 were never enrolled at all. This shameful account keeping involved the breakdown of the

[1] There are enrolled wardrobe accounts available for 1 Edw. II, but no others until 8 Edw. II. After this they are regularly, though very tardily, enrolled (*Enrolled Foreign Accounts*, p. 102). Fortunately there also survive in E.A. 374/6, 15, 375/1, accounts of receipts for 4, 5 and 6 Edw. II, and *ibid.* 375/8, a *jornale* of the wardrobe, 6-14 Edw. II [E.A. 375/9, noted as a king's wardrobe account in the first edition, and so described in the official printed list, is actually an account of Queen Isabella's wardrobe.] Thus the only years entirely unrepresented are 2 and 3 Edw. II.

[2] Benstead died before 20 Dec. 1317, and his lands were seized by the king by reason of his debts to the exchequer (*Cal. Inq.*, vi, 284-7). His widow, Petronilla, and his other executors finally satisfied the exchequer claims (Pipe Roll 168, m. 50). A clerk at the time he held office, Benstead's will was proved by his widow, and his estates inherited by his son, a boy of twelve.

financial system which Walter Langton and Droxford had devised for Edward I. We shall see the remedies devised to end this scandalous state of things later. During the first ten years of the reign, with which alone we are concerned in this chapter, the chaos was yearly becoming more complete.[1]

In these circumstances the Italian bankers were the king's only refuge. The advances of the Frescobaldi enabled Edward II to keep alive the ministers of his household and state. It is clear, however, that only a small portion of the sums received by these greedy foreigners from the king's subjects actually reached the royal coffers. The rest of it remained in their own hands. Yet though hated and unpopular, they were indispensable. Amerigo dei Frescobaldi, their chief English representative, became one of the most important men in England. He was not only chief receiver of customs; he was also keeper of the king's exchanges at London and Canterbury.[2] As constable of Bordeaux, Amerigo was also the head of the financial administration of Edward's duchy of Gascony. Moreover, he was only one of the many foreign exploiters of the English national purse. Gascon bankers rivalled the Florentine societies of merchants in their business-like pursuit of their own game. Conspicuous among these was the family of Calhau, and this clan of Bordeaux capitalists was linked, as we have seen, by close ties of blood and interests to the upstart earl of Cornwall. Bertrand Calhau, Gaveston's nephew,[3] and a valet of the household, was his uncle's financial agent, and stood for the "foreign merchants" to whom Peter was popularly supposed to be engaged in transferring the huge treasure which he had amassed at the expense of Englishmen, that it might be stored up in Gascony against a rainy day.[4] Even in matters of business the king's "brother Peter" had not clean hands. And the outlook was the worse since the men of affairs were now

[1] Mr. Arthur Jones notes similar arrears in the accounts of the chamberlains of Chester. There are no accounts from 1306 to 1312, and other gaps between 1313 and 1316, 1317 and 1319, and 1321-24 (*Flintshire Ministers' Accounts*, Flintshire Hist. Soc., pp. viii-ix).

[2] He was appointed to this office on 20 Aug. 1307 (*C.F.R.*, ii, 2).

[3] Cotton MS. Nero C. viii, f. 88v. "Domino Petro de Gauaston comiti Cornubie de dono regis *per manus Bertrandi Caillau nepotis sui* . . . d. marcas." See above, p. 12. Bertrand and his kinsfolk apparently exploited the earldom of Cornwall, especially its mines (*Ann. Lond.*, p. 199).

[4] Trokelowe, p. 64, "thesaurum . . . mercatoribus transmarinis ad custodiendum tradebat."

become also administrators and politicians. Arnold Calhau, at one time mayor of Bordeaux, was admitted in 1313 as a knight of the royal household,[1] and later became seneschal of Saintonge [2] and keeper of Oléron. Both Gascon and Italian capitalists, then, were laying hands on affairs of state, the natural preserves of Englishmen and in particular of the English aristocracy.

The alert baronial opposition, which the old king had silenced with the greatest difficulty, instantly took advantage of the incapacity and distress of the young king. I need not tell the oft-told tale how, within a few months of the new king's accession, the barons drove Gaveston into his second exile, and how cleverly Edward and his personal advisers broke up the unity of the baronial opposition, but gave way on all points of policy on condition that the favourite was allowed back. The articles of Stamford of 1309,[3] which registered this surrender, were in substance a re-enactment of the *Articuli super Cartas* of 1300. In no way, however, do these articles mark an epoch, and they never had a chance of being carried out. Many of the barons refused to agree to Gaveston's restoration. The Gascon, when he reappeared at court, showed that he had learnt little by his exile. So the same game was played over again. This time the barons would stand no nonsense. It was useless wresting promises from a king who would not keep his word. They fell back on the remedy which their grandfathers had employed so effectively against Henry III. A baronial committee was to "ordain and establish the estate of the realm and the household according to right and reason." London was their meeting-place, and not even a Scottish war could drag them from the work in hand until it had been completed. Eighteen months was allowed them for this onerous task, from March 1310 to Michaelmas 1311. Some preliminary ordinances were issued soon after they first assembled; the complete ordinances were of the later date. The principle which inspired them all was the transference of power from the king and his friends to baronial nominees, and the drastic purging of

[1] E.A. 375/8, f. 5, records his admission on 7 March 1313, to the wages and robes of a "miles simplex," *i.e.*, not a "banneret," of the household. He is described as "ciuis Burdegale."

[2] [Letters patent appointing him were dated 2 April 1313 (G.R. 26, m. 9).]

[3] Printed in *Rot. Parl.*, i, 443-5.

the royal household of its irresponsible and unworthy elements. Such was the genesis of the lords ordainers and of the ordinances of 1311 which they drew up.

### (3) The Ordinances and the Ordainers

The judicious monk of Malmesbury refused to copy out all the ordinances in his chronicle because he had no wish to break into his narrative or to bore his readers.[1] But, he added, anyone can find them in the collection of laws, and, even apart from this, the ordainers had taken good care that they should obtain sufficient publicity.[2] I cheerfully follow the wise monk's reticence, and I do so the more willingly since I have no wish to discuss the ordinances at large.[3] Some five points in relation to them must, however, next demand our attention. These are the composition of the ordaining committee and its mode of appointment, the problem of the participation of the commons in their work, the nature and authority of the ordinances issued, the extent to which they were carried out, and the permanent changes resulting from them. Let us take these points in order.

The ordainers were a purely aristocratic committee, consisting of bishops, earls and barons.[4] They represented, however, very varied types of opinion, and only the thoroughgoing partisans and dependents of the king were excluded. The venerable earl of Lincoln and the youthful earl of Gloucester, the only two earls who, despite strong personal provocation, had been magnanimous enough never to take up a decided line against Gaveston, co-operated with the truculent opposition, represented by Lancaster, Hereford, and Warwick, and the milder opposition, represented by Pembroke. Ancient ministers of Edward I, innocent of all revolutionary aims, like bishop John Langton of Chichester and bishop Baldock of London, went hand in hand with the determined archbishop Winchelsea, who had resumed the leadership of the opposition as soon as he returned from the exile into which Edward I had driven him. The large

[1] Malmesb., p. 171.

[2] A copy was sent under the great seal to every county of the realm (*ibid.*, p. 171, compare *Flores Hist.*, iii, 147). Every cathedral church had also a copy (Murimuth, p. 15).

[3] The ordinances are printed in *Rot. Parl.*, i, 281-6, and *Statutes of the Realm*, i, 157-67.

[4] A list is in *Ann. Lond.*, p. 172.

proportion of Edward's former ministers among the ordainers is particularly noteworthy. But these various shades of policy did not prevent speedy and decisive action. There is no evidence that there was a protesting minority against the vigorous doings of the majority. Of the more royalist element, Lincoln died before he was called upon to make his final election between the son of his old master and his own son-in-law, Thomas of Lancaster; while Gloucester evaded responsibility by taking part in a Scottish campaign, and returning to London only to act as regent after Lincoln's death.[1] With this one exception the ordainers stuck manfully to their task, refusing for instance to participate in the Scottish campaign, on the ground that it was their duty to remain in London to complete their programme of reform.[2]

As regards the method of appointment, the king's face was saved by the election of the ordainers being formally made by virtue of royal letters patent, giving authority "of our free will" to draw up ordinances for the reform of state and household[3] to whomsoever the barons appointed for the purpose. Edward's feelings were also respected by a declaration on the part of the barons that the rights of the king and his heirs should not be prejudiced by his compliance with their wishes.[4] The patent of appointment was, however, based upon the petition of the baronial parliament, assembled at London in the spring of 1310,[5] and therefore substantially took the ordinary course of legislation at that period. Some evidence of haste and informality suggested the purely nominal nature of the royal assent. The ordainers were already at work before Edward gave his sanction to their institution. The letters patent of approval are dated 16 March, and the ordainers were only elected and

[1] *Ann. Lond.*, p. 174. He was made *custos Anglie* on 4 March 1311 (*C.P.R. 1307-13*, p. 333). Lincoln died on 5 Feb.

[2] *Ann. Lond.*, p. 174.

[3] *Foedera*, ii, 105; *Rot. Parl.*, i, 445. With the clear object of giving greater publicity to the concession, the patent was drawn up in French, not in Latin, as most patents were, and fourteen copies of it were ordered to be made. "Et inde fiunt septem paria." [According to the usual interpretation, however, this means not seven pairs, *i.e.* fourteen copies, but seven sets, seven copies. *Cf. Medieval Latin Word-List* (1934), p. 293.]

[4] *Rot. Parl.*, i, 443. It was dated 17 March, and was enrolled on the close roll. Eleven bishops, eight earls, and thirteen barons took part in the act, both the royalists and the opposition being represented.

[5] *Ann. Lond.*, pp. 168-9. This chronicle also sets out in full both the royal consent of 16 March and the baronial declaration of 17 March.

sworn on 20 March. However, the day before, on 19 March, six preliminary ordinances were issued,[1] which laid down the general lines on which the work was to be done, and these, irregular as they were, Edward was forced to promulgate in the following August. While the ordainers held constant sessions in the city, the king and Gaveston kept out of the way by engaging in the Scottish war. It was nearly eighteen months later that the completion of their task brought Edward back to the capital to meet the full parliament of the three estates which met on 9 August 1311 at Westminster. To this body the whole work of the ordainers was submitted, including the six preliminary ordinances of March 1310.

It is in this parliament of the summer of 1311 that any general assent of the three estates to the ordinances must have been given, if such popular ratification were thought necessary at all. I cannot, however, but think that both those who maintain and those who deny the participation of the commons in the passing of the ordinances seek to apply to the early fourteenth century the distinctions and refinements of a later generation, and that the problem they discuss is largely an unreal one. It in fact involves that unhistorical way of looking at history to which ordinary practical lawyers have at all ages been exceptionally prone. They look at the past as a plane surface which has never been altered. They have imperfect appreciation of the idea of development. They assume that the modern categories have existed from all time, and persist in reading them back into an age which knew nothing of them. Take as an ancient example of this mental habit, the attitude of the seventeenth century lawyers of the school of Coke to mediæval antiquities, which led them to read into history the ideas of their own age and profession. Nor has the following of Coke altogether ceased in the land. Our modern peerage law, as Mr. J. H. Round has so incisively shown,[2] is full of these legal perversions of history, notably in its ridiculous doctrine of "calling out of abeyance" thirteenth-century baronies which were in no wise hereditary dignities in the modern sense. It is almost as absurd to expect formal legislation by the three estates in 1311 as it is to imagine that Edward I created an hereditary house of lords in 1295. As, however,

[1] *Ann. Lond.*, pp. 172-4.

[2] See notably Round, *Peerage and Pedigree*, i, 103-283, "The Muddle of the Law."

we are nearing the time when the consent of the three estates did begin to be thought necessary for legislation, it is worth while to pause to deal with the facts.

I have already pointed out that the spring parliament of 1310, at which the ordainers were appointed, was a purely baronial assembly. Accordingly, the view, maintained nearly a hundred years ago by Hallam,[1] that the assent of the commons was given to the appointment of the ordainers necessarily falls to the ground. Its only basis was an inaccurate recital of the royal writ of 16 March 1310, contained in the preamble to the ordinances as they appear in print. In this preamble Edward II's letters patent are quoted as granted to the "prelates, earls, barons and commons of the land." [2] I shall soon have occasion to show that this copy of the ordinances is not older than 1322, the year of their repeal, and is therefore in no real sense the work of the parliament of 1311. Moreover, if we turn to the numerous versions of the letters patent of appointment, we shall find that the king granted the right to nominate the reforming committee, not to the magnates and the commons, but simply to the "prelates, earls and barons." So narrow was the reformers' point of view, that they did not even avail themselves of the power, allowed by the crown, of going outside baronial circles in the selection of ordainers.[3] Besides this, I would also stress the very loose way in which such words as "communitas" and "commons" were used at this time. We want something more than that vague term to prove a real participation of the third estate. Last of all, a law was in those days equally authentic, whether approved by the three estates or by the magnates only. I cannot, however, go as far as some modern teachers, who maintain that in the early fourteenth century the commons were no part of parliament, even when they had been expressly summoned to that body. This, and some analogous points, can, however, be better postponed until we get to the parliament of York of 1322.

The real evidence of popular participation in the passing of the ordinances rests, as I have suggested, on the history of the parliament of 1311. We have the certain evidence

[1] Hallam, *Europe in the Middle Ages*, iii, 42 (1872).

[2] *Rot. Parl.*, i, 281.

[3] The royal letter of 16 March authorised the election of "certeins persones de prelatz, countes et barons, *et des autres*" (*Ann. London.*, p.169). But all the ordainers came within the aristocratic categories.

of the writs that not only the magnates, but the lower clergy and the knights of the shire, and a fair number of citizens and burgesses, were summoned to this assembly,[1] which is further described as "the parliament in which the ordinances made for the common weal are to be completed and confirmed."[2] We can read in print, in the official return of the members serving in parliament, the names of the knights and burgesses who sat in this important gathering. We know, too, from the close roll, that a reasonable proportion of these members received their expenses for a session which began on Sunday, 8 August, and lasted for what was then a long period of two calendar months, until 9 October.[3] Unluckily we have no roll of the proceedings of this assembly. What in the printed rolls of parliament—a collection, I may add, which in no wise corresponds to the needs of modern scholarship—is called the roll of the parliament of 5 Edward II is in truth nothing more than a copy of the letters patent, which were scattered broadcast all over the country, in which the king was forced to declare to the world the contents of the ordinances which he had so unwillingly accepted. Moreover, the memorandum at the end that the ordinances were repealed in 1322 shows that the copy was made in the light of more recent history, and is not, therefore, the best of evidence for the text of the ordinances. Its only help to us is in the date of the letters patent of promulgation. This date is 5 October and shows that the ordinances were proclaimed when parliament was still in session.

The chroniclers help us where the records fail. The monk of Malmesbury relates at length how the king's reluctance to confirm the ordinances was only overborne when his counsellors frightened him with the prospect of another battle of Lewes and another domination of a new earl Simon of Leicester,

[1] *Parl. Writs*, II, ii, 44-57. [2] *Ibid.*, App., p. 41.

[3] The summaries in *C.C.R. 1307-13*, p. 440, and *Parl. Writs*, II, i, 73, show that expenses were allowed from 8 Aug. to 9 Oct. to the knights and to representatives of 21 boroughs. Parliament was then prorogued, and fresh elections held for another one to meet in Nov. The boroughs returning members on these two occasions were strikingly different. On the latter occasion expenses were only allowed to representatives of 13 boroughs. As it is unlikely burgesses in attendance omitted to claim, the inference is that only a small proportion of those returned actually sat. [But for Mr. Tout's later view that "it is absolutely clear that the number of expenses writs issued is no evidence at all as to the number of burgesses who sat in any particular parliament," and his reasons for it, see *Chapters*, iii, 291, n. 1. *Cf.* M. McKisack, *Parliamentary Representation of the English Boroughs* (1932).] For the persons returned see *Return of Members of Parliament*, i, 32-6.

as represented by earl Thomas the inheritor of his estates. Though the monk of Malmesbury says no word of the commons, he quotes that famous sentence from the code of Justinian with which Edward I had made such play in 1295, "quod enim omnes tangit ab omnibus debet approbari." [1] The canon of Bridlington tells us more specifically that the ordinances were published in parliament on 30 September,[2] so that it must have been with the full knowledge that the three estates were cognisant of their contents and approved of their character that Edward yielded his assent five days later. Other authors tell us how the articles were read in St. Paul's cathedral in the presence of the king, prelates, magnates and commons,[3] and that archbishop Winchelsea and his suffragans solemnly discussed the ordinances in provincial synod and ultimately promulgated sentences of excommunication against all who would infringe them.[4] I have already emphasised the great pains taken to scatter official copies of the ordinances all over the country. In the light of these facts it would be most hazardous to affirm that the ordinances were anywise defective by reason of any lack of popular confirmation. That this popular approval was silent and informal followed from the social conditions of the time. Legislation was still by the king, and the authority of the ordinances rested upon their solemn proclamation by the king before his assembled estates, in circumstances of the greatest publicity.

As regards the contents of the ordinances I have little to say. The provisions which loomed largest before the minds of contemporaries were those for the expulsion of Gaveston and of his English and foreign associates. The claim of the barons to nominate the king's ministers had been made many times before, and it may be accounted to them for moderation that they were content with nominating ministers high and low, and did not demand the setting up of a permanent council, like that of the Fifteen in 1258. The point in which the ordi-

[1] Malmesb., pp. 169-71. [The tag was fashionable. In 1323 bishop Cobham of Worcester used it in injunctions to Malvern priory (*Reg. of Thomas de Cobham,* Worc. Hist. Soc., p. 153).]

[2] Bridl., p. 39.

[3] *Ann. Paul.*, p. 270; *Flores Hist.*, iii, 147. The chronicle printed in the appendix to *Liber de Antiquis Legibus*, pp. 251-2, gives curiously different details to those of other writers. Walsingham, i, 124, specifically says, "in praesentia praelatorum, magnatum et communium totius regni," but he may be reading into his texts the language of the late fourteenth century.

[4] *Ann. Lond.*, pp. 177-8.

nances largely differed from the provisions of Oxford lies in the immense particularity with which the men of 1311 pressed for the radical reform of the royal household. In 1258 it was enough to say in one short clause, "let it be remembered to amend the household of the king and queen."[1] Of course the whole of the ordinances are much more detailed than are the provisions of Oxford and Westminster combined. A large amount of the detail is due, however, to the care with which the purging and amendment of the royal household is provided for.

The reasons for the stress laid in 1311 on reform of the household are not far to seek. Under Henry III all the king's ministers had been, so to say, of one sort. The distinction familiar in the reign of Edward III,[2] between ministers of state and ministers of the household, had not yet arisen, and it was part of Henry III's policy that no such distinction should exist. The chancellor and the chancery were almost as much attached to the court as the wardrobe and the chamber. The same line of attack secured a baronial chancellor and treasurer as well as a baronial keeper of the wardrobe. The barons of 1311 were neither clear-headed nor far-sighted, but they could not but take cognisance of the facts that lay straight before their eyes. Among their number were the two prelates who had administered the chancery from the king's accession to within fifteen months of the meeting of the parliament which confirmed the ordinances. They must have known from their own experience of office where the root of the evil lay. It is no rash guess that they were driven into opposition not only by their loss of their posts, but by their consciousness that when in office they were powerless to enforce their will by reason of the organised household system, whose ministers alone possessed the ear of the king. Accordingly the ordainers insisted both on purging the court and on treating ministers of the court as equally responsible to the nation with the ministers of state. This point of view expresses itself in the fourteenth ordinance with its long list

[1] *Select Charters*, pp. 392 and 396. The bad translation copied out by Stubbs calls "hospicium" "place of reception," and finds no clearer word for "hostel" than "hostelry." Unluckily, this unnecessary darkening of counsel has not been removed in the useful new edition by Mr. H. W. C. Davis (1913), p. 387.

[2] It is brought out clearly in Avesbury's characterisation of the ministerial crisis of 1340 as a struggle between the king's "secretarii" (*i.e.*, household officers) and the king's "officiarii in magnis officiis ministrantes" (Avesbury (R.S.), pp. 323-4).

of officials whom the king is to appoint " by the counsel and assent of his baronage and that in parliament." [1] These ministers include the chancellor, the two chief justices of the king's bench and the common bench, the treasurer, chancellor and chief baron of the exchequer, the steward of the household, the keeper and controller of the wardrobe, a suitable clerk to keep the privy seal, two keepers of the forests, and two escheators, one for the north and one for the south of Trent, and the chief clerk of the common bench. The provisions for the appointment of keepers of ports and castles [on the coast], of ministers in Gascony, Ireland and Scotland, and of sheriffs,[2] contained in the articles immediately subsequent, all emphasise the same spirit. A like intention inspired the negative articles. Let us illustrate it from the thirteenth article, which runs as follows: " Inasmuch as the king has been misguided and advised by bad counsellors, we ordain that all the bad counsellors be removed, so that neither they, nor others like them, shall be near the king nor kept in the king's service, and that other suitable persons shall be put in their places. And in the same fashion let it be done with regard to the members of the king's household who are not suitable."

## (4) The Execution of the Ordinances (1311–14)

The questions remain how far the ordinances were carried out, what permanent improvements sprang from them, and how far they remedied the grievances they were drawn up to redress. To answer these questions fully would be to write the history of the rest of Edward II's reign. How little the ordinances were executed could be read in every page of that history.

It was not that the barons did not make every effort to give effect to the ordinances. Their greatest point was

[1] *Rot. Parl.*, i, 282. The interesting thing about the list is the offices that, in the barons' opinion, were important enough to be under their control. The exclusion of the office of king's chamberlain from the long catalogue is quite unintelligible to me, especially as the barons soon afterwards were urging the removal from court of the then chamberlain, John Charlton. I can only guess that it was a piece of complaisance to the king, and a recognition of the peculiarly intimate relation between the king and his " chamber." See for this Fleta, p. 71.

[2] [Mr. Tout's attention was drawn by Miss L. Taylor to the removal of the privilege granted to the county court by the *Articuli super Cartas* of electing if it wished, except where the sheriffdom was hereditary or of fee. The privilege had been sparingly exercised.]

gained when Gaveston withdrew almost immediately beyond seas.[1] The records for October and November are full of minor changes, but not all of them were quite to the barons' liking. It was a matter of small moment that a somewhat colourless official, John Sandall, the treasurer, should yield up his post to another official, Walter of Norwich, though the latter, a knight and a baron of the exchequer, was probably more acceptable to the magnates. In August, and again in December, Walter Reynolds, now bishop of Worcester, resigned the keeping of the great seal to the chancery clerk, Adam Osgodby. The facts that Norwich was merely keeper of the treasury; that Reynolds was still nominally chancellor; [2] and that Osgodby was merely keeper of the seal; suggested to the two new officials that their offices were not meant to be of long duration. It is difficult to understand the principles underlying the minor changes. It is a clear triumph for the ordainers when Amerigo dei Frescobaldi was succeeded on 9 October by John Cockermouth, king's clerk, an exchequer official, as keeper of the exchanges of London and Canterbury [3] and perhaps a more complete victory when, eleven days later, the king's clerk gave place to John of Lincoln, citizen of London.[4] But it was not until 2 December that Gaveston's deputy, John Hotham, king's clerk, acting keeper of the forests north of Trent, yielded up his office, to which Henry Percy succeeded; "and afterwards the ordainers consented to the aforesaid." [5] Again, on the same day, the elder Hugh le Despenser surrendered to the king the keepership of the forests south of Trent "in

[1] [For varying accounts of his movements during brief exile and after secret return see *Chapters*, ii, 195, n. 2.]

[2] Reynolds had at all times so frequently acted by deputy that it is perhaps dangerous to ascribe his abandonment of the seal to political motives. It is, however, probably significant that from 27 Aug. to 28 Sept., and again from 9 Dec. onward, Osgodby and other chancery clerks "kept" the seal. See App. II, pp. 285-8. If Edward II avoided being compelled to accept a chancellor imposed on him by the ordainers, it was found impolitic to allow the courtier prelate, still dignified with the title, to do the chancellor's work.

[3] *C.F.R.*, ii, 104. Cockermouth had been remembrancer of the exchequer since 2 Aug. 1310 (*C.P.R. 1307-13*, p. 273).

[4] *C.F.R.*, ii, 105. John of Lincoln was a citizen of high position. He had been sheriff in 33 Edw. I (*Mun. Gild. Lond.*, II (*Lib. Custumarum*), i, 244) and was in 1311 an alderman (*Parl. Writs*, II, ii, App., p. 41). The "exchanges," in modern phrase the mint, remained in the keeping of London citizens up to 1316, Lincoln being succeeded in 1315 by William Trent.

[5] *C.F.R.*, ii, 116.

compliance with the ordinances of the prelates and barons."[1] But these are the only important personal changes that took place between October and the end of the year, and the new officers held their positions by an exceedingly precarious tenure. Gaveston's partisan Hotham[2] [had ceased in February to be] escheator north of Trent. [His successor Robert of Wodehouse, who had till 31 Jan. been cofferer of the wardrobe,[3] remained undisturbed.] It is of particular significance that no changes whatsoever seem to have been made in the king's household.

It was clear that something more would have to be done if the ordinances were to prove effective. Accordingly the ordainers, though their period of legal office was now at an end, kept up their organisation and assemblies, and deliberated in common as to what further measures were to be taken to carry out their accepted policy of the purgation of the royal household. What these further measures were can be read in print in a remarkable document, which has been preserved for us both in the archives of the city of London and by a London chronicler. The latter version, which is the only complete one, may be seen in Stubbs' edition of the *Annales Londonienses*, where it is described as *ordinationes comitum secundae*.[4] In the imperfect version in the London *Liber custumarum* it is called with greater force " the articles which the earls of Lancaster and Warwick submitted to the king to appoint and remove officers in his household and to observe the ordinances before written in all their points."[5] I specially call attention to these remarkable articles because they have not, I think, met with the attention they deserve. At first sight it might be thought that these articles were the basis of the ordinances of 1311, standing to them as the articles of the barons stand to the Great Charter, or, if we adopt M. Bémont's opinion, as the baronial petition, expressed in the so-called *statutum de tallagio non concedendo*, stands to the *Confirmatio Cartarum*

[1] *C.F.R.*, ii, 116 ; *C.P.R. 1307-13*, p. 464. His successor, however, was the ex-steward, Robert Fitz Payn.

[2] Hotham had been Gaveston's attorney during his exile (I.R. 115, m. 8).

[3] [Bodl. Lib. Tanner MS. 197, f. 63v. *Cf.* App. II, p. 317.]

[4] *Ann. Lond.*, pp. 198-202. " *Postquam* autem supradictae ordinationes per dominum regem pupplicatae et ratificatae fuerunt per totam Angliam, ordinatores tractaverunt *de familia et servis regis*, et supplicaverunt domino regi forma qua sequitur ut eos ab officio removeret." Bridl., pp. 40-1, and Malmesb., p. 174, clearly refer to these.

[5] *Mun. Gild. Lond.*, II (*Liber Custumarum*), ii, 682-90.

of 1297.[1] A very superficial examination, however, shows that these articles pre-suppose the existence of the ordinances of 1311, and are simply another effort on the part of the more energetic earls to give effect to them. They deal almost entirely with the followers and kinsfolk of Gaveston, the alien farmers of the customs, and the members, great and small, of the king's household. A very large number of the king's friends are specified by name and their immediate removal from their offices is urgently demanded. So minute are the personal details given that I have no doubt that a careful study of the articles would enable one to date them with a near approach to accuracy. Meanwhile it is enough to say that they must have been written between the latter part of October 1311 and the reappearance of Gaveston at court before Christmas 1312.[2]

Some few further results seem to have followed this fresh effort of the earls. Among them we are pretty safe in including the final disappearance of Amerigo dei Frescobaldi from English history, the deprivation of the king's French friend, Henry de Beaumont, of the Isle of Man, and the ejection of Beaumont's sister, the lady Vescy, from the castle of Bamburgh.[3] These changes, however, did not bring nearer that purging of the household which was the barons' chief desire. On the contrary, the very demand drove Edward into a fury. He was greatly indignant that the barons would not allow him to keep a single member of his household after his own heart. He complained that he was being treated like a madman when the arrangement of his whole household was to be determined upon by the judgment of others.[4] In great disgust he withdrew to the north. And with the king went to the north the hated household officers against whom the barons fulminated in vain. Among them were the steward, Edmund Mauley,[5] and the three heads of the wardrobe—the keeper, Ingelard Warley,[6]

[1] *Chartes des libertés anglaises*, Introd., p. xliii, and p. 87.

[2] *Ann. Lond.*, p. 202. The article refusing to recognise Gaveston's protection and general attorneys suggests that he was still abroad, though his kinsfolk were still prominent among the king's train (*ibid.*, p. 201). [Mr. Tout later came to the conclusion that the date must be between 25 and 30 Nov. (*Chapters*, ii, 198, n. 1).]

[3] Henry of Percy was made keeper of Bamburgh on 18 Dec. 1311 (*C.F.R.*, ii, 121). But on 28 Jan. 1312, the king, after Gaveston's return, ordered Isabella de Vescy to retain the castle (*C.P.R. 1307-13*, p. 427).

[4] Malmesb., p. 174.

[5] *C.P.R. 1307-13*, p. 428, shows that he was at York by 3 Feb. 1312.

[6] *Ibid.*, p. 434.

the controller, William Melton,[1] and the cofferer, John Ockham.[2] With them went many other enemies of the ordinances. They found congenial spirits among the royal ministers still established in the north, and, as soon as Edward was safe in Yorkshire, a multitude of royal grants and favours was scattered among these too faithful servitors. It was by the advice of these hated *familiares* that Edward now revoked the ordinances and reinstated Gaveston in January 1312.

In the early months of 1312 there were two rival governments, that of the king and his household in the north, and that of the ordainers in the south. But while the ordainers soon began to extend their influence into the king's sphere of action, Edward's attempts to exercise authority south of the Humber proved singularly abortive. In his anxiety to use all men of ability against the barons, Edward had already restored Walter Langton to his bishopric and some share of the royal favour.[3] He now made a desperate effort to avail himself of the skill of his father's old minister to upset the ordinances. On 23 January 1312 the king appointed Langton treasurer of the exchequer to hold office "until the next parliament."[4] But the exchequer was at Westminster, and the "keeper of the treasury," Sir Walter Norwich, was an official in no wise wishful to stand up against the ordainers, who had absolute control of the capital. Accordingly the patent of appointment was disregarded in the south. On 14 March a new patent was issued renewing Langton's appointment, with equally little result.[5] The barons of the exchequer ignored Langton, and the ordainers threatened him so severely that the treasurer, who had lost the magnificent nerve and audacity of his early days, was afraid to take up the office. The indignant king on 12 April told the barons "as on other occasions" that they would incur his severest displeasure unless they obeyed Langton as treasurer.[6] Next day, 13 April, Edward sternly warned Langton not to shirk discharging his duty.[7] Excommunicated by Winchelsea for his violation of the ordi-

[1] *C.P.R. 1307-13*, p. 430 (12 Feb.). [2] *Ibid.*, p. 453.

[3] "Ad semigratiam regis" (Trokelowe, p. 64).

[4] *C.P.R. 1307-13*, p. 413. The limitation "until parliament" was an ingenious attempt not to break the letter of the ordinances.

[5] *Ibid.*, p. 440.

[6] Madox, ii, 38. "Et hoc sicut indignationem regis vitare voluerint nullatenus omittant." This letter is dated from Newcastle-on-Tyne.

[7] *Foedera*, ii, 164.

nances, chased away by the ordainers when he appeared in the exchequer, Langton had no mind to continue the struggle. He appealed to Avignon against the archbishop and made the need of personally prosecuting his suit an excuse for seeking leave to visit the papal curia. On 1 May he received letters of conduct and a warm commendation of his cause to the pope.[1] But Edward soon abandoned his ally's cause. On 17 May he directed Walter Norwich to "continue to act" as treasurer, as the bishop of Lichfield has been "for divers reasons prevented from entering upon the execution of that office."[2]

It was some time between the spring and autumn of 1312 that the king was forced to meet another baronial proposal by appointing a "suitable clerk" to keep the privy seal. Up to this time William Melton remained controller as well as keeper, but before November the offices were separated, and the king's clerk, Roger Northburgh, became the first keeper of the privy seal who was separate from the controller of the wardrobe.[3] Thus within a year a new ministerial office seems to have come into existence at the request of the ordainers.

The real cause of the king's change of front was the conquest of the north by the ordainers. Edward's last resistance was on 4 May ended by his panic flight from Newcastle, and the withdrawal of Gaveston to Scarborough. Two days after the king threw over Langton, Gaveston was forced to yield himself up to the ordainers. He met his fate on Blacklow Hill in June, within six months of his reappearance in England.

The monk of Malmesbury drew the obvious moral that courtiers must learn from Gaveston's death not to despise the barons.[4] But the treachery which ignored the terms of his capitulation profited Edward more than the pity excited by the favourite's tragic end. Public opinion was still so set against the courtiers that Pembroke failed to stir either the university or the burgesses of Oxford to support him against the felon earls who had broken their word to the Gascon.[5] The apathy of even the instructed public forced

[1] *Foedera*, ii, pp. 166-7. [2] *C.P.R. 1307-13*, p. 459.

[3] E.A. 375/8, ff. 8, 11 v., shows Northburgh acting between Nov. 1312, and May 1313, with a staff of clerks. For the influence of the ordinances on the staples see later, p. 224. [4] Malmesb., p. 180.

[5] *Ibid.*, pp. 178-9. "Sed nec clerici nec burgenses rem ad se non pertinentem tractare vel attemptare curabant."

the aggrieved earls to take things into their own hands. From this arose a permanent schism among the higher barons that was never quite repaired. Henceforth Pembroke and Warenne hated Lancaster and Warwick more bitterly than they despised the king. They were thus forced to make common cause with the court, even though it still swarmed with the very men against whom the ordainers had fulminated in vain.[1] The ordinances could now only be enforced at the cost of a civil war, from which even Thomas of Lancaster shrank. Failing the decisive arbitration of the sword, there was no reality in the gathering of armies and the threatenings of war, the insincere negotiations, the hollow compromises, and finally the pretended reconciliation which, two years later, enabled Edward to make a pretence of leading a national army against Robert Bruce. The collapse of the Scots campaign on the fatal field of Bannockburn again threw the wretched king on the mercy of his enemies.

### (5) The Ministerial Changes after Bannockburn

The monk of Malmesbury sketches with spirit and accuracy [2] the political results of the battle of Bannockburn, as they were worked out in a full parliament held at York in September 1314. "The earls said that the ordinances had not been observed, and that therefore things had gone badly with the king, both because he had disregarded his oath to stand by the ordinances, and because the archbishop of Canterbury had excommunicated all violators of the ordinances. Therefore they declared that no good would come until the ordinances were fully observed. The king denied nothing to the earls, and agreed to allow in good faith their complete execution. Thereupon the chancellor, the treasurer, the sheriffs and other officials were removed, and new ones were appointed in parliament in accordance with the tenour of the ordinances." The record evidence shows that the chronicler's statements are almost literally true. The magnates and commons were still in session when a new chancellor and treasurer were chosen. Walter Reynolds, who had recently succeeded Winchelsea as primate, had had since 1312

[1] Malmesb., p. 192. "Sed adhuc remanent in regis curia de familiaribus Petri et ejus familia, qui perturbant pacem totius patriae et regem inducunt vindictam quaerere."

[2] *Ibid.*, p. 208.

so loose a hold over the great seal that he was described more often as keeper than as chancellor, and after 30 March 1314 was not even called keeper, remaining, however, as some sort of adviser and director of the chancery clerks keeping the seal.[1] This ambiguous state of things was now ended. John Sandall, who had returned to the treasury through Pembroke's good offices in October 1312, was sufficiently trusted by the barons to be appointed Reynolds' successor as chancellor. Sandall's fellow worker at the exchequer, Sir Walter Norwich, now became treasurer in name as well as in fact, his appointment being made on 26 September "by the king and council." [2] Next day the commons went home, but there was enough of a baronial element now surrounding the king to secure more drastic further changes. If we turn to the fine rolls, on which at this period the appointment of the sheriffs is recorded, we discover that, with the necessary exceptions of certain hereditary or quasi-hereditary sheriffdoms, new sheriffs were appointed in October and November 1314, in every case except two.[3] Five of the new sheriffs had sat in this parliament as knights of their respective shires.[4] There was certainly

[1] Reynolds' peculiar relations to the chancery are more fully discussed later; App. II, pp. 285-88.

[2] *C.P.R. 1313-17*, p. 178.

[3] *C.F.R.*, ii, 220-1. The hereditary sheriffdoms were Rutland (Margaret, widow of Edmund, earl of Cornwall), and Westmorland (Roger Clifford, a minor). Besides these, earl Thomas had been sheriff of Lancashire since 1298, and stood in a quasi-hereditary relation to that office. So also did earl Guy of Warwick to Worcestershire, of which he had been sheriff from 1298 to his death in 1315 (*P.R.O. Lists and Indexes, no. ix. List of Sheriffs*). The two exceptions were Cumberland and Devonshire. Andrew Harclay, sheriff of Cumberland since 1311, was in effect a military governor rather than an administrative official. He can hardly be called a true exception to this rule of change. The only real exception, then, was Devonshire, where, however, a new sheriff was appointed in Jan., 1315. It should be remembered that the sheriff was usually appointed not only to the custody of his shire or shires, but also to the custody of one or two chief castles within their limits. He was thus a military as well as an executive officer, a fact which makes the importance of securing the right sort of sheriffs the more evident. The order to the outgoing sheriff is generally to deliver the custody of the shire and castle to his successor, "with the rolls, writs, memoranda, and other things touching the office" (*e.g.*, *C.F.R.*, iii, 35). Yet in the London eyre of 15 Edw. II a Justice was told that a sheriff retained his rolls after he had been removed from office. "Donqes cels qe pledent devant les viscontes perdent malement lor trauayle," was his comment (*Year Book of 5 Edw. II*, Selden Soc., Intro., p. xviii).

[4] *Return of Members of Parliament*, i, 46-7. The members of the York parliament (other than barons) who were also sheriffs were Nicholas le Scot, sheriff of Northumberland and burgess for Newcastle; John de Lisle, sheriff and knight of the shire for Hampshire; William of Basing,

a far greater change among the state officials than there had been in October and November 1311.

More important still was the beginning of changes in the personnel of the king's household, which had withstood the ordainers successfully for three good years. Not only was the king now less able to resist. Bannockburn had wrought havoc among the knights and clerks of the household. Edmund Mauley, the steward, had been slain on the field, and Roger Northburgh, keeper of the privy seal, had been taken prisoner along with his two clerks, and the privy seal with him. Northburgh, as we have seen already,[1] is the first recorded keeper of the privy seal who was not also controller of the wardrobe. He is known to have kept the seal since 1312, and we are therefore fairly safe in regarding him as representing the only change hitherto brought about by the ordainers in the royal household. It was more important that Ingelard of Warley, whose removal from office the barons had specifically demanded three years before, was at last deprived of the keepership of the wardrobe.[2] His successor, the former controller, William of Melton, was the only highly placed household clerk against whom the barons had nothing to say. He remained in charge of the wardrobe until his elevation to the archbishopric of York. With Warley there disappeared from office John Ockham, the cofferer of the wardrobe, who had, like Warley, been specially mentioned in 1311 as one of those who were to be removed from the king's service and presence.[3] Even now the earls showed circumspection in the purification of the household. The parliament at York had wished that Hugh le Despenser, Henry Beaumont and several other *curiales* should be driven from court, but had agreed to postpone this requirement to please the king.[4] However, the barons took more drastic steps in the next full parliament, held at London in February 1315. They then turned Hugh le Despenser and Walter Langton out of the king's council. Afterwards, says Malmesbury, they "removed

sheriff and knight for Kent; Richard de Rivers, sheriff and knight for Gloucestershire; and William Trussell, sheriff of Warwick and Leicester, and knight for Leicestershire.

[1] See p. 89, above, and also App. II, p. 317. Northburgh on returning from captivity resumed his "keepership" of the privy seal.

[2] Warley ceased to account on 30 Nov. 1314 (Pipe Roll 166, m. 29). Melton began his account on 1 Dec. [Peter of Collingbourn, described in a note of Mr. Tout's as a "temporary ordainist keeper," had been acting in Jan. and Feb. 1312. See App. II, p. 316.]

[3] *Ann. Lond.*, p. 200.

[4] Malmesb., p. 208.

from the king's court his superfluous household, which had been excessively burdensome to king and kingdom, as was affirmed. And from that removal the king's daily expenses were reduced to £10."[1] A reference to the wardrobe accounts of the period shows us that this statement has absolutely no foundation. The changes in the household *personnel* were not very drastic. The expenses of the *hospicium regis* were in no wise materially altered.[2]

The hopes excited by these proceedings were soon dashed to the ground. The years 1314-16 were among the most distressful and disorderly of the reign. Robert Bruce cruelly avenged his country's wrongs by the systematic devastation of the northern shires; his brother Edward laid low the English power in Ireland. Southern Britain was disturbed by famine, pestilence, floods and private wars. There was war in North Wales where the king's favourite, John Charlton, fought with his wife's kinsmen for the possession of Welshpool. There was war in Glamorgan, where Llewelyn Bren raised the country against the royal agents who misgoverned the Welsh palatinate of the dead earl Gilbert of Gloucester. Lancaster himself had to wage war in Lancashire against his old servant Adam Banaster, but was still strong enough to put down easily the revolt of a discontented *familiaris*. In the more peaceful regions of the south the commons of Bristol carried on an armed resistance to the king for several years on end.[3] Such disorders needed strong government and none of the earls proved his right to be called a strong man. Lancaster's incompetence was already notorious, and it may well have been to remedy it that, early in 1315, Guy of Warwick was, in the words of the chronicler, made "the king's principal counsellor."[4] A few months later Warwick's death again made Lancaster the indispensable man.

[1] Malmesb., p. 209 ["in decem libris." May this not merely mean "by £10"?]

[2] One result of the household changes was that the wardrobe accounts were again enrolled in the Pipe Roll for the first time since 1 Edward II. For the first period of enrolment, that between 1 Dec. 1314, and 1 Feb. 1316, the receipt was £59,903 13s. 7½d. The expenses of the *hospicium* for the same period were £13,028 7s. 8½d, nearer £30 than £10 a day. The fact that by far the greater proportion of the wardrobe receipt, namely £56,707 19s. 1½d., came directly from the exchequer shows that another ordinance was enforced with some strictness (Pipe Roll 166, m. 29).

[3] 1312-16. See E. A. Fuller in *Trans. Bristol and Glou. Archæolog. Soc.*, xix, 172-278, and Seyer, *Memoirs of Bristol*, pp. 88-106.

[4] *Ann. Lond.*, p. 232.

## (6) The Failure of Lancaster (1316–18)

The last real triumph of Thomas of Lancaster was consummated in the full parliament which met at Lincoln on 28 January 1316. All three estates were represented, the proctors of the inferior clergy were summoned, and knights from thirty-three shires and burgesses from eight boroughs received writs for their expenses.[1] We are fortunate in having a roll of the proceedings of this parliament, drawn up in the form of a journal, which traces its transactions from day to day, and therefore gives us a far better idea of what took place in it than the jejune collections of pleas and petitions which form the ordinary "rolls of parliament" of this period.[2] It was characteristic of earl Thomas that neither he nor his baronial supporters condescended to put in an appearance until the king and the estates had been at work for more than a fortnight. On their arrival, there was a sort of second opening of the parliament on 12 February in their presence.[3] After this prelates and barons deliberated separately on the problem of the Scottish war. Various statutes, including an important one relating to the appointment of sheriffs, were now promulgated.[4] Then on 20 February the commons made their grant of funds, whereupon they received writs for their expenses and went home.[5] Their removal did not, however, end the "parliament," and it was only after their dismissal that the most stirring scenes in its history took place. On Sunday, 22 February, parliament met before the king in Lincoln cathedral. Sir John Ros made a violent attack upon the younger Hugh le Despenser, denouncing him in strong language and rushing on him with his drawn sword. Despenser in self-defence hit the aggressor a blow on the face with his fist, which drew blood. The unseemly strife was only appeased by the arrest of the two culprits by the marshal,

[1] *C.C.R. 1313-18*, pp. 320, 326-7. The paucity of borough representatives is interesting. There are no returns extant, so our whole knowledge of the constitution of parliament depends upon the writs for expenses endorsed on the close roll.

[2] *Rot. Parl.*, i, 350-64. It was the work of the chancery clerk, William of Airmyn; see later pp. 165-6. There is internal evidence that the record was added to, possibly otherwise altered, after Jan. 1320 (*ibid.*, i, 352). Some of the petitions and acts of this parliament are also enrolled after the more normal fashion contained in *ibid.*, 337, 343, and 347. See also Mr. A. Hughes' valuable paper on "The Parliament of Lincoln, 1316," in *Trans. R. Hist. Soc.*, n.s., x, 41-58 (1896).

[3] *Rot. Parl.*, i, 351.

[4] *Ibid.*, p. 353.

[5] *C.C.R. 1313-18*, pp. 326-7.

and they only obtained their release when two groups of magnates became sureties for their surrendering themselves to justice. It is not easy to see the relation of this altercation to the business in hand. Perhaps it made things easy for the final scene on 24 February [1] when, on the proposal of John Salmon, bishop of Norwich, as spokesman for the discomfited king, the prelates and barons agreed that Lancaster should be made chief of the king's council, and that the king should be suffered to do nothing of importance without the consent of the earls and barons. Thereupon Lancaster took oath, as chief counsellor, declaring that he assumed office for the common profit of the realm, for the maintenance of the ordinances and in the hope of amending many matters that were in need of reform as regards the condition of the royal household and the state of the realm.[2] Then, or soon after, the magnates began to stream away from Lincoln.

The circumstances of Lancaster's appointment as chief counsellor showed that the work done in the autumn of 1314 had all to be done over again. In the course of eighteen months Edward had gradually brought back to the household, and to office, nearly all the ministers displaced in the parliament held at York immediately after the battle of Bannockburn. If the most unpopular of the former household staff were still kept at a distance from the court, their successors were rather less notorious than less curialistic in their attitude. The purgation of the household was still practically unaccomplished, and while the knights of the chamber and the clerks of the wardrobe still stirred up the king against Lancaster and the ordinances, it was very little use calling him chief counsellor and looking to him for reforms which it was still beyond his power to carry out.

From February 1316, to the summer of 1318 it cannot be said that earl Thomas took a single effective step towards the enforcement of the ordinances or the removal of the "inconvenient" knights and clerks of the royal household. He still drew up schemes of reformation and strove to enforce them on the king. Before July 1317 a gathering of the "wiser and more provident members," that is the baronial section, of the king's council had met in London in conference

[1] [For reasons for believing that this episode had taken place on 17 February, before the commons left, see H. Johnstone, "The Parliament of Lincoln of 1316," in *Eng. Hist. Rev.*, xxxvi, 53-7.]

[2] *Rot. Parl.*, i, 351-2.

with Lancaster, and had drawn up "what seemed necessary to them" for the reform of the household and realm. These requests were transmitted to the king by Bartholomew Badlesmere and William Inge, chief justice of the king's bench, a Lancastrian partisan. The project of the council found no acceptance, and Lancaster in great disgust took up the highly constitutional line that the king should transact no business of importance save in parliament before the peers of the realm.[1] But when Edward summoned parliaments, Lancaster after his fashion refused to attend them, declaring that his life was not safe if he came within the verge of the court by reason of the plots of the courtiers. Edward now categorically refused to drive his *familiares* from the household and sought to coerce Lancaster by force of arms. In September 1317 both king and earl were in Yorkshire, Edward at York and Thomas at his castle of Pontefract. Each feared to approach the other, and surrounded himself with as many armed men as he could raise.

Lancaster now started a new hare. As the representative of the houses of Beaumont and Montfort, he was earl of Leicester, and the earl of Leicester was hereditary steward of England. In the heyday of his power Simon of Montfort had shown a strong disposition to make the most of his position as steward of England, as a means of exercising hereditary claims to control the state and the household, but the battle of Evesham was fought before those claims were settled.[2] Lancaster now took up more decidedly the position once maintained by his predecessor in policy and in dignity. He now strove to guard the bridges and stop armed men from approaching York. "And he declared that he did this because he was steward of England, whose duty it was to safeguard the interests of the kingdom. And if the king desired to take arms against anyone, it was his first business to notify the steward of the fact."[3] Nothing came of the claim for the moment, but we shall hear of it later on, in a more clear and concrete fashion. It is pretty certain, however, that what Lancaster had in his mind was to use his position as steward as a new weapon for purging the court. If the earl of Warwick, as hereditary chamberlain of the exchequer, was suffered without hindrance to nominate one of the working

[1] Bridl., pp. 50-2.
[2] Vernon Harcourt, *His Grace the Steward*, pp. 124-6.
[3] Malmesb., p. 230.

chamberlains, had not the hereditary steward an equal right to claim the nomination of the steward of the household? And if Lancaster could choose whom he would as the lay head of the *domus regis*, had he not at last obtained possession of an effective instrument for ridding the royal establishment of the enemies of the baronial cause?

Edward had already perceived that the reality of earl Thomas' power by no means corresponded to the exalted position in which he had been placed by the parliament of Lincoln. Since the end of 1316 the king had plucked up courage to restore to the administration some of the most hated victims of the parliaments of York and Lincoln. The dispossessed *garderobarii* of 1314 were found safe posts in the exchequer. Ingelard of Warley became a baron of the exchequer in December 1316, and John Ockham received a similar office in June 1317.[1] In November 1316 a glaring breach of the ordinances was risked by suppressing the keepership of the privy seal as a separate office. On Northburgh's promotion to the keepership of the wardrobe, vacated by Melton's appointment as archbishop of York, the king's clerk, Thomas Charlton, brother of the chamberlain, John Charlton of Powys, now again combined the keepership of the privy seal with the function of controller of the wardrobe.[2] Another step in the same direction was taken on 27 May 1317, when John Hotham, Gaveston's former confidant, and now by the king's good will bishop of Ely, replaced Walter Norwich as treasurer. Norwich, a promoted official of no strong political leanings, made the transition easy by petitioning for his own removal to a less arduous office. Thereupon—to follow the official version—the king "relieved him from the burden of the treasurer's office, but wishing to retain him in an office of moderate labour, appointed him during pleasure chief baron of the exchequer, desiring that, when he was able, he should be present at the king's councils, both secret and other."[3] It is significant of the reviving power of Edward that, while Norwich had been nominated treasurer "by the king and council," Hotham's appointment was "by the king."

[1] *C.P.R. 1313-17*, pp. 606, 671.

[2] He is specifically called keeper of the privy seal on 15 Nov. 1316 (*C.C.R. 1313-18*, p. 440). He had been controller since 7 July (Enrolled Exchequer Accounts (Wardrobe and Household), no. 2, m. 1).

[3] *C.P.R. 1313-17*, p. 655; *cf.* p. 657.

The effect of all this was that there were, between 1316 and 1318, two weak rival governments, each bent on thwarting the other, and each only strong enough to give effect to the negative side of its policy. Surrounded by the unbroken phalanx of his household staff, Edward was still able to contend for mastery with earl Thomas. Failing to exert effective control on the machine of state, Lancaster fell back, like his cousin, on his own personal resources. Like the king, the earl now relied mainly upon his own domestic establishment. He also had his own household, as numerous, as disorderly and as factious as that of the king, and directed, we may feel quite sure, with much less intelligence. Lesser magnates followed, as best they could, the examples set by the king and the earl. It looked as if England were breaking up into a group of feudal principalities, each one jealously watching its neighbours, and each seeking to secure its own interests amidst the general confusion. It was well for England that these conflicts were somewhat superficial in character. After all, the machine of state went on by itself, though its movements were increasingly halting and feeble.

The keen-witted monk of Malmesbury sketches with great accuracy the results of this ineffective contest between the king and the earl. "Whatever pleased the king, the household of the earl strove to overthrow. Whatever pleased the earl, the king's household declared to be treasonable. And so, at the suggestion of the devil, the households of the earl and king put themselves in the way, and would not allow their lords, by whom the land should have been defended, to be of one accord."[1] The earl and the king moved through the country attended by great bands of armed followers, and carefully avoided coming into each other's presence. Lancaster loudly professed that it was as much as his life was worth to come within the clutches of his cousin's followers. It is hard to say that he was wrong, but it is impossible to justify his temporising position. He clearly ought either to have given up the game altogether, or have settled the questions between himself and the king by an appeal to arms.

Debarred from exercising the power which parliament had given him, Lancaster threw his chief energy into the pursuit of his own private interests. The most important

[1] Malmesb., p. 224.

of these was now the prosecution of his feud with earl Warenne, which in 1317 led to a fierce private war in the West Riding of Yorkshire. The origin of the quarrel is characteristic of the purely personal politics of the time. Lancaster had long been on bad terms with his wife, Alice Lacy, the heiress of the two earldoms of Lincoln and Salisbury, which had swelled Thomas' earldoms to five. With Warenne's active help and, as was believed, with the connivance of the king, the countess of Lancaster fled from her husband's home and sought the protection of a certain lame squire, Eubulo Lestrange, whom she henceforward lived with and married after her husband's death. In revenge for this insult, Lancaster devastated with fire and sword Warenne's estates in the West Riding, and took possession of some of his castles. In such circumstances the measures projected against the Scots at Lincoln proved utterly abortive. Bruce pursued his way, regardless alike of king and earl. In April 1318 he captured Berwick, and soon afterwards laid siege to Norham. The danger to the last of the border fortresses in English hands brought the barons to their senses, much in the same way as the danger to Stirling had done in 1314. The results of this were to be seen in the great combination against Lancaster which I shall speak about in my next chapter.

# IV

# THE LATER YEARS OF THE REIGN

## (1318–27)

### (1) The Rise of the Middle Party (1316–18)

We have now worked through the political history of the first and longest period of Edward II's reign. It remains to speak in this chapter of the chief features of the later nine years, including especially the critical years 1318-22, to which we shall have to devote most of our attention.

I have already shown the collapse of the power of earl Thomas of Lancaster. For eighteen months he had been disputing with the king for the possession of authority which both alike were incompetent to wield, and his dismal failure had already forced upon the better elements of the baronage the need of some drastic readjustment of political forces. Some of Lancaster's own associates were growing utterly disgusted with him. Conspicuous among these was the Kentish baron, Bartholomew Badlesmere. Up to this time Badlesmere had not been, either territorially or politically, a personage of the first importance, but he had obtained a certain position as a partisan of Gilbert of Gloucester, whose kinswoman he had married.[1] He acted on occasion with the Lancastrian party,[2] but in the main, since Gaveston's death, he had belonged to the Pembrokian group. His quarrel

[1] For his relations with Gloucester see Conway Davies, *Baronial Opposition to Edward II*, pp. 427-8. Early in 1312 Badlesmere was acting with the opposition, for on 20 Jan. he was superseded as constable of Bristol by Edmund Mauley (*C.F.R.*, ii, 122), though he refused to obey the king's order (*C.P.R. 1307-13*, pp. 430, 453). After Gaveston's death, when the Pembroke group rejoined the king, Badlesmere was reappointed at Bristol on Pembroke's information (*ibid.*, p. 483).

[2] Bridl., pp. 50-2, quotes a letter which shows Badlesmere acting closely with Lancaster in July 1317. See above, p. 96. Yet even Stubbs, who fully realised the importance of the letter quoted by the chronicler, put back too far Badlesmere's hostility to Lancaster.

with Lancaster became now the more important, since it occurred about the same time that earl Aymer of Pembroke reappeared on the scene of English politics.

Since the parliament of Lincoln, in which he took a conspicuous part, Pembroke had not been a prominent figure on the political stage. Having interfered with little result to procure peace upon reasonable terms between the king and the men of Bristol,[1] he went in December 1316 on a mission to Avignon, along with Badlesmere and bishops Salmon of Norwich and Hotham of Ely.[2]

The object of the ambassadors was to enlist the sympathy of the new pope, John XXII, for the English king, and in particular to obtain for Edward power to tax the English clergy, and to employ ecclesiastical censures against the Scots. It was even believed that Edward's secret intention was to obtain absolution from his oath to observe the ordinances, but the inclusion in the mission of Badlesmere, at a time when he was hand and glove with Lancaster, makes this piece of chroniclers' gossip improbable. Except Badlesmere, however, the chief personages of the embassy were already ill-affected towards earl Thomas, and it may well have been that the opportunities of repeated discussion of the political situation which the embassy afforded first bound together Pembroke and Badlesmere, Hotham and Salmon, in a common view as to the remedies necessary for the English state. However that may be, it is certain that the pope took no action against the ordinances. On the other hand, John was able, energetic and intent on the large plans which make his pontificate something of a landmark in the history of English relations with the papacy. Of these larger questions we shall have to speak later.[3] For the moment it is enough to mention that John allowed Edward to collect tenths from the English clergy, and to nominate certain bishops who were to receive their sees by papal provision. Moreover, John agreed to mediate between Edward, the Scots and the earl of Lancaster. With that object he despatched two cardinals, Gaucelin of Eauze and Luca Fieschi, to England with a commission to make peace. Close on their heels came a less dignified papal envoy. This

[1] Malmesb., pp. 221-2.

[2] The date of the protections for Aymer and twenty-four of his household is 7 Dec. (*C.P.R. 1313-17*, p. 573).

[3] See below, pp. 207-10.

was Master Rigaud of Assier,[1] canon of Orleans, appointed nuncio, independently of the two cardinals, with the charge of collecting various papal dues. After the fashion of papal collectors, Rigaud soon became a centre of complaints and remonstrances.

By April 1317 the work of the English ambassadors at Avignon was completed, and they started on their way home. Most of the envoys safely returned to England, where Hotham became, as we have seen, treasurer. An untoward accident delayed earl Aymer abroad until the summer. When in the neighbourhood of Etampes, he was taken prisoner by a French gentleman, named John de Molière, who had a grievance against the English king by reason of certain arrears owed to him by Edward for former military service.[2] In lawless fashion Molière held earl Aymer as a pledge for the payment of his master's debts, and conveyed him into imperial territory for safer keeping than France afforded to feudal brigands. In May king Edward was scattering circulars to the kings of France and Bohemia, and to a large number of lesser princes of France and the empire, beseeching their aid in obtaining his kinsman's release.[3] Finally Pembroke escaped a prolonged captivity by the payment of the heavy ransom of £2,500, which was advanced by the Italian financiers who kept Edward II's necessities supplied. The king had the grace to make himself responsible for this sum, so that Pembroke was attached to his cousin by a fresh bond of obligation.[4] He was back

[1] *Foedera*, ii, 343, gives his protection, dated York, 24 Sept. 1317. Rigaud remained in England and became in 1320 bishop of Winchester. He is generally called "Rigaud Asser," an unmeaning name, in English books. He derived his name from Assier, a village in Quercy, cant. Livernon, arrond. Figeac, dep. Lot. See for him later, p. 208.

[2] Murimuth, p. 26, describes Pembroke's mishap, but only speaks of his captor as "unum domicellum cui sibi servienti prius in Anglia non reddidit mercedem." His phrase that Aymer was led "de Burgundia in Alemanniam" is contradicted by the king's letters in *Foedera*, ii, 329, to Philip V, locating the episode at "juxta Staumpes infra potestatem vestram." There is a commune half-way between Etampes and Versailles, called Les Molières, cant. Limours, arrond. Rambouillet, dep. Seine-et-Oise, which may well have given its name to the perpetrator of the outrage. In Richard of Bury's letter book, the outrage was the work of "John de la Mercke and other rogues" (*Hist. MSS. Com., Fourth Report*, p. 385).

[3] *Foedera*, ii, 329-30.

[4] *C.P.R. 1317-21*, pp. 6-7, 9, 11. It was known in England that the money had been paid by 24 July, and Pembroke was probably back home by 3 Aug. (*ibid.*, p. 8) and was certainly at York in Sept. (*ibid.*, p. 23).

again in England by August, at about the same time that the two papal legates appeared there, and soon after Badlesmere had made his last attempt at common action with Lancaster.

The appearance of the papal legates had done nothing to restore tranquillity in England.[1] A misfortune closely resembling the kidnapping of Pembroke showed that public order was as insecure in England as in France. The two cardinals made their way to the north of England, with the immediate object of attending the consecration of Louis of Beaumont, the illiterate bishop of high birth [2] whom papal and regal favour had forced upon that see, and doubtless with the further hope of entering into negotiations with the Scots. On 1 September 1317, as they rode between Darlington and Durham, they were maltreated and robbed by a band of desperadoes. The leader of the gang was one Gilbert of Middleton, a Northumbrian knight of some position, who had taken advantage of the disorders of the times to make his castle of Mitford on the Wansbeck the centre of highway robbery on a large scale. With them were the bishop-elect and his brother Henry, and while the legates were allowed to proceed on their journey, the two Beaumonts were held up for ransom in Middleton's castle. There was a great outcry against the sacrilege involved in robbing the papal legates, and it was even suspected that some of the followers of Thomas of Lancaster had a hand in the outrage.[3] However, the law was still strong enough to secure the condemnation and execution of the knightly culprit.[4] This mischief was immediately succeeded by Bruce's attack on the border strongholds, which showed that the king of Scots was as careless of the pope as he was of the power of England. To the great disgust of the legates, Bruce denied them entrance into Scotland. In revenge the two cardinals excommunicated

[1] It was said that in this year Lancaster executed a knight, formerly of his household, whom he caught on his way north from Pontefract with a blank charter sealed with the king's great seal and letters of credence sealed with the privy seal (*Triveti Ann. Cont.*, p. 24, Walsingham, i, 152).

[2] Son of Louis, viscount of Beaumont, kinsman of queen Isabella and brother of Henry Beaumont and Isabella de Vescy (see above, p. 87). At the queen's request in 1307 the pope had given Louis dispensation to hold a canonry of Le Mans at the same time as several other prebends and benefices (*C. Pap. Lett.*, ii, 49).

[3] This is a natural inference from *C.P.R. 1318-23*, p. 233. [But the Continuator of Trivet represents Lancaster himself as coming to the rescue and escorting the cardinals to York (*Triveti Ann. Cont.*, pp. 22, 23).]

[4] Murimuth, p. 27; Malmesb., pp. 231-3; *Ann. Paul.*, pp. 280-2; Trokelowe, pp. 99-101; *Foedera*, ii, 341-4.

anew the pretender and his adherents, and laid all Scotland under an interdict.[1]

It is not impossible that the two cardinals were more successful in reconciling the king with Pembroke and his associates than they were in their efforts to establish peace between England and Scotland. Anyhow, before the end of the summer of 1317, Pembroke and Badlesmere had come to a perfect understanding. Their aim must now have been to establish a political party, which, while accepting the constitutional standpoint of the ordainers, would save the king and the kingdom from Lancaster, and restore Edward to dignity and some measure of power, on the condition that he amended his ways and ruled by their advice. It was not long before the two confederates enlisted powerful recruits among the baronage. Conspicuous among them were the husbands of the three co-heiresses and sisters of earl Gilbert of Gloucester, among whom, after many disputes, the Gloucester inheritance had been divided in the course of the same year 1317. These three, Hugh Audley, the younger, Roger Amory, and the younger Hugh le Despenser, had not yet conceived the immeasurable ambitions whose growth, four years later, filled all England with their feuds. They were still content to work together, on the lines traditional to those who aspired to continue the historic policy of the house of Clare, and had at least one common point of agreement in distrust of Lancaster. Accident has preserved for us the formal indenture in which Roger Amory bound himself, on 24 November 1317, by the enormous sum of £10,000, to use all his influence with the king to persuade him to be governed by the advice of Pembroke and Badlesmere, and to trust their counsels beyond those of all other people on earth.[2] Though no fellows to this bond are known, it affords clear evidence of the formal and legal character which it was sought to give to the new party. Though Lancaster is nowhere mentioned in the bond, the compact has no meaning unless it be regarded as an organised effort to replace earl Thomas by earl Aymer as the king's chief counsellor.[3]

The new party soon grew apace. It looks as if it soon

[1] Murimuth, p. 27.

[2] *Parl. Writs*, II, ii, App., p. 120; Stubbs, *Chron. Edw. I and Edw. II*, II, lxxx.

[3] [For decisive proof of this see "A Political Agreement of June 1318," in *Eng. Hist. Rev.*, xxxiii, 78-82, cited in *Chapters*, ii, 205, n. 1.]

won over John Charlton, still the chamberlain of the household, and thus obtained intimate access to the king.[1] When Charlton gave up the office of chamberlain, he was succeeded by the younger Despenser, another member of the new party. Sir William Montagu, steward of the household since 1316, also joined the confederacy, whose success was assured when it had thus obtained the support of the lay heads of the chamber and household. It is certain also that the clerical head of the household, the keeper, Roger of Northburgh, took up a similar line, while the second in dignity among the wardrobe clerks, Thomas Charlton, controller and keeper of the privy seal, faithfully followed his brother, the chamberlain, in abandoning the curialist traditions of his earlier career. Up to now the household officers had been for the king against the barons, but the resentment they must have felt in relation to Lancaster's claim, as hereditary steward, to nominate the king's domestic officers at his discretion, gave them special reasons for welcoming a baronial party, strong enough to protect them both from earl Thomas and from the popular indignation of which Thomas was still, to some extent, the mouthpiece. The new party found as much support among the officers of state as among the officers of the household, from prelates as well as barons. Pembroke's companions at the Roman curia, John Hotham, bishop of Ely, and John Salmon, bishop of Norwich, represented its point of view. Hotham's appointment as treasurer, immediately after his return from Avignon, had been one of the first signs of the king's rejection of Lancaster's counsels. A prelate of more authority was Hotham's comrade at Avignon, the judicious bishop of Norwich, whose adhesion added a real measure of weight and independence to the new party. Besides these two, the veteran John Langton, bishop of Chichester, the surviving custodian of the chancery traditions of the reign of Edward I, threw in his lot with Pembroke. Other baronial adhesions included those of the most powerful of the earls. One of these was earl Warenne, eager to avenge on Lancaster the loss of his Yorkshire castles; another was the earl of Arundel, an ancient ordainer, who was, however, Warenne's brother-in-law, and whose eldest son was married to the daughter of the younger Despenser. The third, earl Humphrey

[1] Charlton's political tergiversations are not easy to work out. He remained chamberlain until at least 19 April 1318 (*C.P.R. 1317-21*, p. 133). He was certainly active against his old associates soon after that date.

of Hereford, the inheritor of the fiercest traditions of opposition from his father, Edward I's antagonist in 1297, had up to now been a convinced ordainer, and the rancorous foe of his royal brother-in-law. Hardly less powerful than any of these earls were the truculent Roger Mortimer of Chirk, and his nephew, Roger Mortimer of Wigmore, the ablest and the most powerful of the lords of the march of Wales. Never since 1263 did the Welsh marcher chieftains show so united a front in rallying round the king. Of all the magnates enumerated, none, save Badlesmere and Montagu, were without landed possessions in the western march. The lords of Brecon and Glamorgan, Chirk and Wigmore, Oswestry and Clun, Bromfield and Yale, dropped their mutual jealousies in the new policy of combined action. And beside the traditional magnates of the march now went the upstart Charltons of Powys.

By the spring of 1318 the king was entirely in the hands of Pembroke and his allies. It must have been a pleasing novelty for Edward to be advised by magnates who treated him with respect, and showed some willingness to gratify his personal wishes. It would, however, be most unfair to Pembroke and Badlesmere to regard them as mere traitors to the baronage, who had simply gone over to the court. It was rather a re-shaping of parties, like that which had been brought about in 1263, when a large section of the baronage, headed by the Welsh marchers, abandoned Simon of Montfort for the lord Edward and Henry III. In idea at least the new party was a combination of the more reasonable and moderate elements of the old baronial and curialist parties. The object of the middle party was to put an end to faction and anarchy, and set up a government strong enough to keep England in peace, and wrest Scotland from Robert Bruce. Edward was still to remain in tutelage, but his tutelage was now to be of a milder and more respectful character.

The chief object of the party of mediation was now to make terms with Lancaster, and it is to their credit that they sought to win him over by negotiations rather than by force. This was, however, undoubtedly the more prudent course, since even after the desertion of so many of his old allies, earl Thomas was still a power to be reckoned with. He still had at his back the resources of his five earldoms, the support of a large section of the clergy, and the popularity which enshrined the doughty champion of the ordinances, and of the good old cause of constitutional opposition. He now established himself in his own castles and lordships, gathered his followers around him, and sullenly waited on events.

It was still a hard job to bell the cat. So far back as September 1317, Pembroke had joined Edward at York, when civil war was momentarily expected to break out. By his mediation, and that of the two legates, it was agreed to refer all disputes to a parliament, which was summoned to meet at Lincoln in January 1318. But as the king's army marched in battle array hard by the walls of Pontefract, on its way back to the south, Pembroke was terribly perturbed lest the king should break the understanding by an assault on Lancaster's castle. The loyalists were in equal apprehension lest the earl should swoop down on them from his fortress, and lay hands upon the king.[1] It was only at Pembroke's urgent entreaty that Edward continued his march to London. Thereupon Thomas moved south also, and took up his quarters in his own midland strongholds of Tutbury and Leicester. But the king's new counsellors soon perceived the futility at this stage of expecting a parliament to settle anything. If the king and Lancaster held aloof the parliament was useless; if they came, each would appear with a retinue of armed followers, who would be more likely to settle matters by breaking heads than by counting votes.[2] Accordingly it was thought prudent to postpone the parliament from January to March, and then again from March till June.

Meanwhile a deputation of prelates and barons took the bold step of journeying to Leicester to beard the lion in his den. After some preliminary negotiations between the mediators and Lancaster's counsellors, a numerously attended assembly was held at Leicester in April, which, though in reality a diplomatic conference between the ambassadors of rival powers, is loosely spoken of by the chroniclers as a parliament. Among those attending it were the two papal legates, who had at last found a fruitful opportunity for mediation. Lancaster showed himself fairly conciliatory. He was quite content to make peace, if he could be convinced that the ordinances were at last going to be carried out. He

[1] Malmesb., pp. 230-1.

[2] *Ibid.*, p. 233, puts into the mouth of the king's counsellors these arguments.

only stipulated that, come what would, he intended to pursue his private feud against Warenne. He was even willing to make peace with the two Despensers, and maintain them in his service with a retinue of 200 knights for the term of their lives.[1] Pembroke and his friends protested that they also were zealous for the ordinances, and pledged themselves that they would force the king to secure their faithful observance. Lancaster agreed to attend the parliament at Lincoln in June, and the omens pointed to a rapid conclusion of the negotiations.

Four months elapsed, however, before anything decisive happened. The capture of Berwick in April, and the advance of the Scots as far south as Bolton-in-Wharfedale, did much to strengthen Pembroke's hand. It was still hard for him to redeem his pledges, by reason of the interested opposition of the courtiers, who saw in the confirmation of the ordinances an imminent danger of losing both the lands granted recently in the teeth of the provisions of 1311, and their appointments in the household,[2] which no baronial parliament would continue to them. Affairs were once more so strained that the Lincoln parliament was given up. At last, in June, the archbishops of Canterbury and Dublin, the earls of Pembroke and Hereford, Hugh Despenser and other magnates conferred with the king's council at Westminster, and drafted an agreement of which the main lines can be traced in spite of the gaps and blemishes in the document in which it is recorded.[3] Lancaster was not to use force and armed assemblies in support of the ordinances, was to sit in parliament " come pier du roiaume, sanz sovereinete a li accrocher vers les autres " and was to accept terms suggested for the settlement of the dispute about his wife. It is noteworthy that Hereford was among those coercing Lancaster, whose truculence was emphasised as the cause of the troubles. I imagine that this agreement was announced in St. Paul's on 8 June, when the king, prelates and barons gathered there, and bishop Salmon of Norwich, mounting the pulpit, proclaimed that the lord king was willing in all respects to accept the advice and aid of his earls and barons.[4] Early in July the court moved to Northampton, where the magnates assembled with such numerous

[1] Bridl., p. 55.
[2] Malmesb., p. 235, makes this clear.
[3] Chancery, Parl. Proc. 4/26, printed in *Eng. Hist. Rev.*, xxxiii, 81-3.
[4] *Ann. Paul.*, p. 282 ; *cf. Flores Hist.*, iii, 184.

followers that one might think, says the chronicler, that they had come for a war and not for a parliament.[1] It was, however, in no real sense a parliament, and Lancaster, though repeatedly summoned, refused to risk his head by attending the assembly. Accordingly, there had still for the next month to be a constant interchange of negotiations between the king at Northampton and the earl at Leicester. The cardinal legates and the prelates still took the leading part in the mediation.[2] It must have been during this period that the remarkable conference between the earl and the prelates was held at Leicester, whose proceedings are recorded for us by the Leicester chronicler, Knighton,[3] and to which scarcely sufficient attention has been paid. Lancaster now seems to have interposed further delays by withdrawing to his castle of Tutbury in south Staffordshire.[4] The result was that the concluding negotiations took place at Leake in southern Nottinghamshire, a few miles north of Loughborough.[5] There was drawn up, on 9 August, between earl Thomas and the Pembrokian leaders, who acted in the king's name, an indenture which it is convenient to call the treaty of Leake. Five days later the king came up from Northampton and met Lancaster at Zouchbridge on the Soar, near Hathern, and exchanged a reluctant kiss of peace.[6]

[1] Malmesb., p. 235. " Et hii omnes cum magna sequela, ita ut reputares eos non ad parliamentum venisse, sed potius ad bella." It was hardly a parliament, even of the baronial type. But any deliberative gathering was still loosely called a parliament.

[2] *Ann. Paul.*, p. 283. " Fuit pax reformata per cardinales et praelatos Angliae inter dominum regem et comitem Lancastriae." On 22 June the cardinals received safe conducts to attend the king at Northampton (*Foedera*, ii, 366). [The continuator of Trivet refers to the presence at Northampton " circa gulam Augusti " of the cardinals and the queen, and describes the final agreement as reached on 9 Aug., " procurante indies et viriliter instante regina supradicta " (*Triveti Ann. Cont.*, p. 27).]

[3] Knighton, i, 413-21.

[4] This is Stubbs' inference from Knighton, i, 413.

[5] Stubbs, followed by most modern writers, makes the place of the treaty Leek, in Staffordshire ; but the movements of parties before and afterwards make it quite certain that either East or West Leake, Notts, villages on the right bank of the Soar, below Loughborough, is meant. The calendars of the patent and fine rolls make this clear. The editor of the calendar of close rolls suggests Leake in the North Riding of Yorkshire as the place, but a village near Thirsk would be even more inaccessible than a town in north Staffordshire.

[6] I follow Stubbs' shrewd suggestion as to the place (*Chron. Edw. I and Edw. II*, ii, lxxxii), but the details in the chroniclers are very puzzling.

## (2) The Treaty of Leake and the York Parliaments of 1318 and 1320

The triumph of the middle party was assured by the treaty of Leake.[1] We must now examine its character and terms. Perhaps the most interesting thing about the treaty is that it was an agreement between one single earl and the eleven prelates and barons, representing the middle party, who spoke in the name of the king. Its contents were very simple. The ordinances were to be maintained; Lancaster and his associates were to be pardoned; a parliament was to be summoned, and in the interval a standing council, one of whose members was a banneret appointed by Lancaster, was to remain with the king.[2] It was only with the assent of this standing council that Edward was suffered to perform the ordinary acts of sovereignty, such things, according to the treaty, as could rightfully be done by the king without the co-operation of parliament. If the council exceeded or misused its powers, its acts were liable to be annulled in parliament. When parliament assembled, this temporary committee was to be superseded by a more permanent council of the same sort, to be appointed by it.

The one thing new in the indenture was the standing council. The adoption of this device made the machinery to carry out the ordainers' policy exactly the same as that which had been framed by the barons who had drawn up the provisions of Oxford. The important point is, that this stringent method of coercing the king, by vesting his executive authority in a baronial committee, was first brought into the programme at the moment of the triumph of the middle party. An expedient, so drastic that Lancaster had shrunk from suggesting it, was now brought into play by Pembroke and his friends, at the moment of Lancaster's humiliation. It is absolute proof that Pembroke's "middle party" was no mere group of courtiers

[1] It is printed in *Foedera*, ii, 370, and *Rot. Parl.*, i, 453-4, from the close roll.

[2] The members of the standing council, appointed at Leake, were eight bishops (Salmon of Norwich, Hotham of Ely, John Langton of Chichester, Mortival of Salisbury, Martin of St. Davids, Halton of Carlisle, Orleton of Hereford, Cobham of Worcester); four earls (Pembroke, Richmond, Hereford and Arundel); four barons (Hugh Courtenay, Roger Mortimer of Wigmore, John Seagrave and John Grey), and the banneret to be appointed by Lancaster. Of these at least two bishops, one earl, one baron and Lancaster's banneret, were always to be in attendance at court.

and deserters from the popular cause, such as Lancastrian partisans, then and later, believed them to be. It shows how hopeless the king was, when even his best friend among the responsible politicians found it necessary to rob him of any real power. The coalition had still before it the work of purging the household, and it was wise enough to see that the only effective step towards securing that great end was the virtual suspension of the monarchy.

Two other remarks on the treaty of Leake must also be permitted. It is interesting that there is no reference in it to the co-operation of the two cardinal legates, though they certainly had a large share in the preliminary negotiations. It is more important to realise that, though in form an acceptance of Lancaster's conditions, the treaty did involve the earl's thorough humiliation. It was of course necessary to gild the bitter pill, but from that day Thomas forfeited all right to speak as the leader of a united baronage. A dexterous use had been made of his notorious unwillingness to appear in parliaments and attend councils. The expedient, which gave him the right to nominate one banneret to the standing council, was doubtless devised to flatter his vanity. The great earl, who was strong enough to negotiate on equal terms a treaty of peace with the king and all his magnates, was to preserve his exceptional position by having the unique privilege, not even shared with the king, of appointing his own representative on the select body which was to do all the king's work for him. The boon seemed all the greater since Lancaster's banneret was alone to be in perpetual residence at court, and to secure this without too great a burden upon an individual, the earl had the right to nominate his representative anew, quarter by quarter. Yet it cannot be doubted that the framers of the indenture welcomed this device as a shrewd way of ridding the council of the unwelcome and disturbing presence of the impracticable chieftain. It was characteristic of Lancaster's blindness that he accepted the specious but dangerous proposal. Not one among his followers could really speak with authority on his behalf. So little weight did earl Thomas' banneret possess in this council that, so far as I know, there is not a single record preserving the name of any of his nominees. Of the other members of the council, I gravely doubt whether there was a single one who was not bitterly opposed to Lancaster and his policy. Certain it is that

Lancaster's banneret, at the best, could only see that his lord had fair play, and was acquainted with the proceedings of the executive committee.

The triumph of the Pembrokian party was consummated in the full parliament of the three estates which met at York on 20 October. The proceedings of this parliament are told in considerable detail in one of the rolls of parliament published in Cole's *Records*,[1] and demand, I think, rather more attention than they have hitherto received. We know from the writs that the shires and boroughs were represented in it, and that the boroughs returning representatives were much more numerous than had been the case in 1314 and 1316, though of the fifty-one boroughs which returned members, only seventeen sent representatives who claimed their expenses.[2] As at Lincoln in 1316, the knights and burgesses had a distinctly subordinate share in the work. Nearly all the proceedings recorded in the roll are set down to the credit of the "prelates, earls and barons." It is specifically mentioned that the king charged the "prelates, earls and barons to meet together and treat apart" such high matters of state as the appointment of ministers, the summoning of an army against the Scots, and the reform of the household. We may remember that in 1316 also there was a similar reservation of the higher politics to the baronage. If from one point of view this involves a survival of the old council of magnates, acting within a new-fashioned parliament, from another aspect the deliberations of the magnates in 1316 and 1318 afford early instances of a body, not very different from the later house of lords, acting together as a self-contained unit and having reserved for it the graver matters brought before parliament. The only evidence of the participation of "the commons of the realm" is in a petition that the sheriffs and other local ministers should be changed. Even the mass of the petitions that emanated from the estates seem to have originated with the prelates, earls and barons only. Thus modest was the participation of the members for the shires and boroughs in the parliaments of the reign of Edward II.

The first act of the magnates in the parliament was to approve the treaty of Leake. Steps were taken for the

[1] Cole's *Records*, pp. 1-46.

[2] *Parl. Writs*, II, ii, 184; *C.C.R. 1318-23*, p. 116. Compare *Return of Members of Parliament*, i, 54-6.

publication of its contents, and for the acts consequential on its acceptance. Between 22 October and the middle of November an enormous number of letters of pardon were drawn up, remitting the penalties of all felonies and trespasses committed before 7 August by Thomas of Lancaster and his adherents. We can still read on the patent roll a list of over 600 of earl Thomas's pardoned followers, which should afford excellent material for the minute biographer, topographer, and genealogist.[1] All these pardons were recited as granted with the assent of parliament. No exceptions to the pardon were made, save that a few malefactors still remained responsible for the outrage on the legates.

It goes without saying that the ordinances were once more confirmed. It is more important that parliament itself took two great steps in the direction of their execution. The first was the appointment of a committee of council, of which the former controller, William Melton, now archbishop of York, was the chief member, to draw up a scheme for the reform of the household, to which we shall recur later. The second was the elaborate and systematic review of all the ministers of the crown, the removal of those who were unworthy, and the nomination of sufficient successors to them. Unluckily the part of the roll containing this survey of the royal officers is so imperfectly preserved that we are left to guess many of the details contained in it. However, with a certain amount of knowledge of the official personalities of the period, it is not very hazardous to piece out the document with conjectures that do not go very far from the truth.

Let us first deal with the work of the parliament in the appointment of the king's officers, both of the state and of the household. Every office, high and low, seems to have been passed in review. The fact that a large number of existing functionaries were continued in their offices shows that the victorious coalition was already strongly entrenched, both in the administration and the household. Thus bishop Hotham of Ely, the former treasurer, who had been chancellor since 10 June, was declared to be sufficient, and therefore retained in office. So also were the two chief justices, the veteran William Bereford, chief justice of the common bench, and the chief justice of the king's bench, the high born Sir Henry le Scrope. It was a matter of course that the chief

[1] *C.P.R. 1317-21*, pp. 227-35.

baron of the exchequer, Sir Walter Norwich, was also retained. Of the other ministers whose appointment had been specifically claimed in the ordinances for parliament, the two keepers of the forest, north and south of Trent, the chief clerk of the common bench, and the escheator north of Trent, were all kept in office, as were the chief clerks of the wardrobe, Roger Northburgh, keeper since 1316, and Gilbert Wigton, controller since 8 July 1318. Thomas Charlton, who, in the days when no respect was paid to the ordinances, had been appointed, after the ancient fashion, to combine the controllership of the wardrobe with the keepership of the privy seal, was now, if I interpret rightly a very corrupt text, allowed to remain in charge of the privy seal, as he had probably held it since 8 July, when he gave up the controllership to Wigton. Of the lay heads of the household, Hugh le Despenser, the younger, was specifically continued in his office of chamberlain,[1] while Sir William Montagu, the steward, whom we have seen in association with Pembroke, was removed from his post. But it was made clear that this was not a penalty for bad behaviour, but because Montagu was transferred to the more dignified office of seneschal of Gascony. His successor as steward was Badlesmere, the original and most intimate associate of Pembroke in the formation of the party which now attained its full triumph.

At the moment of the appointment of the new steward, earl Thomas of Lancaster made the only personal intervention, of which we have any record, in the proceedings of this parliament. Already in 1317 he had declared that it was part of his functions, as hereditary steward of England, to interfere in the administration, and perhaps also to nominate the steward of the household as his deputy. This troublesome demand was now specifically put forward by him, and was received with formal respect.[2] Orders were issued that search was to be made in the three offices of state possessing relevant archives, the chancery, the exchequer and the wardrobe, and that the result of this search should be reported to the council by a fortnight after the following Easter, six months hence. Thus decorously was the fallen leader's claim shelved,

[1] Cole's *Records*, p. 4, "Item le roi sest acorde par conseil et a la requeste de grauntz qe Monsieur Hugh le Despenser le fuiz *demoerge* son chamberleyn." John Charlton was still chamberlain on 19 April (see above, p. 105), so that Hugh's appointment was quite recent. It is very hard to piece together precisely the successions of the chamberlains of this period.

[2] *Ibid.*, p. 8; *cf.* p. 3.

and by way of emphasising the stubbornness of the magnates, the appointment of steward of the household went to the deserter Badlesmere. There is no wonder then that, for the rest of his life, earl Thomas hated Badlesmere more bitterly than he hated mortal man. The whole incident was a demonstration to every member of parliament that earl Thomas's period of power was over. Another petition of Lancaster for the restoration to himself of a village in the wolds, anciently appertaining to his Yorkshire manor of Pickering, was similarly treated.[1]

Some other royal functionaries, spared at first, succumbed, after a brief respite, to the reforming zeal of the estates. Among the less dignified of the dispossessed officers was the escheator north of Trent, replaced late in November.[2] The most important officially of the belated sufferers was the treasurer of the exchequer, John Walwayn, a king's clerk who had long acted as escheator, and was of no great personal importance. He had only been appointed on 10 June, when bishop Hotham went from the treasury to the chancery, and perhaps then had been brought in as a stop-gap. There seems to have been some hesitation in parliament as to his "sufficiency," but he was suffered to remain in office for the greater part of its duration, and to take his place among the barons and prelates who, as we have seen, were specially assigned to deliberate on high matters of state. However, on 16 November he was replaced [3] by the veteran exchequer officer, John Sandall, since 1316 bishop of Winchester, who, though also an ex-chancellor, had shared with Sir Walter Norwich the effective charge of the treasury for ten years. For this long period the prelate and the knight had ruled the treasury, save only for two short breaks, the last of which, recently terminated, was the only one which continued for any appreciable time.[4] So little were the changes brought about by the victorious coalition revolutionary in character.

[1] Cole's *Records*, p. 8.

[2] *C.F.R.*, ii, 380-1. Robert of Sapey, a layman, was succeeded by Ralph Crophill, a clerk, on 25 November. Sapey, like his kinsman John, took his name from the Herefordshire village of Sapey, near Bromyard.

[3] I.R. 186, m. 1, says that Sandall entered on his office on 23 Nov., "post amocionem magistri Johannis Waleweyn in instanti parliamento apud Eboracum habito."

[4] I gather from the patents of appointment that Sandall was *locum tenens* for Reynolds, Dec. 1307 [*cf.* below, p. 297 and n.] to July 1310, and treasurer July 1310 to Oct. 1311, when Walter Norwich became *locum tenens*, and acted until Jan. 1312. Walter Langton's renewed treasurership, early in 1312, was never effective, for if he acted at all, it was at the most for

The same rigid regard for propriety characterised some other acts of the York parliament. John of Sapey, then justice of Chester, had been for eight years past one of those permanent officials who clung to office despite the demand of the ordainers for his removal. It was once more requested that this insufficient justice should be replaced by a more competent person. The royal answer was, however, that the offices of Chester touched the king's son, and not the king. Accordingly all that the king could do was to give the boy of six advice as to the wisdom of finding a more efficient justice. Sapey was, however, removed from the posts he held in Wales, because Wales was always in the king's hands. Soon he was removed from Chester also.

A cleaner sweep was made of the lesser officers both of the household and the state. The petition of the three estates that the sheriffs should be changed was exactly carried out. The Bridlington annalist tells us that all the sheriffs were removed on one day.[1] This is only a slight exaggeration, for on 29 November twenty new sheriffs were appointed to exercise jurisdiction over thirty shires, while another sheriff was set over two other shires on 1 December.[2] We may add to these two other cases, where quite recent appointments seem to have been regarded as satisfactory.[3] It is not often that a chronicler hits the mark so nearly in a matter of minute personal detail, but the wholesale changes in the sheriffs in 1318, as in 1314,[4] appealed, it is clear, to popular imagination, and were therefore remembered. It can hardly be expected that the chronicler should have known that the parliament excepted the shires of Cumberland, Westmorland, and Northumberland from its demand. These military posts needed permanence in their officials, and one of them, Westmorland, was an hereditary sheriffdom. It may well have been a corollary to these measures that commissioners were appointed to visit each shire to hear and determine the complaints of the king's subjects against his ministers.[5]

a few weeks in March and April. Anyhow, on 17 May Norwich was ordered to "continue to act." In Oct. 1312 Sandall was again treasurer, "by the king on the information of Pembroke." He gave way on 26 Sept. 1314 to Walter Norwich, appointed by king and council. Hotham's tenure of office, from 27 May 1317 to 10 June 1318, and Walwayn's, from 10 June to 16 Nov. 1318, were the only effective breaks to the power of these two officials, who presided continuously over the exchequer from 1310 to 1317. Sandall now acted till his death on 2 Nov. 1319.

[1] Bridl., p. 56.

[2] *C.F.R.*, ii, 381-3.

[3] *Ibid.*, pp. 367 and 369.

[4] See above, p. 91.

[5] Malmesb., p. 239.

Another important act of the York parliament was the setting up, on a more permanent and legal basis, of the standing royal council, provisionally agreed upon at Leake. It did this by the simple method of accepting *en bloc* the persons who had been acting since August. However, it added to them two additional bishops and seven more barons.[1] The two new prelates were John Sandall, bishop of Winchester, the new treasurer, and Walter Langton of Lichfield, whose days were now nearly run. A piteous recital of Langton's ancient grievances in a petition was pronounced obscure, and was rejected.[2] His post in the council was perhaps some consolation to the veteran prime minister of Edward I. But he was no longer a power in the state. More important by far were such new lay councillors as Despenser the new chamberlain, Badlesmere the new steward, and Roger Mortimer of Chirk, since 1317 the justice of Wales. There were also men of less weight in William Martin, John of Somery, John Giffard and John Botetourt. The effect of their addition was to diminish the relative importance of the prelates, but it would perhaps be fanciful to suggest that this was a result of the loss of authority of that stout friend of the church, the earl of Lancaster.[3] It is more likely that the increased numbers were mainly designed to lessen the burden of residence at court, by allowing longer intervals between the quarters of obligatory attendance on the part of the counsellors.[4] It required some negotiation before this delicate problem of the council could be settled, and we are told that archbishop Melton and earl Humphrey of Hereford presented to the king the petition of the magnates, the acceptance of which involved the extension of the council. It goes without saying that the ordinances and the Great Charter were solemnly read before the estates. But we may pass over such formal acts as these. Let us similarly omit the petitions received and answered in this parliament, and the laws duly promulgated, though one at least of them was memorable. We must proceed straight to the crucial question of the reform of the royal household.

[1] Cole's *Records*, p. 12.

[2] *Ibid.*, pp. 4-5.

[3] There is perhaps a touch of anti-clericalism in the request of parliament that the king "attach" master Rigaud of Assier and his clerks, "if they go against the prohibition ordered by the common council." For Rigaud see above, p. 102, and below, p. 208.

[4] The four who acted on the council during the parliament were bishop Hotham and Cobham, the earl of Pembroke and John Seagrave (Cole's *Records*, p. 13). Where then was Lancaster's nominee banneret ?

During the session of parliament the committee for drawing up a plan of household reform had been at work. On 6 December the result of its deliberations was issued in the form of a royal ordinance, which we may call, for the sake of distinction, the household ordinance of York.

As I am printing a text of this ordinance in the appendix,[1] and shall have to describe its provisions at length, when I deal with the administrative reforms of the reign, there is no need to say much about it now. It suffices perhaps to remark, that, though a codification of pre-existent custom rather than an attempt to embody a new policy of household organisation, it represented a real effort to set down clearly points that had been hitherto matters of doubt and tradition. Moreover, it involved a thorough revision of the methods of household finance and administration, and a drastic attempt to minimise the long-standing abuses that had so long made the royal household a by-word for incompetence, greed and venality. It is some evidence of the reforming spirit that now inspired the new household officers, that the drafting of the ordinance seems to have been entrusted to the four chief ministers of the domestic service, Badlesmere the steward, Despenser the chamberlain, Northburgh the treasurer, and Wigton the controller of the wardrobe. The committee appointed by the estates, of which archbishop Melton, bishop Hotham, Badlesmere, Mortimer of Wigmore, and Walter Norwich were the guiding spirits, seems to have been content to accept the conclusions of the official heads of the domestic establishment. The matter so nearly touched the king's dignity that, even in his humiliation, Edward was allowed to nominate two members of the committee, namely Melton and Hotham.[2]

Three days after the promulgation of the household ordinance, the parliament of York was dissolved on 9 December. In its session of seven weeks it had performed an immense amount of work, and I have ventured to speak at length of its proceedings because they have never been

[1] App. I, pp. 244-81.

[2] Cole's *Records*, p. 12, gives the names of those appointed "ad supplicandum regem quod velit ad reparacionem status hospicii" as Hereford, Badlesmere, Mortimer of Wigmore, John of Somery and Walter of Norwich. The king's two nominees are associated with them by the king "ad intendendum negocia hospicii regis." *Ibid.*, p. 3—a corrupt passage—most of the same names appear, and *lacunae* in the manuscript account for the loss of the rest. But Melton and Hotham here seem appointed by the estates.

studied with any detail, and never, so far as I know, has their importance been properly appreciated. And contemporaries were no more alive to the importance of its work than have been our modern historians. Our chief guide among the chroniclers stresses the reconciliation of the king and the barons, but he speaks rather of the negotiations at Leake in August than of the proceedings of the York parliament between October and December. He is certain, however, that the troubles of the first eleven years of Edward's reign are at last resolved, and believes that, like another Nebuchadnezzar, the king will begin to be prosperous in the twelfth year of his reign. Four signs of improvement are to him already discernible. The pope has excommunicated Robert Bruce and his followers and put Scotland under an interdict, and already miracles are showing that the divine favour has been withdrawn from the rebellious land. Moreover, God has given Englishmen the victory of Dundalk over Edward Bruce and his Irish confederates. Again, the famine is over and the bushel of wheat, which last year sold for 3s. 4d., can now be easily bought for sixpence. But chief of all the signs of better times is the reconciliation between the king and his barons. Now at last Edward listens to the advice of his magnates, and there is no longer anyone to instigate him to evil, since the domestic household, which had been the enemy of the baronage, has now withdrawn from the court.[1]

Subsequent events show that the moralising monk of Malmesbury was somewhat too sanguine in his anticipations. So much of truth, however, was there in his forecast, that Edward and England had between 1318 and 1321 such peace and prosperity as at no other time were experienced during the twenty years of this reign. It is true that trouble still remained. Lancaster obstinately refused to be reconciled, and still loudly claimed control of household appointments. In the next parliament, which sat at York in May 1319,[2] earl Thomas renewed in more outrageous form his demands of the previous year, praying "that the king should grant him the stewardship of his household, which appertains

[1] Malmesb., pp. 237-9. The last change was of course the work of the York parliament.

[2] The parliament, which included knights and burgesses, sat from 6 May to 25 May (*Return of Members of Parliament*, i, 57-9; *C.C.R. 1318-23*, p. 139). Its roll is in Cole's *Records*, pp. 47-54.

to him by reason of his honour of Leicester." [1] The only answer vouchsafed was that he might still have, if he would, the writs ordering a search in the records of exchequer, wardrobe and chancery, which had been allowed in the last parliament, but had never been asked for.

Other petitions of the earl were even more curtly rejected by parliament. There is little wonder then that Thomas's old dislike of attending parliaments broke out anew. He made a merit of taking part in the expedition which at length tardily mustered in July and laid siege to Berwick.[2] The siege was fruitless; the Scots got round the besiegers' lines and invaded Yorkshire; the gallant attempt of the Yorkshiremen to check the enemy collapsed at the battle of Myton on 12 September, and this disaster forced the king to raise the siege of Berwick. It was believed that Lancaster had inspired the Scots to burst into Yorkshire, and the great man condescended to purge himself by the ordeal of hot iron from the injurious accusation.[3] Despairing of military success, the English concluded a two years' truce with the Scots. The truce was another triumph for the middle party, for the negotiations were entirely in the hands of Pembroke and his friends.[4] Henceforth earl Thomas sulked, like Achilles, in his tents.[5] He refused to attend a baronial parliament, summoned to York for 20 January 1320. A parliament, he declared, ought not to be held *in cameris;* he distrusted the men surrounding the king as much as ever.[6] He had some excuse, for the ruling faction treated the baronial assembly as a full parliament,[7] and took advantage of it to make the first important ministerial changes that had been made since the York parliament of 1318. The bishop of Ely now laid down the great seal, and was succeeded by John Salmon, bishop of Norwich; the treasurership, which had been in the hands of Walter Norwich, as keeper, since bishop Sandall's death in the previous November, was entrusted to Walter Stapeldon,

[1] Cole's *Records*, p. 48. [2] *Foedera*, ii, 400. [3] Malmesb., p. 249.

[4] The negotiators, appointed on 1 Dec. 1319, were bishop Hotham, Pembroke, the younger Despenser and Badlesmere (*Foedera*, ii, 410). It was for two years, from 21 Dec. 1319 to 21 Dec. 1321, and was sealed before 24 Jan. 1320 (*ibid.*, p. 416).

[5] Malmesb., p. 251. The comparison is the chronicler's.

[6] *Ibid.*, p. 250. "Non enim decebat habere parliamentum in cameris." Is this a constitutional declaration that the only valid parliaments are parliaments of the three estates?

[7] *Foedera*, ii, 415, "in pleno parliamento."

bishop of Exeter, and Master Robert Baldock, archdeacon of Middlesex, succeeded Thomas Charlton as keeper of the privy seal.[1]

It is difficult to argue that any political motive underlay these new appointments. Those who see in them the beginnings of the ascendancy of the Despensers and of the conversion of the triumph of the middle party into the renewed ascendancy of the king, guided by a new favourite, adopt the somewhat unsafe course of arguing back from the events of 1321 to those of the beginnings of 1320. So far as their antecedents went, the new ministers were of the same stamp as their predecessors. Salmon had been an ordainer and, like Hotham, a member of the standing council appointed in 1318. Moreover, an aged Benedictine, with failing health and a reputation for moderation, was not likely to pursue a more forward policy than the strenuous and pushing Yorkshireman whom he replaced. Stapeldon had been bishop of Exeter almost as long as Edward II had been king, but his main interests seem to have been in the careful administration of his diocese, the completion of his cathedral church, on which he lavished large sums, and the establishment of Stapeldon Hall, now Exeter College, at Oxford, as a place for the training of west-country scholars. So far as he had been a politician, he had taken up a line as moderate as that of Pembroke. Though not an ordainer, he had joined in the petition of the magnates which resulted in the appointment of the ordaining committee.[2] He had been more than once closely associated with Pembroke in embassies and similar employments.

Even Baldock's political record was not clearly against him. The kinsman of that old official and ordainer, Ralph Baldock, bishop of London, he was a well-trained, able and pushing wardrobe clerk, who had recently borne the chief burden of the negotiations of the truce with the Scots, and was no sooner back from Newcastle than he received the custody of the privy seal, apparently as the reward of his activity in this matter. Whatever may have been going on under the surface, no breach in the coalition in power had as yet been disclosed. Nor is any such schism visible

[1] *Ann. Paul.*, p. 287. Salmon was appointed on 26 Jan. in "parliament" (*Foedera*, ii, 415), Stapledon, on 18 Feb. "by the king," after the court had moved to London (*C.P.R. 1317-21*, p. 417), and Baldock at York on 27 Jan. (Add. MS. 17362, f. 9 v.).

[2] *Ann. Lond.*, p. 170.

for the whole of the year 1320. When in the summer the king went over to Amiens to perform his long-delayed homage for Ponthieu and Gascony, he left Pembroke as regent of the kingdom.[1] When a bad ecclesiastical job was to be perpetrated, it was done in favour of the high-born young clerk, Henry Burghersh, raised to the great bishopric of Lincoln before he was thirty, nominally at the petition of the king to the pope, really because he was the nephew of Bartholomew Badlesmere.[2] The London parliament held in October was uneventful, and it was no new thing that Lancaster disdained to attend it.[3] For earl Thomas still stood aloof in sulky isolation, and he alone displayed manifest signs of discontent. [To others, the prospects seemed bright. Bishop Cobham of Worcester, present at this parliament, wrote to the pope that the king was behaving "magnificently, prudently and discreetly," rising early, contrary to his wont, showing a cheerful countenance to prelates and magnates, and even, when parliamentary business was under discussion, "ad eorum emendacionem de suo subtiliter adiciens quod defecit."] [4]

## (3) The Revolt of the March and the Fall of the Despensers (1320–21)

While everything outwardly remained harmonious, however, another political crisis was gradually developing. The two storm centres were the king's court and the march of Wales, and the cause of the new troubles was the same in each, the ambition of the younger Despenser and the strong position which he gradually secured for himself in the king's favour. A few changes in the household staff in the summer

[1] The king was absent abroad between 19 June and 22 July (*C.C.R. 1318-23*, pp. 238, 246-7). During this time writs were issued in England under a small seal of absence, and tested by Pembroke. The chancellor accompanied the king, but the great seal remained in England "closed up and in a secure place."

[2] In April Badlesmere went with Orleton and the elder Despenser on embassy to Paris and Avignon. When at the curia he secured his nephew's provision to Lincoln "et plus quam xv millia librarum expendit ibidem de pecunia regis, sed nihil regi utile procuravit nisi promotionem dicti domini Henrici" (Murimuth, p. 31; *cf.* Bridl., p. 60). Many strong letters were written on Burghersh's behalf (*Foedera*, ii, 414, 418). The bull of provision is *ibid.*, ii, 425.

[3] *Ann. Paul.*, p. 290. Thomas, however, condescended to send a proxy and excuses.

[4] [*Reg. Tho. de Cobham* (Worc. Hist. Soc., 1930), pp. 97, 98.]

of 1320 are symptomatic of what was soon to come. On 7 July Gilbert of Wigton gave up the controllership of the wardrobe, and in defiance of the ordinances Robert Baldock was appointed his successor, though he still retained the custody of the privy seal and his promotion did not receive the approval even of a baronial parliament. In fact the change was made during the king's visit to France, when Pembroke was in England and Badlesmere at Avignon, and must be set down to the growing influence of Despenser with the king. From this time at least, the younger Hugh, as chamberlain, ruled the king and court with absolute authority. A proof of this was the appointment of two of Hugh's personal clerks to positions of importance in the state. On 11 September 1320, one of these, the Burgundian William of Cusance,[1] succeeded Ralph Stokes, a veteran of Edward I's reign, as keeper of the great wardrobe. The other, William of Cliff, already transferred from his master's service to the position of a chancery clerk, was promoted to the king's council, and the opposition soon believed that he was sworn to prevent any writs issuing from chancery to the prejudice of Despenser and his father.[2] The purgation of the household in 1318 was thus partially undone. Henceforth Robert Baldock controlled the king and the household, and for the rest of his career remained the brain and the hand of the younger Despenser. The new favourite, who in some measure had stepped into the place of Peter Gaveston, was not content with becoming the chief power within the household. He now strove to take advantage of the chronic

[1] William of Cusance was still Despenser's clerk on 14 Oct. 1319, though receiving the king's wages (E.A. 378/4, f. 19 v). There were several persons named Cusance in the royal service in the early fourteenth century. Their name seems derived from Cusance in the free county of Burgundy, canton and arrond. Baume-les-Dames, dep. Doubs, and they were connected with Otto de Grandison. For the career of six members of this family in England under the three Edwards see C. L. Kingsford in *Trans. R. Hist. Soc.* (1909), iii, 181-2. To the facts there stated as to William Mrs. W. D. Sharp adds that in Jan. 1326 he was still acting as treasurer of the wardrobe of Edward of Windsor, the future Edward III (Plea rolls of Chester, no. 38, m. 8 d).

[2] The evidence for these facts is not very good, resting upon the complaint of the northern barons in July 1321 (Bridl., p. 67). In many of the allegations against the Despensers there are evident signs of exaggeration. We may, however, accept them as testimony of the undoing of the effects of the purgation of the household in 1318. William Cliff, to be distinguished from the better known chancery clerk, Henry Cliff, was already a king's clerk in June 1316 (*C.P.R. 1313-17*, p. 476) and a clerk of chancery on 24 Dec. 1317 (*C.C.R. 1313-18*, p. 587).

troubles of the march of Wales to build up, on the basis of his third share of the Clare inheritance, a mighty principality which might well make him independent even of his royal master.

Since the conquest of the principality of Wales by Edward I, the palatine franchises of the feudal lords of the march of Wales had become a dangerous anachronism. It was part of the real statecraft of the author of the writs of *quo warranto* that, in the later years of his reign, he had applied the principles of those writs to define and limit the jurisdictions of the marcher barons. Within a few years private war had been prohibited; extravagant claims to extreme regalian rights rejected; the rule of law upheld, and the proud marchers of Glamorgan, Brecon, and Gwent humiliated. There was no part of Britain where the change from Edward I to Edward II made more difference than in the western march lands, and all through our period the disorders of the march stand in strong contrast to the tranquillity of the principality of Wales. But if the Welsh of the principality never rose in revolt against a king born in Gwynedd,[1] their kinsmen in the marches were a constant source of trouble to their local lords. I have alluded already to the most important of these marcher troubles, the war between Owen ap Gruffydd and John Charlton for the possession of Powys, and the revolt of Llewelyn Bren against the royal bailiffs who, after 1314, administered the Clare lordship of Glamorgan.[2] In the absence of central authority, the chief lords marcher worked out a rough and ready method of maintaining the cherished "custom of the march," by a plan of mutual co-operation, a sort of holy alliance to maintain the tradition of baronial rule and uphold a rude balance of power between the various families. Thus the Mortimers went to the help of John Charlton and won back for him his threatened authority in Powys. Again, the Mortimers and Hereford combined to repress the rising of Llewelyn Bren.

The confederate lords of the march bore no illwill towards the younger Despenser, when he took up his wife's rights as lord of the Glamorgan palatinate; but the third of the Gloucester inheritance, assigned to him in 1317, in no wise contented the covetous chamberlain. His chief ambition

[1] Higden, *Polychronicon*, viii, 300, "unum tamen huic regi feliciter obvenit quod Cambria contra eum minime rebellavit." See also later, pp. 187-90.

[2] See above, p. 93.

was now to enlarge his wife's inheritance on every side,[1] and to exercise to the full every claim to exclusive jurisdiction. Within a few months of his accession to Glamorgan, he gave offence to the Mortimers and Bohuns by removing Llewelyn Bren from his prison in the Tower, taking him down to Cardiff, putting him to death as a traitor to his lord, and confiscating all his estates. Afterwards this was regarded as involving a breach of faith not dissimilar to the act of treachery by which Warwick and Lancaster lured Gaveston to his end.[2] For the moment, however, nothing was said. Lancaster, Hereford and Pembroke themselves attested the charter in which on 21 November 1318, "with the assent of the prelates, earls, barons, and other magnates in the king's parliament at York," Despenser and his wife Eleanor received a grant of all "royal and other liberties" in Glamorgan, "which any of the ancestors of the said Eleanor did use."[3] It was thought well that Hugh should be endowed with lands worth 600 marks a year, to meet the expense of the continuous residence at court involved in the chamberlainship.[4] Three days before the date of this charter, he received a grant for life of the historical castles of Drysllwyn and Dynevor in the vale of Towy. Along with them went Cantrev Mawr,[5] the largest district in the royal shire of Carmarthen, which was to some extent removed in his interests from the jurisdiction of the courts and exchequer of the southern capital of the principality, and therefore from the authority of Mortimer of Chirk, the justice of all Wales. A further movement in the same direction was when, in July 1319, Hugh obtained the control of the castle of Newcastle-Emlyn, and of the commote of Emlyn, on the lower Teivi.[6]

[1] Malmesb., p. 254. "Omni studio et tota mente terras vicinas dominio suo nitebatur amplificare."

[2] Bridl., pp. 67-8, gives the version of the transaction accepted by Despenser's enemies in 1321.

[3] *C. Chart. R. 1300-26*, pp. 396 and 398-9, gives the charter in duplicate form. The names of witnesses, not given in the calendar, I have extracted from Charter roll 105, m. 11, no. 38. They are archbishop Melton; bishops Salmon and Hotham; the earls of Lancaster, Pembroke and Hereford; Hugh Courtenay, John Mowbray, and Badlesmere, steward of the household.

[4] Cole's *Records*, p. 9: "les dc marches de terre queux le roi lui deveit pur voir pur sa demore ovesque lui."

[5] *Ibid. C.C.R. 1323-27*, p. 249, shows that the date of the grant was 18 Nov. 1318. But already before 14 Sept. Hugh was "keeper" of Drysllwyn (*C.F.R.*, ii, 375). Roger Mortimer of Chirk had been finally made justice of North and South Wales, *i.e.* of all the principality, on 7 Oct. 1317 (*ibid.*, p. 342).

[6] *Ibid.*, iii, 2. They were granted to a dependent at his request.

The effect of this was to establish Hugh as ruler of the best part of the rich vale of Towy, and of all the uplands and dales between Teivi and Towy. He next turned his attention eastwards, and began to cast greedy eyes upon his brothers-in-laws' shares of the Gloucester heritage, especially upon the region of Gwent, immediately to the eastward of Glamorgan, and now divided between Amory and Audley, who respectively held upper and lower Gwent. So early as 10 January 1320, Hugh Audley and Margaret his wife, the sometime widow of Gaveston, received licence to grant to Despenser the castle of Newport-on-Usk, and other adjacent lands in what is now southern Monmouthshire.[1] By May the Audleys had been induced, or more probably coerced, into accepting an exchange by which they received lands and advowsons in the peaceful south-east, in return for yielding up Newport and Nether Went to the grasping chamberlain.[2] A similar effort to appropriate Amory's share of the Clare lands in Wales failed,[3] but Despenser's agents were successful in preparing the way for his obtaining Lundy island, and with it the command of the Bristol Channel.[4]

Despenser next turned his eyes towards the English-speaking peninsula of Gower, with its castles of Oystermouth and Swansea, with whose lord he had been quarrelling as early as 1318.[5] Gower, now the western portion of the modern Glamorganshire, was no part, either politically or ecclesiastically, of the mediæval Glamorgan which he had inherited from the Clares.[6] Gower would form a bridge to unite Cantrev Mawr with Glamorgan, and thus round off the Clare inheritance in the west, just as Nether Went rounded

[1] *C.P.R. 1317-21*, p. 415. The grant included the castle of Newport, the manors of Stowe, Rhymney, Dowlais, Machen, Ebbw Vale ("Freneboth"), and certain knights' fees in Bassaleg, Coedcarnau, Begansley, St. Bride's, and St. Mellons, and the advowsons of the churches of Machen and Llanvihangel, and of the priory of Malpas in Gwenllwg.

[2] *Ibid.*, p. 456. The exchanges offered were mainly in Oxfordshire, Kent and London. Malmesb. is quite clear as to the involuntary character of Audley's action. Despenser, he says, "castrum de Neuport . . . fraudulenter intravit et tenuit" (p. 254). The exchange of lands was a subsequent attempt to square the injured party. The Tintern annalist says, "traditorie et quasi vi ceperunt Novum Burgum" (*Flores Hist.*, iii, 342).

[3] *Ibid.*

[4] *Eng. Hist. Rev.*, xii, 755-61.

[5] *C.C.R. 1318-23*, p. 96, cited by Conway Davies, "The Despenser war in Glamorgan," in *Trans. R. Hist. Soc.* (1915), ix, 21-64.

[6] The ancient limits of Gower, which extended eastwards into the Welsh-speaking lower valley of the Tawe, are to-day marked by the portion of Glamorganshire—the deanery of Gower—which is still included in the diocese of St. Davids.

it off in the east. It had long been ruled by the once great house of Braose, which held in it the same ample regalian rights that the Clares exercised in Glamorgan.[1] Its then lord, William de Braose, was sonless and thriftless, and had been for some time endeavouring to sell the reversion of his estate to the highest bidder.[2] Among the marcher lords eager to bargain with Braose for his lands were the Mortimers and earl Humphrey of Hereford, to whose lordship of Brecon Gower lay adjacent. Various contracts were made, but in 1320, six years before Braose died, Gower was taken possession of by the husband of his only daughter, John Mowbray, lord of Axholme, Melton, and many other rich lordships in England, by virtue of a contract earlier in date than these.[3] The royal licence for this alienation was neither sought nor obtained, and Mowbray declared that the custom of the march made such a step unnecessary. Thereupon Despenser affirmed that the king had in Wales the same right that he had in England, to insist on his permission being obtained before the heir of any tenant in chief presumed to take possession of his inheritance. As Mowbray had neglected this formality Gower was now regarded as escheated to the crown. If this doctrine had prevailed, it would have been an easy step for the king to re-grant the forfeited lordship to the all-powerful favourite. In that case Despenser would have been lord of South Wales from the Teivi to the Wye, and every other marcher baron would have been at his mercy.

A hastily-formed confederacy of marcher lords against Despenser now radically changed both the course of events in South Wales and the balance of English politics. With the exception of earl Aymer of Pembroke and earl Edmund of Arundel, lord of Clun and Oswestry, every great marcher made common cause against the aggressive favourite. Both of these magnates also were nervous of Despenser's aggressions, but Pembroke was too accustomed to mediation to be able to play a decisive part. Arundel also had been forced to lean upon the king as his best protection from the Mortimers, who had recently been assailing his lordships in North Wales. Of the rest, however, royalists like earl Warenne and John

[1] *C. Chart. R.*, iii, 46-7.

[2] Trokelowe, p. 107: "Quandam portionem terrae habens quae 'Terra de Gowers' nuncupatur, quam multis dominis obtulit venalem."

[3] [The account given of this episode in the first edition has here been modified in accordance with the new light thrown by Mr. Conway Davies's important paper cited above.]

Charlton of Powys, temporisers like earl Humphrey of Hereford, lord of Brecon, and the two Mortimers, united with the Lancasters and other stalwarts of the baronial opposition, to stop the growth of a power which threatened their own inheritance in the march. When in October 1320 the king ordered the seizure of Gower, by the sheriff and sub-escheator of Gloucestershire,[1] the confederate marchers rallied to the support of John Mowbray and prevented the execution of the royal mandate. Their triumph was the easier since Roger Mortimer of Chirk held the great office of justice of Wales and could use all the forces of the principality against the royal officers. The Welsh, who hated the rule of Hugh, cordially co-operated with their alien governors.[2]

Despenser's claim to regard a marcher franchise as an appendage of an English shire gave good colour to the cry of the marchers that the law and custom of the march were in danger.[3] Inevitably the attempt to enforce the seizure involved South Wales in civil war.[4] The fight continued until Despenser had lost all his hardly won possessions, and until the stalwarts of the baronial opposition in England took advantage of his misfortunes to revive the old watchwords of the ordainers and unite with the victorious marchers to procure his ruin. Thus the aggressions of Despenser in South Wales are not only the starting point of the greatest crisis of Edward II's reign ; they broke up the combination of parties which had controlled England since 1318. In 1318 the solid support of the marcher lords had secured the triumph of the middle party. In 1321 the equally solid defection of these same magnates rent the middle party asunder and once

[1] *C.C.R. 1318-23*, p. 268.

[2] Malmesb., p. 256. " Nec Walenses, dominationem Hugonis execrantes, tuitionem inferre procurant." Hugh himself writes to an agent about " la malice de ceux de Breghenok et de Cantrebaghan " (*Eng. Hist. Rev.*, xii, 761). His attitude to the Welsh gentry is suggested by his order that none of the 24 Welshmen " des pluz grant de nostre terre," sent to remain with him by his sheriff of Glamorgan, should be allowed the use of horses, " einz voloms qu'eux soient touz a pie, et touz as ouelles gages " (*ibid.*, p. 760).

[3] Malmesb., p. 255. " Sprevit Hugo et consuetudines et legem marchiae."

[4] Hostilities began about Nov. 1320, when " a great crowd of armed Welshmen " at Kilvey prevented the sub-escheator executing his mandate. Some of the persons appointed to hear and determine the inquest resulting therefrom, such as Hereford, Henry of Lancaster, and John Giffard, became members of the marcher confederacy (*C.P.R. 1317-21*, pp. 547-8). The Tintern version of the Flores (*Flores Hist.*, iii, 344-5) gives the best account of the war in South Wales. [For its details see Conway Davies, " The Despenser war in Glamorgan," cited above, p. 126.]

more compelled a baronial triumph. In both cases, as in 1263, the decisive voice lay with the lords of the march of Wales.

Thomas of Lancaster was the chief gainer by the outrageous conduct of the Despensers. The old champion of the irreconcilables could now say, with good reason, that there was no trust to be placed in the king and his courtiers, and that Pembroke and his associates had been fooled by their own anxiety for compromise and conciliation. The old party of the ordainers, broken up in 1318, was now again reconstituted by the force of events. Of this party earl Thomas was once more the leader. We are again in the atmosphere of the early years of the reign, when in May 1321 the northern lords assembled in the chapter house of Pontefract priory, under the walls of earl Thomas's chief castle, and formed a league to defend their leader and their inheritance,[1] and when in June a gathering of northern clergy, barons and knights met together in the parish church of Sherburn in Elmet, and formulated once more the old demands for the purging of the court and the reinforcement of the ordinances.[2] In pursuing such courses the earl was simply renewing his former game. But this Lancastrian parliament, as Stubbs truly called the gathering at Sherburn, resolved to refer its grievances to a true parliament of England. This body met at London on 15 July, and care was taken to include in it representatives of shires, boroughs and lower clergy.[3] But though experience had taught the barons the wisdom of showing some respect to constitutional forms, the real decision lay, not with the timid estates, but with the lords of the northern and western opposition, who now met in London with thousands of armed followers in their train.[4] Under these circumstances it was easy to banish the Despensers, and to draft articles against them which once more re-echoed the old cries of the ordainers.[5] Late in August parliament separated, after a comprehensive measure of pardon to protect the triumphant rebels.[6]

[1] Bridl., pp. 61-2. Stubbs first indicated the importance of the information given by this writer in his introduction to *Chron. Edw. I and Edw. II*, ii, lxxxvi-xc.

[2] Bridl., pp. 62-5.

[3] *Return of Members of Parliament*, i, 62-3.

[4] *Ann. Paul.*, pp. 293-8, vividly illustrates the real situation.

[5] Bridl., pp. 65-70.

[6] *Ibid.*, pp. 72-3. The names of the persons pardoned are detailed in *C.P.R. 1321-24*, pp. 15-21. The pardons are [of various dates between 20 Aug. and 27 Sept.].

The fall of the Despensers was due not so much to their being royal favourites, as to the incompatibility of the interests of the barons with the personal ambitions of the younger Hugh. It was to little purpose that the lord of Glamorgan cloaked his greed in high sounding, constitutional doctrine, except so far as it shows that his theory was in no wise the point of view of a mere creature of court favour. We have seen how he had posed as a champion of English law and royal prerogative against the anarchic traditions of the march. Even more subtle was his doctrine that obedience was due not to the king's person but to the crown,[1] and that it was lawful accordingly for him, the chamberlain appointed in parliament, to compel Edward to do his bidding. In similar fashion he maintained that as chamberlain he had a right to dismiss and appoint household officers at his discretion,[2] and that, being nominated to his office by the estates, he could be removed by no inferior authority.[3] Such views were too deep for the conservative baronage. They were moreover in utter contrast to the undeviating pursuit of personal advantage, by violence and fraud, which marked each step of Hugh's later career. He had packed the court, the two benches and the great departments of state with his dependents. He had outraged the interests of his old allies and had made the compromise of 1318 utterly unworkable. The result was that he and his father were entirely isolated. They fell because not even their own dependents and nominees would support them. The very fact that their banishment was attended by no wholesale changes in the administrative *personnel* shows that even men like Baldock were in no mind to risk their offices for their sakes.[4] Edward II was more solitary in 1321 than he had been in 1310 and in 1314.

[1] [Mr. Conway Davies has collected various examples of similar distinctions between capacities in England from the Norman Conquest to the reign of Edward I in his *Baronial Opposition to Edw. II*, pp. 22, 23. We might add the case referred to by Dr. J. P. Whitney in *Hildebrandine Essays*, p. 17, of the French bishop described by Orderic Vitalis "who, while preserving the strictest celibacy as a bishop, was married in his capacity of baron."]

[2] *Ann. Paul.*, p. 292. For Lancaster's similar claim as steward see above, pp. 96-7, 114, 119-20.

[3] *Parl. Writs*, II, ii, 231.

[4] The only important change was in the treasury, where Stapeldon was, on 25 Aug. 1321, "discharged at his own request" (*C.P.R. 1321-24*, p. 14). That this had no political significance is shown by Stapledon's employment as a royal commissioner in the south-west (*ibid.*, p. 15). He probably withdrew in order to transact diocesan business. He was continually in his diocese from Sept. 1321 to his reappointment as treasurer in May 1322 (Stapledon's *Register*, pp. 556-7).

The break up of the middle party was complete. Earl Aymer of Pembroke did not openly desert the king, but his private sympathies, as was natural to the lord of a Welsh palatinate, were with his marcher brethren.[1] When the storm burst he withdrew from England, having a good reason for absence in the prosecution of his marriage with Mary of Saint-Pol, an event which took place at Paris on 5 July.[2] Pembroke was, however, back in London on 20 July, soon after parliament had assembled, and faithful to his rôle of mediation urged the king to consent to the banishment of the Despensers.[3] His chief henchman, Badlesmere, when in England, was assiduous in attendance at court in the discharge of his functions as steward until the end of 1320, and again made a sporadic appearance in May and June 1321.[4] After this Badlesmere openly threw in his lot with the opposition, so that he had to receive a pardon in August.[5]

### (4) The Fall of Lancaster and the Reaction of 1322–26

Rapid as was the fall of the Despensers, their return was even more sudden. Within a few weeks of their withdrawal from England, circumstances gave the king a chance of striking a new blow for freedom and his friends. This

[1] Murimuth, p. 33. "Comes vero Lancastriae consensit eis expresse, et comes de Pembroke occulte."

[2] *Ann. Paul.*, p. 292. [This was not, as stated in first edition, his third marriage, but his second and last. His first wife died in Sept. 1320, and by Nov. he was in France. For these and other details see Mr. Hilary Jenkinson's paper on "Mary de Sancto-Paulo," cited above, p. 19.]

[3] Malmesb., p. 259, puts in his mouth a speech addressed to the king on this matter. Richmond also joined in this mediation.

[4] Badlesmere's attestations of charters throw some light on his attendance at court. In 13 Edw. II he regularly attested all charters with two exceptions between 19 July 1319 and 28 Feb. 1320, but none for the rest of that term. In 14 Edw. II he attested charters from 9 Sept. till 29 Dec. 1320. After this his name is not found until 10 May. Between 10 May and 14 June he attested six charters. I can find no evidence of his being called steward after 14 June. As we shall see, he did not resume his functions after his pardon in August. For his attestations see Charter Rolls 106, 107, *passim*.

[5] *Foedera*, ii, 454. On 26 Sept. the custody of Tonbridge castle, which he had received on 17 May, was transferred to Edmund of Woodstock, the king's brother (*C.F.R.*, iii, 57, 71) who had already on 16 June replaced him as constable of Dover and warden of the Cinque Ports (*ibid.*, p. 62). He had received that appointment on 30 Oct. 1320 (*ibid.*, p. 38), perhaps as compensation for handing over to Hugh Despenser the custody of Bristol on 1 Oct. (*ibid.*, p. 33). These changes may possibly be significant in connection with his growing hostility.

opportunity came from the imperfect reconciliation of old enmities which had attended the shifting of parties in 1321. It is particularly seen in the curious position of Badlesmere. Though he pardoned him for his treachery, Edward II clearly found it harder to forgive Badlesmere than most of his associates. Anyhow, for some reason or another the steward was never so fully reconciled to the king as to return to court to discharge his duties.[1] Before long he abandoned his office in circumstances that filled the king's mind with the blackest hatred towards him.[2] But Thomas of Lancaster was even more embittered than the king against Badlesmere. He could not forget his personal grudge against an old ally, whose appointment as steward in 1318 he had regarded as a personal insult, as the flouting of his claim, as hereditary steward, to control the king's household. Badlesmere thus remained isolated alike from his recent associates and his ancient foes. Both sides now equally regarded him as a traitor.

The somewhat mysterious changes of Badlesmere's attitude are worth careful examination, since it was his ambiguous position that first gave the king a chance to strike a blow for freedom. Moreover, his imperfect reconciliation with the northern lords prevented the whole of the baronial party from making common cause in supporting him against the crown. The result was that, within two months of the solemn reconciliation of parties in the London parliament, England was once more plunged into civil war.

It is generally said that the cause of the renewal of hostilities was the refusal of lady Badlesmere [3] to allow queen Isabella to take up her quarters at Leeds castle in Kent, where the wife of the ex-steward was residing in October. The details which I have given of Badlesmere's attitude shows that this was no isolated act of rudeness, as has been often believed, but the natural, if lawless, act of those attached to an avowed enemy of the king. Edward was, however, shrewd enough to lay great stress on the insult to

[1] The steward of the household was the one household officer who normally attested officially the charters issued from the chancery. But the Charter roll of 15 Edward II never mentions his name, though it affords no evidence that he had a successor as steward until Jan. 1322, when Gilbert Pecché began to act. See App. II, p. 315. For the name Pecché or Peachy see *ibid.*, p. 349.

[2] *Flores Hist.*, iii, 199.

[3] The king himself described the contempt as committed by "certain members of the household of Bartholomew de Badelesmere and others staying in the said castle by his precept" (*C.C.R. 1318-23*, p. 504).

the queen, as a pretext for raising a large army to prosecute the siege of Leeds. Edward's appeal for help met with an extraordinarily favourable response, and put at his disposal a large military force. The remarkable circumstance is that many of the magnates who had recently been Badlesmere's closest allies should have joined the besieging army. Among these were Pembroke himself, his fellow mediator Richmond, Arundel and even Warenne, who had taken a leading part in the recent marcher rising. It looks as if Badlesmere's obstinate refusal to reconcile himself with the court had left him absolutely friendless. This, however, does not explain why the earls who followed Edward to the siege of Leeds remained for the rest of the reign staunch in their devotion to the king.

Badlesmere was absent from Leeds, and was therefore free to seek for help to release his wife and followers. It was useless for him to appeal to Lancaster, for his relations with earl Thomas were even more hostile than his attitude to the king. The enemy of earl Thomas could therefore expect no support from the northern baronage which still followed Lancaster's lead. All that happened in the north was that Lancaster summoned another ambiguous "parliament" of his supporters at Doncaster. As a result of this the northern opposition once more slowly armed itself. It stood aside, however, until the fate of Leeds was settled; even after that it took no steps to make common cause with the friends of Badlesmere.

Badlesmere found more effective helpers in the magnates of the march of Wales, who retained the liveliest distrust of the Despensers even in their exile. Hereford and the Mortimers rapidly raised their forces, marched eastwards and joined Badlesmere at Kingston-on-Thames. There the news came that Leeds had yielded to overwhelming forces after a siege of a few days. It was useless for the hasty levies of the marchers to pursue their eastward march into Kent and challenge a battle with the triumphant king. They promptly withdrew into the west, leaving all southern and eastern England in the hands of Edward and his friends.

The king's party showed an energy, a unity, and policy, that contrasted very favourably with the timidity and disunion of their enemies. The host which had mustered at Leeds followed the retreating marchers into their own lands, and the early winter saw a bloodless campaign in the Severn valley, which culminated in the tame surrender of the Mortimers and the other leaders of the west country opposition. In December the Despensers were recalled from banishment and at once began to take advantage of the defeat of their bitterest enemies. Only a few wrecks of the marcher host, under Hereford, escaped and managed to join Lancaster and the northern lords, who were now under arms at Tutbury. On the approach of the king, Lancaster also lost heart and fled precipitately northwards. Just north of Boroughbridge, his retreat over the Ure was blocked by a second royalist army, consisting mainly of borderers commanded by Sir Andrew Harclay.[1] On 16 March 1322 the royalists won their final triumph. The crowning victory of Boroughbridge, where Hereford met his doom from a Welshman's knife, was soon followed by the execution of Lancaster, the wholesale proscription of the "contrariants," and the confiscation of their estates. It is typical of the divisions of those who professed a common cause that, while Lancaster paid the penalty of his treason at his own castle of Pontefract, Badlesmere perished on the scaffold at Canterbury, also in the neighbourhood of his own estates. Thus the enemies were divided in death as in life. The last scene of all in the drama of their fall was the reversal of their common policy in the repeal of the ordinances by the parliament which met at York in May.

The cause of the disgraceful collapse of the opposition is mainly to be found in its division into two separate and unrelated elements, as the result of the feud of Lancaster and Badlesmere. Already in the summer of 1321, the northern and marcher oppositions had had their different points of view and spheres of action, but they were still able to combine for a common cause, and the union of the northern and western lords in London in July had secured them an overwhelming and almost bloodless victory. In the winter of 1321-22, north and west fought separately each for its own hand, and defeat in detail was the natural result of such a fatuous policy. The impracticability of the opposition gives some show of justification for the desertion by Pembroke and Warenne of their old allies. The baronage was so utterly selfish and purposeless in its action, that its triumph

[1] For Harclay's career see Dr. J. E. Morris' article in *Trans. Cumberland and Westmorland Archæological Soc.*, new ser., iii, 307 and following. His name is really "Hartlay," or "Hartley."

might well have led to even greater evils than the victory of the king and the Despensers.

How far were the events of 1322 parallel to those of 1318? Superficially, Edward's later and more complete victory seems more personal to himself than that of 1318, and history has commonly spoken of the years between 1322 and 1326 as the period of the rule of the Despensers. I feel quite sure, however, that without the co-operation of Pembroke [1] and the remnants of the old middle party, the royalist victory of 1322 would never have taken place. Certain it is that between 1322 and his death in 1324 Pembroke still remained a powerful influence on the side of moderation and peace. If his self-defeating love of peace made him no effective check upon the Despensers in matters of internal administration, and still less in the partition of the spoils of victory, he still had a field of his own in the conduct of the relations with the Scots. Two events now showed that it was hopeless to continue hostilities. One was the defeat between Byland and Rievaux, when Edward narrowly escaped capture in the heart of Yorkshire. The other was the tragedy of Carlisle, when Harclay, the victor of Boroughbridge, the new-made earl of Carlisle, paid with his life the penalty of his desperate efforts to take the law into his own hands. All that could be done was to procure a long truce on terms which the Scots would accept. Under these circumstances was concluded the thirteen years' truce of 1323, which virtually concluded the Scottish war of independence by recognising Robert Bruce as the *de facto* ruler of Scotland. This truce was the last work of Pembroke's life, and it is characteristic of his attitude that his fellow negotiators were the younger Despenser and Baldock.[2] He died suddenly in France, on 23 June 1324, leaving no male heir, so that his earldom fell into abeyance. Weak as he had often been in action, doubtful as were some of his subtle changes of front, with him disappeared the best influence that had ever been exerted on the court and councils of Edward II.

[1] On 22 June 1322, a deed was drawn up and enrolled in chancery witnessing that Pembroke, as the king "was aggrieved against him for certain reasons," had of his own accord sworn on the Gospels to obey and aid the king in war and peace, and not to ally with anyone against him. For this promise he charged his body, land and goods and also found mainpernors (*C.C.R. 1318-23*, pp. 563-4).

[2] *Foedera*, ii, 521; Bridl., p. 84.

The repeal of the ordinances by the parliament of May 1322 is, even more than the proscriptions and confiscations, evidence that the triumph of the Despensers had a reactionary character. Yet even in this repeal the constitutionalism of the younger Hugh found its expression. I have spoken already of his strange teaching, condemned by the barons of 1321, that homage is due to the crown rather than to the king's person. It was hardly the part of a mere favourite to appropriate, for his own purposes, doctrines that had seemed natural on the lips of the ordainers of 1311, and which clearly anticipated what the parliaments of the Restoration called the damnable doctrine that war may be levied by the king's authority against the king's person. We must not now interpret too literally the famous declaration of the parliament of 1322, which repealed the ordinances on principles which have seemed to many to be a vindication of the right of all three estates to participate in valid legislation, and therefore to be the most important constitutional advance of the reign. I should prefer rather to accept the more refined explanation of the act which Mr. G. T. Lapsley has recently advanced.[1] Mr. Lapsley suggests that this enunciation of principle was not meant to extend to all legislation, but only to such fundamental constitutional changes as the ordainers had aimed at. If the men of Edward's reign could distinguish between the obedience due to the office and that due to the person of the king, they were surely intelligent enough to grasp the distinction between ordinary legislation and a fundamental law. It was reserved for comparatively modern times in England to consider the same method adequate for passing a private act and carrying out a constitutional revolution.

More important than these theorisings are the solid facts that the York parliament of 1322 was not only a full parliament of lords, clergy and commons, but that it even contained for the first time representatives of the commons of Wales. Even now, however, the commons were sent home after less than three weeks, leaving the magnates in session for six weeks longer. Yet the precedents in favour of popular representation were too strong to be further resisted. The next epoch-making assembly, the parliament of January 1327, wherein the work of 1322 was undone, witnessed again the solemn participation of all three estates,

[1] *Eng. Hist. Rev.*, xxviii, 118-24.

including even the Welsh representatives, in the first formal deposition of a king by legislative act. It is not too much to say then that one result of the reign of Edward II was the establishment of the practice of regarding as true parliaments only those which contained representatives of the commons. It is true that the commons were still in the background; that in many matters of importance they were never consulted at all, and that they were,—mainly, I imagine, to save expense—got rid of at the earliest possible moment. I cannot, however, subscribe to the doctrine that in the early fourteenth century the commons were not yet a part of parliament, but rather an accidental appendage to it, brought together for purely formal and ceremonial purposes. The real distinction between the magnates and the commons seems rather to be, that the latter were not considered to have any natural voice in the problems of administration and government, in which the magnates were the undoubted sole advisers of the crown.

We can trace Despenser's influence in matters of more practical importance than vague enunciations of insincere and premature theory. We see it rather in the care taken that the undoubted improvements brought about by the ordinances should not be jeopardised, when the ordinances as such were repealed. Vital in this relation is the remarkable series of "establishments" accepted by the parliament which repealed the ordinances.[1] By virtue of these, such things as the ameliorations in the forest law, and the limitations of the jurisdiction of the court officers, legalised during Edward I's last years, the provisions as to sheriffs of the statute of Lincoln of 1316, and many similar practical reforms, still remained English law. We see the same spirit still more clearly in the radical reforms of household and chamber, chancery and exchequer, which will be the subject of our next chapter, and which were only seriously taken in hand after the triumph of the courtier element put reforming specialists in the places so long claimed by conservative and sluggish baronial nominees. We can also detect a certain amount of the same radical spirit in some other miscellaneous reforms, which I shall have to lump together in summary fashion in my last two chapters.

The Despensers thus remained reformers until the end.

[1] *Rot. Parl.*, i, 456-7; *C.C.R. 1318-23*, pp. 557-8. *Cf.* Stubbs, *Const. Hist.*, ii, 370.

How then can we account for the universal odium which they excited, and for the suddenness and completeness of their fall? For one thing, Englishmen of the fourteenth century loved neither reforms nor reformers, especially such reformers as made their radical policy a cloak for their personal ambitions. Yet I should not like to say that the Despensers' reforming policy was altogether lacking in sincerity, even though it is easy to admit that many of their reforms were sketched out on paper rather than carried out, even in the imperfect measure in which any mediæval law was really executed. The reason is rather to be sought in the conflict of personal ambitions in the king's environment, the incompetence of the monarch, and the self-defeating greediness of many of his most conspicuous ministers. Most of all, however, is the explanation to be found in the revival of the Despenser plan of a mighty marcher lordship, now that the obstacles which had prevented its earlier realisation were so dramatically removed.

It may be accounted for moderation for the younger Despenser that, when his father became earl of Winchester, he never gave effect to his earlier ambition to be styled earl of Gloucester. The reason may partly be that experience had shown the lord of Glamorgan that men dreaded the appearance of power more than its reality. But I am rather inclined to base it upon the fact that earl of Gloucester was a title too limited to express the fullness of his power, and that he was biding his time to win some more grandiose dignity, such as that which his rival secured a few years later when he caused himself to be styled earl of the march of Wales.[1] A title limited to a single county was inadequate to express the territorial position in Wales and its march enjoyed by Despenser between 1322 and 1326. The stages of this process are too elaborate to be explained here, but I hope that before long they may be worked out in detail.[2] It will be enough now to add that Despenser at once got back all the

[1] *Ann. Paul.*, pp. 342-3. "Et talis comitatus nunquam prius fuit nominatus in regno Angliae."

[2] I must express my indebtedness for the facts in this paragraph to the degree thesis of my pupil, Mr. Harold Kay, B.A., on the *Marcher Lordships of Wales in the first half of the Fourteenth Century*. [Prof. William Rees in his monumental *Historical Map of South Wales and the border in the fourteenth century* (Ordnance Survey, 1933) has now provided workers in this field with a most valuable aid to their studies. His plan, however, did not include entering or listing the names of the families which held each lordship.]

lands that he had lost in 1320-21, and that to these enormous additions were soon made. Gower fell to him, soon after John Mowbray was slain fighting for earl Thomas at Boroughbridge.[1] The shares of Audley and Amory in the Gloucester inheritance were secured for him by Audley's forfeiture and Amory's death. The forfeiture of another "contrariant," John Giffard, put in the king's hands the lordship of Yskennin, with its castle of Carreg Cennin. This was now granted to Despenser, and resulted in his establishment in the district between the Towy and the sea. Along with Gower, Yskennin bridged over the gap between his old lordships of Cantrev Mawr and Glamorgan.[2] The grant of Yskennin was the more valuable since it was to be administered by Hugh with the same ample franchise enjoyed by him in Glamorgan.[3] A parallel eastward extension of his sphere of influence was obtained by the grant to him for life by the king's brother, Thomas, earl of Norfolk, of the honour of Chepstow, and all the old Bigod lands beyond the Severn.[4]

What Despenser did not hold directly he administered as guardian. Several of the greatest marcher lordships had now fallen to minors, and royal favour soon gave him the custody of many of these, including the lands of the young Lawrence Hastings, which comprised not only the Hastings lordships of Cilgerran and Abergavenny, but also the great Pembroke palatinate which he had recently acquired as one of the co-heirs of earl Aymer.[5] Moreover, the elder Despenser, earl of Winchester, obtained possession of the Lincoln lordships of Denbigh, Rhos and Rhuvoniog, the discredited Alice of Lacy and her second husband, Eubulo Lestrange, being forced to yield these fragments of earl Thomas's possessions to his mighty supplanters.[6] Thus Despenser ruled over all South Wales from Milford Haven and Cilgerran to Chepstow and Abergavenny. There the only region outside his direct sway was a little district round Carmarthen, still ruled by the king's sheriff of that shire, and the adjacent lordship of Kidwelly, which was still retained by Henry of Lancaster. North of this, Brecon was in the king's hands by reason of the minority of earl Humphrey's heir. Even in northern and central Wales there was only one strong marcher lord

[1] *C. Chart. R.*, iii, 448. [2] *Ibid.*, 450.
[3] *C.P.R. 1321-24*, pp. 245-6; *C. Chart. R.*, iii, 448.
[4] *C.P.R. 1321-24*, p. 341; *ibid.*, *1324-27*, p. 52.
[5] *C.C.R. 1323-27*, pp. 288-9.
[6] *Ibid. 1318-23*, p. 620. *Cf. C. Chart. R.*, iii, 448.

remaining. This was the earl of Arundel, lord of Clun and Oswestry, who, however, was appeased by the office of justice of Wales, and by the custody of a large share of the Mortimer lands. There was enough in all this to revive the jealousies which had already once destroyed the Despensers' power. But it is a testimonial to Despenser's intelligence that, after 1327, his supplanter Mortimer undoubtedly borrowed his methods, and went one better than he in his efforts to build up a mighty power in Wales and its march.

If the ambition of the Despensers was the ultimate cause of the fall of Edward II, fuel was added to the flame of discontent by the collapse of foreign policy, the French war and forfeiture of Gascony, the insubordination of the bishopric-hunting royal clerks, the eager scramble for wealth and power, and the grave disorders and unpunished acts of aggression which accompanied these developments. The personal wrongs of the queen, the greediness which sequestrated her estates,[1] the fatuousness which sent her to France and allowed Mortimer of Wigmore to escape from prison, brought about the last great crisis of the reign. I have no need to dwell upon the incidents of the fall of Edward II, which Stubbs has worked out with admirable mastery.[2] It proved as light a task in 1326 to overthrow Edward and the Despensers as it had been easy to effect the other superficial revolutions of this reign. It bears upon what I have stressed already that Edward fled from his wife and her paramour into the Welsh dominion which the younger Hugh had been establishing. The utter failure of the lord of south Wales to resist Mortimer in his own chosen ground illustrates the futility of all the laborious efforts of a personal ambition that strove, but strove in vain, to run athwart the natural course of history. After the fall of Edward II, Despenser's dreams are only noteworthy as showing to Mortimer the road to a similar aggregation of Welsh marcher lands. Yet Mortimer's ambition was almost as fleeting as that of Despenser's. If the policy of the aggregation of great

[1] This was on 18 Sept. 1324 (*Foedera*, ii, 569). On 20 Nov. the queen was put on an allowance of 8 marks a day "pro expensis hospicii sui," and of 1,000 marks a year "pro omnimodis aliis expensis necessariis," to be received at the exchequer (Issue Roll 210, m. 14). The household allowance thus amounted to 2,920 marks a year, and was therefore an increase upon the sum of 50 marks a week, *i.e.*, 2,600 marks a year, which she had been receiving from the Bardi in 1318 (*C.P.R. 1317-21*, p. 130).

[2] Introduction to *Chronicles of Edward I and Edward II*, II, xci-cii. [See also Miss M. V. Clarke, "Committees of Estates and the deposition of Edward II" in *Hist. Essays in honour of James Tait*, pp. 27-45.]

groups of marcher lordships, thus initiated, has any permanent importance, it is because it prepared the way for the transference of the march to the direct rule of the crown, which was consummated in 1399 and in 1461, when the heir of the Lancasters and the heir of the Mortimers, successively mounting the throne, added their marcher lands to the direct possessions of the English monarchy. In the preliminaries of this process lies another important feature of the reign of Edward II.

V

# THE ADMINISTRATIVE REFORMS OF EDWARD II

## (1) The Methods and Authors of the Reforms

Great administrative changes were a special feature of the reign of Edward II. Administrative reforms and re-adjustments were going on, more or less, all through the reign. There were even reforms during the long period of the struggle for the ordinances; but these were, so far as conscious, more largely efforts to buttress the court against baronial attacks than honest attempts to improve the machinery of government for its own sake. Apart from these, the only deliberate change of this period that has any permanent importance was the separation of the custody of the privy seal from the general administration of the wardrobe, and the consequential growth of an office of the privy seal. In 1318, however, we have a formal policy of reform enunciated in the household ordinance of York, which followed up the purgation of the *familia regis*, already effected, by a vigorous attempt to overhaul the system on which it was constructed. The subsequent household ordinance of 1323 carried the same process still further. The final steps were the result of the exchequer ordinances of 1323-26, and in particular of the ordinance of 1324. The result of these enactments was to establish the royal household as it existed for the rest of the middle ages, and in most respects as it continued until Burke's economical reform in 1782. By a series of parallel enactments, the exchequer system was reformed only less drastically than the wardrobe. Here the great date is 1323, but the supplementary edict of 1324 and the final exchequer ordinance of 1326 are only less important.

In this drastic re-casting of two of the three great offices of administration, the method of reform was in both cases the same. The changes were effected by ordinances drawn up by the king in council. We are in fact drifting towards the famous distinction between an ordinance in council and a statute in parliament. Already administrative matters were appropriately dealt with by an ordinance, even when, as was the case with the York ordinance of 1318, parliament was actually sitting at the time and was certain to be sympathetic with the changes proposed by the council. Even to revolutionaries, the king's government and its reformation was a matter not even for the magnates, still less for the commons, but for the king himself and the narrow circle of his permanent advisers.

The policy which inspired the reforms is as clear as the method by which they were effected. Before 1318 they were either the result of the baronial effort to enforce the ordinances, or they followed from the attempts of the *curiales* to entrench themselves more securely in the last strongholds of the household. After the drastic purging of the court in 1318, the spirit of the ordinances prevailed for at least the next three years, and it was then that the period of systematic reformation begins. What is most remarkable, however, was that the reaction of 1322 hardly retarded the reforming movement. If we may give the chief credit of the reform of the household to Pembroke and Badlesmere, the completion of their plans was carried out after Badlesmere had fallen on the scaffold and Pembroke had died on his last embassy to France. Moreover, exchequer reform was only attacked with any seriousness after the triumph of the Despensers in 1322 and was persevered in until the very end of the reign. There is nothing astonishing in intelligent champions of a strong monarchy being greater reformers than a conservative aristocracy. This has often been the case throughout English history. It is, however, enough to show that the Despensers and their followers were not mere creatures of court favour, but politicians with ideas which, however unpopular among the magnates, were valuable and attractive in themselves. It would be unfair, however, to give any party the sole credit for these changes. As under Henry III, court and baronage did not greatly differ in their methods, when they approached in a serious spirit a practical problem of administrative reform. What is astonishing, however, is that the men who had repealed the ordinances carried out so many of their innovations in the spirit of the ordinances and often gave effect to the very letter of the legislation which they had so solemnly annulled.

If we cannot claim any special measure of zeal for any one party, still less can we set on a pedestal any individual reformer among the politicians of that age. The credit for the amelioration of the household is to be divided among many, among whom Badlesmere and the younger Despenser, archbishop Melton, the two keepers Northburgh and Waltham and the controller Robert Baldock must certainly be included. The lion's share of the improvements in the exchequer may clearly be assigned to bishop Stapeldon, who, reappointed treasurer in May 1322,[1] remained in office until 3 July 1325, and was therefore treasurer when the ordinances of 1323 and 1324 were issued. But Stapeldon, one of the most puzzling characters of the reign, was no mere ministerial bishop. During his three years of office he left the exchequer for long periods to the care of his deputy, Sir Walter Norwich, and his absence was on his own as well as on the king's affairs.[2] However busy with affairs of state, Stapeldon was always extremely active in the administration of his diocese. Not even his zeal as a bishop saved him from the ill will of the chroniclers. His supersession by archbishop Melton was clearly a popular act.[3] Nevertheless Melton's policy was not different from his predecessor's. It was while Melton was treasurer that the third exchequer ordinance of 1326 was promulgated, and this was in no wise the least important of the series. Nor must we forget that the apostate Lancastrian knight, Sir Roger Bellers, also had his place among the exchequer reformers.[4] But the strongest and most active personality in the later years of the reign was, beyond doubt, Robert Baldock. Keeper of the privy seal from 1320, his elevation, on 20 August 1323, to the chancellorship, in succession to bishop Salmon, marks the flood tide of reaction at its height, though he retained office till he fell with his master. Able as he was, he was neither respected nor trusted. What authority was to be expected from a chancellor for

[1] The appointment was significantly "per regem," though parliament was still sitting (*C.P.R. 1321-24*, p. 112).

[2] *C.C.R. 1318-23*, p. 613. R.R. 241 speaks of his "recessus" from York on 8 Dec. 1322, though Norwich became his deputy on 3 Nov. Norwich was again acting in 1324 (*ibid.*, 250).

[3] Malmesb., p. 283, emphasises this. Stapeldon, he says, was "ultra modum cupidus et durante officio suo vehementer dives effectus."

[4] See later, pp. 180-1. *Ann. Paul.*, p. 310, calls Bellers the king's principal councillor.

whom all the good offices of his master could not procure the humblest bishopric? Chancellor for three years, Baldock, when he succumbed to a fate as cruel, but probably better deserved, than that of Stapeldon, still remained simple archdeacon of Middlesex. The chroniclers look upon Baldock, Stapeldon and the two Despensers as chiefly responsible for the fall of Edward II.

Baldock's successors in the wardrobe were men of little personal importance. When Roger Northburgh, treasurer of the wardrobe, got his bishopric, he gave way to Roger Waltham, whose advent to office on 1 May 1322 coincided with the supreme triumph of the Despensers. In October 1323 Robert Wodehouse, Baldock's successor as controller, stepped into Waltham's place, and by a timely desertion of his master managed to retain his post until 1328. More loyal was the new controller, Robert Holden, who followed Edward to his last refuge in Wales, and only lost power on his capture by Mortimer in November 1326. The lay officers of the household seem to have been overshadowed by the chamberlain. Neither Gilbert Pecché, nor Simon Dryby, nor Richard Amory, the stewards between 1322 and 1325, had great personal weight, while the last steward, Thomas le Blount, is only remembered by his symbolic breaking of his official wand which declared the reign to be over. Altogether there is little to be got from studying the ministerial changes of this period. The most significant feature is the appointment of magnates on the king's side to some of the great dignities. Thus Arundel was from 1323 onwards justice of Wales and Pembroke and Winchester were, in succession, keepers of the forests south of Trent. In general, however, the ministerial history of the last years of the reign strengthens the impression that the real work was done not so much by the higher dignitaries as by the obscure clerks and knights whose personality is now so difficult to grasp.

Let us turn from the methods and the men to the changes themselves. Here there is some little difficulty as to the best way of going to work. The reforms of the different departments of state are only intelligible in their relation to each other, and yet clearness requires that we should take the various offices separately. To do this with any effectiveness will involve an occasional repetition, for which I shall have to apologise. With this caution I shall attempt to speak, first, of the changes in the household departments;

secondly, of those in the chancery; and, lastly, of those in the exchequer.

## (2) The Household Reforms

### A. The Privy Seal [1]

Reforms of a sort in the household departments were going on all through the reign. Though the general attack on the courtiers, made in the ordinances, failed for nearly seven years to effect its purpose, one important permanent change was brought about in the household as the direct result of the provisions of the ordainers. We have spoken already [2] of the demand of the ordainers of 1311 that there should be a "suitable clerk" appointed to keep the privy seal, and that this clerk should, with other great household dignitaries, be appointed in parliament. The result of this was that by 1312 we have in Roger of Northburgh such a "suitable clerk" assigned to keep the privy seal, specially and personally responsible for the employment of the instrument of the domestic chancery, and liable to be called to account if the king went beyond the narrow limits laid down by the ordinances for the use of the privy seal. It is clear that along with this keepership of the seal went the custody of the household archives and responsibility for the preparation of the numerous writs and rolls drawn up under the privy seal. Accordingly it was necessary that Northburgh should have round him a staff of clerks, who were inevitably soon differentiated from the ordinary wardrobe clerks, and were almost at once spoken of as the clerks of the privy seal. I shall soon speak further of this office of the privy seal, which I regard as a direct result of the ordinances of 1311.

There were ebbs and flows before the separation of the keepership of the privy seal from the controllership of the wardrobe became permanent. Roger Northburgh, the first known keeper of the privy seal who was not also controller, held office from 1312 to 1316. During that period, the capture of keeper and seal, clerks and records of the seal, at Bannockburn, suspended for a short time the use of the instrument, without damaging the routine which its existence involved. For a time the king used as a substitute for the lost privy

[1] [For fuller treatment, and authorities, see *Chapters*, ii, 282-313.]

[2] Above, p. 89.

seal the privy seal of queen Isabella, and, as we shall see, the development of a new domestic seal, the "secret seal," was stimulated by this accident. Before long, however, Northburgh came back from captivity and resumed his interrupted functions, and a ransomed knight was allowed to bring home with him to England the captured seal itself.[1] But the separation of keepership and controllership was a hated thing, because it was imposed by the ordinances. Accordingly, in 1316, when Edward felt himself strong enough to flout the ordainers, he put Northburgh in Melton's place as keeper of the wardrobe, but once more combined the keepership of the privy seal and the controllership of the wardrobe in the person of Thomas Charlton, brother of the chamberlain, John Charlton, lord of Powys. Little comfort came to the king from this, since the Charltons went over to the Pembrokian party. Accordingly, in 1318, Charlton was continued keeper of the privy seal, but out of regard to the ordinances a new controller was appointed.

By the York ordinance of 1318 [2] the "office of the privy seal" was henceforth to remain a separate sub-department of the household. The keeper was in status and emoluments slightly inferior to the controller and cofferer of the wardrobe. If he only had wages "until he was advanced," it was because the king seldom paid a clerk a salary when he could provide for him more cheaply by ecclesiastical preferment. Under him were the four "clerks who write for the privy seal." But the department was not yet autonomous. The wages of these subordinates were fixed by the steward and keeper of the household. Yet the distinct privy seal organisation was kept up, even when Robert Baldock, appointed keeper of the seal in 1320, became a few months later controller of the wardrobe as well as keeper of the privy seal, after the ancient fashion. When Baldock left the wardrobe in 1323 to become chancellor, the differentiation of the two offices had become permanent. It followed from the separation that the keeper of the privy seal, now gradually becoming an important

[1] [On condition, however, that it should not be used again (*Chapters*, ii, 295). Meanwhile, a new seal had been made, which was in use as early as 13 July. *Cf.* the case of John Rose of Greenwich, sent to buy wine in Gascony by a London merchant, who was arrested on suspicion of having forged letters of safe-conduct, since two of these, one sealed with "our privy seal which we used before the fight at Stirling in Scotland," the other with "our privy seal which we now use," bore the same date (G.R. 35, m. 20 d).]

[2] Printed in App. I, pp. 244-81.

political officer, was destined, like the chancellor a few generations earlier, to drift out of close relations with the court. Even Northburgh had been constantly absent from court with his privy seal; his successor resided still less regularly. Not only did the barons approve of this; the king soon accepted the inevitable, and giving up the office of privy seal, as no longer under his direct control, established a new domestic chancery in the revived chamber. While the privy seal became, under Edward III, a seal of state, a new personal seal for the king had been found in the "secret seal" of the chamber.

Some remarkable results followed from these developments. Of the revival of the chamber I shall speak later on, but I should like here to emphasise the fact that, as a result of the separation of the privy seal from the household, and its development as an office of state, England had, after the middle of the fourteenth century, two independent secretarial and sealing departments of state, in addition to the third secretarial and sealing office which, we shall see, grew up to supply the wants of the household.[1] To these we must of course add the exchequer, which had had its seal, its secretariat and its chancellor *eo nomine*, since the end of the twelfth century. This growth of four separate "chanceries," to use the best mediæval word for any secretarial department, was the more complete since the great seal, the privy seal, the secret seal and the exchequer seal were each served by a separate staff of clerks. Each constituted a distinct and self-contained department, out of any fixed relation to the other secretarial offices, and jealously preserving its own independent existence and separate traditions. A very different result followed from that which obtained in most western countries, and notably in France, the one country of the west with which England had constant and intimate relations, whether of friendship or of hostility. Now in France there were several royal seals, as in England, though not quite so many seals as in this country. In France, however, there was only one secretariat, the royal chancery, controlled by the chancellor.[2] The

[1] Even under Edward I there was a tendency in this direction, for Fleta tells us that the keeper of the privy seal, that is, of course, in 1290, the controller of the wardrobe, was independent of the chancellor, being the only keeper of a royal seal in England outside his purview.

[2] For all that follows see P. Morel, *La Grande Chancellerie royale, 1328-1400* (Paris, 1900).

French *clercs du secré*, the counterpart of our clerks of the privy seal, first appear in records in 1316, just at the very moment when Edward II's privy seal office was coming into being. In numbers, emoluments, dignity, the four clerks of Edward II's privy seal correspond nearly enough to the three *notaires suivant le roi* of Philip V. In the next generation, however, the secretariat of the French secret seal became infinitely more important than the narrow and self-contained department of the English privy seal. This was inevitably the case, since the French secret seal now acquired a much wider scope than the English privy seal. Both seals alike lost their original private character and became official, but while the English privy seal degenerated into becoming one link in a long chain of forms, the French secret seal took the place of the great seal as the regular means of authenticating an important branch of the public royal correspondence. While English "letters close" required the great seal, French letters close were habitually sealed with the *sceau du secret.* This was possible without breaking up unity of administration, because, since the days of Philip the Fair, the French kings possessed a single centralised clerical department, served by officials of a common type, subject in all cases to the chancellor as their official head, and soon developing a strong corporate tradition. This was the great corporation of royal notaries and secretaries, of whose power and influence French administrative history is so full. While in England each office had an independent staff of its own, the French system was to assign members of a single notarial corporation to perform secretarial functions in the various offices of state. But while thus told off to write for the chancery, the *chambre des comptes*, or the secret seal, the French civil service clerks still remained members of the single corporate body, and therefore continued subject to the jurisdiction of the chancellor. This characteristic difference of English and French administrative history can be explained by the fact that all the French departments of state remained closely attached to the royal court. The centralising bureaucratic spirit, which, except in the judicial sphere, was so much stronger in France than in England, is largely to be accounted for by the different complexion of French and English political history. The struggle of monarchy and aristocracy in France was fought out normally in the field, and only in exceptional times, like those after Poitiers, in parliaments and councils. In England parliamentary conflict was normal, armed conflict exceptional. Thus the French administration remained royal and domestic, even when it became national and political. It followed that there was no real counterpart in France to that differentiation between the departments of the state and the departments of the household, which the power of the baronage under Edward II was permanently establishing as a central fact of English administrative history. The unity of secretarial organisation in France explains the lateness and the rarity of French departmental seals. Even the *chambre des comptes* had no corporate seal during the whole of the fourteenth century.

Never were French analogies and French methods more appreciated by English administrators than under Edward II. Accordingly, it was only after some experiments in the French direction that the system of separating the privy seal office from the chancery was triumphant. By 1323 the privy seal office, though still in the wardrobe, had acquired a distinct organisation within it. But the chancery itself had only gone "out of court" a generation or two earlier, and it was still, perhaps, an open question whether the co-existence of the seals did, or did not, involve the existence of two chanceries, one for each seal. No sooner was the organisation of the privy seal office complete than the experiment seems to have been consciously tried of introducing the French fashion of one chancery, or secretariat, for the two seals. The period of these experiments was between 1323 and 1326, when Robert Baldock, whom we remember as controller of the wardrobe and keeper of the privy seal between 1320 and 1323, acted as chancellor. Despite his long connection with the wardrobe, Baldock seems to have definitely tried to subordinate the privy seal office to the chancery. This was, in effect, the reversal of his previous policy of maintaining the privy seal in the wardrobe in the custody of a general wardrobe officer, and therefore in strict separation from the chancery. We have seen that henceforward the offices of keeper of the privy seal and controller of the wardrobe remained permanently in different hands. The natural result of this was the acceptance of the old device of the ordainers of treating the office of the privy seal as a semi-independent secretarial and administrative body. Baldock, however, seems to have gone back on this policy. He now imposed upon the wardrobe a succession of keepers of the privy seal who had had no previous connection with the royal household. Up to this every official head of the wardrobe, every keeper of the privy seal, had been a promoted *garderobarius*. Each of the three obscure keepers of the privy seal who held office between 1324 and 1326 had been, before his appointment, clerk of the chancery itself. To send a chancery clerk to keep the privy seal was but a first step towards the amalgamation of the office of the privy seal with the office of the chancery. Had Baldock's policy become established, there might well have resulted a unity of the secretarial offices in England as in France. The privy seal would have become not a small independent chancery, restricted in sphere yet complete in itself, but a branch of the great chancery under the high chancellor. Baldock was, however, among the most hated of Edward II's later ministers, perhaps because fourteenth-century English opinion disliked all innovators. Like the other great reformer, bishop Stapeldon, he fell victim to the Londoners [1] during the troubles that attended the fall of Edward II. With him perished all his schemes. This future secured for the office of the privy seal its independence of the chancery. In the next generation it also became independent of the household. The result was to limit its functions and prevent it attaining any really great importance. By the fifteenth century the privy seal became an additional otiose wheel in an over-complicated administrative machine, and in modern times the seal and the office have been abandoned as impediments to speedy and efficient administration. All that remains of the privy seal is a sinecure ministerial dignity.

## B. The Chamber [2]

In the course of the reign the king's chamber, which had vegetated in obscurity for some eighty years, attained once more a position of importance, worthy of the original institution from which both the exchequer and the wardrobe had risen. The beginnings of this reorganisation of the chamber

[1] [After trial at Hereford in Nov. 1326, he was claimed as a clerk by Bishop Orleton, from whose London house he was afterwards carried off by the citizens to Newgate, where he died in 1327 (*Ann. Paul.*, pp. 320-1, Baker, pp. 25-6).]

[2] [For fuller treatment see *Chapters*, ii, 314-60.]

took place in the earliest years of Edward II's reign, but the movement became much more important after the passing of the ordinances.

The revival of the chamber under Edward II cannot but be regarded as the king's direct answer to the attempts of the barons since 1300 to secure for the exchequer the absolute control of all the king's finances. At the very beginning of Edward II's reign two great forfeitures swelled the king's scanty resources. These were the confiscated estates of the disgraced treasurer, Walter Langton, and the much more extensive temporalities of the knights Templar, which, taken into the king's hands while the pope and the council were settling the fate of the order, remained to a large extent under the royal control many years after the pope and council had assigned them to the knights of St. John. A certain proportion of the lands of both Langton and the Templars was put into the hands of keepers, who were instructed to account for them, not in the exchequer, but in the king's chamber. The new departure was made very cautiously at first, but soon began to assume larger dimensions. Accordingly, the chamberlains—Gaveston perhaps, certainly John Charlton and Hugh Despenser the younger—soon had in the chamber an organised office at their disposal. Astute clerks, the first of whom was Ingelard Warley, supplemented the unlettered knights and valets who mainly officered the chamber when it meant little more than the king's bedroom. The ordainers strove to stay this process by demanding Charlton's exile from court and by insisting that the issues of the land should be paid and accounted for in the exchequer. On the rare occasions when some show was made of executing the ordinances, a few perfunctory orders were issued that lands hitherto accounted for in the chamber should henceforth be accounted for in the exchequer. Unluckily, the desire of the ordainers that the king should " live of his own " led them to acquiesce in the appropriation of certain parts of the royal domain to the support of the household and induced them to allow the revenues of specific royal manors to be paid directly into the wardrobe. It was but a step from the wardrobe to the chamber and, as soon as the baronial pressure on the court was reduced, it was an easy thing to revive the system of the appropriation to the chamber, not only of these lands, but of a great many others as well.

As the result the chamber grew immensely in importance

in the confused years between Bannockburn and the treaty of Leake. It was easier to widen its scope, since there was so little directly about it in the ordinances. Disregard for a merely domestic office, important only to the king as a man, unwillingness to wound the king's feelings unnecessarily by meddling with a department which concerned the royal privacy and dignity so nearly, may well have combined to make the barons neglect it. Anyhow, the ordainers left the chamber to the king and did not even insist upon the appointment of its head, the chamberlain, in parliament, though in 1318 parliament rectified this omission, as we have seen, when it confirmed Hugh Despenser in that office. The baronial attack on the courtiers, as a whole, was a very questionable success, and the household, dealt with by the York parliament of 1318, remained as useless, as superfluous, as greedy and as irresponsible as the household of the heyday of Gaveston's influence. But while the barons were besieging to little purpose such outworks of the wardrobe as the marshalsea and the stewardship, the astute *curiales* were successfully building up an innermost keep of royal privilege by their resuscitation of the chamber. It was not likely that this elaborated court organisation, this concentric castle of defence, as deftly articulated as Caerphilly, or Carnarvon, or Coucy, would yield to the casual and unsystematic siege operations of the disorderly and unruly baronage. It was the stronghold, possession of which enabled the younger Despenser to worm his way into court favour and win for himself the highest influence in the state.

These years saw the revival of the chamber at once as a royal privy purse, as a source of "secret" and court expenses, and as virtually withdrawn from all responsibility to the exchequer. The chamber, too, became again a court chancery, the source of writs, letters, administration and sealing, so that it reproduced the characteristic dual aspects, administrative and financial, of the king's wardrobe. Side by side with the privy seal, the seal of the wardrobe, the sometime personal instrument of the king, which the barons aspired to turn, like the great seal, the seal of the chancery, into another seal of state, there now arose a new domestic royal seal, the secret seal, to enable the king still to have some individual and private token of his wishes, independent of the official seals, which were in danger of being used only as the barons directed.

It is a pure accident that the " small seal " of the English kings had become known as the " privy seal." Similar seals had arisen all over western Europe and were almost universally known as " secret seals." Now *secretum* and *privatum* are of course the most absolute synonyms. Moreover, the instrument which English officials called the king's privy seal had engraved upon it *secretum regis Edwardi.* With *secretum* staring in the faces of all who examined an impression of the king's small seal, the wonder is how Englishmen ever came to call it habitually *sigillum privatum* and not *sigillum secretum.* It is not to be marvelled at that in thirteenth and fourteenth century documents alike this seal was occasionally called the " secret seal." Up to the very end of the thirteenth century " secret seal " and " privy seal " were simply different names for the same thing.

In the latter portion of the reign of Edward I a " secret seal " begins to be mentioned which is perhaps something different from the privy seal. At first this was a small stamp, used for sealing up enclosures that accompanied letters of privy seal, just as when letters of the great seal were despatched along with schedules, rolls and writs, these latter were sent *sub pede sigilli*, " under the foot of the seal." It is quite possible that this secret seal was still only the privy seal, though I am inclined to think that it was something else. However, in the years immediately succeeding the ordinances, we get undoubted traces of a secret seal which was demonstrably different from the privy seal. I have not come across any impressions of this seal showing its nature and inscription, but the mark of the wax on the parchment shows that it was slightly smaller than the privy seal of the same period.[1] The first letter so authenticated that I have examined is dated 1313. An order under the secret seal dated May 1318 has been preserved among the chancery warrants, which instructs Thomas Charlton, whom we know to have been at that date keeper of the privy seal, to draw up a letter under the privy seal. Such letter must clearly have been sealed with a stamp that was different from the privy seal. It is accordingly the first absolute demonstration

[1] The most accessible material for this investigation is contained in the P.R.O. series of Chancery Warrants and the corresponding series of Exchequer Warrants, a large proportion of each series consisting of writs of privy and secret seal. The chancery secret seals are mainly contained in Chancery Warrants, files 1328-30. See Déprez, *Etudes de diplomatique anglaise*, pp. 73-86 [and *Chapters*, v, 164-70].

that the secret seal of Edward II was an independent instrument. Moreover, there is evidence under Edward III that the secret seal was kept "in the chamber." There is earlier evidence that, before the organisation of the wardrobe, the privy seal had also been the seal of the chamber. There is, moreover, a curious passage in an obscure chronicle of Edward II's reign, which connects in a muddled way this duplication of the king's personal seal with the falling of the privy seal into the king of Scots' hands at Bannockburn, and associates with one of these seals a clerk named Wingfield, whom we know to have been a clerk of the king's chamber.[1] Now the beginnings of the secret seal occur, as we have seen, absolutely at the same time, and that time the period immediately after the ordinances. On all these grounds I feel justified in the conjecture that the secret seal was from its origin the seal of the chamber. This is the more likely since the development of Edward II's chamber system was clearly suggested to his *familiares* by the great extension of the chamber and the chamberlain's office in other lands and notably in France. In the year 1312, the year before Edward II's secret seal can first be proved to be other than his privy seal, we learn that the secret seal of his father-in-law, Philip the Fair, was kept by one of his chamberlains.[2] And in the distinction already existing in the French court between the *sceau du secret* which, as in England, was becoming officialised, and the king's personal *cachet*, or signet, we get exactly the same differentiation of the personal royal seal into two, which henceforth also characterises English history.

The importance of the chamber was much increased after the triumph of the court party in 1322. The system of reserving certain lands to the chamber, and exempting them, at least in the first instance, from the jurisdiction of the exchequer, was now openly developed on a large scale. An opportunity for this was afforded by the vast estates forfeited to the crown by reason of the treason of Lancaster, Hereford, and the other stalwarts who had fought at Boroughbridge. A large proportion of these "contrariants'" lands

[1] *Nicolai Triveti Annalium Continuatio* (ed. A. Hall, Oxford, 1722), p. 15.

[2] Morel, *Grande Chancellerie*, p. 258; *cf.* the more sceptical view in Giry, *Manuel de Diplomatique*, p. 653. The text of Bardin's chronicle, our source for this much-contested statement, is quoted in *Histoire Générale du Languedoc*, t. x. pref., col. 30 (ed. Privat).

in the king's hand were now annexed to the chamber, and their keepers were ordered to account not in the exchequer but in the chamber. Such forfeitures were not destined to remain long in the king's hands, and the typical chamber manors are rather to be sought in escheats that from motives of policy were to be regarded as permanently incorporated in the royal domain. Such was notably the Fors inheritance of Holderness, which Edward I had permanently appropriated for the crown. Burstwick was in those days the *caput* of the crown possessions in Holderness and perhaps the most typical of chamber manors. It is now an obscure little place, with the faintest suggestion of the remains of the manor house where Edward held his court, and with a church that compares very unfavourably with the magnificent structures that, in the neighbouring parishes, still tower over the flat fields and dull villages of Holderness to testify to its ancient greatness. But the best features of the church of Burstwick belong to the reign of Edward II; and the fair image of a young king, preserved as an ornamented corbel of a fourteenth century chapel, may not impossibly be an attempt to represent in stone the king who first annexed Burstwick to his chamber, and made it his most usual northern home. In other cases also chamber manors were specially attractive as places of royal residence. Such a chamber manor was King's Langley, in Hertfordshire, Edward II's favourite home in the south, where the body of the beloved Gaveston reposed in the chapel of the convent of Friars Preachers, chosen to enshrine that precious dust.[1] It was a matter of policy, then, to withdraw the king's chief abiding places from the national jurisdiction and submit them to the special personal authority of the sovereign. In modern times a king would attain the same end by reason of the distinction between the private and official estate of the crown with which the middle ages were unfamiliar. Langley and Burstwick stood to Edward II as Osborne and Balmoral to queen Victoria, or as Sandringham to Edward VII.

Chamber organisation now grew apace. Chamber accounts survive in the Public Record Office after 1322 for

[1] [The foundation of this priory originated with the Dominicans of Oxford, to whom Edw. II granted a site at King's Langley as early as 1307. Before Gaveston's death, Edward had already provided endowment for 45 friars there. After it, he raised the number first to 55, then to 100 (Rev. C. F. R. Palmer, "The Friars Preachers of King's Langley" in *Reliquary*, xix (1878), especially pp. 37-43, 74-6).]

the rest of Edward II's reign. The chamber, though independent of the wardrobe, accounted at that time to the exchequer and the exchequer has luckily retained some of the accounts thus tendered to it for verification. They reveal to us a whole hierarchy of chamber officers, receivers and controllers, stewards and auditors, knights and clerks, gentle and simple, influential and obscure. They show that the chamber had a revenue of its own, though that income was still small, and that both in its receipts and expenses it constantly overlapped the wardrobe. Moreover, they show Despenser, the chamberlain and therefore head of the chamber, constantly exercising a personal influence on the details of its work. I feel pretty sure that this revived chamber system was a conscious result of the Despensers' policy, and that by it they hoped to retain one centre of household authority untouched by the reforms which, as we shall see, tended to limit the influence of other branches of the royal household. Perhaps the best proof of this is that after the fall of Edward II the chamber lands and accounts entirely disappear. They were revived after 1330, when Edward III began to govern as well as reign. For a time this king stressed his chamber even more than his father had ever done, refusing, for instance, to allow it to account to the exchequer, and instituting an additional seal for specifically chamber business in the "griffin seal."[1] These arrangements did not, however, last long. They collapsed almost entirely before the financial embarrassments of a king compelled to wage continual war for his "heritage of France." After about 1355 the chamber, as restored by Edward II and revived by Edward III, became a shadow of its former self. The chamber lands were transferred to the exchequer; the griffin seal disappeared, and, if the secret seal still remained, it took a new shape as the king's *signet*, the custody of which was henceforth in the hands of the king's secretary, who ceased speedily to be a chamber officer, having a department of his own in the signet office. From these modest beginnings arose the secretaryships of state of the Tudors, and all the modern administrative departments that centre round the secretaryships. Thus history again repeated itself. When the old court offices became ineffective, they gave rise to the signet office and the secretariat of state, which from the Tudor period stepped

[1] [For this see *Chapters*, v, 181-92.]

into the position of the mediæval chancery. Thus the most characteristic modern offices of state arose, like the mediæval departments, from the king's domestic establishment.

## C. The Wardrobe [1]

Having dealt with the privy seal and the chamber, we must go back to the wardrobe in the narrower sense. The establishment of a privy seal office, and still more the revival of the chamber and the beginnings of the secret seal, must have tended to limit the functions of the wardrobe proper, by lopping off from it spheres of work with which it had previously been specially concerned. The same tendency was strengthened by the changes brought about by the York ordinance of 1318, and the later exchequer and wardrobe ordinances which were consequential upon it. In the minds of the men who drew up the ordinance of 1318 there was no intention of extending, or strengthening, the authority of the wardrobe. Their chief object was to purge the household of its unworthy members, and to take precautions to prevent the revival in the future of the disorders of the *familia regis*, against which the ordainers had fought so long and so unsuccessfully. The best way to do this was by a rigid definition of the constitution and functions of the household. Both the disorder and the strength of the king's household had in the past been derived from the same source. This was the absence of precedent and definition, which allowed every official to work for his own and the king's interests in his own way. Thus in the heart of the fourteenth century there still survived the primitive undifferentiated household establishment of our early kings, in which every royal officer was jack of all trades, administrator, judge, collector, book-keeper, paymaster, store-keeper, auditor, surveyor, scribe, secretary, as occasion demanded. What had perhaps seemed in the past to be the strength of the household now seemed to the reformers its weakness. Up to this point, they tell us in their preamble, the officers of the household had always been in arrears, and, " uncertain what they should do and what they should take of the king by reason of their offices, so that no control could be exercised over these offices, nor the officers charged as they ought, to the great damage and

[1] [For fuller treatment see *Chapters*, ii, 224-81.]

dishonour of the king." [1] This suggests that the extraordinary arrears into which the household accounts had fallen, referred to in an earlier chapter, were regarded as inherent in the disorderliness of the household system, and were not solely the result of the financial embarrassments which Edward II had inherited from his father. To remedy this the ordinances entered with great detail into the duties and emoluments of every member of the household. It is for that reason that the ordinance was a much longer and more elaborate document than the first household ordinance which still survives, namely the ordinance of Edward I of 1279.[2] Innovations were not aimed at. The object of the reformers was to maintain the existing office under conditions that made further disorders more difficult. Their goal, then, was definition rather than reformation. The trend of all their enactments was to emphasise the need of division of labour in every state department. The plain reason for this was the fact that it was impossible to call a royal officer to account for doing his work ill, so long as there was no certainty what his true work was. Subject to this limitation, we are not to expect innovations in documents of this character.

Even the elaborate definition in the ordinance of the functions of the office of the privy seal, of which I have already spoken, was doubtless little more than the statement of the existing usage. But it is worth while to notice here that the duties of the controller are defined with special particularity, and that he is given such an immense amount of detailed supervision of the household and its accounts that he could have had little leisure or opportunity to concern himself with general business of state. The same spirit of definition and limitation marks the provisions of the ordinances relative to the great wardrobe. Here again we have complaints of " the great damage and loss which had arisen from the wasting and ill-spending of things that came for the household by delivery of the clerk of the great wardrobe, for want of setting down the certainty of the price every day upon the account of the household." [3] To remedy this the clerk or keeper of the great wardrobe was to deliver the commodities in his keeping by indenture, specifying details

[1] App. I, p. 244. Only the domestic work of the household is emphasised in this document ; the political side is ignored.

[2] [Printed in *Chapters*, ii, 158-63.]

[3] App. I, pp. 247-8.

and prices. In other ways also, the keeper of the wardrobe was to keep a tight hand over his subordinate. As some compensation, the clerk of the great wardrobe was allowed more authority over his own staff, which included the armourers, tailors, tentmakers, and other craftsmen of the household. Though stress was laid upon his residence in court, the exigencies of the great wardrobe office now required it to maintain permanent headquarters in the city of London, so that, even earlier than the office of the privy seal, the great wardrobe began to acquire an independent status.

So much for the ordinance of 1318. It was supplemented by a second household ordinance issued at York in June 1323, about the same time as the first reforming ordinance for the exchequer. Both the York household ordinances seem to me so valuable that I have published the French text as an appendix to this book, and need therefore say the less about them now. For our present purpose, it is enough to mention that the ordinance of 1323 is mainly taken up with pleas for the reform of the system of drawing up and tendering the accounts of the household.[1] The details show that the reforms of 1318 had been but little acted upon and the interesting thing is that here also the policy of 1318 remains the policy of 1323. The semi-independent "foreign" officers who account in the wardrobe, such as the clerk of the great wardrobe and the butler, are to render their accounts twice or thrice a year. There is clear evidence that the delays in tendering the general wardrobe accounts were not yet over and it was particularly complained that the last year's account was very diffuse and that the staff was inadequate to grapple with it. Studied in connection with the exchequer ordinance of 1324,[2] it enables us to state shortly what remedies were devised to prevent such difficulties recurring in the future.

The remedy of 1324 was this. The wardrobe was to be relieved by the various semi-autonomous branches being pushed still further on the road towards independence. The keeper of the wardrobe has been "charged with many foreign accounts, whereof he can have no knowledge, . . . so that thereby the account has been delayed and put in arrear."[3] Henceforth the clerk of the great wardrobe was to account to the exchequer, and, like the keeper of the wardrobe, was

[1] App. I, pp. 281-4.

[2] This is printed, like the other exchequer ordinances, by Hubert Hall, *Red Bk. Exch.*, iii, 908-29.

[3] *Ibid.*, p. 908.

to receive his funds direct from the national exchequer, his chief subordination to the wardrobe being the strict control which the keeper still exercised over him in details. Similarly, the king's butler was to account at the exchequer, and only that part of the wines dealt with by him which was used for the royal household was to be charged to the keeper of the wardrobe. In the like fashion the receivers of stores and victuals were to account directly to the exchequer, "so that the keeper of our wardrobe shall not meddle with such victuals, except such as shall be received for the entertainment of our household."[1] The same was to hold good of the keepers of the king's horses, the clerk of the hanaper of the chancery, and the messengers who went on royal embassies and missions. The effect of this was to bring all these departments into direct relations with the exchequer, which soon made their relation to the wardrobe exceedingly nominal.

The great result of these changes was the separation of the "foreign accounts" from the pipe rolls in which they had hitherto been embedded and their separate enrolment by themselves. For our immediate purpose, however, the most important consequence was that these innovations relieved the wardrobe proper of a large amount of its national work and tied it down much more closely to the regulation and administration of the affairs of the royal household. It is significant, then, that the exchequer ordinances of these years speak repeatedly of the wardrobe as the "wardrobe of the king's household," the phrase which a generation or two later became the ordinary method of describing it.

I do not say that all these changes were rigidly carried out, but they were sufficiently executed to make a real difference in the future history of the wardrobe. It is true that, under Edward III, the early years of the Hundred Years War saw a recrudescence of political and martial wardrobe activity on a large scale, but it dried up before the hostility of parliaments, the stubborn prejudices of the exchequer, the growing complexity of the machine of state, and the increasing tendency to distinguish between the king's private and public capacities. Thus the reign of Edward II, which marks the culmination of wardrobe activities from one point of view, marks also the beginning of its decline. Continuing under Edward III, this declension went on so rapidly in the

[1] *Red Bk. Exch.*, iii, 918.

second half of the fourteenth century that Richard II made much less conscious effort to exalt his prerogative through the traditional channels of household organisation than did any of the three Edwards. Thus in the long run the constitution overshadowed the household. No longer did the clerks of the wardrobe exercise a concurrent jurisdiction with all the great administrative officers of state. They gradually ceased to be administrators, judges, revenue collectors, arrayers and equippers of armies and navies, ambassadors, victuallers, clothiers, and all the rest of it. In the great days of the wardrobe, the wardrobe clerk worked at functions as diversified as those of the most isolated and solitary Indian civilian of the present day, to say nothing of having as his primary duty to attempt to put order into a royal establishment as vast and disorderly as that of any eastern sultan or rajah. But when he lost this many-sidedness, he lost his influence and importance. After the fourteenth century he was a mere court officer, limited and circumscribed by the dull work of routine and ceremonial. During that same century he took for the last time the lion's share in the government of the country. And the reign which first suggests the marshalling of the forces which were soon to narrow and restrict his sphere is the reign of Edward II. It marks, therefore, a turning point in the history of English administration.

## (3) The Chancery Reforms

I have now spoken of the reforms carried out under Edward II in the administrative departments dependent on the court. My next task is to deal with the results of the spirit of administrative reform as it affected the two traditional departments of state, the chancery and the exchequer. Let us treat first of the chancery.[1]

The chancery was the office which altered least during the reign of Edward II. There is absolutely no chancery legislation corresponding to the reforming ordinances which between 1318 and 1326 changed the face of the wardrobe and the exchequer. Such reforms as were brought about in it were due either to the indirect effect of these ordinances on a closely allied department of government, or to the result of a gradual process of administrative change brought about from within and for no other motives than practical convenience. In some respects the chancery went back on

[[1] For fuller details see Dr. B. Wilkinson, *The Chancery under Edward III*.]

ancient lines, though these experiments in reaction, if numerous, were seldom long continued. I explained in an earlier chapter how, nearly up to the Barons' Wars, and again in the days of bishop Burnell, the custom had been to hand over the "issues of the chancery" to a magnate chancellor to make his own profit out of them, and how ultimately this system had been superseded in favour of the more economical and bureaucratic device of paying these revenues over to the wardrobe, and giving to the chancellor a fixed "fee" for the remuneration of himself and the clerks of his office, and for the several expenses of carrying on his department. It is with some surprise that we find that under Edward II there was an intermittent harking back to the old system, which treated the chancery as the personal property of the chancellor, which he might exploit in his own interests. Thus as early as May 1311 the keeper of the hanaper was ordered to hand over the issues of the seal to chancellor Reynolds, until a loan of £1,000, which Reynolds had advanced to the king, had been repaid.[1] This patent was at once cancelled, because it was found that Reynolds could be satisfied with a sum of rather less than half the debt, and that the hanaper was at once able to pay over to him such a proportion of his due.[2] Its significance cannot be stressed because, like the handing over the customs to the Frescobaldi, it was plainly due to financial embarrassment rather than to a conscious desire to exalt Reynolds. As ever, the barons were the conservatives and the king and his following the innovators. Accordingly, it was only when the ordainers of the school of Pembroke got the upper hand that the restoration to the chancellor of the issues of the seal became a matter of deliberate policy. It is rather surprising to find that, three years after he had become chancellor, the baronial official, John Sandall, bishop of Winchester, received in 1317 all the issues of the seal by the king's gift "for the sustentation of his household and of the other burdens of the said chancery."[3] It looks as if the barons not only wished that the king should "live of his

[1] *C.P.R. 1307-13*, p. 345. I owe this reference and all the following ones about the chancery to the kindness of Miss L. B. Dibben, who has put at my disposal the great mass of information she has collected on the early history of that office.

[2] *Ibid.*, p. 346. Mandate to William Thorntoft, keeper of the hanaper, to deliver out of the issues of his office £418 6s. 8d. to Reynolds in part payment of the £1,000 which the king owes him.

[3] E.A. 211/7, m. 1.

own," but that the chancellor should do the same. Anyhow, it seemed to the magnates that it was better that the surplus profits of the seal should swell the state of the chancellor than that they should be diverted to increase the resources of the household. When Sandall resigned the chancery in June 1318 the king again received the issues of the seal.[1] Only a month later, however, a similar grant of the issues of the seal was made to the succeeding chancellor, John Hotham, bishop of Ely, and in October the royal grant was formally renewed, or sanctioned, in parliament. The result was that Hotham exploited the profits of his office until his resignation in January 1320.[2] The reactionary experiment was now dropped for six years. Both the baronial nominee, bishop Salmon, chancellor from 1320 to 1323, " whom the king nominated his chancellor in full parliament," and Robert Baldock, the curialist chancellor for the rest of the reign, had to content themselves with the " accustomed fees " of their office. These were exceedingly moderate, and, I imagine, rather presupposed that the chancellor was able to make both ends meet from the revenues of the bishopric he normally held and perhaps even from the unmentioned opportunities of doubtful gain which accrued to the king's ministers. Now Baldock held no higher church preferment than the archdeaconry of Middlesex, and the king's repeated efforts to procure him a bishopric had ended in failure. This must have meant that the legitimate profits of the office were hardly adequate for Baldock's requirements, and may account for fresh grants to him of the issues of the seal at the very close of the reign.[3]

Save for these experiments in reaction, the chancery, so far as it moved at all, moved on progressive lines. The persistence of the ordainers in upholding the rights of the great seal against the privy seal was all in its favour, though it was somewhat neutralised by the tendency to legitimatise the privy seal and make it official, within certain definite lines. I do not think, however, that the solicitude of the barons for the traditional rights of the exchequer had any prejudicial

[1] He resigned on 9 June, " a quo tempore rex habuit omnes exitus predictos " (E.A. 211/7, m. 4).

[2] *Ibid.*, 211/8. Hotham held the issues from 8 July 1318 to 23 Jan. 1320. This grant was expressly approved by the parliament of York of Oct. 1318, " jesqes au fin du procheyn parlement " (Cole's *Records*, p. 10). The limitation of the parliamentary grant was not observed.

[3] Baldock was granted the issues of the seal from 3 Feb. 1326 to Easter, and then from Easter 1326 to the Easter following (Chancellor's Roll 118, m. 42.)

effect on the fortunes of the chancery. Neither do I find, in the history of the early part of the reign, the decisive turning point in a long conflict between the chancery and the exchequer, such as has sometimes been imagined.[1] On the contrary, I can discover no traces of such a struggle, and believe that the theory reposes on a misconception of the earlier position of the exchequer which is based, in the last instance, on an undue following of the great authority of Madox. Most certainly it is a misreading of history to assert that the transference to the chancery of the nomination of sheriffs, required by the ordinances of 1311, by the parliament of Lincoln of 1316, and by the establishments of York of 1322, was in any wise the culminating issue of this hypothetical struggle. This change was rather a part of that policy of definition and differentiation of function which underlay all the really good side of the administrative reforms of Edward II. There was, in fact, absolutely no reason why the chancery should carry on an imaginary feud with the exchequer. Its enemy was rather in the administrative offices of the household, against which it had a common ally in the exchequer. There was a certain amount of give and take in the adjustments of duties and spheres, but nothing that could cause any active rivalry between the two offices.

Only indirectly embarrassed by the financial disorders that nearly overwhelmed the exchequer, the chancery showed in the early years of the reign more capacity for self-reformation than the exchequer was in a position to manifest. We may attribute this not to the chancellors themselves so much as to the able band of chancery clerks, whom the general lack of control, perhaps, set free to order their office after their own fashion. Conspicuous among these chancery clerks was William Airmyn, who is spoken of as the "principal clerk in the chancery," and sometimes, less officially, as "vice-chancellor." He was the man to whom the foremost place was generally given among the keepers of the great seal, when the custody of the seal was put into the hands of a commission of chancery clerks. Moreover, he was the second chancery clerk to combine the offices of keeper of the

[1] Notably by the late Mr. A. Hughes, in his paper on "The Parliament of Lincoln, of 1316" in *Trans. R. Hist. Soc.*, new series, x. 41-58 (1896); see above, pp. 38 and 94-5. Unluckily Prof. Baldwin is among his disciples (*The King's Council*, pp. 210 and ff.).

rolls of chancery and keeper of the *domus conversorum* in which these rolls ultimately found their home. Airmyn, doubtless, had his weak points, as witness the sharp practice which got for himself the bishopric of Norwich, which he had been empowered to seek for his chief Baldock in 1325. Yet, in his office, he was a reformer, and for one reform brought about by William historians have good reason to be grateful. This was the composition of the first full and intelligible record of the proceedings of a parliament. Up to 1316 the rolls of parliament, whether short or long, are an unsystematic putting together of odds and ends, eked out by a varying number of petitions of very unequal importance. The roll of the parliament of Lincoln of 1316, made by William, who was specially appointed to compile it, is the first parliamentary roll which gives us, in the form of short dated minutes, a record of parliamentary proceedings, day by day, and so enables us to get an intelligible idea of what the estates actually did.[1] It set an example not always followed even in the rolls of some of the later parliaments of the reign, which we have already found of such value to us. But all rolls of parliament were, at this period, similar in their origin to Airmyn's roll of the parliament of 1316. I mean that they were the works of clerks of chancery. It is true that many of the rolls surviving, both before and after this roll of 1316, whose origin is so certain, are preserved in the records of the exchequer, as is notably the case with the rolls of 1318 and 1319, printed by Cole in his Records. There is no need, however, to imagine that there was a time, perhaps in 1316, when, as a result of the hypothetical triumph of chancery in a purely imaginary battle with the exchequer, the duty of compiling the parliamentary roll was transferred from the beaten exchequer to the victorious chancery.[2] The simpler but absolutely sufficient explanation is, that as was the case with many other records several copies of them were made, one of which was for convenience of reference deposited in the exchequer.

We may also thank the clerks of Edward II's chancery

[1] *Rot. Parl.*, i, 350-64 : "Memoranda de parliamento domini Edwardi regis Angliae . . . facta per Willelmum de Ayremynne, clericum de cancellaria prefati regis, ad hoc nominatum et specialiter deputatum." [For a detailed description, by H. G. Richardson and G. Sayles, see *Bull. Inst. Hist. Research*, vi, 151 (1929). They do not regard the roll as a precedent for others, or as a true journal, but as an *ad hoc* production, written up later from notes. See *ibid.*, pp. 141-2.]

[2] This was Mr. A. Hughes' view in the article already referred to.

for the increasing orderliness, detail and method of the chancery rolls. The result is that the patent and close rolls of Edward II's twenty regnal years contain as much matter, roughly speaking, as do the similar records of the thirty-five years of Edward I. Nor is this all. The bulk of the patent rolls was lessened by the systematic relegation of certain matters to other rolls, such as the fine rolls, which now contain exceedingly important enrolments of appointment. The result is, that while the calendar of the fine rolls of Edward I is contained in one volume, a similar calendar for the reign of Edward II requires two volumes. What the additional matter had to do with fines no one has as yet told us. These things seem very unimportant, yet they must needs be set down. We must remember that in any age, and particularly in the middle age, it is dangerous to despise forms. In the wise words of Maitland, "all this formalism is worthy of study; it is the necessary groundwork for ministerial responsibility and government by discussion."[1] But the increased formalism and bulk of the records of Edward II's reign are in no wise limited to the chancery records. They are equally found in the archives of the wardrobe and the exchequer, and were assigned by contemporary officials as one of the chief reasons for administrative reforms.

More important than improvements in form was the completion of the emancipation of the chancery from the court, which was the indirect effect of the exchequer reforms of 1323. We have seen already how the separation of the hanaper department from the wardrobe was effected, when the clerk of the hanaper was ordered to account directly to the exchequer for the issues of the seal. Perhaps the apparent reaction in 1317-20 towards the old fashion of the chancellor exploiting the seal for his own advantage was a step in the same direction. Anyhow, it was better for the independence of the office than the system of accounting for the profits of the seal in the wardrobe. When the profits of the seal were accounted for in the exchequer, the chancery sheds the last vestiges of its original position as a dependent office of the court, and stands forth in its later character as a self-sufficing office of state. This was the real chancery reform of the reign. It was not, however, so much a conscious change, as the last link in a long chain of development.

[1] *Memoranda de parliamento*, p. lxxi.

## (4) The Exchequer Reforms

Let us now turn to the course of exchequer reformation in the reign. Here we have to distinguish between the slow changes worked out, either within the department by its own officers, or by political action from the outside, and the more deliberate and conscious reforms of the years succeeding 1323. At first the exchequer had its work cut out in vain efforts to pay the king's debts and to provide him with the means to live. It derived some profit from those remedial elements in the ordinances which strengthened its position by defining and limiting its scope. The ordinance that the issues of the land should all be paid into the exchequer was the starting point of a long development, which was ultimately to make the exchequer supreme in all national finance. Though it cannot be said to have been carried out to any great extent, it went so far with the general tendency of the times, that all through the reign the "foreign receipt" of the wardrobe is—so far as we know the figures—insignificant, save at one or two exceptional crises, as compared with the receipt from the exchequer. Accordingly, to that extent the exchequer made a clear gain. The limitations to the hearing of pleas in the exchequer and to the use of the exchequer seal for other than departmental business, were, after a fashion, a set off to this. I have already given reason for hesitation in accepting the existence of an "exchequer chamber" or an "administrative exchequer" at this time.

All through its history, the exchequer was competent to make of its own initiative useful administrative reforms. Such, early in the thirteenth century, had been the clear and intelligible issue and receipt rolls, which give us the best conception of the general scope and direction of national finance. A study of these issue and receipt rolls of the early years of our reign shows both a remarkable continuity of the administrative personnel of the exchequer, irrespective of politics, and the persistent carrying on of the methods and traditions of the reign of Edward I. With the ever increasing embarrassment of the finances, the issue rolls, which had gained in complexity under Edward I, became under Edward II increasingly and hopelessly complicated. Even the simpler receipt rolls show how bad were the business methods then adopted. The form of the issue roll now made it very difficult to ascertain anything like a balance of accounts, or to discover a clear statement of the gross amount of issues for the term. The easy-going officials of Edward II did not even take the trouble to add up the totals of the receipt rolls, which were at least arranged intelligibly and easy to sum up. Sometimes by accident the totals of the receipt for a term are recorded in the roll. More often the clerks were content to set down the sums received day by day or week by week. Sometimes even the weekly totals are not added up, and often the despairing auditors' entry "examinatur, non summatur"—"examined, not added up,"—warns the student that he can only extract the information he desires by infinite labour on his own part. At last, for the sixth exchequer year of Edward II—1 October 1312 to 29 September 1313—we have the receipt rolls of both terms (nos. 202-5) added up. The amount of exchequer receipt recorded is just less than £50,000, though we must never forget that these are bookkeeping figures, made up by entries and re-entries of tallies, and that they in no wise necessarily show the sums actually touched by the crown. It is the same in the issue rolls. We must not, therefore, overstress the significance of the totals, when next year, 7 Edward II, we find that the issue roll (no. 167) for Michaelmas term is added up for the first time in the reign, and attests payments totalling £47,541 8s., almost as great in amount as those of the receipts for all the previous year. These are dull things to tell, but the modern student will feel deeply grateful to treasurer Sandall, in whose time the king's exchequer, by first adopting the ordinary precautions of a man of business with his accounts, has spared him much weary labour of uncertain result. Later on, such additions became usual, at least as regards the receipt rolls, while even the issue rolls gradually become less complicated and unpractical in their form. Unluckily, there were a good many cases of reversion to the earlier and worse type, and the gross amount of exchequer revenue, for much of Edward II's reign, still awaits complete statement. In both types of rolls, after 1316, we note the gradual establishment of exchequer control over the wardrobe. If this process was retarded in the years 1322-23, it was once more to be pushed forward during the last few years of the reign.

There is perhaps a suggestion of conscious reformation even so early as October 1310, when auditors of foreign accounts in the exchequer were appointed,[1] probably as a first result of ordaining pressure. But they languished in numbers and influence until Stapeldon started reforms on broader lines in 1323. In 1318, after Sandall's third appointment as treasurer in November, groups of clerks were assigned for scheduling the debts owed to the king, and for their classification between the recoverable and irrecoverable ones.[2] This shows that the problem of the bad debt, imperfectly grappled with when Edward I removed the most hopeless of the debts due to the crown from the pipe roll, and put them on a special *exannual roll*, was beginning to be seriously tackled. During Stapeldon's first treasurership, from 1320 to 1321, much wider schemes were mooted, involving the arrangement and ultimately the calendaring of the mass of the exchequer archives. Within a few months of Stapeldon's entrance into office, the treasurer, barons, and chamberlains were ordered to appoint "such of the king's clerks as shall be necessary to survey, dispose, and put into a proper state, before Michaelmas, the king's things in his treasury and the Tower of London, and the rolls, books, and other memoranda touching the exchequer of the times of his progenitors, which, the king understands, are not so well disposed as is needed for him and the common weal."[3] This order was only issued in August, and it shows some optimism on the part of the chancery to expect the work to be accomplished within less than two months, even with the promise of "reasonable expenses,"[4] to stimulate the zeal of the clerks engaged upon the task. Immediately afterwards, we find that both the two chamberlains, Master James of Spain and Master William Maldon, were assigned, with two clerks apiece, to discharge this important work.[5] Up to Easter, 1321, James and William with a large staff of clerks were still at work at the "arrayment" of the "rolls and other things in the king's chapel in the higher part of the Tower of London."[6] With Stapeldon's first retire-

[1] See D. M. Broome, "Auditors of the Foreign Accounts of the Exchequer, 1310-27," in *Eng. Hist. Rev.*, xxxviii, 63-71 (1923).

[2] I.R. 186, m. 7.

[3] *C.C.R. 1318-23*, p. 258.

[4] *Ibid.*

[5] I.R. 191, m. 8.

[6] "In summa turri Londonensi" (*ibid.*, 193, m. 4). This is doubtless the Romanesque chapel of St. John on the second storey of the White Tower, or keep, which is thus proved to have been a place of deposit of exchequer records under Edward II. [For full details, with a plan, see "The Tower as an Exchequer Record Office in the reign of Edw. II," by Mr. V. H. Galbraith, in *Essays . . . presented to T. F. Tout*, pp. 231-47.]

ment, in August 1321, the business seems to have flagged; the division of the archives, between those stored in London and those which had been taken by the exchequer to York at this period, could not have made it easier.

A further development soon followed when it was found desirable that certain sections of the exchequer archives should be "calendared" as well as "arrayed," and calendared, moreover, in connection with the relevant archives of the chancery and wardrobe. Practical reasons as usual brought about this new reform. No records were more constantly referred to in the course of the endless controversies between the agents of the English and the French crowns than those relating to Gascony, and a fire at the castle of Bordeaux had already compelled the English negotiators to rely largely on the documents kept in England. A royal clerk, Master Elias Johnston, who had in a subordinate capacity been assigned by Edward I to sort out and keep ready all documents that might be needed for such negotiations, was, in 1309, appointed formally keeper of the "processes" and memoranda touching Aquitaine and held this office until 1336.[1] But this new class, set apart for practical reasons, was inaccessible, and so early as 1315-16 a petition from Gascony reached the English chancery, begging that a register of documents relating to Gascony should be sent to the castle at Bordeaux, and specifying the documents which it was suggested were to be transcribed.[2] It may well have been that this circumstance attracted Stapeldon's attention. Anyhow a calendar of certain types of archives, "papal and royal letters, charters, bonds, quittances, remembrances and other muniments," was ordered to be compiled and as a first instalment documents of these classes relating to Gascony were dealt with. In August 1320 Master Henry of Canterbury, king's clerk, was ordered to make a calendar of such records for the use of the king's advocates of his claims in the "parliament of France"[3] and in July 1321, just before Stapeldon went out of office, Master Henry was

[1] E. Déprez in *Mélanges Charles Bémont*, p. 226. [For additional information see Galbraith, *op. cit.*, p. 242.] Johnston's predecessor was Mr. Philip Martel. His style was "custos processuum et memorandorum regis ducatum Aquitanie tangentium."

[2] Chancery Miscellanea, 29/8 (8). [M. Marcel Gouron, archivist of the department of Gard, has published an interesting *Essai de reconstitution du trésor des chartes du château de Bordeaux et de son mobilier au moyen âge* (Bordeaux, 1934), much of which relates to Edward II's reign.]

[3] *C.C.R. 1319-23*, pp. 319-20.

ordered to complete the work without further delay and to associate with himself in its execution two other experts, one of whom was Elias Johnston.[1] With Stapeldon's retirement, however, further delay seems to have ensued, for, though the calendar was completed, it remained in Stapeldon's custody and no use seems to have been made of it.

Stapeldon's second treasurership began on 10 May 1322, and the spirit of reform was once more unloosed. On 21 May Henry of Canterbury's calendar, in two books, was delivered into the exchequer by Stapeldon and put in the keeping of the chamberlains.[2] On 5 December 1322 it was delivered by the exchequer to Robert Baldock, the keeper of the privy seal, no doubt for custody in the wardrobe.[3]

Two days before the Gascon calendar was handed to Baldock, the preliminary steps towards completing the scheme of making an inventory of archives were taken by the issue of a new order to the treasurer and chamberlains to cause the "arrayment" and "calendaring" of all bulls, and of all other charters, deeds and memoranda touching the king and his estate and liberties in England, Ireland, Wales, Scotland and Ponthieu, existing in their custody in the treasury and elsewhere. "Sufficient persons" were to be appointed "at the king's expense," by the treasurer and chamberlains who were to "cause these things to be done as conveniently as they can be."[4] In the autumn of 1322 there was the further complication of the division of the exchequer into two sections, for while Walter Norwich, keeper of the treasury, was at York with most of the exchequer staff, Stapeldon went to London and received moneys and transacted business there.[5]

[1] *C.P.R. 1321-24*, p. 5.

[2] L.T.R.M.R. 92, m. 18 d.

[3] This "Kalendarium litterarum processuum et memorandorum ducatus Aquitanie" is now preserved in Misc. Bks. Exch., T.R., no. 187. It has never been printed, but a full account of it and its origin has just been published by Professor Déprez of Rennes in *Mélanges offerts à M. Charles Bémont* (1913), pp. 225-42. M. Déprez, however, proposes to publish it in full with copious annotations. He has already printed the headings and the formal introduction, with its lofty enunciation of principle, similar in conception to that of the published "Stapledon's Calendar."

[4] *C.C.R. 1318-23*, p. 688. Dated 3 Dec. 1322 at York. It is curious that the Channel Islands are not included in the list of places whose records were dealt with. Among the sufficient persons assigned were Robert of Hoton and Thomas of Sibthorp, clerks, whose function was to array and order "quedam scripta et monumenta in quibusdam castris et locis regni Anglie" (I.R. 201, m. 6).

[5] R.R. 241. [For a similar arrangement in 1298 see *Chapters*, ii, 105, n. 4.] Stapeldon's "recessus" from York was on 8 Dec. 1322; after 20 Dec. he received £3,988 7s. 1d. at London.

There were, therefore, two exchequers working simultaneously at York and London. At last the re-transference of the exchequer to Westminster, in time for the autumn session beginning in 1323, facilitated the completion of the task. The result of all this labour was the well known "Bishop Stapeldon's Calendar," wherein we can still study the arrangement and description of all the bulls, writs, charters and other documents then kept in "the treasury of the exchequer."[1] A generation in which scholars are still concerned with the problems of the custody, arrangement and calendaring of our ancient records, cannot feel too much gratitude to bishop Stapeldon for this timely work, and it is hardly too much to say that we owe to Stapeldon, more than to any other one person, the fact that our vast collection of exchequer records before 1323 is still preserved to us. Without such an effort the exchequer records may well have gone the way of the archives of the wardrobe and the privy seal, which, as separate collections, have wholly disappeared. It is worth remembering, too, that the effort was not a merely departmental one. Stapeldon's aim was to include in his survey the records of the wardrobe and those scattered in various castles and places throughout England. It was, therefore, an admirably designed plan to group together in a single synopsis an inventory of the administrative archives of the crown, outside those of the chancery. I imagine that these chancery records were safe enough under the keeper of the rolls of chancery, but that there was no similar responsibility clearly imposed on the chancellor of the exchequer or the remembrancers, the natural custodians of exchequer archives. In modern days the process of concentration was the other way about. By the act of parliament which marks the starting point of our modern centralised system of record keeping, the Master of the Rolls, historically only the keeper of the rolls of chancery, became also the custodian of the archives of practically all the central offices of state and law.

The first of Stapeldon's reforming ordinances of the exchequer was issued in June 1323 at Cowick in Yorkshire.[2] It was in form, like the household ordinances, an ordinance of the king in council. It was entitled "the articles ordained

[1] It is printed in i, 1-155 of Palgrave's *Antient Kalendars and Inventories of the Exchequer,* Record Com., 3 vols., 1836.

[2] This was while the exchequer was still at York, which it left at the end of July. [For dates and references see Dr. D. M. Broome's "Exchequer Migrations to York" in *Essays . . . presented to T. F. Tout,* p. 292, n. 1.]

and provided for the arrayment of matters in the exchequer." [1] The idea at its root was that the incredible confusion of the exchequer accounts and the deplorable arrears of the accounting were due, not only to the embarrassed finances of the crown, but also to the old-fashioned and unbusinesslike way in which the accounts were kept. I have illustrated this already from the muddled arrangement of the issue rolls and the indifference to arithmetic in even the comparatively orderly receipt rolls. But these rolls were the most modern and up-to-date of the exchequer records, so modern that they were enrolled from their beginning, under Henry III, after the so-called "chancery fashion" of fastening the various membranes together in one unending roll. Those who have had to unroll a hundred feet of parchment to verify one entry, will almost regret that the "exchequer system" of "filing" the membranes at the top, as is done with the pipe rolls, was not extended to these also, though they will admit that the "make up" of the pipe roll is almost as painful to him who would consult it, as is the "make up" of the chancery roll, winding out its endless length. The other new thirteenth-century rolls, the memoranda rolls of the two remembrancers, have hardly yet been studied with sufficient care for it to be safe to lay down the theory of their arrangement or development.[2] Yet even the memoranda rolls seem by this period to have settled down on the fixed, though not very clear lines on which they were afterwards carried on, doubtless as an indirect result of the strengthening of the remembrancers' staff and the definition of their duties by the ordinance of 1323, as we shall soon see. But the "great roll," or the "year roll" of the exchequer was still what we call the pipe roll, the oldest and most authoritative record of its work.[3] It looks as if the later rolls of issue and receipt had arisen to give a general conspectus of the revenue and expenditure of each half-yearly term, and so to remedy the system which treated the finances of the year as a series of separate accounts of the king with the sheriffs and other ministers of the crown. Even on their own lines, however, the pipe rolls were becoming

[1] Hall, *Red Bk. Exch.*, iii, 848-907, gives the French text and an English translation.

[2] [A description of their characteristics and the duties of the remembrancers, 1282-1350, has since been given by Prof. Willard in *Essays . . . presented to T. F. Tout*, pp. 215-29.]

[3] "Great Roll of the Exchequer," not Pipe Roll, was, I may note in passing, the ordinary mediæval name for this roll.

impossible. For one thing the amount of business, and therefore the size of the yearly roll, was now inordinately swollen. The ordinance tells us that in one department only of the exchequer, that of the treasurer's remembrancer, "the rolls and writs made by him in the time of this king amount to more, in a single year for the same time, than the rolls and writs of the same office in five years or six together, in the time of the king his father."[1] It is not likely that this was the rate of progress of every branch of the clerical work of the exchequer, but it is undoubted that both exchequer and—as we have seen—the chancery records are enormously greater in bulk for the reign of Edward II than for that of Edward I. One has only to wield the colossal pipe rolls of the period to experience this truth in a very practical way. According to the ordinance "the great rolls"—*i.e.* the pipe rolls—"are larger for one year of the time of the king that now is than they used to be for three years, or four, in the time of his predecessors."[2] And again, as regards the mass of individual documents apart from the rolls, "there have been more writs and letters made and delivered into the exchequer under the great and privy seal in every year at this present time than used in former times to be in ten years or more."[3]

The pipe roll was growing not only in size but in complexity. The ordinance speaks feelingly of the "overweighting of the great roll by much writing, whereby the settlement of the account has been, and is, delayed." To its proper material, the individual accounts of the sheriffs and bailiffs, directly responsible for the "farm" of lands and offices under the crown, had gradually been added a large number of "foreign accounts," including the accounts of the wardrobe and its various subsidiary branches. All these "foreign accounts" had hitherto been entered upon the pipe roll, either at the end or wherever there was room for them. And, as we have seen, the accounts of the wardrobe had included, up to this date, the accounts of all the great "spending departments" that were affiliated to it. Another cause of the overweighting of the "great roll" was the continued appearance of ancient and irrecoverable debts to the crown on the pipe roll, despite the remedial legislation of Edward I, which seems to have been as ineffective as most mediæval legislation was. A mass of new business was

[1] *Red Bk. Exch.*, iii, 884.
[2] *Ibid.*, p. 860.
[3] *Ibid.*, pp. 862, 864.

transferred to the exchequer during the reign, for example, the accounts for the issues of contrariants' lands, which till 1322 had been presented to the chamber.[1]

A further trouble was the inadequacy of the exchequer staff, especially in certain departments, for the business of the ordering of the national accounts. And this inadequacy was intensified since the most important officers after the treasurer, the barons, had the habit of keeping sheriffs and bailiffs waiting, when they came to tender their accounts, because these dignitaries preferred to hear pleas rather than do their proper work of examining the ministers' accounts. Moreover, exchequer pleas were often held in the same room as that in which the "full exchequer" was sitting, so that the barons were supposed to be listening with one ear to the lawyers and with the other to the sheriffs. This is a typical picture of the easy-going mediæval ways of transacting business. The barons certainly showed feats of dexterity which can only be compared to the intellectual resource of the fashionable modern "leader," conducting cases in two courts at once. We need not wonder that, in the words of the ordinance, "these accounts cannot be sufficiently rendered, heard or concluded with great diligence and perfect quiet."

The Cowick ordinance of 1323 provided a remedy for all these obstructions to the punctual and effective working of the exchequer. Strict directions were issued for the drawing up of the yearly roll, which was to be written after the ancient fashion "in great letters in full exchequer." "And if by chance he who wrote it erred, let him not presume to erase the mistake, but to cancel it, and to write beside it that which was correct." "And inasmuch as the said roll has such great force in itself, let all the pipes and accounts be henceforth well and fully examined, before they be put together, and the roll made of them at the end of the year." Moreover, the pipes—that is the individual membranes—of the "foreign accounts" were to be "put by themselves, and the other pipes of the sheriffs' accounts by themselves." Two rolls, in fact, were henceforth to be made, "with such titles as are fitting." The "foreign accounts" are enumerated as including the accounts of the king's wardrobe, of Gascony, Ireland, Wales, the customs, the escheators, the custody of the temporalities of vacant bishoprics, the profits

[1] [*Cf.* Tout, *Chapters,* ii, 338-43 and Miss Broome's article on the auditors cited above, p. 170.]

of abbeys and priories in the king's hands, the aids of the clergy and laity and every kind of aid, and accounts of castles, honours, forests, manors and other king's possessions, "such as have not been committed to farm but to custody."

Besides this great measure of relief, the debts to the king, which, seeming still recoverable, were left by Edward I in the annual roll, were now to be removed, and written only in the *exannual roll*, whose title was to be "the roll of debts extracted out of the year rolls," on which also summonses for the payment of these overdue sums were to be based. These debts were for the future not to be entered afresh in the exannual roll of future years. To perform all this new work and to catch up arrears, large additions to the exchequer staff were ordered. The special "apposal" of debts not in the great roll was entrusted to a baron and clerk assigned for the purpose, so that the two accounts could go on at the same time. The "engrosser of the exchequer," the clerk responsible for the writing of the rolls, was to "take to himself at the king's expense as many helpers as may be needed, so as he may with greater haste" perform his old and new duties becomingly. Among these fresh assistants were two clerks "appointed at the king's wages to engross the foreign accounts."

Very elaborate provisions were made to distinguish the work of the two remembrancers, whose offices had now considerably more than a century of history behind them. These two clerks appear originally acting as colleagues, like the two chamberlains. But the remembrancers had already become so far distinct as regards their functions, that one was called the king's remembrancer and the other the treasurer's remembrancer. Nevertheless, "the office of the two remembrancers has been much confused for long time past, and is so still," so that "down to the present time it has not been made certain what the one ought to have in keeping and what the other." To remedy this, definite functions were assigned to each, so that their work was not in the future to overlap. Thus, the king's remembrancer only was to "make remembrance of," that is to say, enrol on his memoranda roll, writs under the various seals received in the exchequer. He was also to keep the estreats of lands concerning the king, the taxation rolls, the red book, the books of the fees and the statutes and transcripts of charters.

The treasurer's remembrancer had "memoranda rolls" of his own, and had the custody of the "estreats" (extracts) from the chancery rolls, sent by that office to the exchequer for the sake of acquainting it with any political acts affecting the revenue and pleas of the exchequer. The enumeration of the functions of the two remembrancers is elaborated in immense detail. The effect, as Mr. Charles Johnson says, was that "henceforth the king's remembrancer was more particularly concerned with the casual, and the lord treasurer's remembrancer with the fixed revenue."[1] Great additions were made to the staff under the remembrancers, so that in effect their respective spheres developed into two sub-departments of the exchequer.

A fifth baron of the exchequer was now for the first time appointed,[2] as also "four sufficient men with their clerks" as auditors, and a special clerk to keep matters touching the forfeited lands of the contrariants. Moreover, the barons were tied down to their financial work as the first charge upon them, by the provision that they were not to engage any day in holding pleas, until the sheriff who was accounting had rendered his accounts in "full exchequer." "And let the barons take heed that no plea from henceforth be held in the exchequer without the king's special mandate, or unless the pleas concern the king in things appertaining to the place or his ministers there. And these things must be done in such a fashion that the execution of the accounts be not delayed or disturbed." Discipline in the whole office was braced up by the order that no accounting officer was to be represented by attorney, save by the king's leave, or through inability to travel, or other sufficient cause. Similarly, no clerk or other officer of the exchequer, or of the receipt, was to be admitted as an attorney in any manner of plea or account. Moreover, while the various clerks were bound to look closely after the rolls, the "chamberlains of the tallies" were "to put in order all the foils of tallies in their keeping."

In May 1324 the second ordinance of the exchequer was issued by the king and council at Westminster.[3] It supple-

[1] *Encyclopæd. Brit.*, eleventh edition, *s.v.* Exchequer.

[2] [He was not, as suggested in the first edition of this book, and in Mr. Johnson's article quoted above, "cursitor baron." *Cf.* Dr. Broome in *Eng. Hist. Rev.*, xxxviii, 67, n. 8. Fulburn, appointed 1323, ceased to act when Edward III became king. During the division of the exchequer, 1324-26, there were seven barons.]

[3] *Red Bk. Exch.*, iii, 908-29.

mented that of 1323. It was almost entirely devoted to speeding up the accounts of the keeper of the wardrobe by disembarrassing him of the many "foreign accounts" for which he had hitherto been responsible. It was now that the great wardrobe, the butlery, the victualling departments, the stud and stables, the hanaper, and the rest, were separated, as we have seen, from the wardrobe and made to account directly to the exchequer. The control of the exchequer over these offices was thus better secured, as it also was by such supplementary measures as the forbidding of "imprests," or partial advances, out of the wardrobe in times of peace, in lieu of the full wages and salaries due. The same object was furthered by the provision of a special clerk to recite and enrol documents from the household office sent to the exchequer, and, above all, by the ordering that the yearly accounts of the wardrobe, which were reckoned by the king's regnal years, which ended early in July,[1] should be put in order, so as to be presented to the exchequer at the beginning of its Michaelmas session next following.

A small but significant modification of tradition, now indirectly brought about, shows how the spirit of reform was in the air. About the time this ordinance was issued a remarkable change in the method of appointing escheators was effected. Up to 1324 there had been appointed one escheator for the counties north of Trent, and another for the district to the south of that river. Apparently two escheators were not regarded by the reformers as sufficient to accomplish the detailed and important work assigned to them. In the course of 1324 the two escheators were replaced by nine, or, if we include the escheator for North Wales, ten. Each of them had charge of a group of counties, such as, for example, Wiltshire, Hampshire, Oxfordshire, Bedfordshire, Buckinghamshire, and Berkshire. This system of a separate escheator for a small group of counties lasted for the rest of the reign. In 1327 Isabella and Mortimer

[1] *Red Bk, Exch.*, iii, p. 928. The regnal year of Edward II ended on 7 July. The wardrobe year, according to the ordinance, ended on 3 July. I do not understand why there was this difference of four days, since most accounts did as a matter of fact run through the regnal year of 8 July to 7 July. [The problem vanishes when it is noticed that the "feast of the translation of St. Thomas" named was almost certainly that of St. Thomas of Canterbury (7 July), not that of St. Thomas the apostle (3 July).] The vital point is that the keeper of the great wardrobe and the butler were to have their accounts ready by 30 Sept., and the keeper of the wardrobe a fortnight later.

went back to the old system, which was carried on until 1335. It was then definitively abandoned in favour of a modification of the plan first started in 1324. It is curious that the fashion of appointing escheators should thus vary with the vicissitudes of contemporary politics. Probably the relegation of the duties to more numerous officials was regarded by the court party as a more effective way of securing the rights of the crown.

Another projected exchequer reform of this period was said by a hostile chronicler to have arisen from the greediness and ambition of one of the barons of the exchequer. This was Sir Roger Bellers, a Leicestershire squire and a former Lancastrian partisan, who had won knighthood and his place at the exchequer by a timely desertion of earl Thomas in 1322. On 9 August 1325 Bellers was appointed as *locum tenens* of the treasurer, until the return of archbishop Melton, "who is going for some time to the north by the king's command." [1] Bellers is said to have proposed the division of the exchequer into two parts, hoping that he would himself be set over one of them, as proved to be the case.[2] Such a proposal was particularly appropriate when the northern metropolitan, anxious to spend part of his time in his province, was treasurer. Anyhow, a plan for legitimatising a fashion by which the exchequer could both have its headquarters at Westminster and also follow the court in its wanderings, may well have been an honest device to secure its more effective control of all finance by giving to the exchequer some of the mobility of the wardrobe. But the enemies of reforming courtiers looked upon it as a wanton attack on the tradition which regarded the exchequer as from all time one and indivisible.[3] The murder of Bellers in January 1326, as the result of a private feud in Leicestershire, was looked upon as God's judgment on the innovator. Every

[1] *C.P.R. 1324-27*, p. 159.

[2] [Mr. Tout printed in *Eng. Hist. Rev.*, xxxi, 462 (1916), the royal writ, dated 16 June 1324, which ordered this division into two parts, of one of which Bellers was to be chief baron. *Cf. Chapters*, ii, 211 and n. 2, and Conway Davies, *Baronial Opposition to Edw. II*, App. of documents, p. 562 (1918).]

[3] *Flores Hist.*, iii, 232: "Scaccarium domini regis apud Westmonasterium, prima sui institutione semper indivisum, superba sui praesumptione in duas partes dividi procuravit, ut et idem . . . coram ipso medietati praesideret, reliquam vero partem caeteris baronibus permisit regendam." But division was far from unprecedented. See above, p. 172 and n.

fresh change of exchequer arrangements, however, was in the direction of increased differentiation.

Even later than Bellers' collapse came the third exchequer ordinance, published at Westminster on 30 June 1326. The issue of so important a scheme of reformation when archbishop Melton was treasurer shows that Stapeldon was not the only radical head of the exchequer in these years. This ordinance was largely a re-enactment of that of 1323, in terms which suggest that the new system had not as yet become practical politics. Some useful new provisions were added, notably that which, while providing that the sheriffs' accounts shall be heard "in the full exchequer," since the exchequer of accounts has been of old a single body, and thus abolishing Bellers' division,[1] also ordered that the "foreign accounts" be heard and rendered in another house adjoining. It also provided for increased severity of audit, for the half-yearly control of the remembrancers by the treasurer and barons, for the annual enrolment by the "chancellor of the great seal and keeper of the privy seal" of all writs for payments in the exchequer,[2] and for the delivery by the escheators of their inquests and rolls into the exchequer. Some relief to the accounting officers was provided by the exchequer recognising writs of great or privy seal addressed to those functionaries, by virtue of which they had made payments from their revenues. Up to now such ministers had been put to the trouble and expense of obtaining a special mandate to the exchequer under great or privy seal, directing it to make the allowance aforesaid. Sheriffs and bailiffs were to be "sufficient persons" with "good estates of land in their counties." "And let not the sheriffs be so often changed as they have been."

How far were these ordinances executed? This question is an important one, but it can only be answered with any fullness by a scholar who will take the pains of working carefully through the exchequer records of the decade immediately succeeding the reforming ordinances, and comparing exchequer procedure at the end of Edward II and the

[1] [See *Red Bk. Exch.*, iii, 930: "qe leschequier des accountes soit un, come auncien temps fut establi."]

[2] *Ibid.*, 950. If this order was carried out by the keeper of the privy seal, there is no evidence of the present existence of what may be called a privy seal "liberate" roll. There are, however, numerous files of original privy seals, preserved by the exchequer, many of which are orders for the payment of money and therefore kept as "warrants for issues."

beginning of Edward III's reign with the business methods in use before 1322.[1] Such a task would be well worth attempting, and when some of the chief exchequer records are calendared in print, like the records of chancery, would not be an impossibly difficult one. One who has but dipped here and there into these records can only offer a strictly provisional and personal answer. There can be no doubt, however, that a real effort was made to put things straight, and the best proof of this is the fact that no subsequent accounts, either of the wardrobe or of the great wardrobe, figure in the pipe rolls, but are carefully audited by themselves and entered as "enrolled accounts," in rolls distinct from the pipe rolls of each year. However, the arrears in accounting were not to be made up in a day, and before the new system was well in working order, the disorders culminating in the revolution of 1326 stood in the way of immediate reform. If, then, these separate "enrolled accounts" go back as far as 1315-16, this circumstance is only evidence that they were made up years later than the time that they covered. It is more significant that the last pipe roll containing wardrobe accounts proper is that of 1322-23, when Benstead's belated accounts of 1307-9 were at last settled by his executors. The wardrobe accounts of 1315-16 and of subsequent years all appear in separate enrolments. But it was not until after 1330 that the final straightening out of these arrears was accomplished. The results are still to be seen in those magnificently written and finely bound volumes, which tell us, in meticulous detail and with many quite modern facilities for reference, what were believed, under Edward III, to have been the correct accounts of the wardrobe transactions in the days of his father. The feeling that they after all are not quite contemporary documents must rather chasten those who wish to use them. We can only hope that they are an honest attempt to get at the belated truth, and not faked for some ulterior purpose.

In some respects the Stapeldon-Melton reforms were slow in being executed. Thus, we find, in defiance of the ordinance of 1326, the hanaper accounts, the butler's accounts, the accounts of the king's horses, of the forests, of various

[1] The comparison of the memoranda rolls of the two remembrancers for these two periods should be of special interest, as showing to what extent the elaborate differentiation of the king's and treasurer's remembrancers' functions were actually carried out. [*Cf.* Prof. Willard's article cited above, p. 174.]

subsidiary wardrobes, some fragmentary chamber accounts, and many analogous accounts still appearing normally in the pipe rolls of the greater part of Edward III's reign, though the ordinance specifically classed most of them with the wardrobe accounts proper as "foreign accounts"[1] and ordered that they should be rendered and audited separately from the ordinary sheriffs' and ministers' accounts, and in the same fashion as those of the wardrobe. It seems that these accounts were separately audited,[2] but it was not until 42 Edward III that a separate roll of "foreign accounts," in addition to the "enrolled accounts" of the household and wardrobe series, became a matter of course. Thus slowly the ideas of the reformers of Edward II's exchequer became realised. But I should be much surprised if the more minute study, which some day may be expected to be bestowed on these problems, did not make it clear that the concluding years of our reign were even more emphatically a turning point in the history of the exchequer than they are in the history of the household.

[1] *Red Bk. Exch.*, iii. 932.

[2] See P.R.O. *List and Indexes*, no. xi, *List of Foreign Accounts*, and, especially, Introduction, p. iii.

## VI

# FOREIGN AND IMPERIAL POLICY, WARFARE, AND THE CHURCH

Up to this point, our interest in the reign of Edward II has rarely strayed from the administrative and constitutional fields. I would gladly have extended my survey to other aspects of Edwardian history, but it is impossible to do so within the limits prescribed to me. In two concluding chapters, I shall, however, endeavour to suggest in outline the general lines on which such a survey might be undertaken. The space that I shall devote to the consideration of the very miscellaneous subjects which I shall attempt to discuss, will, I must add, be determined not so much by their relative importance, as by my general wish rather to indicate new points of view than to emphasise once more a well recognised standpoint. Subject to this limitation, I now propose to deal briefly in the present chapter with Edward II's reign in its relation to external policy, the art of war, and the church, and, in the concluding chapter, to treat the social and economic development of the period. As in the previous chapter, nearly all that I have to say will have relation to the later and more eventful years of the reign. These sections may be regarded as supplementary to the story of political and administrative reform already told.

## (1) Foreign and Imperial Policy

There is no need to speak at any length on the external history of the reign of Edward II. The main facts concerning both Edward's relations to the British Islands and the foreign policy of the reign are sufficiently well known. The former seem a record of disaster; the latter a catalogue of futilities. Yet the failure of Edward II to carry out his father's imperialist plans produced permanent consequences in all the three kingdoms. Even the foreign policy of the reign, centring as usual round English dealing with France, is worth a little more attention than it usually receives. Let us deal with these subjects in turn.

## A. Scotland

I need not dwell once more on the collapse of the imperialistic visions of Edward I. The old king had half realised the forcible union of England with Scotland and Wales, and made some little effort to strengthen the decaying supremacy of the English lords of Ireland. Most of this work was now undone, and only in Wales did Edward I's policy leave behind it the results which he designed to accomplish. The successful vindication of Scottish independence by Robert Bruce made it certain, before Edward II's reign was over, that even Britain was to consist of two states and not one. Moreover there was trouble in the future when Edward II's successors strove from time to time to hark back to his inherited policy. There was also permanent danger to both countries, when the smaller northern state was constantly compelled to maintain its independence by playing into the hands of the foreign enemies of England. Yet we must never forget that the downfall of English ambitions was brought about almost as much by the slackness of the English baronage as by the valour of Bruce and his Scots and the ineptitude of Edward II. As far as claims went, the ordainers maintained their right to control the whole inheritance of Edward I. They formally included in their sphere the direction of the government of Scotland, Ireland and Gascony, as well as the direction of that of England.[1] We need not see in this either a prophetic vision of an imperial Britain in the future, or a simple suggestion of greediness, though in it there was more of the latter than of the former. The stolid indifference of the barons to great plans of premature centralisation was, I imagine, in no small measure due to the consciousness that the cause of Bruce was not altogether dissimilar to their own. We must not overstress their want of patriotism. Their instinct was that of their class all over Europe, and it in no wise made

[1] This comes out clearly in the "ordinationes comitum secundae" in *Ann. Lond.*, p. 202, where the barons added to the list of officers to be appointed by the baronage in parliament "bons et suffisaunces ministres en Gascoigne, Irelaunde et Escoce."

altogether for evil. Good peace and administration, disciplined government, and social progress were only obtainable, under mediæval conditions, by the establishment of many centres of political influence. We may no longer give to the monarchs of a few great countries all the credit for the building up of the modern nationalities of Europe. A good duke of Brittany or of Burgundy, a good duke of Austria or of Saxony, did the same sort of work of discipline and direction, within his sphere, as did any French king or Roman emperor of the German nation. And in the same way it is thinkable that the ultimate unity of Britain was better brought about by the failure of Edward II in Scotland than it would have been by the establishment of an over-great monarchy, based solely on force, yet too weak to control the remoter regions wherein it claimed to exercise power. The rule of English kings in Scotland might have been as bad for real national unity as was the domination of German monarchs in Italy for the national union of Germany.

## B. Ireland

Against the successful revolt of Scotland under Robert Bruce may be set the failure of Edward Bruce to destroy what remained of the English power in Ireland. Yet Edward Bruce's collapse was not so much to the benefit of the English crown as it was to the advantage of the Norman-Irish barons and the more purely Irish clan chieftains, who, for the next two hundred years, were to divide among themselves the government of Ireland, after a fashion which, if disorderly, was also picturesque and by no means incompatible with some real development of Irish civilisation. One potential means of developing Irish culture was secured under Edward II by the bull obtained from Clement V by archbishop Leek of Dublin in 1312 for the foundation of a university in Dublin.[1] This was not quite a "paper university," for after the war with Bruce was over, we find evidence that there were in the Dublin schools of the later years of this reign a few masters and scholars, for whose use archbishop Bicknor drew up statutes in 1320. In the next generation, however, the whole thing died out. The growing weakness of the central power made a university in Dublin impossible.

[1] Denifle, *Die Entstehung der Universitäten des Mittelalters*, i, 639-43; Rashdall, *Universities in the Middle Ages* (2nd edn., 1936), ii, 325-27.

Irish historians have generally admitted that the expedition of Edward Bruce was the turning point in the history of the Anglo-Norman "colony" in Ireland, and I have no reason for quarrelling with a view that fits in so agreeably with my general theme. We should be more confident in the justice of the verdict, were the history of fourteenth- and fifteenth-century Ireland worked out in the detail which the abundance of documents, both of official and national provenance, may well admit. Irish history has, of late years, been rightly receiving more attention than it has met with in the past.[1] But there is still a regrettable tendency for enquirers to limit their attention to one side of the evidence, and to select from it facts which seek to prove some modern political doctrine. We shall never get a real history of mediæval Ireland unless we are able to include both the "English" and the "Celtic" material in our survey, and unless we abandon the well-worn and meaningless generalisations about national characteristics, which have made historical study a buttress of prejudice and error on both sides alike. Celtic Ireland can only be understood when Celtic scholars will appreciate the importance of the archives of the governments, preserved in Dublin and London. Anglo-Norman Ireland can only be properly interpreted in the light of sympathetic appreciation of the Celtic point of view. For my part, I find it difficult to see much difference in practice between the methods of government of the Fitzgeralds and Butlers and those of the great Celtic clans. Feudal Ireland and Celtic Ireland are not so far apart as they are sometimes imagined. And both are a long way off any modern conception of an Irish nationality.

## C. Wales

The same revival of local independence which is characteristic of Scottish and Irish history under Edward II also manifested itself in the history of Wales, though conditions restricted the revival within narrower limits. Yet even if the Welsh of the principality made no more serious efforts to reverse history, the march of Wales was constantly alive with new movements, and there was constant interaction between the principality and the march. The politics of the

[1] [Since these words were written, Prof. Edmund Curtis has published his *History of Mediæval Ireland* (1923) and Dr. Orpen vols. iii and iv, covering the period 1216-1333, of his *Ireland under the Normans* (1920).]

Welsh march are so closely allied with the broadest streams of English history that I have perforce had to say much upon this subject at an earlier stage of this book. The recrudescence of feudal separatism in the march of Wales which at once followed the removal of Edward I's strong hand has already been noted. The agglomeration of groups of small marcher states in the hands of great houses, such as those of Mortimer, Fitzalan and Despenser, was the more emphatic when a Mortimer and a Fitzalan controlled in turn the government of the principality, which, nominally, was a source of strength to the king or a training ground for his son. But Edward of Windsor, the future Edward III, was never made prince of Wales, though he became earl of Chester in 1312,[1] and count of Ponthieu and duke of Aquitaine in 1325.[2] Between the rule of a Mortimer and an Arundel there was no room for a young prince. However, the unity of direction, which was common to principality and march alike, made for peace. Wales "rebelled very little" against Edward II. The plan of concerted action between Edward Bruce and the Welsh came to nothing,[3] collapsing with his Irish failure; and Sir Gruffydd Llwyd, of Trevgarnedd, the bardic hero of Welsh resistance to Edward II, is still of unproved historicity.[4] But this quietness of Wales is not to be set down so much to the sympathy of the Welsh for a Welsh-born king,[5] as some

[1] There is no record of Edward of Windsor's creation as earl of Chester, but on 24 Nov. 1312, when he was only eleven days old, he received by charter the counties of Chester and Flint (*C. Chart. R.*, iii, 202-3). Henceforth the chamberlain's accounts of Chester and Flint speak of him as earl, as, for instance, A. Jones' *Flintshire Ministers' Accounts, 1301-28*, p. 65, "the lord king . . . gave to the lord Edward his son, *now earl of Chester*." The undated account is with good reason assigned by Mr. Jones to the year 1312-13. In 1314, when aged two, Edward was first ordered as earl of Chester to supply troops against the Scots (*Parl. Writs*, II, ii, 427). In 1320, at the age of eight, Edward was summoned to parliament as earl of Chester (*ibid.*, II, ii, 219). [For further details see *Chapters*, iv, 69-70.]

[2] The appointments, by patent, not by charter, are dated 2 Sept. and 10 Sept. 1325 respectively (*Foedera*, ii, 607-8).

[3] Malmesb., p. 211.

[4] [Mr. J. G. Edwards in *Eng. Hist. Rev.*, xxx, 589-601 (1915), has shown that Llwyd was "no martyr in a national cause," but a loyal official of Edward's both as king and prince. *Cf. Chapters*, ii, 172 and n. 2, 209, n. 1.]

[5] Yet E.A. 373/15, a wardrobe book for 1307-8, shows *passim* wages paid to Welsh foot serving in the war against the Scots, or guarding the carriage of the king's wardrobe (f. 17 v°). Two Welsh trumpeters "made minstrelsy" before the king on various occasions (ff. 13, 13 v°, 19, etc.) [For other details as to Welsh in the service of Edw. II see *Chapters*, ii, 137, and for Welsh in his household when prince of Wales, *ibid.*, p. 172. On

people have imagined, as to the coercive power of the great English families, who in fact governed both principality and marches.

Some practical amelioration of the hard conditions of a conquered people undoubtedly took place, both in the principality and in the march. This process was begun in Edward's replies to the Kennington petitions, issued when he was still only prince of Wales,[1] and continued in the Lincoln ordinances for north and south Wales, issued on 7 February 1316.[2] But these ordinances, though referring markedly to the king's natural interest in his native land, cannot in any wise be set down to the personal action of Edward, who, as we have seen, was at the moment deprived of all real power in the interests of Thomas of Lancaster. Similarly, we cannot safely attribute to the Welsh-born prince's individual initiative either the repeated efforts made to remedy abuses and constrain the king's Welsh ministers to moderation,[3] or the issue of charters to additional north Welsh towns.[4] They are rather to be assigned to the gradual spirit of administrative reform which was so marked a feature of the time. In Wales, as in England, no one party or person can claim the credit of these. Mortimer of Chirk, as justice, promoted native-born Welshmen to sheriffdoms and other offices, against the commands of the central authority,[5] and Hugh Despenser strove to advance the economic prosperity of his south Welsh principality by making Cardiff, its capital, the seat of the staple of wool.[6] I have spoken elsewhere of the representation of Wales in the epoch-

his introduction at his court of the Welsh national instrument, the *crwth*, see Intro., pp. xlv-xlvi, in Johnstone, *Letters of Edw.*, and *cf.* Brit. Mus. Add. MS. 22923, f. 5 v.]

[1] *Record of Carnarvon* (Record Com.), pp. 212-25.

[2] *Foedera*, ii, 283-4. Prof. E. A. Lewis, in his excellent study of the *Mediæval Boroughs of Snowdonia*, pp. 232-7, gives some interesting observations on Edward's Welsh administration, which I have found very useful. [See also W. H. Waters, *The Edwardian Settlement of North Wales, 1284-1343* (1935).]

[3] *Cf.* letters patent dated 26 July 1320, which empowered commissioners sent by the king to Wales for the reformation of that land to remove inefficient sheriffs, constables and other ministers, except those holding office for life, whose acts, however, and "malpractises if any," were to be enquired into (*C.P.R. 1317-21*, pp. 492-3).

[4] Lewis, *op. cit.*, pp. 283-7, prints Edward's charters to Newborough (1303) and Bala (1324).

[5] *Rot. Parl.*, i, 273.

[6] *C.P.R. 1324-27*, p. 274. See also later, p. 235. Some glimpses of the state of trade in both the principality and the march at this period may be obtained from the summary of mediæval Welsh customs accounts in E. A. Lewis' "Contribution to the Commercial History of Mediæval Wales," in *Y Cymmrodor*, xxiv (1913).

making parliaments of 1322 and 1327.[1] As far as numbers went, the forty-eight Welsh representatives bulked larger than the corresponding members for English districts of the same size and importance; but it is noteworthy that on each occasion it was the principality only that sent representation. The march, not being in the king's hands, had no more claim than Cheshire or Durham to send members to an English parliament. We may connect, then, the beginnings of Welsh representation with the fact that Edward II always kept the government of the principality directly dependent upon himself. When the continuous English line of princes of Wales begins with the Black Prince, the principality had no more reason for being represented than any other palatinate. But I must not be tempted to develop any further a subject on which I would gladly have lingered. I have said enough to show the importance of the reign of Edward II in the conciliation and administration of Wales and its march. It is quite a mistake to think that the history of Wales stops short with the conquest of Gwynedd by Edward I, to be resumed, after a century and a quarter, with the meteoric appearance of Owen Glendower on the historic stage. However, until the history of fourteenth-century Wales has been written at length, it would be highly rash to indulge in confident generalisations about it. All I need say is that the subject is crying aloud for treatment, and that the materials for its investigation are extraordinarily ample.[2]

[1] See above, p. 136. On 18 April 1322, Arundel, as justice of Wales, was ordered to summon twenty-four "de discretioribus, legalioribus et validioribus hominibus" from South Wales, and a similar number of like persons from North Wales (*Foedera*, ii, 484). No return, however, is known to have been made to this writ. In 1327 similar writs were issued, and North Wales returned six members from both Carnarvonshire and Anglesea, and six from Merioneth, as well as two burgesses each from Beaumaris, Carnarvon and Conway boroughs (*Return of Members of Parliament*, i, 77). [On the peculiarities of the Merioneth writ see Mr. J. G. Edwards in *Eng. Hist. Rev.*, xxx, p. 595.] The absence of extant returns on the earlier occasion does not justify the conclusion that the Welsh members did not sit at York.

[2] My former pupil and colleague, Mr. Arthur Jones, Reader in History in the University of London, tells me that he is engaged on the study of this neglected subject. His edition of the *Flintshire Ministers' Accounts, 1301-28*, published through the enterprise of the Flintshire Historical Society (1913), is an excellent first step in that direction. Another pupil, Mr. J. G. Edwards, has also been devoting himself to the history of Wales between the Edwardian conquest and the death of Edward II. [The results of his studies were embodied in a thesis presented for the M.A. degree of the University of Manchester in 1915.]

## D. France and Gascony

Edward II ruled over his mother's county of Ponthieu and over such fragments of the Gascon inheritance of Eleanor of Aquitaine as the constant and successful aggressions of the French crown still left to him. As he held both Ponthieu and Gascony as fiefs of the French king, his feudal relations to his overlord immensely complicated the national relations of the English and French states. Indeed it is hard to disentangle the political relations of England and France from the problems of vassalage and feudal franchise which were so constantly bound up with them. Neither the general dealings of Edward II with his French neighbour and kinsman, nor his efforts to uphold his authority in Ponthieu and Gascony have as yet been examined in the detail which the copiousness of the materials allows, but the investigations are well worth making, even admitting that no great modifications of our general views of his policy can be expected to result from them. Enough, however, has been written by French historians of the general relations of Edward II to the four kings who governed France during his reign [1] to enable us to remedy to some extent the incuriousness of our English historians in the matter.[2] We find that, despite the near kinship and double marriage relation between the English and French royal houses and despite the very close social, political and commercial intercourse between the subjects, high and low, of the two realms, there was, underlying their apparent friendliness, a deep incompatibility of position which rendered a cordial understanding impossible. There was the constant problem of the relations of the French overlord to his Gascon vassal, the interminable debates as to the interpretation of the treaty of Paris of 1259 and of the subsequent explanatory

[1] Conspicuous among these I may mention M. Gavrilovitch, *Le Traité de Paris de 1259*, pp. 96-111 (1899); P. Lehugeur, *Histoire de Philippe le Long, 1316-22*, pp. 240-66 (1897), the best consecutive study of Anglo-French relations for any part of Edward II's reign with which I am acquainted; and E. Déprez, *Les Preliminaires de la Guerre de Cent Ans*, pp. 14-26 (1902). To them may be added E. Albe, " Les suites du traité de Paris de 1259 pour le Quercy," in *Ann. du Midi*, 23^e^ année, pp. 472-91; 24^e^ année, pp. 54-78, 218-31, 396-410 (1911-12). All these also touch on Anglo-Gascon questions. Miss H. Johnstone informs me that she has made collections to illustrate this subject, notably as to the " War of Saint-Sardos " and its preliminaries.

[2] [Miss E. Pole Stuart has printed in *Eng. Hist. Rev.*, xli, 412-15 (1926) a memorandum preserved among Chancery Miscellanea of a discussion between Philip V and Edward II at Amiens in July 1320.]

treaties. The "process" of Périgueux [1] of 1311 was as ineffective as the "process" of Montreuil had been before Edward II came to the throne. As time went on, there was a gradual intensification of the strain, which under Edward III was to make the Hundred Years' War inevitable.

In dealing with these questions, we are no longer working out the after results of the policy of Edward I. We see ourselves rather anticipating the special problems of the reign of Edward III. The personal friendliness between the courts made slow and doubtful the development of the strong forces which made for hostility. Yet in the conflict of these opposing tendencies, we discern how, insignificant as is the foreign policy of Edward II, it has some prospective importance by reason of the fact that the whole relations of the two realms centre round the constant undermining of the English power in Gascony and the vain efforts made by the agents of the English dukes to resist it. In the ineffective attempts to gloss over differences of policy by marriage bonds and personal ties we see the beginning both of the great war of the next reign and of the long efforts of diplomacy which retarded its outbreak until a good ten years after Edward II's death. Passing over minor difficulties that were for the moment smoothed over, we have, at the end of the reign, a real, though short, outbreak of hostilities in the "War of Saint-Sardos," whose whole course showed the futility of the previous efforts of the two courts to maintain the peace. In the inability of the English to resist French aggression; in the feverish efforts to raise armies, which would not materialise, to fight for the king's Gascon inheritance; in the occupation of Gascony by Charles of Valois almost without resistance; we learn that the inevitable struggle could have in the long run but one inevitable end. Gascony was, as under Edward III, the root of the troubles between the two kings; but already we have the contributing causes of the later and more famous rupture at work in the French championship of the Scots, in the rivalries of English and French sailors and traders, and in the close commercial relations of England with the great Flemish cities, at this time on quite irreconcilable

[1] There is a very convenient and clear summary of these negotiations in Madame Lubimenko's *Jean de Bretagne, comte de Richmond*, pp. 80-91. Gavrilovitch, *op cit.*, pp. 124-44, prints the minutes of the *processus* and the long grievances of the English.

terms with their French overlord. Nothing essential is wanting, save the English king's claim to the French throne, and that, as we now recognise, was not at the root of the Hundred Years' War.

Turning from Edward II's general French policy to his administration of Ponthieu and Gascony, we see the same notes of normal feebleness of control, and spasmodic, though earnest, efforts towards reform, which characterised his policy in numerous other directions. With regard to Ponthieu I have nothing to say, but am content to leave the subject to the competent scholar who is now engaged in investigating it.[1] As regards Edward's southern dominions,[2] the ordinances of 1311 had declared that Gascony, like Ireland and Scotland, was in peril of being lost for lack of good ministers, and provided that "good and sufficient ministers" should be chosen by the baronage to replace these unworthy officers.[3] The ordinances were so far respected that they saved Gascony from the heavy hand which the Frescobaldi had laid upon its finances, but it can hardly be said that any other material amelioration of its condition resulted from them. The short-lived seneschals of Edward II[4] had not a sufficient tenure of power to be able to carry out any real reforms, even if they had actually ruled at Bordeaux for the whole of their brief periods of office. But they were sometimes absentees; were sometimes engaged in negotiations at Paris or some nearer centre of French diplomacy; and were all hopelessly crippled by the embarrassed state of the finances of the duchy and the constant calls for pecuniary assistance made by the English king for his own purposes. In any case, officials who were changed more than twenty times in the twenty years of the reign could hardly have hoped to exercise any real authority. On the whole, it is a wonder that they did so well as they did.

The financial officers of Gascony, the constables of Bordeaux, held office [rather] longer than the seneschals.

[1] [For Edward's administration of Ponthieu before his accession to the English throne see H. Johnstone, "The County of Ponthieu, 1279-1307," in *Eng. Hist. Rev.*, xxix, 435-52 (1914).] For its seneschals see App. II, p. 352.

[2] [For recent English work on these, see Dr. Eleanor Lodge's *Gascony under English Rule* (1926) and summary in *Bull. Inst. Hist. Research,* v, 171-4, of an unpublished London Ph.D. thesis on "Some Aspects of the political and administrative history of Gascony, 1303-27," by Miss E. Pole Stuart.]

[3] *Rot. Parl.*, i, 282.

[4] For personal details see App. II, pp. 349-50.

There were only [thirteen] constables during twenty years, and some of them had a reasonable period of authority. But in Gascony, as in England, the real element of continuity was supplied by the officials of secondary rank. The best instance is the case of the controller of the castle of Bordeaux, the minister who stood to the constable [1] in the same relation as that in which the chamberlains stood to the treasurer of the exchequer, or the controller of the wardrobe to its keeper. To this office Edward I appointed John Guitard to act during the king's pleasure, from 30 March 1305. Guitard retained this place for the whole of Edward II's reign, and was still in office in the early years of Edward III. This is the more significant as Guitard was a Gascon clerk, working with Gascon subordinates, and often called upon to discharge higher functions when the constable was absent from his post.[2] In him and his subordinate Aubert Mège [3] lay the real continuity of Gascon administration, which went on much in the same way, whatever English nobleman, or English clerk, happened from time to time to be sent out to represent the home authority. Thus in Gascony, as in England, the subordinate officials did most of the work, and upheld under great difficulties the traditions of orderly and sound government.

The finances of Gascony were closely conditioned by those of England and the constable and controller were expected to account regularly before the exchequer at Westminster. The worst troubles of Gascony were financial, and between 1309 and 1311 the duchy was the prey of the grasping Amerigo dei Frescobaldi, who was made constable of Bordeaux, though he never resided there, but acted through his deputy, Ugolino Ugolini. The ordinances did Aquitaine the good service of getting rid of the Frescobaldi, though they also turned loose on their native land spoilers

[1] His function was "ad audiendum et testificandum reddicionem compotorum" of the constable of Bordeaux and the receivers of customs at Bordeaux (*R.G.*, iii, no. 4718). This function was supposed to involve annual attendance at the exchequer at Westminster.

[2] Guitard was also "custos sigilli quo in Burdegalesio utimur ad contractus" (G.R. 24, m. 23). He often acted as deputy of the constable. [In 1297 he had been in the household of John of Brittany (Lubimenko, *op. cit.*, pp. 50, 137).]

[3] He was for many years "contrarotulator maiorie ville nostre Burdigale et scriptor scribanie prepositure Umbrarie nostre Burdigale." "L'Ombrière" was the castle of Bordeaux. Aubert became constable in 1326.

so expert as the Calhaus, whom the favour of their kinsman, Gaveston, had for a time attracted to wider fields of exploitation in England. The remedy now adopted was the renewal of the system of Edward I's reign. But the restoration of the financial control of an absentee English constable, acting through Gascon agents, was not a sufficiently strong measure to retrieve the difficulties of the situation. The English government, whether controlled by Edward or by the barons, expected to get from Gascony appreciable subventions for carrying out its ambitious schemes in England. Failing these, it saw no remedy save the pledging of Gascon revenues as a security for loans absorbed in the general service of the English crown.

A temporary salvation was now to come from pope Clement V. What Clement had done as pope for Edward II we shall soon see.[1] But Clement never forgot that he was a Gascon nobleman, a born subject of the Gascon duke, and a former archbishop of Bordeaux. From 1305 to 1308, it looked as if his only difficulty was whether he should rule the church universal from Gascony or from Poitou.[2] He never lost a chance of restoring to their ancient opulence the family of the Gots, and his nepotism, unsatisfied with five cardinal nephews and as many duchies and rectorships in Romagna, ultimately took the form of providing his numerous kinsfolk with castles, lands, treasure and churches in Gascony.[3] At his native place, Villandraut,[4] he erected one of the completest and most dignified of Gascon castles, and there and at Uzeste[5] he endowed colleges of secular clerks for whose service he erected stately churches.[6] Two

[1] See below, pp. 206-7.

[2] This is clearly brought out even by the skeleton itinerary of Clement, in Mas Latrie, *Trésor de Chronologie*, pp. 1124-7.

[3] Ehrle, in *Archiv für Literatur- und Kirchengeschichte*, v, 148, enumerates 10 brothers and sisters and 22 nephews and nieces of Clement V.

[4] Villandraut, chef-lieu de canton, ar. Bazas, dep. Gironde. It was anciently styled Saint-Martin du Got.

[5] Uzeste, cant. Villandraut (5 kilometres), ar. Bazas, dep. Gironde.

[6] Details of Clement's position as a Gascon nobleman are given in E. Berchon, "Histoire du pape Clément V," in *Actes de l'Académie de Bordeaux*, 3me série, 55me année, 1893, pp. 493-535. See also F. Lacoste, *Nouvelles Etudes sur Clément V* (Bordeaux, 1896); C. Wenck, *Clemens V und Heinrich VII* (Halle, 1880); and Ehrle, "Process über den Nachlass Clemens V," in *Archiv für Literatur- und Kirchengeschichte*, v, 1-158 (1889). Both Ehrle's comments and the texts throw special light on Clement's financial relations with Edward II. Clement's *Regesta* have been published *in extenso* in eight magnificent folios at the cost of Leo XIII (Rome, 1884-1892).

of his kinsfolk entered the higher circle of Gascon nobility when his nephew Bertrand de Got became viscount of Lomagne and Auvillars,[1] and when Bertrand's daughter and heiress, Reine, became the wife of John, count of Armagnac.[2] The resources of the papacy swelled the scanty patrimony of the house of Got, and the pope, as a private person, was ever willing to embark on any speculation which, if of doubtful financial attractiveness, would at any rate glorify his family and increase his hold on his fatherland.

The necessities of Edward II now gave Clement his opportunity. After long negotiations conducted by papal agents, Clement agreed, *tanquam persona priuata*, to advance him a sum of 160,000 golden florins of Florence, the equivalent of £25,000 sterling, on condition that the whole "issues" of Gascony were handed over to the pope or his nominees to administer.[3] A small sum, of £30,000 *chapotenses* for each of the first two years and £18,000 *chap.*[4] subsequently, was to be paid back by the pope to Edward to enable him to meet the expenses of maintaining the duchy. The contract was announced on 28 October 1313; the whole sum was paid down in the course of March 1314, and the issues were handed over to the pope's nominees on 16 March.[5] But Clement died on 20 April, and, when his remains were entombed in his own church of Uzeste, there was an end to any schemes he may have entertained for establishing his family in Gascony in such a position as to anticipate, however slightly, the glorious territorial nepotism of the popes of the Renascence.

[1] Lomagne, capital Lectoure, comprised most of the modern arrondissement of Lectoure, dep. Gers, and the cantons of Beaumont and Lavit, dep. Tarn-et-Garonne. Auvillars is an adjacent canton of that name in Tarn-et-Garonne, the three cantons constituting the whole of that department south of the Garonne.

[2] This was the John I of Armagnac who survived to be the great enemy of the Black Prince. His marriage with Reine took place in 1311, but on her death in 1325 (*Foedera*, ii, 609) Lomagne went to John and became permanently part of Armagnac, Lectoure later becoming the capital of that county.

[3] The contract is printed in *ibid.*, 231-2, from the Gascon roll. Pains were taken to procure its confirmation by Philip V (*ibid.*, ii, 232). For the method of payment see Ehrle, *op. cit.*, p. 45.

[4] The "libra chapotensis" or "chipotensis," a usual currency in Aquitaine, was of lower value than the *livre tournois*, £1 5s. *ch.* being equivalent to £1 *tour.* As the pound sterling was worth £4 *tour.*, it was equivalent to £5 *ch.* Such sums as £6,000 and £3,700 sterling were ridiculously inadequate to pay for the expenses of government in Aquitaine.

[5] *C.P.R. 1313-17*, p. 205. Each florin was evaluated as three shillings and three halfpence sterling. Clement also lent 100,000 florins or more to Philip the Fair (Ehrle, p. 91).

In his testament Clement V left the bulk of his vast accumulated treasure to his nephew Bertrand, on the condition, which may or may not have been a real one, of employing the major part of it on the projected crusade and other pious uses. The possession of this great store gave the viscount of Lomagne continued importance during the long papal interregnum, but the unfulfilled conditions afforded John XXII an opportunity of attacking him, which involved a famous trial in the years between 1318 and 1321, and ended in the unconditional submission of Bertrand. A side issue of this process was the question of Clement's loan to Edward II. By the terms of the contract, Bertrand and the other executors and heirs of Clement V continued to receive the issues of Gascony for several years. This period, between 1314 and 1317, is called in Gascon history the "time of the obligation," [1] and the Gascon rolls give abundant evidence of the difficulties in which the government was involved by the appropriation of the local revenues to foreign collectors. There was appointed, doubtless on the Gots' nomination, a new constable of Bordeaux, a clerk named Aicard Barbe, who accounted for the receipts on behalf of "those having a claim for the receipt of the issues of the duchy by reason of the obligation." [2] The subordinate receivers of Saintonge and Agenais equally acted as the agents of the king's inexorable creditors.[3]

To make matters worse, Edward II got little benefit from Clement's loan. The whole sum was paid over to Antonio di Passano [4] of Genoa, who after 1311 stepped into the place left vacant by Amerigo dei Frescobaldi, and recouped himself after this fashion for the advances which he doled out to keep up the king's household and government.[5] It is

[1] "de tempore obligacionis" (Misc. Bks. Exch. T.R., 187, p. 191).

[2] "Recepta de compoto domini Aicardi Barbe, constabularii Burdegale, pro causam habentibus in recepcione exituum ducatus predicti virtute obligacionis" (*ibid.*, p. 192).

[3] *Ibid.*, p. 191.

[4] [Mr. Tout adopted the form Passano instead of Pessagno for this surname in the belief that Antonio came from Passano in the Riviera. For reasons and details see *Chapters*, ii, 315, n. 1.]

[5] *C.P.R. 1313-17*, pp. 203-6, records payments made by Anthony amounting to £111,505 15s. 8½d., for which he had accounted at the wardrobe and received bills of the wardrobe. Among his receipts were the £25,000 from Clement V (*ibid.*, p. 205). The date of Anthony's quittance is 27 Nov., 1314. He was appointed on 18 Oct., 1313, to receive Clement's loan (G.R. 28, m. 10). In 7 Edw. II the receipts of queen Isabella's wardrobe were "de Antonio de Pysane £5,303 11s.; summa totalis recepti £5,559 18s. 11d." (E.A. 375/9). Anthony thus practically supported the queen's establishment for the whole of the year.

no wonder that Edward strove to go beyond his ordinary taxes in Aquitaine, and that he sent on a special mission to his duchy Sir John Benstead and Thomas of Cambridge, the ex-chief baron of the exchequer, to solicit contributions from the Gascons towards the expenses of his war against the Scots.[1] There is no evidence that these efforts were rewarded by any considerable success.[2]

The "time of the obligation" continued until November, 1317, when a remarkable attempt was made to set things straight. This was no less than the appointment of Passano, the king's chief creditor, as seneschal of Gascony.[3] The financier is no longer "our beloved merchant" but "Sir Anthony of Passano, knight." His nomination is worth recording as the first instance of a creditor of the merchant class being advanced to a great office of state hitherto limited to noblemen. His mission was to resume into the king's hands the issues of Gascony from the executors of Clement V and to obtain their consent to this step.[4] But the appointment was not a success, and was not of long duration. Anthony was only a year in office and spent part of that in negotiations with John XXII at Avignon. However, he won over the consent of the viscount of Lomagne to the termination of the obligation, and so fulfilled the great object of his mission. Bertrand, already involved in his litigation with John XXII, was in no position to make a stiff fight and the English king made a serious effort to pay his debt to him. Accordingly, in July 1318, the accounts of the "time of the obligation" were rendered before the archbishop of Bordeaux.[5] But it was no great change for the

[1] G.R. 30, m. 20. Their credentials are printed in *Foedera*, ii, 273-4, under the date 17 July 1315. Among the persons they solicited for aid was the viscount of Lomagne himself, from whom a further loan of 60,000 gold florins was sought (*ibid.*, ii, 259). Cambridge's account for expenses is in E.A. 309/22.

[2] Their report is in Chanc. Miscell., 26/10.

[3] *Foedera*, ii, 345. The date is 3 Nov.

[4] G.R. 32, m. 16, "ad resumendum in manum nostram omnes exitus ducatus predicti de executoribus testamenti bone memorie domini Clementis nuper pape quinti," etc.

[5] *Ibid.*, m. 7. The relevant documents, now probably lost, were calendared in "Stapeldon's Calendar" as including "Instrumentum principale super fine compotorum exituum ducatus Aquitanie factum coram archiepiscopo Burdegale," and the "Ratificatio . . . per dominum B. vicecomitem Leomanie et Altiuillarie" (Misc. Bks. Exch., clxxxvii, f. 192). Bertrand recovered a large part of what the pope had advanced to Edward (Ehrle, *op. cit.*, pp. 40, 57). He got nothing back of his uncle's loans to the French king (*ibid.*, pp. 57, 135).

better to get out of the hands of the old pope's executors into those of Anthony. The complaints which invariably followed his appointments to any office [1] had already begun to flow to England, and he was in November charged to attend in person at Westminster to render his own account of his stewardship.[2] He was at once replaced by Sir William Montagu, and with that practically ends the Genoese adventurer's connection with English history. He was never seen in England for many years, though so late as 1320 he was still offered safe-conducts to induce him to tender his accounts to the exchequer.[3] Later on he became a bitter enemy of Edward II, and in 1325 was accused of inciting his brother Manuel, the admiral of the king of Portugal, to send an armada for the invasion of England.[4]

The administration of Gascony went back to normal lines under the seneschalship of Sir William Montagu, after whom there was sent to Gascony the ex-wardrobe clerk, Richard of Elsfield, as constable of Bordeaux.[5] There ensued, however, a continued series of changes in the office of seneschal, which prevented a real improvement. The period of confusion had relaxed the duke's hold over his duchy, and made it impossible for his officers to resist the steady encroachments of the French king on his sovereign rights. Appeals to the French court were encouraged, and it was but natural that sufferers from such an intolerable régime as that of Arnold Calhau, the English seneschal of Saintonge, should carry their complaints to a powerful and sympathetic overlord.[6]

[1] See, for example, the complaints of the Cornish tinners against him, when, after the fall of Gaveston, Anthony obtained a commission to buy all the tin produced in Devon and Cornwall. In 1316 the tinners procured the revocation of the patent (G. R. Lewis, *The Stannaries*, pp. 142-3, 241-2, *Harvard Hist. Studies*, 1908).

[2] G.R. 32, m. 5.

[3] *C.P.R. 1317-21*, p. 508, a safe-conduct dated 11 Oct. 1320, and available till the Michaelmas following. Compare *C.C.R. 1318-23*, p. 85, an order to the exchequer of 8 June 1319, to audit with all speed the accounts of what Passano had received in Gascony for the king's use.

[4] G.R. 37, m. 12d. The king speaks of Anthony as "quidam A. de P. noster olim familiaris." Next year, however, Manuel was an ambassador from Portugal to Edward offering an alliance (*Foedera*, ii, 625). In 1332, Anthony, though still having doubtful relations with the exchequer, was again the king's counsellor and ambassador to France.

[5] Elsfield was *ostiarius garderobe* in 1314-15 (E.A. 376/7). [Miss E. Pole Stuart, who is preparing for publication an article on Richard's constableship, finds that he was still usher in 1318. She has printed in *Bull. Inst. Hist. Research*, x, 178-80 (1933), a letter written by Elsfield when constable to Richard of Ferriby, formerly his colleague in the wardrobe.]

[6] See for these *Foedera*, ii, 351-2. We must not overstress his acquittal in 1317. He was a relative of Gaveston. See above, p. 12, n. 1.

So early as 1314 the suzerain was sure enough of his power to forbid the circulation of "sterling" and the minting or circulation of Bordeaux moneys within the duchy, as infringing the uniformity of monetary standard which was claimed to be the law of France.[1]

All through the reign strong external and internal sources of evil had been acknowledged, and frequent proposals for reform had been sent to England by the seneschal and his council. Moreover, the need of reform was recognised by the despatch from time to time of commissions from England, which, if possible sources of reformation, must also have restricted in various ways the not over great authority of the seneschals for the time being. Bishop Salmon of Norwich, John earl of Richmond, Guy Ferre and the other English representatives at the abortive Périgueux conferences of 1311 had also been charged with ordering the king's affairs in Aquitaine.[2] They busied themselves with such matters as setting up a court of appeal in Gascony, to avoid the necessity of recourse to the parliament of Paris, with the organisation of public archives in Gascony, with the remedying of troubles in Bordeaux and the like.[3]

More systematic commissions of reform began when the Pembrokian triumph established a wiser rule in England. The first commission was that of Hugh le Despenser the elder and Bartholomew Badlesmere, despatched in February 1320 to enquire as to the excesses of the seneschal and inferior officers of Gascony.[4] Next came the appointment of John Hotham, bishop of Ely, and Amaury de Craon, the former seneschal, in February 1324,[5] and that of Alexander Bicknor, archbishop of Dublin, Edmund, earl of Kent, and William of Weston, doctor of laws, in March 1324 for the reformation of the rule of Gascony.[6] Their destination in the first instance was Paris, to appease the troubles which the "affair of Saint-Sardos" had recently exacerbated. Nothing effective was done there and on 20 July 1324 Edmund's appointment as king's lieutenant threw on him the responsibility of resisting French invasion as well as of retaining the duchy. Kent's failure in the first task gave him the opportunity of under-

[1] *Foedera,* ii, 240, 250. See also Déprez, *Les Préliminaires de la Guerre de Cent Ans*, p. 24.

[2] G.R. 25, m. 6.

[3] See for these matters Lubimenko, *op. cit.*, pp. 91-101.

[4] *Foedera,* ii, 418; G.R. 33, m. 11.

[5] *Ibid.*, 35, m. 7.

[6] *Ibid.*, m. 5; *Foedera,* ii, 547-8. The commissions vary, as do the names of the commissioners.

taking the second. However, before the end of 1324, all Gascony save Bordeaux, Bayonne and Saint-Sever was in the hands of Charles of Valois.[1]

Negotiations for peace soon followed ; and it was arranged that the king's son, Edward, earl of Chester, should receive Aquitaine and perform homage to Charles IV for it. On 10 September 1325 Edward was appointed duke.[2] He soon made his way to France, accompanied by his mother, and did homage to his uncle. A partial restitution of Gascony followed, leaving the Agenais in French hands. But Edward II never allowed his youthful son more than the title of duke of Aquitaine. The administration was still continued in the name of the king, who styled himself " governor and administrator " of his son's lands.[3] Accordingly, he appointed the last seneschal, Oliver of Ingham and the last constable, Aubert Mège, who ruled what was left of his son's duchy until the return of both son and wife precipitated the revolution which hurled Edward II from the throne.

Such periods of war and invasion naturally left their mark on the history of Gascony. Accordingly, the last important Gascon reform was that embodied in the royal ordinance issued on 8 February 1323 at Pontefract.[4] By it a serious effort was made to give unity of administration to the whole of the king's dominions in southern France. It sought to maintain the supremacy of the seneschal over the whole of the duchy, by the provision that the subordinate seneschals of Agenais, Périgord, Saintonge and the Landes, and the hardly less important mayor of Bordeaux, should receive their commissions under the Gascon seal, instead of directly from the English chancery. Similarly, the financial supremacy of the constable of Bordeaux was secured by the enactment that henceforth he should appoint the treasurers and receivers of the minor *sénéchaussées* and that they should account to him. It was also laid down that a Gascon chancery should be erected under a " sufficient clerk, learned in written law, as chancellor and keeper of the seal," who was to " live on the profits of the seal," and be appointed by the seneschal and council. The policy of setting up " seals for

[1] *Cont. Guillaume de Nangis,* ii, 58, ed. Géraud, Soc. de l'histoire de France, 1843.
[2] *Foedera,* ii, 607-8.
[3] " Edwardi filii nostri primogeniti, Aquitanie ducis, ac comitis Cestrie, Pontiui, et Montisstrolii, ac terrarum ac rerum ipsius gubernator et administrator."
[4] *Foedera,* ii, 505-6.

contracts," hitherto only allowed at Bordeaux, was to be extended to Blaye, Libourne, Saint-Macaire and La Bastide de Créon.[1] Moreover, the number of ministers in Gascony and their fees were strictly defined.

This interesting ordinance shows how the reforming spirit, so strong in England, was also extended to Gascony. It had hardly become law when the political troubles with France came to a head. The results of the war of Saint-Sardos and the ensuing conquests of Charles of Valois gave the friends of the English king's power in southern France no further opportunity of putting their house in order.

## (2) The Art of War

Let us now turn to the chief lessons of the military history of the reign. As most of the fighting that mattered took place within the three kingdoms, its more obvious morals have always been brought home to us. That Bannockburn was a turning point in tactics, as well as in politics, is among the commonplaces of history. Yet most of the recent accounts of the great battle seem to me to be constructed on essentially wrong lines. I may say this without giving offence, since my own attempts at describing the battle are among those open to reproach. We have assumed that Bannockburn was a defensive battle of immobile Scottish pikemen, holding a carefully prepared position, north of the Bannock, in the broken and wooded land through which ran the direct route from the south to Stirling. The recent writings of Mr. W. M. Mackenzie,[2] and a visit to the traditional site of the engagement, have convinced me that the true story of the battle is something quite different. Though Bruce had carefully prepared to fight in the spot where he is generally supposed to have fought, his success in the skirmishes of 23 June made it desirable, and possible, for him to change his whole plan of operations. Disheartened

[1] [This is the correct form of the name given in the first edition as Craon. M. Bémont pointed out to Mr. Tout that the name of Amaury de Craon's *bastide* underwent this modification, just as Roger de Leyburn's became Libourne, the bishop of Bath's Baa, and so on.]

[2] These are "The Real Bannockburn," in *Transactions of the Glasgow Historical Society* (1910); the notes to Mr. Mackenzie's edition of Barbour's *Bruce* (1909), and his *Battle of Bannockburn: A Study of Mediæval Warfare* (1913). [Some of Mr. Mackenzie's conclusions have recently been challenged by Rev. Thomas Miller, a native of the district, in a pamphlet entitled "The site of the battle of Bannockburn" (*Hist. Assoc.*, 1931).]

by Gloucester's failure in the scuffle along the high road, alarmed at the defeat of Clifford's horsemen by Randolph's pikemen in the "carse" to the north-east, the English army abandoned, on the evening of 23 June, all intention of accepting battle in the place carefully prepared for them, and moved bodily into the carse, where the troops encamped for the night "upon a plain near the water of Forth, beyond Bannockburn, an evil, deep and wet marsh, having sadly lost confidence through the events of the day." [1]

The sore plight of the English was well known to Bruce. Accordingly, on the morning of Midsummer day, he took the bold course of leaving his strong position and marching into the carse. This movement was a virtual challenge to the English to fight further to the north-east in the level ground nearer the Forth, a position very much to their disadvantage. Bruce's success on this field meant the ruin of the English, but victory could only be secured by the defeat of cavalry by infantry in a level plain. The battle of St. John's day was fought between armies facing each other on lines running almost north and south. The English right rested on the Forth, opposite Cambuskenneth, and was in easy communication with Stirling. Its left extended nearly to the lower Bannock, and retreat was only possible, save in the direction of Stirling, by crossing the Forth or the Bannock. Mr. Mackenzie emphasises the fact that the Scots attacked the English. It is perhaps injudicious to press this point too far. I should admit, however, that they threw themselves into the way of their enemy and deliberately forced a battle. It is hard, however, to believe that Bruce in 1314 ventured upon what the English commanders of the Hundred Years' War never dared to risk, namely, to attack with dismounted followers a heavily-mounted army of men-at-arms. On the contrary, it seems almost certain that, when the two hosts got into close quarters, the English horse took the immediate initiative by charging the dense "schiltrons" of Scottish pikemen.[2] But when the attack failed to break through the impenetrable array, the Scots in their turn assumed the offensive. The English horsemen were easily beaten; the infantry hardly got into action; of both arms, the luckiest were those who fled towards Stirling and

[1] *Scalacronica*, p. 142.

[2] *Chron. de Lanercost*, p. 225. "Et magni equi Anglorum irruerunt in lanceas Scottorum, sicut in unam densam silvam."

thence escaped home by circuitous routes. Great numbers were drowned in the Forth and the Bannock, and so, in one day, the freedom of Scotland was secured.

Two of the chief authorities for the battle compare the struggle in set terms with the Flemish victory over the chivalry of France at Courtrai, twelve years before.[1] How close the analogy was will not be realised until some one takes the pains to compare in detail the incidents of the first two victories of pikemen over feudal cavalry in western Europe. Here it is enough to say that, while the shame of Courtrai was soon wiped out for the French by the glories of Mons-en-Pevèle, there was no reversal of the verdict of the victory of St. John's day. Important as is the position of Bannockburn in the history of tactics, it is not quite a precedent for purely "defensive battles" such as Crécy and Poitiers. The lessons that the Scottish tactics were only safe in a defensive fight was only learnt at Halidon Hill, which saw the easy discomfiture of the Scottish schiltrons, charging up the slope against the men-at-arms, flanked by archers, who were stationed to meet them on the crest of the hill. We must not, however, treat the Scottish pikemen as if they were light-armed irregulars, like the Welsh and Irish auxiliaries of the English. On the contrary, they were, like the Flemish infantry at Courtrai, solidly equipped, well disciplined and adequately armoured warriors, who if not technically "men-at-arms" were fitted to cope with them on equal conditions.[2] The superiority of such a force over mounted men-at-arms was at once made clear to every English warrior who had experience of northern warfare. It was driven home still more when, in 1319, the aggressive schiltrons of Scotland scattered the "disorderly array"[3]

[1] Malmesb., p. 206, and *Scalacronica*, p. 142.

[2] The Scots, who fought on foot, rode horses on the march; *cf*. Trokelowe, p. 84, "equos suos penitus dimittebant." Lanercost, p. 239, shows that at Myton in 1319 the Scots forming the schiltron of pikemen, on winning the day, "equos suos ascenderunt, et Anglicos sequebantur." Malmesb., p. 203, also speaks of the Scots in terms which suggest dismounted "hobelers," if not men-at-arms. He describes them as ready for battle "cum magna multitudine armatorum." "Et nullus eorum equum ascendit, sed erat unusquisque eorum *levi armatura munitus, quam non faciliter penetraret gladius*." No very light armour could have warded off sword thrusts. Compare what *Annales Gandenses* (p. 32) say of the Flemings at Courtrai—where the French men-at-arms succumbed to infantry, but not light infantry, for they were opposed "vulgaribus Flamingis et peditibus, licet fortibus et virilibus, bene armatis et cordatis, et expertos gubernatores habentibus."

[3] I borrow the phrase from the *Scalacronica*, p. 148.

of Yorkshire in the battle of Myton, and, in 1322, drove Edward II to panic flight from Byland or Rievaux to Bridlington.[1]

That the English soon learnt their lesson is clear from the details of the battle of Boroughbridge, where the Cumberland knight, Andrew Harclay, governor of Carlisle, and a warrior of great experience against the Scots, easily defeated the demoralised Lancastrians by holding the passage over the Ure with a force of dismounted knights and men-at-arms arranged in a schiltron after the Scottish fashion.[2] Engaged in a purely defensive battle, and strengthened by better archery support than the Scots had at Bannockburn, Harclay made short work of the followers of the rebellious earls, though they also dismounted their men-at-arms for the assault on the bridge. Boroughbridge, with its defensive tactics and its effective archery, is a step nearer Crécy than Bannockburn, and deserves a more prominent place than has always been allowed to it in military history, just as Harclay, for his quick adaptation of Bruce's methods, and his shrewd improvements on them, merits a permanent fame among our mediæval masters of the art of war. Nor did Harclay stand alone, for in the abortive expedition of 1322, the last attempt under Edward II to invade Scotland in force, the English deliberately preferred heavy infantry to cavalry and even to archers.[3] I have now said enough to show that the reign of Edward II was a turning point in military history, since it witnessed the critical stages of the transition from the fashion of fighting under Edward I to the English military system of the Hundred Years' War.

## (3) Ecclesiastical Policy

We must now make an abrupt transition to the ecclesiastical history of the reign. Edward II inherited from his

[1] The battle was on the steep hill north of Byland. It is uncertain whether Edward was at Byland or Rievaux (*Chron. de Melsa,* ii, 346). Bridlington (p. 79) says at Byland, and he ought to know, but several chroniclers say at Rievaux. Sir James Ramsay over emphasises the evidence for Rievaux (*Genesis of Lancaster,* i, 133). I regret that the precise and valuable account of Edward II's reign given in this work was published too late for me to use it as much as it deserves.

[2] See my note on "The Tactics of the Battles of Boroughbridge and Morlaix," in *Eng. Hist. Rev.*, xix, 711-13. [Republished in *Collected Papers,* ii, 221-31.] The source for the details is *Chron. de Lanercost,* pp. 243-4.

[3] See J. E. Morris, "Cumberland and Westmorland Military Levies," in *Trans. Cumberland and Westmorland Archæological Assoc.*, new ser., iii, 324.

father the two rather conflicting points of view which, at various times, had determined the old king's attitude to problems of church and state. There was the heroic, but rather fruitless, policy of conflict, which had come to a head in the struggles with Peckham and Winchelsea, and had made its mark in legislation in the anti-clerical statute of Mortmain and the anti-papal statute of Carlisle of 1307. There was also the more normal feeling that it was as well for an orthodox king to keep on friendly terms with the ecclesiastical authorities and that, with an accommodating pope, like Clement V, it was a waste of energy to carry on the old heroics. Though Winchelsea came back from exile as soon as Edward II was on the throne, and though the returned archbishop threw all his weight on to the side of the ordinances, it was the policy of mutual accommodation that prevailed in this reign and so secured the general friendship of crown and papacy, of church and state. Accordingly, there is no period of the reign in which there is the least suggestion of the renewal of the chronic mediæval conflict of the "two swords." On the contrary, the time may be regarded as one in which the loosely grasped secular sword was pushed aside by the more skilfully directed sword of the church. Under Clement V, the first of the two popes of the reign, friendly relations were facilitated by reason of the pope's willingness to resign to the crown the lion's share of the material spoils of the church. Under the dominating and dogmatic John XXII, his successor, the renewal of the higher style of papal assumption brought even more solid fruits to the church than had been secured by the pliant complaisance of Clement. The dividing line between the two pontificates corresponds pretty accurately with the deep line of division between the two political periods of the reign.

While Clement V was still pope, papalism secured a double triumph in the abandonment of any effort to enforce the statute of Carlisle and in the permanent establishment of annates, first imposed by a bull of Clement in 1306, as a regular source of papal revenue from the English church.[1] Besides these new exactions, so called "crusading" tenths continued as of old to be levied, not only in England and Wales, but also in Ireland and, so long as Robert Bruce

[1] Clement V's bull has been recently published, from a Salisbury episcopal register, by Prof. W. E. Lunt in his valuable article on "The first levy of Papal Annates," in *American Hist. Rev.*, xviii, 62-4.

allowed it, in Scotland. In the result, these levies produced much more benefit for the English kings than for the crusading cause, or even for the papal authors of these taxes.[1] But papal taxes collected by English bishops, like John Halton of Carlisle, represented alien authority in a shape little calculated to offend national susceptibilities, at least south of the border.

The alliance of church and state was never more close than when the business in hand was the spoil of the church. And the reign of Edward II first saw the suppression of a great monastic order in the abolition of the knights of the Temple by Clement V, in the council of Vienne. Though this was the work of the ecclesiastical authorities, the state took a good share of the spoils. Though the lands of the Templars were assigned to the knights of St. John of Jerusalem, a considerable portion of them remained permanently in the possession of the crown or its nominees. The Hospitallers found that the only way to secure part was to renounce the rest. Despite the large alienation of church property thus effected, the dissolution of the order of the Temple must still be accounted as a manifestation of papal authority. And it is significant that the case against the Templars first brought into England agents of the papal inquisition.

Winchelsea, the last of the zealots for ecclesiastical privilege among the Edwardian bishops, died in 1313, and Clement V in 1314. When, after a vacancy of nearly two years, James of Cahors became John XXII, the real Avignon period of papal history began.[2]

I must pause for a moment to emphasise the deep mark which John XXII's masterful personality imprinted on English ecclesiastical history. Under him "first fruits" became a universal and permanent obligation, and the "good asses" of England bore this new burden with their accustomed docility.[3] It was owing to John that foreign ecclesiastics were permanently established in England as collectors of papal taxation, instead of the English prelates

[1] I may refer to my remarks on crusading tenths during this period, especially in Scotland, in my introduction to the *Registrum Johannis de Halton* (Canterbury and York Soc.). [Republished in *Coll. Papers*, ii, 106-21.]

[2] Clement V was made pope in 1305, and mainly resided in Gascony and Poitou until the end of 1308. After 1309 he partly lived at Avignon, which only became the permanent papal headquarters after John XXII took up his residence there.

[3] Murimuth, p. 28. "Anglici, sicut boni asini, quicquid eis imponitur tolerantes"; *cf. ibid.*, p. 175.

to whom that duty had sometimes recently been delegated. Notable among these was the papal nuncio, Master Rigaud of Assier, canon of Orleans, a Cahorsin like the pope, who was promptly despatched to collect arrears of tenths, of Peter's pence, of king John's tribute money, and of other dues from England to the apostolic see.[1] It was not long before Rigaud's activity provoked an order forbidding his attempting anything to the prejudice of the crown, as complaints have arisen " that he is exercising various new, unusual and inconvenient practices against religious and other ecclesiastical persons and laymen in this realm." [2] It was clearly the personal work of John XXII that appointment to English bishoprics, hitherto only exceptionally made by direct papal nomination, became henceforth normally and almost invariably effected in that fashion, not only in this reign but for the rest of the middle ages.[3] Robert of Reading tell us that John reserved the nomination of English bishoprics to himself, because he was disgusted with the appointments which had been made hitherto through the instrumentality of Edward II. The hostile Westminster monk approved the pope's action as that of a restorer of the English church to its pristine purity.[4] But John's policy would have been better justified if he had not on several occasions pushed his complaisance to the king to the extent of " providing " to English sees notoriously unworthy clerks. It may, however, be set down against this, that John stopped some of the worst jobs which the English government wished to perpetrate.

How completely John carried out the policy of papal nomination can be realised from the fact that, while between 1307 and 1316 there were only two individual English pre-

[1] Rigaud de Asserio's *Register* (Hampshire Record Soc.), App. pp. 555-8, prints his various commissions. See also above, p. 102, and *Cal. Pap. Lett.*, ii, 127.

[2] *Foedera*, ii, 356 ; *C.C.R. 1313-18*, p. 593 (6 Feb. 1318).

[3] [Mr. Tout's pupil, Miss D. M. Bridge, pointed out to him that this statement needs qualification. It was not till Clement VI became pope, in 1342, that provision became invariable. From 1327 to 1342, *i.e.*, during the latter part of the pontificate of John XXII and that of Benedict XII, 10 out of the 23 bishops appointed were elected, 13 provided. Three of the provisions confirmed a choice already made by the chapter, 5 set such choice aside.]

[4] Robert of Reading in *Flores Hist.*, iii, 175-6. Perhaps the Westminster monk is more intent on abusing Edward II than praising the pope. But John's extension of the system of papal nomination was not limited to England.

lates appointed by the pope,[1] there were between 1317 and 1326 ten bishops established by papal reservation and provision.[2] While in the former period ten English bishops owed their sees to capitular election,[3] in the days of John XXII only four were so appointed, two of whom obtained their sees after great difficulty and a long contest. Moreover, the last of these appointments dates no later than 1319.[4] Between 1320 and 1326 there was not a single case of successful capitular election, and five chapter appointments in succession were quashed by the pope. Among John XXII's nominees were aristocratic youths like Louis of Beaumont and Henry Burghersh, who stood well with pope and government; respectable officials like Roger Northburgh, the old *garderobarius;* and scandalous self-seekers of the official type, such as Adam Orleton, John Stratford and William Airmyn. Two of John's bishops were Frenchmen, namely, Beaumont and Rigaud of Assier. Only one represented a high spiritual type, and this was Thomas Cobham, the "good clerk," the "flower of Kent," the distinguished academic teacher, who received in his promotion to Worcester some consolation for his election to Canterbury being set aside in favour of Walter Reynolds. The two other bishops made by John had at least the merit of not being politicians, but they appear so seldom in the chronicles that it is somewhat rash to generalise as to their character. After 1322, however, John XXII

[1] These were Walter Reynolds, appointed in 1308 to Worcester and translated in 1313 to Canterbury, and Walter Maidstone, made bishop of Worcester in 1313.

[2] These were:—1317: Thomas Cobham to Worcester, Adam Orleton to Hereford; 1318: Louis of Beaumont to Durham; 1320: Rigaud of Assier to Winchester, and Henry Burghersh to Lincoln; 1322: Roger Northburgh to Lichfield; 1323: John Eaglescliffe to Llandaff, and John Stratford to Winchester; 1325: John Ross to Carlisle, and William Airmyn to Norwich.

[3] These were:—1308: Walter Stapledon to Exeter; 1309: Eineon Sais to Bangor, and John Droxford to Wells; 1310: John Keton to Ely; 1311: Richard Kellaw to Durham; 1313: Gilbert Seagrave to London; 1314: David ap Bleddyn to St. Asaph; 1315: Roger Mortival to Salisbury; 1316: John Hotham to Ely, and John Sandall to Winchester. The last four were elected during the long papal interregnum between 1314 and 1316. The reservation of Durham had already been ordered by Clement V (*Foedera*, ii, 313).

[4] These were:—1317: William Melton to York, and Richard Newport to London; 1319: Stephen Gravesend to London, and Hamo Hethe to Rochester. Of these, Melton, elected in 1316, before John was pope, had to wait eighteen months at Avignon before he could obtain confirmation and consecration. Hamo Hethe, elected in 1317, had his election referred to Rome, and was only confirmed in 1319 (*Cal. Pap. Lett.*, ii, 188-9).

deserves undoubted credit for rejecting the nominees of Edward II as rigorously as he ruled out the elect of the chapters. It may be accounted to him for righteousness that he quashed the election of Robert Baldock to the see of Norwich and so saved England from a most unworthy bishop.[1]

We may also count among the good deeds of pope John that in 1318 he issued a bull of foundation which technically made Cambridge a university established by papal authority. He was more successful in this than was Clement V, when in 1312 he set up a university in Ireland. Another meritorious act of John XXII was the authorisation of the "new taxation" of the dioceses of the province of York in 1318, by which the districts which had felt the chief stress of the Scotch invasions were relieved by a substantial reduction of their assessments.[2] The pope was also actuated by excellent motives when, following the example of Clement V in 1312,[3] he sent, in 1317 and later, legates to England to mediate between the king and both his Scottish and baronial enemies. The firm attitude of Bruce prevented any great success in the former quarter, but it was in some measure due to the papal legates that the pacification of 1318 was effected. The mission of the cardinals Gaucelin of Eauze and Luca Fieschi in 1317, and still more that of the archbishop of Vienne and the bishop of Orange in 1324, anticipate the mediation of the inevitable two cardinals who moved uneasily between the English and French camps in the early campaigns of the Hundred Years' War.

In strong contrast to this long series of papal encroachments on the authority of a weak king stand the vigorous measures adopted in the end of the reign to protect the interests of the state on the outbreak of war against France. Improving upon the rather tentative measures taken by Edward I against "alien men of religion," during his war with Philip the Fair, Edward II in 1324 laid his hands upon all the alien priories, lest the French monks who held them

[1] In this paragraph on papal nominations to bishoprics under Edward II I have been much indebted to the material collected by my pupil, Miss Ethel Hornby, M.A., in her degree thesis on that subject. The details of appointments given in text and notes are largely taken from her work. The dates and details collected by her compelled the conviction that John XXII was responsible for the change described in the text. Stubbs, *Const. Hist.*, iii, 312-23, has some weighty paragraphs on this subject, but does not emphasise sufficiently the extent to which the policy of John XXII exceeded the action of Clement V.

[2] See for more details on this subject later, pp. 212-13.

[3] *Ann. Lond.*, p. 210.

should send their incomes out of the country to support the cause of the enemy. Nor were the alien religious the only sufferers. French secular clerks beneficed in England had to endure a similar suspension of their revenues. A monastic chronicler reckons the sufferings of beneficed foreigners, who for a great space obtained nothing from their cures save scanty food and raiment, as among the chief inconveniences arising from the French war.[1] However, in 1326, the crown agreed to allow the alien priors and also the beneficed aliens to "redeem" their property by contracting to pay fixed amounts of money and corn to the state.[2] The precedent of Edward II was carefully followed when the beginnings of the Hundred Years' War involved the alien priories in a larger and more famous suspension. The whole transaction was a mere move in the political game, but some of the chroniclers accuse Edward on this account of sacrilege. They are equally angry at his laying hands on temporalities of his personal enemies among the bishops.[3] But it requires a robust faith to believe that political reprisals against an Orleton, a Stratford, and Airmyn and a Burghersh have any real ecclesiastical significance. There is, however, a slight suggestion of future anti-papalism in some of Edward's later poses. In 1325 he forbade a prior of Lewes going out of the realm to answer a citation procured by his chief, the abbot of Cluny, "considering the prejudice done thereby to our royal dignity, since no one ought to be drawn to answer outside the realm for anything whereof the cognisance belongs to the king."[4] Here is the language of the statute of Praemunire, if not of the statute of Appeals. Years before this, the well-known outbursts of indignation of the monk of Malmesbury against the greed of the curia of Avignon showed what some English clerks thought of the administration of Clement V.[5] But we must distinguish between purposeless grumbling, such as every generation saw, and definite steps towards a remedy, such as came from the state alone, and were therefore sadly to seek in the reign of Edward II.

[1] Blaneford, pp. 150-1; *Flores Hist.*, iii, pp. 225-6, says the sustentation allowance to foreign prelates was three shillings a week and to foreign religious eighteen pence a week each. [Alien seculars transferred inland from benefices near the coast were to receive 18d. a week for sustentation and 40s. a year for clothes and shoes (G.R. 36, m. 25).]

[2] *Ann. Paul.*, p. 313; *cf. ibid.*, p. 307.

[3] See for example *Flores Hist.*, iii, pp. 218-19.

[4] *C.C.R. 1323-27*, p. 529.

[5] Malmesb., p. 198. "Domine Jesu, vel papam tolle de medio, vel potestatem minue quam praesumit in populo."

## VII

# SOCIAL AND ECONOMIC HISTORY. ORIGINS OF THE STAPLE

### (1) State of Society under Edward II

The social and economic history of the reign of Edward II is still an unworked field, and I can only suggest in outline a few points which on first examination have struck me as interesting, leaving others to work them out and to test the truth of my impressions. It has been a commonplace of both contemporary and modern historians to emphasise in exaggerated terms the miseries from which England suffered under Edward II. In all ages there are prophets of evil and the chronic disorders of society always gave mediæval pessimists plenty of material for pointing their moral. But if we analyse the chroniclers with any care, we shall find that a large part of their dreary picture is drawn with relation to particular districts or to particular periods of the reign. The north, which was exposed to the incessant ravages of the Scots, and was the scene of much of the civil strife, was in these respects in an exceptional condition. Here the misery and desolation were real enough. A comparison of the figures of the "new valuation" of the churches of the province of York, effected in 1318, with that of the "taxation of pope Nicholas," made in 1291, is more eloquent than the rhetoric of any annalist. By the later assessment the two sees that felt the worst burden of Scottish invasion had their valuation cut down enormously, Durham falling from nearly £11,000 to a little over £2,000, and Carlisle from over £3,000 to £480.[1] On the other hand, the taxation of the diocese of York was only reduced by two-sevenths. The reason is clearly that, though the northern part was open to occasional forays of the Scots, the greater part of Yorkshire, Nottinghamshire and North Lancashire was outside the area

[1] See the table in Stubbs, *Const. Hist.*, ii, 580.

of constant and devastating attack. Indeed, such decline as there was may be as much set down to the general disorder of the times as to Scottish inroads; though these were mitigated for Yorkshire by the frequent presence of the court and government departments. The utter collapse of the two border dioceses speaks for itself.

The worst times were the black years between Bannockburn and the treaty of Leake. For these four successive years there were cold, rain, flood, famine and pestilence, involving such mortality as had not been seen for a century.[1] The north suffered worse than the south, and tales were told how, in Northumberland, men could only keep body and soul together by devouring the flesh of dogs and horses. The Scottish invasions and the exceptional feebleness of the government brought the troubles to a head.

In 1318 a rapid improvement followed immediately upon the better political conditions then established. The bushel of wheat, which in the previous years had sold for three shillings and fourpence, could now be easily procured for sixpence. There were more favourable seasons, less fighting and wiser government. The revenue began once more to yield better results[2]; and though there were constant threatenings of war, there was very little fighting outside Yorkshire and the march of Wales. Mediæval society was always disorderly, and the effectiveness of government was so circumscribed that, just as good kings could not make earth an Eden, so bad kings had strictly limited opportunities of doing mischief. The worst signs of continued political trouble, the marchings and counter-marchings of the rival armies of king and barons, were not in themselves sufficient to throw the land into confusion. The skilful policing of London in July 1321 by the mayor, Hamo of Chigwell, made it possible for the huge trains of the northern and western barons to be assigned separate quarters in different suburbs, so that the parliament passed over without any disorder.[3]

[1] The trouble began in 1314 (Malmesb., p. 214) and was at its worst in 1315 and 1316. The relevant passages in the chronicles are: Malmesb., pp. 209, 214, 219, 238; Bridl., p. 48; *Ann. Lond.*, p. 237; Murimuth, p. 24; Trokelowe, pp. 89-98; *Flores Hist.*, iii, 174, 340-1.

[2] Prof. Willard informs me that the subsidy roll from this time begin to show an increased yield. [*Cf.* the tables of assessment in 1307, 1313, 1315, 1316 and 1322, printed by him in *Eng. Hist. Rev.*, xxix, 317-21. Certain deductions must be made from these figures when estimating the sums actually received (*ibid.*, xxviii, 517).]

[3] See *Ann. Paul.*, pp. 294-5. "Et sic in pace unusquisque et sine strepitu hospitabantur."

When a threatened civil war could thus be averted by good management, there was a very practical guarantee for the maintenance of the public peace, so that there were few signs of abnormal trouble and distress during the concluding years of the reign.

Even in the worst period of the reign, the general machinery of administration went on much as usual. At every possible stage the administrative records were kept with remarkable fullness and care, even though the financial records fell, as we have seen, into terrible confusion. The judges went on circuit, or sat at the courts at Westminster or York, just as regularly and worked through their lists just as carefully as if all had been well with the state. Thus the Year Books of Edward II's early years are exceedingly copious and instructive. Maitland, who began the great scheme for their republication, has well emphasised their importance for social history. Yet we may search the published four volumes of reports of trials, for the years 1307 to 1311,[1] without finding evidence of more disorder or more difficulty in administering the law than was chronic under mediæval conditions. Even more evidence of the normal course of public business despite days of trouble and distress is found in the three volumes which record the proceeding of the general eyre of Kent, the "longest eyre ever holden," when five justices sat at Canterbury for the whole year preceding Bannockburn, and hundreds of jurors, suitors, and officials from every part of the richest shire in England flocked together to the county town, while Hervey of Staunton and his comrades heard all manner of pleas, alike on Sundays and week-days, in term time and vacation time, only interrupting their unceasing labours for a short month's holiday in August.[2] The reported cases of the eyre form an extraordinary picture of brutal crime and greedy treachery, but they are not worse than the criminal records of any other mediæval assize, in what are generally considered more orderly and prosperous times.

Another sign that the reign of Edward II was not altogether unprosperous is the remarkable number of pious foundations. I will not say that the dedication of wealth to the church is

[1] *Year Books of Edward II*, Year Book Series, i, ii, iii, and iv (Selden Soc.).

[2] See the three volumes of the *Eyre of Kent, 6 and 7 Edward II* (Selden Soc., Year Books Series, nos. v, vii, and viii), and especially Mr. Bolland's introduction to vol. v, sections 1, 3, 4, 5, and 15. [*Cf.* also B. H. Putnam, *Kent Keepers of the Peace*, 1316-17.]

in itself a sign of material prosperity. In the darkest days of feudalism men set up cloisters in their despair of the secular world. But no such thoughts as those which in the days of Stephen drove a Walter Espec to a monastery inspired the comfortable benefactors of religion and learning under Edward II. They gave, not of their necessity, but of their superabundance, and those of them that we know best were rather benevolent and prosperous worldlings than enthusiasts for high ideals. It is not then off the point to appeal to the new foundations of our period as a sign that there was superfluous wealth available for pious purposes. The reign saw the creation of two universities in Edward's dominions, though one of these was in fact over a century old, and the other barely struggled into a short existence. The intercession of the government of Edward II procured, in 1318, the bull of John XXII, which formally founded the university of Cambridge, and so converted the unordered and struggling schools of that city into a *studium generale*, established, like Toulouse or Montpellier, by papal privilege.[1] Moreover, a bull of Clement V had, in 1312, established the short-lived mediæval Irish university at Dublin.[2] But these were formal rather than munificent acts. A much more characteristic aspect of the benevolence of the reign assumed the shape of collegiate foundations at Oxford and Cambridge.[3] Indeed in no period of twenty years, except perhaps the generation after the Black Death, were so many new colleges established in the two English universities. No doubt the foundations of the reign were small, but they showed the drift of fashion in such things, and it is significant that the king and his ministers took the lead. At Oxford Edward II refounded, and provided a habitation in his own palace for, the monastic college of the Carmelite friars, and at Cambridge Edward set up the King's Hall for the children of his chapel. Again at Oxford bishop Stapeldon, afterwards treasurer, founded what was later known as Exeter College,[4] and Adam of Brome, the chancery

[1] Denifle, *Die Entstehung der Universitäten der Mittelalters*, pp. 374-6.

[2] *Ibid.*, pp. 639-43. There was a real, if small, university of Dublin in 1320 and also in 1358. See also above, p. 186.

[3] Rashdall, *Universities in the Middle Ages* (2nd edn., 1936), iii, 201-7, 299-302.

[4] Stapeldon founded "Stapeldon Hall" before his ministerial career began. His statutes are printed in Hingeston-Randolph's *Stapeldon's Register*, pp. 304-10. They are dated 1316, one of the worst years of distress.

clerk, founded Oriel College, while Michaelhouse, at Cambridge, owed its establishment to the judge and exchequer official, Hervey of Staunton. The saintly bishop Cobham of Worcester set up a university library for Oxford.[1] He is the chief non-ministerial benefactor of the universities during the reign. To complete our list, however, we must go on for a few years and record the two great foundations at Cambridge by the widows of prominent actors in our drama, that of Clare Hall by the Gloucester co-heiress, Elizabeth of Clare, widow of Roger of Amory, and that of Pembroke Hall by the widow of earl Aymer, Mary of Saint-Pol.

Other undoubted signs of social progress are to be found in the growth of English towns, as is witnessed by the large share which London and Bristol took in the politics of the reign, and by the inter-relation of municipal and political changes during the period. The growth of the political and economic importance of London is especially remarkable. Hamo of Chigwell, the clerk who turned fishmonger and became mayor, was one of the most important minor personalities of the reign. His career has hardly been worked out sufficiently for it to be safe to dogmatise about it, but his political leanings seem, like those of most sensible people, to have been towards the Pembrokian policy.

Of great significance for the period was the growth of an English capitalist class, which was able to compete with the Italian bankers for royal favours and commercial privileges. Indeed, most of the names of the monied houses which later financed Edward III, for instance, the Poles and the Conduits, began to appear under Edward II. The result was that when the Frescobaldi were driven from the realm by the ordainers there were English merchants able to carry on their work, not only in controlling the export trade, but also in helping to finance the king's government. If they were not sufficiently wealthy to do all that the king wanted, they prepared the way for the famous merchant princes of the reign of Edward III. They were strong enough, however, to compete vigorously with the Bardi, who aimed not unsuccessfully at stepping into the place of the banished Frescobaldi, and had their position further strengthened by the withdrawal of the Genoese financier knight, Sir Anthony

[1] [See his own letter on the subject in *Reg. Tho. de Cobham* (Worc. Hist. Soc. 1930), p. 201, and *cf.* Pearce, *Thomas de Cobham*, pp. 244-6.]

of Passano,[1] from English politics and business. It was a sign of advance that so brisk a struggle between English and alien merchants was now become possible.

## (2) The Establishment of the Compulsory Staple

The chief points of the economic history of Edward II's reign are all well illustrated by that remarkable consolidation of the staple system, which is, perhaps, the most characteristic feature of its commercial progress. Accordingly, leaving other matters aside, I shall venture to suggest in some detail the most important turning points in the development of the staple of England under Edward II. It will show that much of the credit of a system often supposed to have been the result of the conscious policy of Edward III, is to be set down to the period of his father.

In the thirteenth century there were in various parts of Europe markets of a special sort called staples.[2] These staples were in essence great depôts of merchandise, established at convenient places on the chief trade routes, and it was natural enough that the townsfolk of a place possessing a staple should do what they could to attract trade to it, sometimes no doubt by compulsion.[3] Thirteenth- and fourteenth-century England was a land of farmers and graziers, and its chief general exports were wool, skins and leather, to which tin and lead, from the mines of Devon and Cornwall, must also be added. The chief demand for these commodities came from the only neighbouring regions where commerce was organised on large lines, and where textiles were manufactured on a wholesale scale for a universal market. This was the Netherlandish district, including

[1] For Passano see also above, pp. 197-9. His interesting career is well worth working out in detail.

[2] The general economic histories have little to say on the origins of the staple. They are treated with more fullness in Miss Adaline Jenckes' *Origin, Organisation and Location of the Staple of England*, a Philadelphia doctoral dissertation of 1908. But the author covers too wide a field for her work to be final, and the authoritative monograph has still to be written. I am glad to say that my colleague, Prof. Unwin, is devoting his attention to the subject. I owe much to his suggestion and advice in what I have written here. I have also been helped by the earlier part of the thesis of my pupil, Mr. L. H. Gilbert, B.A., on the *History of the Staple of English Wool, 1313-1353*.

[3] See for this R. Häpke, *Brügges Entwicklung zum mittelalterlichen Weltmarkt* (1908), pp. 222-33. "Dieser Stapel ist mit *Nederlaghe* oder *depositio mercimoniorum* identisch." It was not until 1323 that a "Zwangstapel" was established for Bruges.

the counties of Flanders and Artois, the duchy of Brabant, and, though to a less extent, the united counties of Holland and Zealand. Accordingly it was to the ports of these regions that English produce was mostly directed, and its course was the more free since, until the end of the thirteenth century, the greater part of the export trade from England was in foreign hands. Up to that period English traders had neither the capital and organisation nor the enterprise and imagination necessary to compete successfully with the Netherlandish, French and Italian merchants, who were as successful in controlling the sea trade to and from England as they were in dominating English banking and finance.

Fiscal, political and economic reasons combined to make it important to English monarchs to control the export trade as strictly as possible. The easiest way to do this was to encourage merchants to frequent some particular favoured markets. Accordingly, since the days of Henry III, there had arisen a staple of English wool in the Low Countries, though this staple was a voluntary one and there were no penalties on traders who preferred to take their wool elsewhere.[1] Under Edward I the organisation of the customs revenue on a large scale made it imperative that trade should go in certain definite channels, to facilitate the collection of so important a branch of the royal income. Accordingly, in 1297, an ordinance of king and council laid down that no "passage of wools or leathers, of messengers or of merchants" was henceforth to be allowed save from certain specified British and Irish ports, where collectors of customs were established, where a "cocket seal" was to be kept, whose stamp was the official notification that wool had paid customs, and where staple commodities were consequently to be concentrated for export after due payment of the royal duties.[2] This device, however, was a simple plan for the collection of revenue, complicated by the immediate

[1] *C.C.R. 1318-23*, p. 235. There is no reason for doubting the statements to this effect by the English merchants of 1320.

[2] *Ibid., 1296-1302*, pp. 86-7, prints at length the ordinance of 1 March 1297. The specified ports for England were Newcastle-on-Tyne, Hull, Boston, Yarmouth, Ipswich, London, Sandwich, Southampton and Bristol. The ports of Wales and the March were Chester, Beaumaris, Milford and Haverford, but the words "nul passage des leynes ne des quirs" are here omitted, and the monopoly only extended to the "passage des messagers ou des marchauntz." For Scotland the monopoly was vaguely given to the "leus ou sont les coketz, e a Kircudbright," when a cocket seal has been sent to that town.

political necessities of a critical period.[1] It only became important as a stage in the growth of the staple because of its connection with other measures which gave Edward I some claim to be regarded as the father of the English staple system. It is true, however, that the "home staples" of a later period did grow out of these special centres of export, established to facilitate the collection of customs.[2]

The beginnings of the staple system in the later part of Edward I's reign are due to the combination of the new plan of giving a monopoly of the export of wool and leather to special customs ports with the old plan of a "foreign staple," and the new importance given to the staple trade by the political and fiscal exigencies of the most critical years of the great king's reign. There is some evidence, though it is not of a very conclusive character, that already certain ports in Flanders, such as Bruges, and in Holland-Zealand, such as Middelburg, had been recognised by Edward as "foreign staples," though there is no proof that any compulsory foreign staple had as yet been devised. But after 1295, the war with France, the dependence of Flanders on Philip the Fair, and the alliance of the count of Holland and Zealand with the French, excluded English merchants from frequenting any of the usual staples of Flanders or Holland. However, a remedy was at hand in the alliance of Edward I with his son-in-law, John, duke of Brabant, which opened up the great Brabançon port of Antwerp to the exporters of English wool, excluded from their usual haunts. Edward I was able to confer a real benefit on the duke by making his dominions a market of English wool, and the export of that commodity to Antwerp created a fund equally available for financing a foreign ally or maintaining an English army. In 1296 duke John showed his gratitude by a remarkable charter to English merchants.[3] This was emphasised in 1297

[1] For instance the careful measures taken for the exclusion of Lombard merchants, and the prevention of the introduction of treasonable correspondence.

[2] The statement that in 1291 "Edward I assigned staples to certain towns in England, Ireland and Wales" (Jenckes, *op. cit.*, p. 8) is based upon the mistake of the editor of the calendar of the Lincoln municipal archives in *Hist. MSS. Comm.*, 14th Report, App. viii, pp. 6-7, where a document of 19 Edw. II is misdated "19 Edw. I," *i.e.* 1291 instead of 1326. The document in question is a copy of the ordinance of 1326. See later, pp. 234-6.

[3] See H. Obreen, "Une charte brabançonne inédite de 1296," in *Bulletin de la commission royale d'histoire de Belgique*, t. lxxx (1911). Prof. Unwin, *Eng. Hist. Rev.*, xxvii, 810-11, suggests that this is the document calendared in an inventory of the charters of the merchant adventurers in 1547, printed in Schanz, *Handelspolitik*, ii, 577.

when duke John took the strong step of granting Antwerp, the staple town and the chief port of his dominions, to Edward I, to be held by Edward of the duke in fee.[1] The charter was renewed in 1305 in ampler form.[2]

The details of these charters of John of Brabant prove that there was in 1305, if not also in 1297, a "staple" at Antwerp, which was something much more than a simple market, like the earlier staples. It proves that the "merchants from the realm of England"[3] were established as an organised corporation, under a "mayor, captain, or consul," and empowered to treat with the municipality, hire houses, purchase goods at reasonable prices, pay a definite scale of tolls and duties, punish offenders, and discharge other semi-political as well as commercial functions.[4] We are quite near the staple of the next reign, but not quite at it. We have a society of merchants, under a mayor, established in a foreign "staple town." But the name staple does not occur in the charter and is found very scantily in the records of Edward I's reign. We have the thing rather than the name, and the thing is still hidden away in the background. Above all, there is no evidence that all wool from England was necessarily sent to Antwerp. Antwerp was, indeed, a favoured, privileged and organised market, but it was not yet a compulsory one. Moreover, difficulties soon arose from the new state of things. Before long English merchants raised bitter complaints of the exactions of the duke of Brabant and commercial relations were broken off for a time in 1302.[5] In 1306, after maritime Flanders had, by its successful revolt, shaken off the yoke of Philip the Fair, Edward I allowed merchants to go to

[1] *Foedera,* ii, 206, from a patent of 6 Edw. II. [On this and other aspects of John's Anglophil policy see articles by Dr. J. V. de Sturler on "Les relations politiques de l'Angleterre et du Brabant (1272-1326)," in *Revue belge de philologie et d'histoire,* xi, 627-50 (1932), and "Le trafic Anglo-Brabançon dans ses rapports avec les origines de l'étape d'Angleterre" (Congrès de Liège, 1932); for fuller survey his book on *Les relations politiques et les échanges commerciaux entre le duché de Brabant et l'Angleterre* (1936).]

[2] This is also printed by Obreen, *op. cit.*

[3] They are always "mercatores de Anglia" or "les marchanz de reaume de Angleterre." It is not quite certain from the phrase whether they were Englishmen or traders from England. Probably both.

[4] Obreen, p. 25. "Praeterea volumus . . . quod mercatores de Anglia . . . maiorem, capitaneum, sive consulem sibi si voluerint eligant." This is in 1305, but in 1297 the merchants could hold "lor assemblees, courts et congregationz." It is, then, hardly rash to say that there were mayors of the staple before 1305.

[5] *C.C.R. 1296-1302,* pp. 439, 540, 551. In 1303 commerce was resumed on the duke's apology (*ibid., 1302-7,* p. 110).

Aardenburg in Flanders, "as they had been wont to go to Bruges."[1] But the market at Aardenburg, like the earlier market at Bruges, was only a special wool market, favoured and protected by royal decree. There was no compulsory foreign staple under Edward I.[2] But apart from compulsion, there were all the elements out of which the later monopolistic and compulsory staple grew.

The reign of Edward II saw the establishment of a compulsory staple system for English merchants, and therefore marks a decided advance on the reign of Edward I in this relation. With the advent of coercion also came judicial proceedings, through which the establishment of the English staple system is revealed with absolute clearness in the English records. In the early years of the reign things remained much as they had been since 1297. The merchants trading to Brabant had to run the gauntlet of French and Flemish hostility, and the early chancery rolls of the reign are full of complaints of the outrages perpetrated by the Flemings and men of Calais on them. On the other hand, the duke of Brabant complained in his turn that, by 1310, English merchants had ceased to hold staple at Antwerp, and induced Edward to issue a proclamation that access to that port was still safe and open.[3] Various circumstances were now drawing English trade into more southerly regions. The increasing cordiality of the political relations of England and France made commercial dealings the easier, and the possession of Ponthieu by the English king made him a near neighbour of the Artesian cloth centres. Thus it was that the city knight and alderman, Sir John Bakewell, who was seneschal of Ponthieu between 1299 and 1305, and became in 1307 a baron of the English exchequer, had been, up to his death in 1308, "used to attend to the affairs of the merchants of England and France,"[4] doubtless by the royal direction. Moreover, the absolute dependence of Edward II on Italian merchant financiers such as the Frescobaldi naturally tended to divert our commerce into more southern channels.

With the exile of the Frescobaldi by the ordinances, the chance for the English merchant was again come. A few

[1] *C.P.R. 1301-7*, p. 435.

[2] Häpke, *op. cit.*, p. 68. "So lag noch kein Staplezwang vor."

[3] *C.C.R. 1307-13*, p. 293, 18 Dec. 1310.

[4] *Ibid.*, p. 53. For the problems involved in this person's career see later, App. II, pp. 301, n. 6, 306, n. 1.

months after the ordinances, we find two negotiations carried on simultaneously in the interests of English traders beyond sea. In 1312 Richard Stury, burgess of Shrewsbury, was sent to treat with the count of Flanders as to the wrongs of English merchants.[1] The reason for Stury's selection is clearly that he was "mayor of the merchants of our realm," the first holder of that office whose name seems to have been preserved.[2] It looks as if the "mayor of the merchants" were arranging for the transference of the staple of wool from Antwerp to Flanders, probably to Bruges. Whatever was the case with the court and its alien capitalistic advisers, the bulk of English mercantile opinion seems still to have been in favour of having the staple located in the region where our chief commercial interests were centred, that is in Flanders. Accordingly, not much later, there was a second negotiation in progress, whose origin seems to be due to the efforts made by the French to secure the staple for some French commercial centre. While these opposing currents were still ineffective, the decision of the problem was transferred from foreign courts to the merchants, by the first known ordinance of the staple, issued by the king and council on 20 May 1313.[3]

The ordinance of the staple of 1313 is a landmark in English economic history, and shows the definite establishment of the system towards which things had been drifting since 1296. It put an end to the merely preferential staple, and set up a monopolistic staple in its place.[4] It recited

[1] *Foedera*, ii, 188.

[2] Richard Stury, burgess of Shrewsbury, represented Shrewsbury in the "model" parliament of Nov. 1295, the Lincoln parliament of 1301, and the Westminster parliament of 1313 (*Return of Members*, i, 5, 14, 40). He was sent on 26 Nov. 1312, as one of two envoys to Flanders (*Foedera*, ii, 188), and when so acting on 15 Feb. 1313, is called "major mercatorum de regno nostro" (*ibid.*, ii, 202). On 22 Aug. 1313 he is called "mayor of the wool staple" (*C.P.R. 1313-17*, p. 15), that is after the "charter" or "ordinance" of 1313. He was violent in his methods, being accused in 1303 of breaking into a barn at Shrewsbury (*ibid.*, *1301-7*, pp. 198-9). In 1320 he was defendant in an action of novel disseisin (*ibid.*, *1317-21*, p. 536). Two other mayors of the staple under Edward II, Charlton and Béthune, were also members of parliament, both for London.

[3] Issued as a patent (*C.P.R. 1307-13*, p. 591), it is spoken of sometimes as the "charter," and more often as the "ordinance of the staple." It is printed in Jenckes, *op. cit.*, appendix, pp. 61-2, and Varenbergh, *Relations diplomatiques entre le comté de Flandre et l'Angleterre*, pp. 440-1.

[4] Häpke, *op. cit.*, pp. 67-8, puts the extent of the innovation very clearly. "Die Urkunde seines Nachfolgers vom 20 Mai 1313 spricht es selbst aus dasz es sich um *eine neue Einrichtung*, Schaffung eines gesetzlichen Stapels, handelt." "Stapelzwang" now begins.

that up to this time merchants, both natives and aliens, had been free to take their wool and wool-fells at their discretion to various places in the lands of Brabant, Flanders and Artois, but ordered that henceforth both classes of merchants should export their commodities "to a fixed staple, within one of the aforesaid lands, to be appointed by the mayor [1] and community of the same merchants of our realm." The same body was also to have authority to change the staple place. Power was given to the mayor and his council to exercise jurisdiction over all exporters, notably by imposing fines on both alien and English merchants who contravened the ordinance.

The staple of 1313 was in a sense a new departure, but the ordinance accepted, without alteration, the organisation that was already in existence, and Stury remained mayor after as before the ordinance. But he is now called mayor of the wool staple, as well as mayor of the merchants. The novelties involved in the ordinance were the fixing of the staple by the merchants themselves, the power to change the staple place at their will, the right the staple officers now had of fining and exercising jurisdiction over all merchants, the restriction on free trade, the subjection of the foreign merchants to the organised "merchants of this realm," and the virtual conversion of a private society, privileged by foreign monarchs, into a public association, backed up by the authority of the English state. The ultimate control of the society was in the hands of the representatives of the chief boroughs of England, whose nominees were henceforth summoned in quasi-parliamentary form through the sheriffs, whenever any problems of the staple needed discussion.

There was naturally a strong opposition to the new system, and the general neglect of merchants to observe the ordinance led to strongly worded "writs of aid," addressed to the collectors of customs on behalf of Stury and his colleagues. The ports to whose officers these writs of aid were addressed were clearly the ports which had collectors of customs and "cocket seals," and to which staple commodities, now as in 1297, compulsorily went for export.[2]

[1] The mayor now had a seal, a symbol of corporate life. See *C.P.R. 1313-17*, p. 15. It is not impossible, however, that this had been the case since 1297.

[2] *Ibid.*, pp. 15 and 56, dated 22 Aug. 1313. The ports enumerated are Newcastle-on-Tyne, Hartlepool, Hull, Lynn, Yarmouth, Ipswich,

It would be rash to call these places "home staples" as yet, but the writs of aid show that the co-operation of the cocket ports was necessary, if the "foreign staple" was to become a reality. The home staple was, therefore, already in germ, although its association with the foreign staple was still in the future.

It is impossible not to connect the staple ordinance of 1313 with the issue of the more famous ordinances of 1311. The organisation of the first compulsory staple, then, is like the institution of an independent keepership of the privy seal one of the permanent marks left by the ordainers on our institutions. To the ordainers the staple ordinance doubtless seemed the necessary corollary of the exile of the Frescobaldi, who had up to now controlled the wool trade, collected the customs, and acted as the chief bankers and loan-mongers of the king. Apart from this obnoxious family, the ordainers made no attempt to exclude foreign merchants from the export trade.[1] That would have been impossible at a time when English shippers were only just struggling into prosperity, and were often only able to freight a single ship by an elaborate combination of interests. But even more definitely than in the Brabant charter of 1297, the aliens were now subordinated to "the merchants of this realm" with whom the directive force of the ordinance lay. Unluckily the times were not yet ripe for English control of the English export trade. It is, however, a sign of the new tendencies at work that we are able to claim for the ordinances of 1311, so often regarded as a mere illustration of baronial reaction, a modest place of their own in English economic development. Yet, though for fourteen years, 1313-26, strenuous efforts were made to carry out the ordinance of the staple, the attempt was not much more successful than was that to execute the ordinances of 1311.

At first there was great competition between French, Artesians, Flemings, and Brabanters to secure within their own lands the coveted "fixed staple." The mayor and his

London, Sandwich, Chichester, Southampton, Bristol and Chester. The English and Welsh ports are not quite the same as those mentioned in 1297; see above, p. 218. Hartlepool has displaced Boston, and Lynn and Chichester are new English ports. The disappearance of the Scotch towns and the limitation of the Welsh trade to Chester are interesting.

[1] [On Mechlin merchants resident in London in this period see Dr. J. V. de Sturler, *In Engeland gevestigde Mechelsche Kooplieden uit de XIII^e en XIV^e eeuwen* (Mechlin, 1935).]

council had a valuable privilege to sell, and there was no want of customers for it. If Antwerp and Brabant soon dropped out of the running, Flanders and Bruges had in their favour the natural trend of the wool trade to the greatest manufacturing centres and most cosmopolitan port of the west. It is not unlikely that a staple in France was proposed. However, the chief seats both of commerce and of political authority were passed over, and the prize went to Artois, then ruled by the countess Maud, whose daughter Joan was the wife of Philip of Poitiers, the future Philip V, and who had neither the strength nor the wish to set herself up independently of her overlord. The town chosen was Saint-Omer, a place best known for its rival churches, but economically conspicuous as a venerable seat of the cloth trade, whose wimples were famous, and which had, so far back as the days of Henry II, already sent to England the most famous financier of his age.[1] Like most mediæval ports, Saint-Omer was at some distance from the sea, but it was easily accessible by sea-going ships up the river Aa, and was not, therefore, necessarily an impossible or an inconvenient seat of the English staple. Its selection was probably due to the fact that Philip the Fair, preferring that the staple should be within his kingdom, and alive to the danger of its location at Bruges among rebels who had thrown off his sway, agreed to take under his protection the staple at Saint-Omer.[2] Anyhow, the English staple was already established there by May 1314.

The fixing of the staple place did not involve the better keeping of the ordinance. Robert, count of Flanders, pleaded urgently for the transference of the staple to Bruges,[3] and the power of the staplers to change the staple place at their will left no finality in the matter. The king's interest in the English merchants was limited to what he could get out of them. He doubtless obtained loans and advances in return for the ordinance, but the English traders' capital was not great enough for him to be able to rely upon them altogether. Before long the society of the Bardi of Florence stepped into the place left vacant by the Frescobaldi, as the king's chief financial agents and bankers. They

[1] The conjecture of Prof. Haskins that William Cade came from Saint-Omer seems to me to be a happy one (*Eng. Hist. Rev.*, xxviii, 730). For Cade see also above, p. 41, n.

[2] *Foedera*, ii, 248, 251.

[3] *Ibid.*, 252.

had to be rewarded by licences to send their wools to ports more convenient than Saint-Omer for their trade, part of which was the export of wool to Italy.[1] Wool ships still sailed to Brabant, though the French did their best to stop them.[2] Saint-Omer pleased no one; not even the French king. In May 1314 Philip the Fair was complaining to Edward that the staplers shut themselves so closely in Saint-Omer that the fairs of Lille, at the moment within the royal domain, were deserted by them.[3] In 1315 Louis X was suggesting the transference of the staple to some place within his dominions between Calais and the Seine.[4] His suggestion was taken so seriously that writs were issued for a parliamentary conference of merchants, to be held side by side with the Lincoln parliament, to consider what was best to be done.[5] At the same parliament of 1316,[6] the complaints of the Flemings were discussed; and more seriously three years later.

Besides the rivalries of Flemish and French claims to the staple, which combined to make precarious its location at Saint-Omer, a new point of view was soon raised that went still deeper into the root of the matter. This was the policy of fixing the staple in England itself instead of beyond sea.

By 1318 the mayorship of the staple had passed to the London mercer, John Charlton, who represented the city in the important York parliament of October 1318.[7] There, with his brother member, Roger Palmer, Charlton had made a spirited protest against the encroachments of the household jurisdiction on the liberties of the city, which, set down on the roll, clearly shows the sympathy of London with the general Pembrokian policy.[8] Accident, however, has informed us that among the discussions of this assembly were certain important debates on economic problems, no suggestion of which is recorded on the roll of that parliament. The question, already ventilated in earlier parliaments, was seriously raised whether it was to the profit of king and kingdom that certain places should be established within England, where wool and other staple articles should be exclusively bought and sold. One special argument adduced

[1] *C.P.R. 1313-17*, p. 169, may be an early example.

[2] *Ibid.*, pp. 545-6.

[3] See Philip IV's complaints in *Foedera*, ii, 248, that the staplers attended the fairs at Lille less than when the staple was at Antwerp.

[4] *Ibid.*, 281.

[5] *Ibid.*, 281.

[6] *Rot. Parl.*, i, 356-7.

[7] *Return of Members*, i, 55.

[8] Cole's *Records*, p. 31.

was that under the existing system counterfeit moneys were introduced into England from foreign parts, to the loss of the king and to the special detriment of merchants whose main business was within the English realm.[1] No conclusions were arrived at for the moment, a negative result fully justified by the extraordinary press of business with which, as we have seen, the York parliament had to deal. It is pretty clear, however, that there was a large body of mercantile opinion in favour of the proposed policy, and quite certain that important steps were immediately taken to give effect to it.

The chief difficulty in the way was the conflict both of mercantile and of political interests. There was a strong desire in some quarters to put the staple back at Bruges, and this question had to be settled before the English staple could be fairly considered. The "mayor of the merchants of the realm" had stayed behind at York "on business touching the state of the said merchants," until 19 November, when he had a safe-conduct to go to Flanders,[2] doubtless on business connected with the staple. But, though Charlton's safe-conduct lasted until Easter, he was back in London early in the new year, for on 20 January 1319 he was directed to set forth the king's pleasure to a quasi-parliamentary assembly of representatives of the chief commercial towns, brought together to discuss the expediency of the staple of wools being removed to a Flemish city.[3] It looks as if the

[1] E.A. 457/5 includes a series of writs and returns for a conference on 24 April, for knowledge of which I am greatly indebted to Mr. A. E. Bland, of the Public Record Office. The preamble runs: "Licet inter alia regni nostri negocia in parliamentis nostris hactenus habitis ventilata, de stabiliendo certa loca infra idem regnum in quibus, *et non alibi*, in ipso regno lane venderentur et emerentur, fuerit sepe tactum, et in parliamento nostro habito ultimo apud Eboracum inde seriosius quam alibi tractaretur, idem tamen negocium utrum ad nostrum et incolarum dicti regni proficuum cederet, vel quibus locis commodius, ex certis impedimentis finaliter non fuit deductum; super quo, ac eciam super illo quod diuerse monete, que de cuneo nostro non sunt, nostre monete contrafacte, in dictum regnum de partibus exteris in dies apportantur, ut dicitur, in subuersionem monete nostre, in nostrum preiudicium manifestum, in quibus tam quorundam burgensium quam mercatorum et aliorum precipue, qui infra regnum nostrum, et non in partibus exteris, merchandisis utuntur, informaciones siue consilia sunt plurimum opportuna." The sidelight thrown on this hitherto unknown aspect of the York parliament justifies, I venture to think, the narrative I have constructed in the text. Compare *ibid.*, 457/32, to which Mr. Bland also kindly directed my attention.

[2] *C.P.R. 1317-21*, p. 239.

[3] *Ibid.*, p. 250; the writ to York is printed in *Parl. Writs*, II, ii, 196. It was to treat "super stapula lanarum in partibus Flandrie tenenda,

need of French friendship, and the vested interests created by the charter of 1313, had put an abrupt end to Charlton's negotiations in Flanders. Anyhow, if Charlton had urged the expediency of the English staple to the Flemish authorities, it is not likely that he received any encouragement from them to persevere in a policy so detrimental to continental interests. It may well be, then, that the English government sought to strengthen his hands by a further reference of the whole policy of the Flemish staple to an assembly of merchants. Unluckily, we have no information, save that contained in the writs, as to the meeting of 20 January. It is clear, however, even if it never met at all, that little favour was shown to the revival of the staple at Bruges.

Events had moved apace. No more was heard of the Flemish staple, but on 8 and 9 March writs were issued summoning, through the sheriffs, representative bailiffs and other citizens or burgesses of the chief commercial towns to meet on 24 April at Westminster, to consider the advisability of fixing the staple at certain places within the realm of England.[1] A very large number of towns were returned by the sheriffs as having chosen their representatives,[2] and it is certain that the assembly was actually held.

The importance attached to the meeting may be inferred from the fact that it was delayed until the exchequer got back to Westminster from its lengthened absence at York.

juxta formam carte nostre inde confecte, necnon et super aliis diuersis statum mercatorum regni nostri tangentibus." Two citizens or burgesses were summoned from each constituency. Charlton is described as "per consilium nostrum plenius informatus." He was, then, the official spokesman of the government.

[1] This is the assembly from whose writs the preamble has already been quoted. The return to the writs is written usually on the dorse. That of Oxford records that the borough was ordered to send "unum balliuum et quatuor de probioribus et potencioribus burgensibus ville nostre ad tractandum simul vobiscum ac cum ceteris mercatoribus regni Anglie de stabilienda certa loca infra idem regnum in quibus et non alibi," etc. (E.A. 457/5).

[2] *Ibid.* Though this large bundle of writs is clearly incomplete, it is very full for certain shires of the south and east. For instance, the sheriff of Somerset and Dorset sends returns of representatives chosen from Bridport, Shaftesbury, Dorchester, Lyme, Weymouth, Melcombe and Ilchester. The returns from the midlands and north seem to have been mainly lost. The variety of phrase and form, and the rudeness of the handwriting of some of the returns, especially of those sent in separately from the writs, is curious. London was asked to return two bailiffs and six citizens (*Letter Books of the City of London, E.*, p. 105). This is the only reference I know to this assembly that had found its way into print until the publication of Mr. Bland's note referred to later, p. 230, n. 1.

This return had been fixed since January for the fortnight after Easter, that is Sunday, 22 April 1319.[1] The Easter session of the exchequer would, under such circumstances, naturally begin on Monday, the 23rd. The very day after, the treasurer and barons were diverted from their natural business of the Easter "view" of the sheriffs' accounts to assist, with certain members of the council, in the discussions of the assembled merchants. The whole problem of the staple touched finance so nearly that it was looked upon as exchequer business. Accordingly, the writs were issued from the exchequer,[2] tested by Norwich, the chief baron, and the returns were made to the exchequer,[3] where, it is likely, the meeting was held. All these little details suggest that considerable importance was attached to the deliberations of the assembled merchants.

Unluckily, we are not completely informed as to the results of this Westminster conference. One remarkable document, preserved in the exchequer archives, suggests that no general resolution was come to, by reason of divided counsels, but that a strong party had been formed to uphold a definite policy, which this writing expounds at length. On its back are written out the names of the shires and towns which accepted the policy it advocates. The list includes London and Stamford and perhaps Shrewsbury, and fourteen counties ranging up the Thames valley from Essex to Gloucestershire, and then up the Severn valley by Herefordshire, Worcestershire, Warwickshire, and Shropshire to Staffordshire and Cheshire.[4] But it excludes the counties south of the Thames, save Berkshire, excludes the whole south-west, all the north, the east midlands north of Buckinghamshire and Bedfordshire, save Stamford, and the whole of the east, north of Essex. There was as much wool-growing in the excluded as in the included shires, so that it is very difficult to suggest other than local reasons for the lines of division.

[1] *C.C.R. 1318-23*, p. 175, records writs dated 22 Jan. ordering the restoration of exchequer and common bench to Westminster for the quinzaine of Easter.

[2] [Not, as stated in the first edition, from the chancery. For this correction Mr. Tout was indebted to Mr. R. C. Fowler.]

[3] The Bristol returns were addressed, for instance, "dominis magnificis, venerabilibus, atque discretis thesaurario et baronibus de scaccario et aliis de concilio domini regis."

[4] The inclusion of Cheshire, a palatinate, with the ordinary shires, is very unusual, but is quite certain.

The policy advocated in this remarkable document was, no doubt, suggested by London to the shires of the Thames valley and the west. It was that there should be two staple towns set up in England, one to the north and the other to the south of Trent, and that for this purpose places should be chosen which were capable of defence, well situated for the repair of foreign merchants and the protection of their lives and property, with a good harbour in the place itself, and where they could use the law merchant and no other law or customs. Moreover, foreigners visiting these staples were to be prohibited from going farther into the realm, or sending agents to purchase goods on their behalf elsewhere than in the established staples. It was also forbidden to introduce foreign money into the staple towns, though bullion and plate could be brought in. By such a policy the impoverished English towns, it was urged, would be enriched and revived; English merchants, who had suffered grievous wrongs in foreign markets, would have their own; stores of specie would flow into the realm and afford material for coining good money in the royal mints; the circulation of foreign or counterfeit money would be prohibited; the king would be discouraged from borrowing from foreigners; English resources would not be used to help lands at war against us; and the treasure now in the hands of aliens would be diverted to the enrichment of Englishmen. It is a strongly-worded manifesto of the patriotic English merchant who sees his own and his country's gain in the exclusion of the foreigner and the diversion of native products from continental to English markets. It represents, doubtless, the point of view of the London capitalists, who, like Charlton himself, regarded this policy as satisfying their economic interests as well as their patriotic prejudices.[1]

The division of the Westminster conference of merchants made any immediate settlement impossible. Even those who wished for an English staple might well dispute as to which were to be the staple towns, and the Londoners' policy of centralisation of the staple in their own city,[2] even with

[1] The manifesto of the Londoners and the southern and western shires, written in French, is contained in E.A. 457/32. This important and illuminating document has now been printed *in extenso* by Mr. Bland, its discoverer, in his note on "The Establishment of Home Staples, 1319," in *Eng. Hist. Rev.*, xxix, 94-7 (1914).

[2] I assume the Londoners intended that the southern staple was to be at London, though nothing is said openly to that effect.

a single northern staple thrown in, was not likely to commend itself to the men of the north and east, who, up to then, had had the choice of six places of export, north of the London-Bristol line. In particular it was against the interests of the wool-growing districts of the eastern counties, which saw direct exportation of their wares cut off altogether, and high freights chargeable for bringing their commodities to either of the two proposed staples. But there were still strong advocates of the foreign staple, not only among the aliens, but among English merchants whose interests centred in the Flemish trade. To defend his policy against their attacks on it, Charlton preferred to continue the staple, as long as it was abroad, at Saint-Omer, which was convenient to few on economic grounds, though it had political advantages in the eyes of the friends of the French alliance. His insistence on the Saint-Omer staple soon brought Charlton into conflict not only with the Anglo-Flemish interests but also with the Bardi, whose opposition to Saint-Omer was based on their dislike to any fixed staple at all. The attitude of the Bardi was the more dangerous, since they were the bankers both of Edward II and of the Despensers,[1] and by simply withholding the advances on which the government depended could at any time stop the machine of state. Moreover, their point of view was shared by many Englishmen, though not quite for the same reasons. The wool-growers, the smaller merchants, who bought up wool locally and took it to the ports, were anxious, like the Bardi, for a more open market than that which suited the London capitalists. It was to no purpose that the foreigners were bribed to accept the law by liberal dispensations from the operation of the ordinance. They were allowed to export wool direct to Italy; to take it to other ports than Saint-Omer; to act as if the ordinance had never been passed. These concessions stimulated rather than abated the agitation for the repeal of the ordinance of 1313 altogether.

In the York parliament of 1319 the question again cropped up. The policy of the Bardi drove all friends of fixed staples, whether home or foreign, to make common cause in defending the charter of 1313. Complaints to the king of the non-execution of the law led to the appointment of Charlton, as mayor, to take judicial proceedings against violators of

[1] *Ann. Paul.*, p. 321.

the staple and impose heavy fines upon them.[1] Charlton's zeal in carrying out these instructions soon brought him into conflict with the merchants interested in free export. Their complaints to the council resulted in a remarkable meeting, held before the king, his ministers, the justices of both benches, the barons of the exchequer and others of the royal council "in the green chamber of his palace of Westminster" on 13 April 1320.[2] The Bardi voiced the opposition to the foreign staple. They declared that they had "never consented" to the "charter of 1313," and declined to be bound by it, because Magna Carta gave all foreign merchants leave to trade freely in England on the sole condition of paying customs.[3] Against them were arrayed all the great men of the city of London, Charlton himself, Prior and Prentice, Hackney and Nasard, Swanland and Piggsflesh. All these urged the maintenance of the ordinance of 1313, and argued that this could only be done by exacting the penalties imposed under it. The council accepted the English merchants' pleas and ordered the immediate enforcement of heavy penalties against all contraveners of the act. This measure threatened both those who wished the transference of the staple to Bruges and those who wished its removal to English ports. A commission was issued to Charlton, Adam of Brome and others, who were henceforth styled the king's justices deputed to try contraventions of the staple.[4] They showed great energy and impartially fined and imprisoned both classes of offenders.

The friends of the Flemish staple were the easiest to hit. Even before the green chamber conference, Henry Northwood and other English merchants at Bruges had made a confederacy to restore the staple to Bruges and to hinder merchants transferring themselves to Saint-Omer.[5] Accordingly, the council issued a prohibition of any attempt to set up a staple at Bruges. By August, Charlton himself

[1] *C.C.R. 1318-23*, pp. 234-5; *Parl. Writs*, II, ii, 218.

[2] This date, the quinzaine of Easter, was exactly the same as that of the colloquy of merchants of the previous year. The letter close summarising the deliberations is printed in full in *Parl. Writs*, II, ii, 217-18.

[3] Among the agenda for the Lancastrian assembly at Sherburn in Elmet in 1321 was discussion of the injury to "mercatoribus extraneis atque notis qui . . . coguntur adire limina Sancti Omeri, ut ubi [*rectius ibi*] contra suum gratum et libertates per cartas regias antiquitus sibi concessas vendant" (*Bridl.*, p. 63).

[4] For these commissions see, for instance, *C.P.R. 1317-21*, pp. 477, 489, 603.

[5] *C.C.R. 1318-23*, pp. 186-7.

imprisoned Henry Nasard, one of his chief supporters in the green chamber, for taking wool to Flanders.[1] The commissioners were equally severe on the Italian exporters. But it was little use condemning offenders of all types, when the government impartially opened the prison doors to all alike. The Bardi in particular had their offences condoned, and received constant dispensations for their open breaches of the law.[2] At last the Flemish exporters had their turn also, for in 1323 a truce was arranged with Flanders on the condition that freedom to export wool from England to Flanders was to be allowed. On 22 July 1323 Charlton was despatched to Saint-Omer to inform the staplers there that their monopoly was suspended till Easter.[3] Then, in 1324, came open war between England and France, which necessarily put an end to the Saint-Omer staple altogether. The prolongation of the Flemish truce for another year made the position of Bruges increasingly favourable. It was now, in fact, if not in name, the foreign staple for English wool.

Charlton had ceased to be mayor of the staple before the final collapse of his policy. His successor, the obscure William of Merewell, was charged to make permanent the temporary arrangements with the Flemings. In August 1324 he was commissioned to renew the negotiations for a staple at Bruges.[4] Next year Merewell was replaced as mayor of the merchants by Richard of Béthune, a very prominent London pepperer, whose name suggests an Artesian origin.[5] The negotiations were transferred to London, where delegates of the "three towns" of Flanders appeared and prolonged the truce for another year.[6] It was virtually a condition of this further treaty that the staple

[1] *C.C.R. 1318-23*, pp. 253-4.

[2] *Ibid.*, pp. 250-1, gives a typical group of such licences to export without reference to the staple. Compare *ibid.*, pp. 303, 392; *C.P.R. 1317-21*, p. 518; *ibid.*, *1321-24*, pp. 193, 300; *ibid.*, *1324-27*, pp. 6, 122. There are in E.A. 120/14 and 15, two rolls, delivered by Charlton into the exchequer on 21 May 1321, which contain copious details of the fines imposed by him and Adam of Brome on offenders against the ordinance of the staple. Such prominent Londoners as Swanland, Conduit and the Prentices were among the victims, but the foreigners generally had to pay the biggest fines.

[3] *C.C.R. 1323-27*, p. 9.

[4] *Ibid.*, pp. 307-8; *C.P.R. 1324-27*, p. 13; *Foedera*, ii, 566.

[5] He is recorded as acting as mayor between 2 May and 27 Nov. at least. He is generally called "Betoigne" in the rolls, but so is the count of Flanders, Robert of Béthune. For his trade see *Calendar of Wills in Court of Husting*, i, 445, note.

[6] *C.C.R. 1323-27*, p. 378; *C.P.R. 1324-27*, p. 134.

should be established at Bruges, and on 2 May 1325 mayor Richard was formally ordered to transfer himself and the merchants thither and hold the staple there.[1] It was, however, stipulated that this should only last as long as the truce endured, and that it should not prejudice the rights of the merchants nor establish a precedent. It looks as if Béthune was already, as he was a little later, a partisan of the foreign staple, as was not unnatural in a man of foreign origin, who was more interested in the import of spices than in the export of wool. But a licence to the Bardi to disregard the new staple showed there was no finality in this settlement.[2] And a new danger arose, when William, count of Holland, an ally of France, seized English ships, loaded with staple commodities, and took them into Flushing.[3] Thus the staple at Bruges was soon in as precarious a position as the staple at Saint-Omer had been. And if Bruges were impossible, what hope was there of setting up a staple in any less favoured foreign town? At last the final blow was given to the policy of 1313 by the younger Hugh le Despenser.

We are now at the very end of Edward II's reign. Queen Isabella had refused to return to England, had taken her son to the Netherlands and was negotiating the Hainault marriage as preliminary to the invasion of England. France was again hostile. Not content with occupying most of Aquitaine in 1324, and still keeping its grip upon it, France also threatened a descent on the British coast. Desperate efforts were made by the Despensers and Baldock to meet the imminent dangers. It was now more necessary than ever to secure popular support. It was at this crisis that there was issued the exchequer ordinance of 1326, but administrative reform was a matter for the administrators only, and, so far as known, was not always welcome to the public. The real proof of Despenser's desire to win popular favour, the certain evidence that the younger Hugh was a reformer to the last, lies in the ordinance of the staple, the second of this reign, issued by king and council from Kenilworth on 1 May 1326, "for the common profit and relief of the people of all our realm and power."

By the ordinance of Kenilworth[4] the policy of 1313,

[1] *C.C.R. 1323-27*, p. 378. [2] *C.P.R. 1324-27*, p. 122.
[3] *C.C.R. 1323-27*, p. 508.
[4] *C.P.R. 1324-27*, p. 269, but better in *ibid.*, *1327-30*, pp. 98-9, which gives a full but not always very precise summary. The Irish ordinance, which was identical, can be read in Berry's *Early Statutes of Ireland*, pp. 314-21.

already broken down in practice, was formally reversed. The foreign staple was abolished, and the staple of merchants of wools, wool-fells and hides established in eight fixed places in England, three in Ireland, and three for Wales, while that of tin was to be restricted to one Devonshire and two Cornish markets.[1] At all these places, and nowhere else, aliens were compelled, under penalty of forfeiture, to purchase staple articles. When the payment of customs on the goods was certified by letters under the cocket seal, merchants were free to take them to whatsoever land they liked, provided that it was not at enmity with the king. Merchants of England, Ireland and Wales were allowed to carry goods, bought at the staples, to sell where they would, but only after they had tarried for fifteen days at a staple in the hope of selling them. "Confederations" of British or Gascon merchants to obstruct the staple or lessen the price of staple articles were forbidden and merchants, both foreign and native, were to be governed by the law merchant in all transactions made at staple places. The wool merchants were to have a mayor of the staple, and foreign traders were to be scrupulously protected.

To these regulations for the markets of the raw material, provisions for encouraging the manufacture of cloth in England were added. After Christmas, 1326, no persons in England, Ireland or Wales were to use cloth which was not made in those lands, save only the king, the nobles, knights, and their families, and persons, ecclesiastical or lay, who could spend £40 a year from their rents. Cloth of any length was allowed to be manufactured in England, Scotland and Wales, and the king, "in order to encourage people to work upon the making of cloth," in England, Ireland and Wales, promised "suitable franchises to fullers, weavers, dyers and other cloth-workers who live mainly by this craft."

The chief agent of this novel legislation was the younger Despenser, and he had his reward when the staple, assigned to his own town of Cardiff, was put under his control, "because he was the principal mover with the king and

[1] The staple towns established were: England: Newcastle-on-Tyne, York, Lincoln, Norwich, London, Winchester, Exeter, and Bristol. Ireland: Dublin, Drogheda and Cork. Wales: Shrewsbury, Carmarthen and Cardiff. For tin only—Cornwall: Lostwithiel and Truro. Devon: Ashburton. These places, though often ports, were primarily great commercial centres, and were not identical with the places where a collectorship of customs and a cocket seal were established. Thus Boston had a cocket seal in March 1327 (*C.P.R. 1327-30*, p. 57).

council that the staples should be held in fixed places in England, Ireland and Wales and not elsewhere." [1]

There can be no doubt that the change was almost universally popular in England. The foreign staple had been tried but had failed to establish itself. It never suited the interests of the Italian societies, who financed the crown and controlled the wool exports, and therefore never had a fair chance. It had remained so long because of the division of English interests. But with its complete abolition men saw a way to a partial reconciliation of the conflicting interests. Thus a judicious policy of moderate protection to each of the English industrial and commercial groups united traders for the first time on a common economic platform. The English staples were good for the wool-grower, and for the small merchant. They attracted foreign dealers to English commercial centres, and allowed enough competition to make prices brisk. They were especially favourable to the clothing trade. They were welcomed even by the majority of the London capitalists who had in 1319 fought for another type of English staple. No doubt the great merchants of London would have preferred to concentrate the southern staples at London and put off the north with a single staple of its own. But they had failed to carry this policy, and, probably, realised that the country would always oppose a programme of economic centralisation in the interests of their own big city. Accordingly, though they did not get quite all they wanted, they were now content to share staple privileges with seven other English towns, rather than accept the hated Flemish staple, or the still more unwelcome free trade that the alien capitalists had demanded in all English ports. It was to avoid these evils that they had somewhat insincerely upheld the Saint-Omer staple, as the least objectionable alternative to English staple towns. And if welcome to the average Londoner, the act of the Despensers must have been peculiarly grateful to John Charlton, who was henceforth a partisan of the English staple as defined in the ordinance. The London capitalists regarded the English staple not only as advantageous to their commercial interest but as the condition precedent to the encouragement of the English wool manufacture. Though the course of industry could not be changed in a day, it was significant that the establishment of the English staple should go

[1] *C.P.R. 1324-27*, p. 274.

hand in hand with the most systematic effort that had been made as yet to divert the export of raw material to foreign workshops and give Englishmen a chance of working up their own wool into cloth. The Bardi and their like were not pleased, for they wished for absolute free trade, were indifferent to English interests and were hostile to the encouragement of English manufactures. But they at least got rid of the Saint-Omer staple, which they very much disliked, and so were comparatively contented.

The change was equally necessary from the point of view of the diplomatic situation. The Saint-Omer staple was dead so long as there was hostility with France; the Bruges staple depended upon precarious truces. Yet with freedom to take wool to any foreign port, the way to negotiation with France was kept open and there was no need to break faith with the "three towns" of Flanders, which had accepted the truce on the virtual condition of the staple being restored to Bruges. The situation was so tangled, that the only way to deal with it was to cut the knot. There is no need to see in this any special wisdom or foresight; but it was a practical and intelligent way of dealing with the difficulty. Few statesmen, earlier or later, have looked much further forward than did Despenser in this matter.

The ordinance was issued in May and in September Isabella and Mortimer landed on the Essex coast. Under the circumstances it is surprising how much effort was made in one short summer to execute its provisions. Elaborate publicity for the new law was procured by its proclamation through all sheriffs and in all staple towns.[1] It attracted so much attention that it was the first regulation of the staple that was noticed in any of the chroniclers.[2]

The first step towards the execution of the new ordinance was the appointment of a mayor of the staple. The method of choosing was singularly democratic for the period. Each of the staple towns of England and Wales was ordered to send "two of its more respectable, wealthy and law-worthy burgesses, trading in wool and other staple products," to a convocation held in London on 12 June to nominate this officer.[3] The choice of this assembly fell on John Charlton,

[1] *C.C.R. 1323-27*, p. 571.

[2] *Ann. Paul.*, p. 312, notices its proclamation in London on 12 May.

[3] *Parl. Writs*, II, ii, Ap. 287; *Letter Book E*, p. 211. The delegates were to appear at the Blackfriars on 12 June, before Hamo of Chigwell,

who at once entered upon office. After eight years of conflict and compromise, Charlton was at last in a position to give effect to the policy which had, no doubt, always been the one nearest his heart. He lost no time in getting to work. By 30 June, orders were issued that no wool was to be exported, save when certified by Charlton, as mayor, as purchased at some English staple.[1] His energy soon brought him once more into collision with the Bardi, who complained that he would not allow them to export wool purchased by them before the ordinance, on the ground that it had not passed through a staple. On 30 July the crown gave the Bardi permission to deal as they would with wool bought by them before the ordinance, on condition that they observed the ordinance for the future.[2] It may well have been difficulties of this sort that made it advisable that Charlton's position should be strengthened by his further appointment on 30 July by letters patent.[3] The mayor of the staple was henceforth a royal officer, not only the president of a mercantile society. In this capacity it was part of his business to prevent staple merchants smuggling into England the correspondence of Mortimer and other rebels.[4] To prevent such abuses, no merchants subject to the French king were to enter the realm, save Flemings and Bretons.[5]

The premature effort to encourage home industries was not quite a dead letter, since the clothiers of Flanders and Brabant were sufficiently alarmed to take immediate steps to stay the growth of cloth-making in England. Their method of effecting this end was a quaint one. They tried to buy up " the thistles called teazles," fuller's earth, madder, woad, " burs " and other things necessary for the making of cloth available in England, in order to send them to the parts beyond sea. " And what is worse they have bought the herb and roots of the thistles, and have caused them to

John Charlton, Reginald Conduit and Henry Darcy of London, and two Norwich citizens, deputed by the king to obtain fuller information. The names show that the chief London merchants were now in favour of the English staple.

[1] *C.C.R. 1323-27*, p. 585. [2] *Ibid.*, pp. 593-4.

[3] *Parl. Writs.*, II, ii, Ap. 291 ; *C.P.R. 1324-27*, p. 301. The appointment was declared to be at the request and on the nomination of the merchants of the staple places. But Charlton was already acting on 30 June (*C.C.R. 1323-27*, p. 585).

[4] *Ibid.*, p. 640. [5] *Ibid.*, pp. 634-5, 636, 643.

be pulled up by the roots in order to send them to parts beyond sea." [1]

This is a curious anticipation of the economic legislation of Edward III as regards the development of the English cloth trade, just as the staple legislation of Edward II left Edward III nothing to do but to go on with it. We are not to believe that the effort to strangle the cloth trade had any great effect, because it is more than unlikely that any real development of the English cloth industry resulted from it. Certainly the action of the foreign clothier did not, as was anticipated, lead to the extermination of teazles from our land!

The battle between the English and the foreign staple was not yet fought out. An early act of the reign of Edward III was the confirmation of the ordinance of 1326. But Béthune, the friend of the foreign staple, became mayor of London and representative of the city in the York parliament of 1328. His fight with Chigwell was, as before, a drawn battle.[2] In despair of reconciling the two factions, the bewildered government abolished staples altogether. But we must not carry on the story past our limits. Enough has been said to show that there was scarcely any detail of staple organisation under Edward III that was not already put into practice under Edward II. The ordinance of 1326 anticipates the statute of the staple of 1353; the ordinance of 1313 prepared the way for the Calais staple of the later middle ages. But this was in the main the result of the working of natural forces, economic, fiscal and political. It is seldom that the prescient legislator arises who takes definite steps towards realising a clearly formed ideal. And statesman of this stamp were particularly rare in the middle ages. Certainly the ministers of Edward II were as blind to the future as are politicians in general. The next move of the game is the thing that looms largest before their eyes, and all that we can claim for Despenser is that he had a

[1] *C.C.R. 1323-27*, p. 565. *Cf. Letter Book E*, pp. 210-11. The motive of the Flemings was "to subvert the staple." The French word "bure," quaintly mis-translated "butter" in the Calendar of Close Rolls, is, as Dr. Sharpe points out, probably "bourre," not "beurre."

[2] Dr. Sharpe's *London and the Kingdom*, i, 171-8, gives from the London archives a good account of this struggle, the study of which is the necessary complement to the history of the staple under Edward II. Unluckily, he confuses the London John Charlton with John Charlton, lord of Powys, the sometime king's chamberlain.

touch of that saving political insight which sees that the best trick to outwit an opponent is something valuable in itself. Thus unconsciously, or half-consciously, the men of Edward II's court worked out their destiny, and in doing so contributed their share in winning for these twenty years a little place of their own in English history.

# APPENDIX I

## THE HOUSEHOLD ORDINANCES OF EDWARD II

THE circumstances under which the Household Ordinances of 1318 and 1323 were drawn up have been sufficiently explained in the text. They are here printed because, though almost exclusively dealing with the domestic routine of the court, they are too important in the history of administration to remain accessible in type in a bad seventeenth-century English translation only. This is to be found in the Chaucer's Society's *Life Records of Chaucer*, ii, 1-62, Edward II's Household Ordinances (1876). The late Dr. Furnival published these ordinances because of their interest to him as illustrating Chaucer's life at court as valet and esquire of the king. Unluckily he was content to set out the unsatisfactory English translation by Francis Tate in 1601, which he found in the Bodleian, MS. Ashmole 1147, pt. iii. He thought, however, that no original text was known, and described how he failed to find one either in the British Museum or Record Office. As his interest in the document was limited to the light it threw on Chaucer's career, he took no pains to elucidate it and fell into error in what little he says about it. For instance, he dates the document in 1323, ignoring the internal evidence which shows that it includes two different ordinances, and that only the second and shorter ordinance belongs to that date, being issued at York in June of that year. The chief interest of the second ordinance is that it illustrates the failure of the earlier ordinance to do the work it set out to do, and the remedies it provided, mainly by reforming the system of drawing up the accounts. The more important document is, however, the earlier ordinance, issued, on St. Nicholas Day, 6 December 1318, at the conclusion of the parliament of York that met in October. The names of the committee and of assenting councillors are enough to show that it could not possibly be in 1323.[1]

Both the ordinance of 1318 and that of 1323 are to be found in the French original in two manuscripts in the British Museum.

[1] See below, p. 244. It gives Badlesmere as steward, but he was executed in 1322; Northburgh as keeper, but he had resigned on his appointment to the bishopric of Lichfield in the same year; and Hotham as chancellor, though he gave up office in Jan. 1320.

16

Both of these manuscripts, however, are of much later date, and neither can be regarded as affording the basis for a very satisfactory text. The earlier of the two is contained in Add. MS. 32097. This manuscript, formerly in the possession of the Lancashire family of Towneley, mainly consists of matter relating to the coronation ceremonies of kings of England and France, but also contains the *modus tenendi parliamentum*, a copy of the treaty of Brétigni-Calais, and ordinances for the regulation of the army in the Scottish expedition of 1385. It is beautifully written, and presents few palæographical difficulties. It is certainly not older than the reign of Henry IV, and may be later. There are a few Elizabethan additions, such as "Lordre de la Maundye, 1572," and occasional annotations and headings of that date. These seem to be the work of the antiquary William Lambard, who notes that he had the book "ex dono Ricardi Atkyns, Lincolniensis" in 1571. The ordinances are to be found between folios 46$^{v}$ and 70. I have called this manuscript A.

It is not very likely that the text of the manuscript is a very faithful transcript of the originals of some eighty years earlier, and certainly it is in places corrupt and impossible to construe. Another British Museum manuscript, Cotton MS. Tiberius E VIII, ff. 54$^{v}$-74$^{v}$, gives us some but not very certain help in elucidating doubtful points. This is a fine folio manuscript, written on paper at very various dates and by very different hands, containing very similar contents to those of the Towneley manuscript, with later additions, as, for example, the titles of queen Elizabeth. The older parts of it, perhaps, belong to about the latter half of the fifteenth century, and include our two household ordinances. It was in some places damaged by the Cotton fire, but the part where our ordinances are found is almost entirely intact. Though later in date, it is easier to understand than the Towneley MS.; but one has a fear that its superior intelligibility is not so much due to higher accuracy and authority as to a rough and ready effort to normalise the grammar and spelling of the original on the lines of later French style. It is, however, distinctly useful in some places where the earlier text is corrupt and contains more headings than the Towneley MS. This MS. I have called B.

In preparing these ordinances for the press I have based my text on MS. A., which has been kindly transcribed for me by Miss C. M. Calthrop. I have noted at the bottom of the page the more important variants found in B., and have sometimes, but not often, incorporated these variants into the text. Most additional matter in B. I have also worked into the text. I have, for instance, put into the text the numerous headlines in B. not found in A. I have not been meticulous about small points that seemed to me of little importance to the understanding of the meaning of the original. Thus I have mainly put down at the foot of the page variants that seem to make A. more intelligible. The capitals and punctuation are my own, but I have avoided any attempts to normalise the text, and have not even tried to make it grammatical or intelligible. Accordingly I have not even added accents, but here and there I have supplied a fairly obvious word in square brackets, generally, but not always, on the authority of MS. B. I feel that it is more important to give scholars Anglo-French as it was actually written, than to make it easier or more correct. The folios of the Towneley MS. are recorded in the margins, and also the English summaries which are found in A., in an Elizabethan hand, and are apparently the work of Lambard.

[A fresh comparison of the printed text in the first edition with the manuscripts has resulted in a certain number of corrections, but treatment has been in accordance with Mr. Tout's wishes expressed above. For clarity's sake, *ou* has been printed *ov* where it is the equivalent of *avec.*]

The ordinances printed here belong to a common type, but very few others seem to have been preserved. The starting point of the series is the well-known *Constitutio domus regis* of 1135, or thereabouts, printed in Hall's *Red Book of the Exchequer*, iii, 807-13, and in Hearne's *Liber Niger Scaccarii*, i, 341-59.[1] The only intermediate ordinance that I have come across is the ordinance of Edward I of 1279, which I hope to print in my forthcoming volume on the wardrobe.[2] Much indirect light is thrown on the subject by the account of the plan drawn up in 1305 for the reform, on English lines, of the Scottish state and household, published by the late Miss Bateson from a C.C.C. MS., No. 37, in the *Juridical Review*, 1901-2, and *Scottish History Soc.*, *Miscellany*, ii, 1-43, 1904. Some later household ordinances were printed in 1790 by the London Society of Antiquaries in a *Collection of Ordinances for the Government of the Royal Household from Edward III to William and Mary.* It is likely that more systematic search than I have been able to give would add considerably to the number of extant household ordinances. Among them may be mentioned the ordinance of Woodstock,[3] referred to in the York ordinance of 1318,[4] and the statute of St. Albans *de aula non tenenda in hospicio regis* of 13 April 1300.[5]

[1] This was quoted by the treasurer and barons of the exchequer in 1300 as authority for the fee of Humphrey Bohun as constable, under the title of "constituciones domus domini Henrici *secundi*" (*Lib. quotid.*, p. 201).

[2] [See *Chapters*, ii, 158-63.]

[3] [Perhaps issued in May 1310. For discussion of date see *Chapters*, ii, 248, n. 3.]

[4] See below, p. 275.

[5] [See *Chapters*, ii, 49-51.]

## A. The Household Ordinance of York, 6 December 1318

Fol. 46v. Pour ceo qe les officers del lostiell nostre seignour le roi ount estez toutz iours en arere, et [1] noun certein de ceo qils deueront faire et prendre du roi, par reason de leur officez, par quoy due examinement dez ditz officers ne poiat estre fait, ne les officers chargez si come estre deuoient, a grand damage et dishonour du roi et en desarament [2] de soun hostiell; et nostre dit seignour le roi, eiant regard al estat de son dit hostell meyns bien garde, et a ses chosez en autre manere despenduez qi estre ne duissent: si comanda a monsieur Berthelmeu de Badelesmere, seneschall de soun hostiell, monsieur Hugh le Despenser, chamberleyn, sire Roger de Northborough, tresorer, et a sire Gilbert de Wyggetone, contreroullour de sa garderobe, qe eux ordinassent sur la remedie, lez queux par vertue du dit comaundement ount ordeigne les chosez souzescritz en amendement dez defautez desusditz: lez quelez ordinauncez furont leuez et assentuez deuaunt le roi et en presence larceuesque

Steward. de Deuerwik, leuesque Dely, chaunceller Dengleterre, leuesque de Northwich, et leuesque de Sarum, monsieur Henry de Scrope, et monsieur Henry Spigurnell, justicez, qi sensuit: cest assauoir qi le roi eit vn seneschall de son hostiell suffisant, qui, sil soit baneret, eit vn chiualer, trois esquiers et vn clerk pur les plees qi appartement a la seneschaucie, mangeantz en la sale. Et prendra pur sa chambre chescun nuyt vn sexte de vin, xij chaundelx, ij tortis pur viu, et vn torche, et pluis quant il auera affaire, et litere pour tout lan, bouche de la vielle de toutz Seintz iusques al vielle de Pasque, pur la soison dyuer, de luscher de la sale, et vn liuere pour soun chamberleyn, cestassauoir vn dare de paine, vn galoun de seruoise, et vn messe de gros [3] de la cusine, et diners et sopers quant il lez vudra auoir; et pur fees xx marcz par an a lez festez de Noell et de Pentecost par owelx porteons. Et sil soit chiualer simple, il prendra feez et robes si come autrez chiualers simplez de lostell, et auera deux esquiers et soun clerk mangeantz en la sale.

### *Le Tresorer* [4]

Treasorer of the Wardrobe. Vn tresorer de la garderobe, qi eit vn chapellain, vn clerk et ij esquiers mangeantz en la sale. Et prendra pur sa chambre vn sexte de vin, xij chaundelx, ij tortis, vn tortis pur viu, et vn torche, et pluis quant il auera affaire, et litere pur tout lan, et busche pur la seison dyuer, cestassauoir entre lez viellez de toutz Seintz et le Pasque, de lussher de la sale, et diners et sopers quant il plerra; et vn liueree pur son chambirleyn, cestassauoir vn darre de payn, vn galon de seruoise, et vn messe grosse de la quissine, et robes

[1] en in MSS. [2] B. disaraiement.

[3] [The constantly recurring gros' or gross' with abbreviation mark, rendered in 1st edn. variously as gros, grose, gross and grosse, has here been standardised as gros. This follows the practice recommended by a committee of scholars in 1923 in the case of MSS. of the 15th or 16th centuries where such abbreviation marks in suspension of final letters are inserted without apparent meaning. (*Bull. Inst. Hist. Res.*, i, 11).]

[4] B. only.

en drap pur sey autre, ov xvj marcz par an a les festez de Noel et Pentecost |[1] par ouelx porcions. f. 47.

*Le Chamberleyn* [2]

Vn chambirleyne qi, sil soit baneret, eit vn chiualer et trois esquiers, mangeant en sale. Et prendra pour sa chambre demi sexte de vin, xij chaundelx, ij tortis, et vn torche, et litere pour lan, et buche pour la [3] soison dyuer de lousshere de la chambre, et diners et sopers de v.s. le roi, et vn liueree pour son chambirleyn, cestassauoir vn dare de payn, vn galon de seruoise, et vn messe de gros de la quissine ; et fees et robez sicone [4] baneret del hostell, cestassauoir pour feez xx marcs, et pur robez xvj marcs par an, sil ne soit serue en drap. Et sil soit chiualer simple, il prendra feez et robez si come vn chiualer simple del hostell, et auera deux esquierz mangeantz en la sale. Chamberleyn

*Le Counterrollour* [5]

Item vn countreroullour, qi doit countrerouller au tresourier de la garderobe toutz lez recceitez et issuez touchantz mesme le garderobe ; et lez testimoignera en leschequer sur la compte du dit tresourier. Et serra a la recette dez vyns en gros. Et suruerra toutz les offices del hostiell, come de panetrie, botillerie, celerie, lardrie, espicerie, auenerie et autres officez, qi les vins, vitaillez, qil trouera en les ditz officez, soient bons et conuenablez pour les dispenses du dit hostell solonque lez achatez. Et sil troue qi null dez ditz vitaillez soient meyns sufficiantz, lez monstra a prochein accompte deuant le seneschal et le tresorer, et sue deuers eux tanque amendement soit fait par reasone. Et doit entrer mesmez lez officez chescun lundi pur veer lez remenantz, issint qil veie qi lez ditz remenantz et les dispenses de la semeyne passe accordent oue lez receitez de la semeyn auantdit. Et serra a quissine a coupere de la chare, et au departier de pissoun. Quant il verra qi soit affaire, sert garne [6] ove le chief vssher, chiualer, et le clerk de la quissine de veer qe lacat de chare et de pissoun soit bon, et le messe coupez en due manere solonque lordinement de ceo fait a la counte, et le pissoun departi sicome estre doit. Et serra chescun iour, sil neit resonable enchesoun, a lez accountez ove le seneschall et le tresorer. Et mesme celluy countreroller de la garderobe eit vn clerk et vn esquier, mangeantz en la sale. Et prendra pour sa chambre demi sexte de vin, vj chaundelx, ij tortis et vn torche, et litere pour tout lan, et bushe pour la seison diuer del vssher del sale, et vn liueree pour soun chambirleyn, cestassauoir vn dare de payn, vn galoun de seruoise, et vn messe gros de la quissine, et robez en drap, | ou viij marcz par an a lez festez de Noel et Pentecost par owelx portions. Et sil soit seigne ou maladez, preigne sa liueree pour son mangier, cestassauoir ij dare de pain, j piche de vin, ij messes en gross de la quisine, et vn messe de rost. Et serra a gagez de v deniers [7] le iour, tanque il soit auancez par le roi. Controller. f. 47v.

[1] A straight line in the text ( | ) marks the beginning of each fresh page of MS. A. [2] B. only. [3] Sa in MS. [4] B. sicome. [5] B. only. [6] B. soit garny. [7] B. xv deniers le iour.

*Le Cofferer* [1]

Cofferer.

Item vn cofferer qi serra mytz pour le tresorer, et eit mangeant en la sale vn esquier. Et prendra pour sa chambre demi sexte de vin, vj chaundelx, ij tortys, vn torche, et pour la table de laccompte xij chaundelx, et pluis quaunt boisoigne serra, et litere pour tout lan, et bousche pour la soison dyuer del vssher de la sale, et vn liueree pour soun chambirleyn, cestassauoir vn dare de payn, vn galoun de seruoise, vn messe de gros de la quissine. Et sil soit seigne ou maladez, preigne pour soun mangere au tiel liuere come countreroullour, cestassauoir ij dare del payn, vn piche de vin, ij messes de gros de la coisine, et vn messe de rost, et toutz autrez coustagez en court, du tresorer.

*Deux Clerks de la table daccompte* [2]

Clerkes of the Greneclothe.

Item deux clerks de la table de la countee, sufficiantz pour escriuer et faire toutz chosez touchantz la garderobe et laccompte dicel, desouz le coffrer, dount chescun prendra le iour pour gagez vij d. ob., ou iiij d. ob., solonque ceo qil serroit destate, a la discresioun le tresorer, ij robes par an en drap, ou xlvj s. viij d., et en dyners.[3] Et prendrent entre eux et le clerk le countrerouller, qi girount ensemble en la garderobe, pour lour coche ij piche de vin, vj chaundelx, et ij tortis, ov [4] litere par tout lan, et busche tout la soison dyuer del vssher de la sale. Et syl dynent en garderobe pur serteyne resoun, ou per conge le tresorer, dieux eient vn liuere a diner et a manger en garderobe, chescun vn liuere de sergeant, cestassauoir j dare de payne, demi piche de vin, demi galoun de seruoise, vn messe de gros de la coisine, et vn messe de rost. Et si nul soit seigne ou maladez, eit mesme le liuere.

*Le Clerk de la priue Seal* [5]

Clerk of the privie seale.

Item vn clerk suffisant gardein de priue seal, qi eit vn esquier mangeant en la sale. Et prendra pour chambre demi sexte de vin, vj chaundelx, ij tortis, et vn torche, et litere par tout lan, et busche pour la soison diuer del vssher de la sale, et vn liuere pour soun chambirleyne, cestassauoir vn dare de payne, vn galoun de la seruoyse, et vn messe gros de la coisine, et robez en drap, ou viij
f. 48. marcz par an, al fest | de Noell et Pentecost par ouelx portions. Et sil soit seigne ou maladez, preigne sa liueree, cestassauoir ij dare de payn, vn piche de vin, ij messes de gros de la cuissine, et vn messe de rost. Et sil soit a gagez tant qil soit auancez. Item iiij clercz pour escriuer au priue seal, qi prendrount toutz ensemble pour lour chambre ij piche de vin, vj chaundelx, ij tortis, et litere pour tout lan, et bousche pour la soison dyuer de la vssher de la sale. Et sils dynent ou maungent al loustell par certeyn reasoun, deux vn liuere a dyner et chescun vn liuere a manger, sicome lez clercz de la countee desuis nomez. Auxint si null' soit seigne ou maladez, eit mesme la

[1] B. only. [2] B. only. [3] B. en deniers. [4] B. et.

[5] From this point the headings are in both A. and B., those in A. being in red ink.

liuere. Et chescun a gagez, a pluis ou a meyns, solonque ceo qil serroit destate, et al discrecion du seneschall et tresorer, tanque ils soient auancez par le roi ; et ij robez par an ou deniers solonque lour gagez.

*Le Clerk purueour de la graunde Garderobe*

Item vn clerk purueour pour la grande garderobe, qi doit giser en garde quaunt il est en court. Et auera mangeant en la sale vn esquier. Et prendra pour sa chambre vn piche de vin, iiij chaundelx, vn tortis, et liuere pour vn chambirleyn qi garde soun lite, cestassauoir vn dare de payn, vn galoun de seruoyse, vn messe de gros de la cuissine. Et sil soit seigne ou maladez en court, preigne ij dare de pain, j galoun de vin, ij messes de gros de la cuissine, vn messe de rost, et ij robez par an en drap, ou viij marcz en deniers. Et hors de court prendra soun fee, cestassauoir xx liures par an, tanque il eit par le roi c marcz de rent. Et quaunt lez auera, serue le roi a sez costagez demein hors de court. Et ferra ceo qi appartient a luy solonque ceo qi est contenu en le statute fait dedeinz soun office.

Clerke purveior of the great Wardrobe.

*Le Clerk de lespyceryе*

Item vn clerk de la spicerie, chief vsser de la garderobe, qi resceiuera du clerk purueour de la grande garderobe cere, napperie, linge, teille, canauas, espicerie, et toutz maneres dez autrez chosez qi apparteignent a son office, par endenture faisant expresse mencioun de price, de aunes, de pois, et de coustage. Et ferra peiser le cere qi le chaundeler ferra ouerer, et repoiser quaunt ele serra oueree. Et suruerra, et ferra escriuer par soun souz clerk, lez liuerez de la chaundelarie qi se ferront chescun iour en garderobe. Et suruerra lendemein le reposer dez torchez, tortis de viu et dez mortere. Abbreuera chescune iour lez parcelx dez toutz maners dez chosez liuerees et dispendues en son office, come de la iourne deuaunt en pris, et en respondra a la countee del hostiell. Et suruerra lez | cariagez appartenauntz a la garderobe, auxibien dez coffers et autres chosez de soun office, come dez litz clercs de la garderobe qi doyuent cariez. Et alleuera en soun roll lez cariagez et portagez resonablement faitz pur iournez le roi. Et prendra pur sa chambre vn piche de vin, ij chaundelx, j tortis, et trois chaundell pour soun office, et litere pour tout lan et busche pour la soisone dyuer del vsshere de la sale. Et sil soit seigne ou maladies, preigne pour sa liuere vn dare de pain, demi piche de vin, demi galoun de seruoise, j messe de gros de la cuissine, et vn messe de rost. Gagez iiij d. ob. tanque il soit auauncez par le roi, et neint pluis par enchesone qil auera cariage pour soun lite en garderobe, et ij robez en drap, ou xlvj s. viij d.

Clerk of the Spycerye.

f. 48$^{v}$.

Et pour ceo qi troue est qi boun et verroi examinement qi nostre seignour le roi ait de cea en arere graundz damagez et perde,[1] par enchesoun qi toutz lez chosez qi sount venuz deuers lostiell par la liueree du clerk et purueour de sa graunt garderobe, come cere, espicerie, et autrez appartenauntez soun officez, ount este malement

Clerk purveiour with Clerk of the Spycerie.

[1] B. perte.

despenduz et gastez par defaut qi certeins price et parcelx nount mye estez renduz iour sur la accompte de lostiell deuaunt le seneschal et le tresorer come dez autres officez, ordeigne est et assentu de par luy et les euesqes, seneschal, et tresorer, chambirleyne et autrez du counseil, qi le clerk purueour de la graunde garderobe deliuere dezhors enauant toutz chosez, et touchent loffice de lespicerie, au clerc de mesme loffice, come de cere, gros espicerie, linge, teile, et canauace, et toutz lez parcelx a luy ensy lyuerez ensemblement ove le price et lez coustagez ; et mesme celluy clerk de lespicerie, ensi charge en certein, serra chescun iour a lez comptz del hostiell, si come lez clercs dez autres officers, a presenter et accompter deuaunt le seneschal et le tresorer toutz lez parcelx et le price de chacun chose, qi serra deliuere et dispenduz de soun office en lostiell a la iourne. Et qi lez pois de la graunde garderobe et de lespicerie soient accordantz, et tiel come lem troue Dengleterre. Et en mesme le manere doit le dit clerc et purueour de la graunt garderobe charger le taillour le roy, et armurer, pau[illon]illoner,[1] confectioner dez espicez, par endenturez dez toutz chosez qil lour deliuera pour lour officez hors de soun office, par endenturez faisantz mencione du price et de la quantite dez chosez ensy liuerez, et qi lez partiez de mesme cels endenturez demuranz deuers le dit clerc, et lez parcelx de toutz les autres liuerez et donnes le roy, qil auera fait hors de soun office, soient quatre foitz par an monstrez au tresorer de la garderobe, issint qil puisse pleinement estre certifiez de lestate de cel office, et charger duement lez dit clerc de lespicerie, taillour, armurer, pauilloner, confectioner dez
f. 49. espicez, sur lour accomptz qi se deiuent | rendre dezhors en auaunt deuaunt le dit tresorer en garderobe, auxibien dez issuez dez telz parcelx, issint resceiuez du dit clerk, come dez coustagez misez par eux entour le fesure et leuereyne dicelx. Et qi la dit clerc pourueour demurge en court tant auant come soun office lem pourra suffrere, sil ne soit par especiall counge du roi.

### *Le Second Clerc de lespicerie* [2]

Et le dit clerc de lespicerie eit vn clerc en eyde de luy, de faire lez chosez qi appartinent a mesme loffice et descriuer lez parcelx del issue qi se ferra de toutz maners dez chosez de cel office solonque lauisement et lordinaunce de dit chiefe clerk. Et prendra vn liueree le iour, cestasauoir j darre de payn, j galon de seruoise, j messe gros de la cuissine, et j robe de clerc par an, ou xx s. par an en deniers.

### *Le Sargeant soubz Vssher de la Garderobe* [3]

Usher of the Wardrobe. Item vn sergeant soutz vsshere de la garderobe qi herbegera le garderobe, et girra dedeinz leushe de la garderobe pour saument[4] garder toutz les chosez qi sount dedeinz. Et respondra, si peril aueigne en defaut de luy. Et querra lez liuereez dez officez pour toutz ceux de la garderobe et entendra a lour comandementz. Et prendra pour couche iij chaundelx. Et sil soit seigne ou maladez,

[1] B. pauillour. The letters bracketed seem repeated.
[2] B. only. [3] B. only. [4] B. sagement.

preigne pour liueree j denier [1] de payn, demi piche de vyn, demi galoun de seruoise, j messe gros de la guissine, et vn messe de rost. Et iiij d. ob. pour gagez le iour, ij robez par an en drap, ou quarrant solds, et soun lit cariez en cariage garderobe.

### *Un Porter de la Garderobe* [2]

Item vn portour de lez garderobe, qi portera coffrez et autres harneys de la garderobe az charettz, et lez chargera et deschargera. Et serra sur le car[ette] [3] en chemyn. Et veillera lez nuytez, si le car[ette] [3] soit dehors measoun en errant par pays. Et prendra en le roulle de lespicerie chescun iour pour gagez, ij d., et chescun de trauaille ij d., en mesme le roulle de lespicerie, outre sez ditz gagez certeins par enchesoun de veille et trauaille ; et vn robe de vallet de mestre par an en drap, ou vn marc en deniers, et pour chaussour iiij s. viiij d. a deux seasouns del an, sicome vallet de mestre, au Nowelle et a la Pentecost per ouelx porcions. Portor of the Wardrobe.

### *Un Esquier Frutier* [4]

Item vn esquier frutier qi resceiuera et leuera [5] confecciouns et autres | espiceries, figes, et reisons du clerk de lespicerie pour la bouche le roy. Et abbreuera chescun iour au dit clerk de ceo qi serra despendu la iourne deuaunt, auxi bien dez ditz espiceriez et fruyt, issint resceux du dit clerk, come de pomes, pers, ciris, et autrez fruytez qi le dit fruitier puruera, mesme le quelle fruit issint par luy purueu, ensemblement lez coustagez misez entour le cariage dicell serra suruou per la dit clerc, auaunt qi rien soit despenduz. Et sil en face taillez as vendours, il doit liuerer lez foillez au dit clerc tantost sur la vieu auauntdit, par quelez taillez ils serrount payez en garde [robe]. Et le dit esquier frutier prendra chescun nuyt pour coche vn galoun de seruoise, iij chaundelx, et pour soun office iij chaundelx ; pour gagez vij d. ob. le iour ; ij robez par an en drap, ou xl. s. en deniers. Et sil soit seigne ou maladez, ij deners [6] de payne, demi piche de vin, demi galloun de seruoise, j messe gros de la cuissine, j messe rost. Et auera vn vadlet soutz luy, qi prendra manger, boyuer et chaucer, sicome vn aultre vallet de mestre del houstell. Esquier Fruterer. f. 49v.

### *Le Sergeant Chaundelere*

Item vn sergeant chaundelere, qi resceiuera la cere et lymyn par pois du clerk de lespicerie, et lez ferra ourir, solonque lassise qi est ordeigne dedeinz en lestatuit. Et la cere et limine, ensuit ouerez, repoisera en la presence du dit clerk. Et en ferra la liueree, et seruira lostiell, par la vieue du dit clerc, ou de soun souz clerc, qi escriuera lissue de mesme la cere. Et la dit sergeant fera queiller torche, tort de [7] et mortere qi serrount liuerez ; et lez ferra repoiser lendemayn par vieue de dit clerc, ou de soun souz clerc, Serieant Chandeler.

[1] B. darre ; certainly the right reading.
[2] B. only. [3] B. cherett. [4] B. only.
[5] The reading of B. [6] A. darre is probably the right reading.
[7] A blank space for one word in both A. and B.

issint come puis sauoir lez despeirs de la iournee al compte. Et soit la liuere de la chaundellarie faite chescune iour en garderobe deuaunt manger, ou si tost apres qi lez ditz sergeantz et clercs ne soient mye destourbez qi ne puissent seruir le roi et lostell. Et prendra pour couche j galoun de seruoise, iij chaundelx. Et sil soit maladez ou seigne, prendra pour liueree j dare de payn, demi piche de vin, demi galoun de seruoise, j mes gros de la quissine, et vij d. ob. pour gagez, ij robez par an en drap, ou xlvj s. viij d. en deniers.

*Deux Vallettes soubz le Sergeant* [1]

2 Groomes of the Chandellrye.

Item deux vallettez de mester, qi deiuent ouerer la cere, desouz le sergeant, et prendrount le iour qils ouerount pour liuere ij dare de payn, ij galloun de seruoise, ij messe de gros de la quissine ; et chescune de eux prendra vn robe en drap par an, ou vn marcz en

f. 50.

| deniers ; et pour chauser iiij s. viij d. par an. Et sil soit maladez ou seigne, prendra pour liuere j dare de pain, j galoun de seruoise, j messe gros de la quissine.

*Le Confessour* [2]

Confessour.

Item vn confessour le roi, et soun compaignoun, prendrent pour tout le iour pour liuere iij dares de payn, ij piche de vin, iij galoun de seruoise, iij messes de la quissine, dount lun serra chare par iour de chare, iij chaundelx, j tortis, litere pour lour lites par tout lan del vssher de la sale, et feuale pour lour viande par tout lan, et pour lour chambre par le seisoun dyuer,—cestassauoir de la veille de toutz Seintz tanque a la Pasque,—de lesquillerie, et liuere dez robez et dez litz de la graunde garderobe, et pour solez, botes, linge, teille, et autres menus necessariez pour lour corps, en deniers en garderobe solonque la discrecion du seneschal et tresorer ; feins et aueinz, littere et ferrure, et autres necessariez pour iiij chiualx, et gagez pour iij garceons, chescune a j d. ob., et robez pour vn keu, qi fera sa viande et mangera deuers soun meistre. Et lez ditz iij garceons en drap, ou pur chescune x s. per an. Et pur chescun de eux iiij s. viij d. pour chauceur a deux soisouns del an, et ij napes et ij towaillez par an du clerc de lespicerie, a Nowell et a Pentecost.

*Le Chief Chapellein* [3]

Chapleyns.

Items vn chief chapellein, qi eit vn esquier mangeant en la sale, et serra as gagez le roi tanque il soit auancez du roi ; et v chapelleins, chescun a vij d. ob., et vj clercs, chescune a iiij d. obole le iour tanque ils soient auancez de roi. Et entre eux toutz prendront pour lour coche ij piche de vin, ij galoun de seruoise, vj chaundelx, j tortis, et littere pour lytes par tout lan, et fouail pur lour chambre en la seisoun dyuer de la vssher de la sale. Et si le chief chapellein soit seigne ou maladez, prengne pour liuere ij dare de pain, j piche de vin, ij messes de gros de la quissine, et vn messe de rost. Et si nul dez autrez chapelleins et clercs soient seigne ou maladez, prengne pour liuere j dare de pain, j galoun de seruoise, j messe grose de la

[1] B. only. [2] B. only. [3] B. only.

quissine, et vn messe de rost. Et le chief chapellein prendra ij robez par an en drap, ou viij marcz en deniers ; et chescune autre chapellein ij robez par an en drap, ou iij marcz et demye en deniers ; et chescune clerc ij robez par an en drap, ou xl s. en deniers.

### *Le Ausmoner* [1]

Almoner. f. 50v.

Item vn ausmoner chapellein, qui eit vn esquier mangeant | en la sale. Et prendra pour chambre j piche de vin, ij chaundelx, j torche, et littere par tout lan, et fouail pou[r] la seison dyuer del vssher de la sale. Et sil soit seigne ou maladez, prengne pour liuere ij dare de pain, j piche de vin, ij messes de gros de la quissine, et vn messe de rost ; ij robez per an, ou viij marcz en deniers ; et serra a gagez a vij d. ob. tanque il soit auance par le roi. Et chescune iour de soiourne xiiij dares de pain, xiiij galoun de seruoise, en roulle panetrie et butillerie, et xiiij messes de la cuissine pour office de lammosenerie ; et chescune iour de trauaille le roi xiiij s., ou [1] deniers de la garderobe, qi serrount entre en le graunt roulle de lez despensez de loustiell a la fyne de la iournee.

Clerk of the Almosenerye.

Item vn clerc qi prendra garde al amoisne desoutz luy, qi mangera en sale et prendra le iour iij d. en roulle de marchauce pour la sustenaunce de soun hakene, tanque il soit auauncez par le roi. Et son garson viuera del amoisne, et auera vn robe par an en drap, ou xx s. en deniers. Et sil soit seigne ou maladez, preigne pour liuere j dare de pain, j galoun de seruoise, j messe de gros de la quissine.

Item vn vallett de mestere de mesme loffice, qi mangera en la sale entre lez autrez vallettz de mestere. Et prendra vn robe per an en drap, ou j marc en deniers ; et pour chauceour iiij s. vii d. par an. Et sil seit seigne ou maladez, preigne pour liueree j dare de pain, j galoun de seruoise, j messe de gros de la cuissine.

### *Le Phisicien* [2]

Physition.

Item vn phisicien prendra pour liueree par tout le iour iij dare de pain, j galoun de vyn, ij galoun de seruoise, j messe de gros de la cuissine, ij messes de rost ; pour chambre iij chaundelx, j tortis et littere par tout lan del vssher de la sale, et fouaille pour sa viande par tout lan et pour sa chambre pour la seison dyuer de lesquillerie, et ij robez par an en drap ou viij mars en deniers [3] ; feins, aueins, littere, ferrure pour iij chiualx, et gagez pour iij garceouns, chescun a vij d. ob., tanqe il soit auance par le roi.

### *Le Cirurgien* [4]

Surgion.

Item vn cirugien mangera chescun iour en la sale, sil ne soit occupiez par resonable enchesoun, tesmoigne deuaunt le seneschall et tresorer. Et adonqes eyt sa liueree, sicome vn chiualer de loustiell seigne | ou maladez, cestassauoir ij dares de payn, j piche de vin, ij messes de gros de la quissine, j messe de rost. Et prendra chescun iour pour sa chambre viij [5] piche de vin, iij chaundelx, vn tortiz, et

f. 51.

[1] B. en. [2] B. only.
[3] B. A. diners or diuers. [4] B. only. [5] B. vn.

littere pour tout lan, et fouaille pour seisoun dyuer del vssher de sale. Et prendra xij d. le iour pour gagez, tanqe il soit auauncez par le roi, ij robez par an en drap, ou viij marcs en deniers. Et prendra pour chosez mediceuls xl s. par an.

### *Le Clerc de marche* [1]

Clerke of the market.

Item vn clerc de marche, corouner de loustiell le roi, qi ferra examinacion lassise de pain, vin et seruoise, et lassise de toutz maners dez mesurez, poys et alnez dedeinz la viergez de la presence notre seignour le roi. Et ferra puny [2] les trespassours qi auereount efreint lassise, ou qi soient trouez ove faux mesurez, par mise ou par fyns, et ceo chescun trespassour solonque son trespas. Et qil ne charge citees ne burghs nautrez villez, et ceo pour vn nuyt et vn iour; tant soulement sil ne soit en defaut dez gentz de la ville, adonquez en demourge en celle ville outre ij iours az coustagez de ville. Et lez denirs qil leuera de fyns et amerciamentz de celle office loialment ferra, de iour en autre, mander au garderobe. Et qaunt le roi sen va le pays, voise deuaunt par lez iournez le roi pour faire soun office, et face bracer et fourner solonqe lassise countre la venue le roi et son houstiell. Et face crier en chescune ville marchaunde dedeinz la vierge lassise de pain, vin, seruoise et auene. Et la dit clerc sount [3] countre-rollour le seneschall az pledez de la sale, et purueour dez cariage[z]. Et auera vn clerc souz luy qi mangera en sale et puruerra lez cariagez de loustell, solonqe ceo qe commaunde luy serra par seneschall et tresorer. Et le dit clerc de marche, countrerollour, receyuera toutz lez deniers surdantz dez pledez de la sale deuaunt le seneschall et mareschall, et lez liuera, ensemblement ov lez estrestez, en garderobe; et illoquez accomptera chescune semayne dez ditz deniers. Et quaunt il sera en court, il prendra de liuere [4] pour sa chambre j piche de vin, ij chaundelx, j tortis, ij robez par an en drap, ou iij marcz et demy en deniers; et sil soit seigne ou maladez, prengne pour liuere j dare de payn, j galoun de seruoise, j messe gros de la couissine, et vn messe de rost.

Pleas in the halle.

The wardes within age with their exhibition.

Item qi toutz lez enfauntz qi chetent en la garde le roi preignent gagez et liuereez et toutz autrez necessares solonqe lour estate, et lauisement et discrecion de seneschall et tresourer. Et mesmez celez enfauntz soient mytz hors dez liuereez et dez gagez, si tost come ils eyent lour terrez, ou qi le roi eit done ou venduz. Et adonquez soient

f. 51v.

az | coustagez de ceux qi lez auerount de dount ou dachat.

### *Un Escuier surueour dez viandes pour le Roy* [5]

Esquiers for the Mouthe as Sewers, Carvers.

Item qi le roi eit vn esquier surueour et gardein dez viandez pour sa bouche, et assaeour de sa table; et vn esquier trenchant deuaunt le roi, et vn esquier pour luy seruire de sa coupe; de queux iij esquiers chescun prendra pour sa chambre pour nuyt demi piche de vin, ij chaundelx, j tortis, et litere pour tout lan, et bouche par la seison dyuer de vssher de la chambre. Et si null soit seignez ou maladez, il prendra liuere come sergeant, cestassauoir j dare de payn,

[1] B. only.
[2] B. punyer.
[3] B. Et ledit clerc soit.
[4] B. de liueree.
[5] B. only.

demi piche de vin, demi galoun de seruoise, j messe gros de la coissine, vn messe de rost ; et chescune az gagez de vij d. ob. le iour, ij robez en drap par an, ou xl s. en deniers.

*Deux Escuiers Ushers de la Chambre le Roi* [1]

Item le roi auera deux esquiers vsshers de la chambre, dount lun serra sergeaunt pourueour del busche et littere pour loffice [1] de la chambre, qi countra lez messes chescun iour en la chambre, et lez tesmoignera a lez accomptez faitz chescun iour de loustell en garderobe, par quel tesmoignance lez officers aueroumt allouance de lour officez sur laccompte. Et mesme celluy sergeant prendra pour soun coche j galoun de seruoise, iij chaundelx, et chescun iour prendra vij d. ob. le iour pour gagez ; et ij robez par an en drap, ou xl s. en deniers. Et si null soit [2] seigne ou maladez, prendra pour liueree j dare de payn, j galoun de seruoise, j messe de gros de la cuissinz et vn messe de rost. Et le sergeaunt purueour auera vn vallet de mestier en eide de luy pour purueance faire, ij d. le iour pour gagee en roulle de la cuisine.

Vshers del Chambre.

*Dez Valletz de la Chamber* [3]

Item viij valletz de la chambre a pee qi seruiront en la chambre en litz faire, tenir et porter torchez, et autrez diuers sez chosez solonqe lez comaundmers et le chambirleyn le roi,[4] lez quelx mangerent en la chambre deuaunt le roy. Et si nulle de eux soit seignez ou maladez, eit pour la liueree j dare de payn, j galoun de seruoise, j messe de gros de la cuissine ; et j robe par an en drap, ou j marc en deniers ; et pour chaucere iiij s. viiij d. a deux seisouns del an. Et si nulle de eux soit mandez hors du court es bosoignez le roi par soun comandement, preigne iiij d. le iour pour soun despensez.

Gromes or pages of the chambre.

*Les Sargeantz darmez*

Item le roi eit xxx sergeantz darmez, sufficeantment armee et moun | tez, cestassauoir chescun de vn chiuall darmez, vn hakene et somer ; qi chiuachent armez chescune iour deuaunt le corps le roi en cheminant par pays, sils neyent autre comaundement le roy ou le seneschall. Et serrount lour gagez chescun iour alloez en rolle de marche,[5] quaunt ils serrount en court issint, cestassauoir qi chescune de eux, qi chiualx darmez eit, xij d. le iour. Et si cel chiaul soit reuenuz en garder[obe],[6] ou moerge en le seruise le roy, li serront alloez en mesme le roulle viij d. le iour pour gagez, tanque il eit autre chiuall darmez ; et a pluis tost qil auera restor de soun chiuall, issint rendue ou mort, luy soit assignez certein iour par la discressioun de seneschall ou de tresorer dauer soun chiuall darmez prest pur seruire le roi, sicome appent. Et sil neit prest a ceo iour, adonques soit de gagez nettement tanque il eit. Et sil ne veut ou le [7] doigne,

30 serieantz at armes.
f. 52.

[1] B. only. [2] In A. et si null soit is written twice. [3] B. only.
[4] B. et autres dyuers chosez solonqe lez commaundements et le chamberleyn le roy.
[5] A. and B. Marechaucie or marechal seem the most likely extensions.
[6] B. en garde. [7] B. ne.

soit auxint mytz hors de gagez tanque il se soit purueu dune autre chiualle sufficeant. Et adonquez soit mytz en gagez, sicome deuaunt. Dez queux xxx sergeantz lez quatre, quelx le roi voudra nomer, serrount toutz iours entendantz al vssher de la chambre en eide de la vsshere ; qui coucheront dehors mesme lusshe, et si pres come ils pourrount. Et aueront pur choche j piche de vin, ij chaundelx, j tortis. Et les xxvj sergeantz girront en la sale lez, pur estre prest quaunt le roy auera affair de eux. Et auerount pour coche iij piche de vin, vj chaundelx, j tortiz. Et chescun de lez xxx seriantz auerount ij robez par an en drap, ou xlvj s., j messe de gros de la cuissine, et vn messe de rost.

Item le chiualer qi est de parte le dit countee mareschall, le clerc, et le sergeant mangeront en la sale saunz riens autre chose prendre de roi.

*Le Chiualer chief Ussher del Sale* [1]

Cheif husher of the halle. Item vn chiualer, chief vssher de la sale, qi prendra garde de lusse de la sale soit bien gardez par lez sergeantz et valletz vssher, sicome apent. Et suruerra qi la sale soit bien et honourablement seruy, et null manguisse forsque ceux qi y deyuent de droit, sauuez toutz foitz qi lez estraungez soient receux et honourez, solonque qil deiuent estre. (Strangers to eat in the halle.) Et deit chescune iour entrer et suruer lez officez del hostiell qi les chosez, qi y serrount enuoiez par lez purueours, soient sufficeantz solonque lachate, et qi null nessoit soeffret en mesmez lez officez forsqe de deiuent estre.[2] Et auera vn esquier mangeant en la sale. Et prendra pour sa chambre vn piche de vin, iiij chaundelx, j tortiz, et litere par tout lan, et busche pur la seison dyuer et j liuere pour soun chambre, cestassauoir | j dare de payn, j galoun de seruoise, j messe gros de la cuissine. (f. 52v.) Et sil soit seigne ou maladez, prengne pour liueree ij dare de payn, j piche de vin, ij messe gros de la quissine, j messe de rost ; pour feez x marcz par an a la seint Michell et a la Pasque ; et ij robez par an en drap, ou viij marcz en deniers a Noell et a la Pentecost par ouelx portions.

*Deux Sergeantz Usshers de la Sale* [3]

Serieants Vshers of the Halle. Item ij sergeantz vsshers de la sale, dount lun serra pourueour del busche et de littere pour loffice de la sale. Et ferra liuerees de littere et busshe a ceux de loustell qi deiuent auoir de droit. Et mesmez celluy ij sergeantz gardent lusshe de la sale, et countrount lez messes en la sale chescun iour, cestassauoir lun a lun mangier, lautre a lautre mangier. Et lez tesmoignerent a la compte. Et chescune de eux prendra pour coche j galoun de seruoise, iij chaundelx, et chescune iour vij d. ob. pour gagez, ij robes par an en drap, ou xlvj s. viij d. en deniers. Et sil soit seignez ou maladiez, prengne pour liueree j dare de pain, demi piche de vin, demi galoun de seruois, j messe gros de la cuissine, j messe de rost.

Groomes or yeomen of the halle. Item ij vallettz de mestre desoutz, qi garderont lusshe de la sale, et serrount en eyde du sergeaunt purueour de faire purueance de busshe et de littere, quant mestre serra. Dez queux lun prendra

[1] B. only. [2] B. Forsqeeaux quy doiuent estre. [3] B. only.

garde a busshe desouz le sergeaunt, lun a lun mangier et lautre a lautre mangier, enter lez autrez vallettz le mestre. Et hors de court entour lour office chescune eit ij d. le iour en la roulle de la quissine. Et si null de eux soit seigne ou maladez, preigne pour liueree j dare de pain, j galoun de seruoise, j messe gros de la quissine, j robe par an en drap, ou vn marc en deniers, et iiij s. iiij d. pur chauceur.

Item j vallett suer, qui [1] soit desoutz le chiualer chief vssher de la sale. Et gardera lez baunkers, et parchers mettera, et apparaillera la sale. Et mangera en la sale entour lez vallettz de mestre saunz rien autre chose aprendre de roi. Et sil soit seigne ou maladez, preigne liueree come vallett de mestre.

### *Deux Chiualers Marchals de la Sale* [2]

Item deux chiualers marchals de la sale, dez queux lune herbergera et lautre serra entendant a la sale. Et pres le herberagage fait en soiorne lun et lautre soient entendantz a la sale.[3] Et assaient | lez gentz en la sale solonque ceo qi lour estate demaunde, issint qi lun soit alant par mye la sale et en lez officez al vn manger, et lautre a lautre. Dez queux chescune prendra pur sa chambre j piche de vin, iij chaundelx, ij tortis entour ceux deux. Et si null de eux soit seigne ou maladez, preigne pur liuere ij dare de payn, j piche de vin, ij messes gros de la quissine, j messe de rost ; et pour feez x marcz, ij robez par an en drap, ou viij marcz par an en deniers ; et littere et busshe sicome le chiualer vssher.

Marshals of the Halle.

f. 53.

### *Deux Sergeantz Marshalx de Sale* [4]

Item ij sergeantz mareschalx de la sale, dez queux lun herbergera, et lauter serra entendant a la sale. Et apres la herbergage fait en soierne, lun et lautre soient entendantz a la sale, et assedent lez gentz en la sale solonqe ceo qi lour estate demande, si come cest suisdit dez chiualers marshalls. Dez queux chescune prendra pour la chambre j galoun de seruoise, iij chaundelx ; et, sil soit seigne ou maladez, pour liueree j dare de payn, demi piche de vin, demi galoun de seruoise, j messe gros de la quissine, j messe de rost, vij d. ob. pour gagez le iour ; ij robez par an, ou xlvj s. viij d. en deniers.

Serieant marshals of the halle.

### *Le Serieant Surueour du dresour pour la Sale* [5]

Item vn sergeant surueour de dressour pour la sale, qi deit auiser dez luez de lour seruice, solonque ceo qi les gentz de graunde estate et autres serrount assiz en la sale. Et prendra pour coche j galoun de seruoise, iij chaundelx. Et sil seit seigne ou maladez, preigne liueree j dare de payn, demi piche de vin, demi galoun de seruois, j messe gros de la cuissine, j messe de rost ; vij d. ob. le iour pour gagez ; ij robez par an, ou xlvj s. viij d. en deniers.

Surveior of the Dressour.

Item trois esquires, asseours de messe en la sale, deiuent mettre le messe en la sale ; et serrount par si bien auisement come il pourrount issint qi lez gentz destate et autrez soient seruiz solonque lour

Esquiers Sewers of the Halle.

[1] Qui supplied from B. only. [2] B. only.

[3] This sentence is omitted in B. The next paragraph shows apres is the right reading for pres.

[4] B. only. [5] B. only.

estate, et nulle part emporterount la viande forsqe la ou ly deiuent de droit. Dez quelx chescun eit pour coche j galoun de seruoise, ij chaundelx ; vij d. ob. le iour pour gagez ; ij robez par an, ou xl s. en deniers. Et seigne ou maladez, eit pour liueree j dare de pain, j galoun de seruois, j messe de gros de la quissine. et vn messe de rost. |

f. 53v. xxiiij Esquiers of the Halle.

Item xxiiij esquiers, saunz lez esquiers de la chambre et toutz lez officers de loustell qi serrount en la sale. Et ferount toutz autres chosez qi appendent a lour estatez par lez commandementz de seneschall et tresorer, ou de ceux qi teignent lour lieus. Dez queux chescune prendra vij d. mail [1] le iour pour gagez ; ij robez par an en drap, ou xl s. en deniers. Et si null soit seigne ou maladez, preigne pour liueree j dare de pain, j galon de seruoise, j messe gros de la cuissine, et vn messe de rost.

*Un chief Clerk de la Panetrie et Boutelerie* [2]

Clark of the pantrye.

Item j chief clerk de la panetrie et de la buttellerie, qi doit faire lez abbreuientz [3] de soun office. Et respondra chescun iour a la countee de loustell de parcelx liuerez et toutz autres chosez qi appartenent a soun office. Et serra al resceit de pain, vyn, [et] seruois. Et suruerra et examinera qil soient de pois, mesure, et value qi deiuent estre. Issint qi null defaut y soit, face monstrere a lez souereins pour faire en demandez [4] sil ne puis mesme amender. Et seruira chescune iour al vn mangier et mangera a lautre. Et prendra pour coche j piche de vin, ij chaundelx, j tortiz ; et seigne on maladez, j dare de payn, demi piche de vin, demi galoun de seruoise, j messe gros de la cuissine, j messe de rost ; vij d. ob. pour gagez le iour ; ij robez par an en drap, ou xlvj s. viij d. en deniers.

Item j southclerc vssher de mesme loffice, qi serra chescun iour al receit de pain en la panetrie, et la ferra counter. Et receyuera et escriura lez foilez dez taillez, et nouns dez vendours de mesme le payn. Et si le pain soit fourni de ble le roy, en ferra taile encountre le peisour le roi. Auxint face de la seruoyse en la butellerie. Et ferra liuereez de pain, vin et seruoise, cestassauoir de payn en la graunt panetrie, de vin et de seruoise en la graunde buttillerie. Et soient cestez liuereez faitz chescun iour enauant manger, sil ne soit par resonable enchesoun. Et seruira en la sale al vn manger, et mangera a lautre. Et seigne ou maladez, il prendra pour liueree j dare de pain, j galoun de seruoise, j messe gros de la cuissine ; et prendra j robe par an en drap, ou xx s. en deniers. Et auera soun lite cariez en la cariage de panetrie.

*Le Sergeant chief Panterer.* [5]

Serieant del pantrye.

Item vn sergeant chief panterer. Et resceiuera le pain en gros par le vieu de clerc ou de southclerc, et respondra de lez despensez au chief clerc chescun iour sur le breuement. Et prendra pour coche j galoun de seruoise, [et] iij chaundelx. Et seigne ou maladez, preigne pour liueree j dare de payn, demi piche de vin, demi galoun

f. 54.

de seruoise, j messe gros de la cuissine, j messe de rost ; | vij d. ob. le iour pour gagez ; ij robez par an en drap, ou xlvj s. viij d. en deniers.

[1] B. vijd. ob. le iour. [2] B. only. [3] B. abreuyaments.
[4] B. en amender. [5] B. only.

Item j vallett de mestier desoutz, qi seruira en la sale al vn manger, et le dit sergeant a lautre mangier ; et ij vallettz portiers de mesme loffice, dount lun portera le pain al vn mangier [et] lautre a lautre. Lez quels iij vallettez chescun eit vn robe par an en drap, ou j marc en deniers ; et pur la chauceur iiij s. viij d. par an. Et seigne ou maladez, eit pour liueree le iour j dare de pain, j galoun de seruoise, j messe gros de la cuissine ; et pur le vallett j lite pour le deux vallettz, cariez en mesme loffice.

*Le Sargeant Panterer pour la bouche le Roy* [1]

Item vn sergeaunt panterer pour la bouche le roi, qi receiuera le pain pour le roi et pour sa chambre chescun iour de grande panterie, et nulle part aillours. Et de ceo respondra au clerk de breuementz. Et prendra pour coche j galoun de seruoise [iij seruoise],[2] et pour soun office vj chaundelx. Et seignez ou maladez, eit pour liueree j dare de pain, demi galoun de vin, demi galoun de seruoise, j messe gros de la quissine, j messe de rost ; vij d. ob. le iour pour gagez ; ij robez par an en drap, ou xlvj s. viij d. en deniers. Serieant panterer for the mouthe.

Item j vallett de mestier desouz luy mesmez loffice deuers le chambre, qi prendra j robe par an en drap, ou vn mars en deniers, et pur chauceur iiij s. viij d. par tout lan. Et seigne ou maladez, eit pour liuerree j dare de pain, j galoun de seruoise, j messe gros de la cuissine, et j lite cariez, pur luy et le vallett de la cuphous, en le cariage de pantre.

Item j vallett de mestier qi puruera le pain pur lostiell, et ferra taillez a vendours maintenaunt sur lachate, auant qi le pain soit emporte du dit vendour. Et le ferra veignir et liuerer en la panetrie az custagez le roi a soun perile demene. Et mangera en la sale entre lez autrez vallettz de mestier, sil ne soit destourbe par resonable enchesoun touchant soun office. Et adonqes soient alloez ij d. le iour pur gagez en rolle de la panetrie. Et sil soit seignez ou maladez, eit pour liueree j dare de payn, j galoun [de] seruoise, j messe de rost de la quissine ; et robe et chauceur come desuis est dit de autrez vallettz de mestier. Le paine.

Item waferer, qi seruira le roi le sale et le chambre de wafers | solonqe ceo qi affiert. Et prendra pour soun office en le roulle de panetrie viij d. le iour, sugurr de la garderobe, et dez ouez de la pulletrie, et fouaille de lezquillerie, solonqe ceo qil auera affair pur la seruice le roi, sicome il voudra auoir, deuaunt seneschall et le tresorer si de soit arresonez.[3] Et prendra gagez vij d. ob. le iour ; ij robez par an, ou xl s. en deniers ; et seigne ou maladez, preigne pour liueree j dare de pain, j galoun de seruoise, de la cuissine j messe de rost. The Waferer. f. 54v.

Item j sergeant pistour qi furnra [4] tout manere de pain pur lez expensez del hostiell le roi, auxibien pain rounde pur tout la communite, come payn de mayn pur la bouche le roy, solonqe ceo qil voudra responder a la compte. Quant il serra charge par le seneschall et tresorer de faire purueance de furment, deit faire lez achatez en due manere a greignour profit le roy, et a mendre greuance de people, Serieant of the Pastrie.

[1] B. only.
[2] Omitted in B.
[3] B. Si ne soit arresonez.
[4] B. suruira.

faisant paiement ou taille az vendours de price de mesme le blee issint purueu, tantost sur lachate, auaunt qi la dit furment soit mesurez hors de poer de vendour. Et liuera lez foillez et taillez, ensi faitz as vendours, au chief clerc de la panetrie dedeinz le sept iour apres lachate fait a pluis tort, par quelx taillez et foillez les vendours en serrount paiez en garderobe et le roi en serui pleinement; le quell sergeant prendra, pur fornage de payn de mayn pour la bouche le roi, chescune iour iij dare en certeyn; pour coche j galoun de seruois, et iij chaundelx, et pur soun office ij chaundelx; pour gagez vij d. ob. le iour; ij robez par an en drap, ou xlvj s. viij d. en deniers. Et sil soit seigne ou maladez, preigne pour liueree j dare de pain, demi piche de vin, demi galoun de seruoise, vn messe gros de la cuissine, j messe de rost. Et hors de court entour soun office, il prendra iiij d. ob. le iour pur sa bouche en la roulle de panetrie.

Item ij vallettz de mestier de pistrine, dount lune serra entendant a fourn, et lautre a molyn pour moler le frument. Et chescune deux prendra ij d. le iour pour gagez en roulle de la panetrie; j robe par an en drap, ou j marc de deniers; et pour chauceur iiij s. viij d. par an, et j lite cariez pur eux deux en le cariage de pistrine.

Serieant of the Naperie. Item j sergeant naperer, qi seruira en la chambire le roy et la sale de soun office. Et receiuera la naperie de clerk de lespicerie, et respondra ent a la compte toutz lez foitz qil en serra apposez. Et fera reporter le veillez nappez en garderobe au dit clerc. Quaunt

f. 55. ils ne purrount pluis longe | ment seruire illoques, serrount liuerez al aumoisne. Et prendra le dit sergeaunt iiij d. ob. le iour pour gagez; ij robez par an en drap, ou xl s. en deniers; pur soun office chescune iour ij chaundelx. Et sil soit seignez ou maladez, eit pour liueree j dare de pain, j galoun de seruoise, j messe gros de la quissine, j messe de rost, et soun lit cariez en la cariage de soun office.

Item j vallett doffice desouz luy en mesme loffice, qi prendra j robe par an en drap, ou j marc en deniers; pur chauceur iiij s. viij d. par an; et seigne ou maladez, preigne pour liueree j dare de pain, j galoun de seruoise, j messe gros de la quissine.

Ewerer of the Chambre. Item j ewere pur la chambre, qi seruira en la dit chambre de par soun office, et prendra iiij d. ob. le iour pur gagez; ij robez par an en drap, ou xl s. en deniers. Et prendra pour soun office ij chaundelx, qaunt mestier serra. Et sil soit seigne ou maladez, preigne pour liueree j dare de payn, j galoun de seruoise, j messe gros de la cuissine, j messe de rost.

Item j vallett de mestier de ewerie, qi seruira de office en la sale, et prendra j robe par an en drap, ou vn marcz en deniers; pour chauceur iiij s. viij d. par an. Et seigne ou maladez, preigne pour liueree j dare de payn, j galoun de seruoise, j messe gros de la quissine.

Launder for the Chambre. Item j lauendre pour le chambre le roi; qi auera tout manere de linge taille pour corps le roy, et tout loffice de ewerie, auxibien deuers la sale come deuers le chambre, pour lez couertures del office deuers le chambre. Et prendra chescune iour pour liueree j dare de payn, ij galoun de seruoise, ij messes de gros de la quissine, ij chaundelx; iiij d. ob. le iour pour gagez; j robe par an ou xxvj s. viij d. en deniers, et pour cendrez et pur busshe xxvj s. viij d. par an de la garderobe.

Item j lauendre de la naperie, qi lauera tout maner de linge taille qi partient a loffice de la dit naperie, et lez couerturez dez officez deuers la sale. Et prendra chescune iour pour liueree ij dare de payn, ij galouns de seruoise, ij messes de gros de la quissine, ij chaundelx ; iiij d. ob. le iour pour gagez ; j robe par an en drap, ou xxvj s. viij d. en deniers ; et pour cendrez et busshe xxvj s. viij d. par an de la garderobe. Launder of the Napery.

*Le chief Botiller Sergeant* [1]

Chief Butler and Serieant purveior of Wynes.

Item j chief botiller sergeant, purueour de vins, qi prendra le iour, qaunt il serra en court, pour coche j piche de vin, iij chaundelx, et tortis ; ij ro | bez par an en drap, ou xxvj s. viij d. en deniers ; et pur soun fee xx marcz par an. Et seigne ou maladez, preigne pour liueree j dare de payn, demi piche de vin, demi galoun de seruoise, j messe gros de la quissine, j messe de rost. Et ferra ceo qi appartient a luy solonque ceo qi est contenue en le statuit de soun officez desoubz. f. 55v.

*Le Sergeant Botiller de Lostell* [2]

Item vn sergeant botiller de lostiell, qi receiuera et despendra tout la vin et seruoise qi serra despendu en lostiell. Et seruira le sale, et respoundra chescune iour abreuement au clerc de la butillerie dez parcelx issint despenduz. Et ferra lez achatez des hanaps de fust par la vieue de clerc, qi lez allouera en le roulle de la butillerie solonqe ceo qi serrount resonablement despenduz, cestassauoir le demange [3] pur semayne passe. Et auera en sa garde lez hanaps dargent, barrilx ferrez, tankars, et tout manere de vessell de la butillerie pur la seruice de la sale, et ent respoundra en garderobe. Et prendra pour liueree demi piche de vin, iij chaundelx ; vij d. ob. le iour pour gagez ; deux robez par an en drap, ou xlvj s. viij d. en deniers. Et prendra pour soun office de la butillerie vj chaundelx, et pur le celerie pur trere le vin iiij chaundelx, quaunt mestier serra. Et seigne ou maladez, prendra pour liuere j dare de pain, demi piche de vin, j galoun de seruoise, j messe gros de cuissine, j messe de rost. Serieant Butler.

*Le Sargeant Botiller pour le Roy* [4]

Item j sergeant botiller deuers le roi, qi receiura tout la vin, et le seruoise, qi serra despendu en le chambre le roi, de butiller de lostell ; et seruira a la chambre et ent respondra chescune iour as breuementz a clerc de la butillerie. Et auera en sa garde lez pees et hanaps dargent pour seruice de la dit chambre, et en respoundra en garderobe. Et prendra pour coche j galoun de seruois, iij chaundelx ; vij d. ob. pur gagez ; ij robes par an en drap, ou xlvj s. viij d. en deniers. Et prendra pur soun office, qaunt mester serra, viij chaundelx. Et seigne ou maladez, preigne pour soun liueree j dare de payn, demi piche de vin, j galoun de seruoise, j messe gros de la cuissine, j messe de rost. Serieant Butlers.

Item j vallet de mestier de cuphous qi seruira la chambre solonqe lordinaunce de soun mestre sergeant auaunt dit ; et prendra j robe The Cuppe house.

[1] B. only. [2] B. only. [3] B. lez damages. [4] B. only.

par an en drap, ou j marc en deniers ; et pur chauceure iiij s. viij d. par an ; et seigne ou maladez, preigne pour liueree j dare de pain, j galoun de seruoise, j messe gros de la quissine, et j lite pur luy et le vallett de la panetrie deuers le roi, cariez en [la charette de] [1] la panetrie.

Drawers of Wyne. f. 56.

Item j vallett de mestier, treour de vin, qi terra [2] tout la vine qi serra despendu en lostell, et eydra seruire en la sale, | quant mestier serra, par comaundement de sez soueraignez. Et prendra vn robe par an en drap, ou j marc en deniers, et pur chauceure iiij s. viij d. Et seigne ou maladez, pour liueree j dare de pain, j galoun de seruoise, j messe gros de la cuissine, et j lite cariez, pur luy et pur versour, en la charette de butillerie.

Item j vallett versour de mestier de la butillerie, qi versera vin et seruoise qi serrount despenduz en lostell pur lez liuerez, et eidra a discharger lez charettez qi venerount ou vin et seruoise, et pur lez dispenses de lostell auauntdit. Et prendra j robe par an, ou j marc en deniers, et pur chauceure iiij s. viij d. par an. Et seigne ou maladez preigne pour liueree j dare de pain, j galoun de seruoise, j messe gros de la quissine.

Purveior of the ale.

Item j vallett de mestier, purueour de seruoise, qi ferra la purueaunce de seruoise. Et mesme celluy purueour ferra taillez a chescune homme de qi il auerra achate la seruoise mentenant sur lachate, deuaunt qi la seruoise isse la meisoun du vendour, et luy ferra veignir en la butillerie az costagez du roi. Et prendra chescune iour ij d. pur gagez en rolle de la butillerie ; j robe par an en drap, ou vij marcz en deniers ; et pur chauceure iiij s. viij d.

Pycher house.

Item ij vallettz de picherous, qi seruiront la sale de vin et de seruoise solonque lauisement de lours soueraigns. Et laueroumt lez tankartz, hanaper, et tout manere de vesselle qils ount en garde, desoubz le butiller de lostell. Et prendrount pur loffice, quaunt mestier serra, ij chaundelx ; dez queux chescune prendra j robe par an en drap ou vn marcz en deniers ; et pur chauceur iiij s. viij d. Et ils deux auerount j lite cariez en le cariage del picherous, et, seigne ou maladez, j dare de pain, j galoun de seruoise, j messe gros de la quissine.

Porters of the Buttery.

Item ij vallettz de mestier, portours de la buttellerie, qi laueront lez barilx feriz,[3] et lez porterount, auxibien de vin come de seruoise, pur la seruoise de la chambre et de lostell, cestassauoir hors de celere tanque al butillerie et cuphous, si la dit celare ne soit de la court herbergez. Et si issi soit, et il busoigne qe le vin soit cariez de celere par charette, ou par botelx, pur defaut de herbergage de celere, qi nest pas herbergez si pres come il comeneit,[4] adonqes lez ditz portours porteront lez barilz ferez dez ditz charettz et botelx tanque en le butillerie a cuphous auauntdit. Et reporteront lez ditz barilx ferez, quaunt ils serrount voidez, quelle partie qi le | butiller de lostiell, qi lez ad en garde, lour chargera pur le seruice le roi. Et mangerount en sale, sil ne soit hors de court en bosoignez le roi par commaundementz de lour soueraignez. Adonqes prendra chescune deux ij d. le iour en la rolle de butillerie pur gagez, et chescune prendra j robe par an en drap, ou j mars en deniers ; et pur chauceure

f. 56v.

[1] Words in brackets supplied.
[2] B. triour de vyn qi triera.
[3] B. le barils ferres.
[4] B. conueneit.

iiij s. viij d. Et ils deux auerount j lite, cariez en la cariage de la buttillerie ; et, seigne ou maladez, j dare de pain, j galoun de seruoise, j messe gros de la cuissine.

*Le chief Clerk de la Cuisine* [1]

Item vn chief clerc de la cuissine, qi doit faire lez abreuientz [2] de soun office. Et respondra lez parcelx liuerez et toutz autrez chosez qi appartienent a soun office chescune iour a la compte en garderobe deuaunt seneschall et tresorer. Et serra a [3] coper de la chare et au departir de pissoun. Et suruera lez achatez et le price de chare et de pissoun, et de toutz autrez chosez appartenauntz a soun office ouesque leide le countrerollour, lussher de la sale chiualer, ou mareschall chiualer, et del asseour de la table le roi.[4] Presentra lez defautez qil verra en soun office a sez soueraigns a toutz lez foitz qil verra qi soit affaire pur le roi. Sil mesme ne portera et seruira a lune mangier chescune iour en sale et mangera a lautre. Et prendra le iour pour soun coche j piche de vin, ij chaundelx, j tortis ; vij d. ob. pour gagez, tanque il soit auaunce par le roi ; ij robez par an en drap, ou xlvj s. viij d. en deniers. Et sil soit seigne ou maladez, preigne pour liueree j dare de payn, demi piche de vin, demi galoun de seruoise, j messe gros de la cuissine, j messe de rost.

Clarke of the kytchyn.

Item j southclerk de mesme loffice, qi doit chescun iour faire lez liuereez de chare et de pissoun et de la pulletrie. Et dez mesmez cez liuereez respoundra chescune iour au chief clerc del office as breuementz, et escriuera lez parcelx del office. Et mangera chescune iour en sale a lune mangier, et seruira a lautre. Et prendra j robe par an en drap del sute dez clercs, ou xx s. en deniers. Et sil soit seigne ou maladez, preigne pour liueree j dare de pain, j galoun de seruoise, j messe gros de la cuissine, j messe de rost.

2 Vnder Clerkes.

*Deux Achatours pour les dispenses de Lostell* [5]

Item deux achatours, qi ferunt lez achatez de chare et pissoun pur lez despensez de lostell. Et ferount venir le price chescune iour au clerc de la cuissine, ou lez bens,[6] issint qi lussher de la sale, chiualer, et lasseour de table le roi, a le dit clerc pourrount ver frechement qi lez ditz biens soient sufficiantz a despender et de bone value, solonque le price, pur le roi. Et ferount lour achate en due manere a greindre profit du roi et a mendre greuance de peple, fesantz paiement | ou taillez a chescune homme de qi ils auerount f. 57.
achatez lez biens al oeps le roi, tantost sur lachate, auaunt qi mesmez lez biens issint purueux issint hors de poer de vendours. Et liueront lez foillez de mesme lez taillez au chief clerc de la cuissinc deinz lez viij iours apres lachate fait a pluis tarde, puruue [7] qi en lez taillez lez vendours en seront paiez en garderobe, et le roi serui pleinment dez biens auauntditz. Dount chescune dez ditz chatours prendra pour coche j galoun de seruoise, iij chaundelx ; vij d. ob. pour gagez ; ij robez par an, ou xlvj s. viij d. en deniers. Et seigne

2 Chators.

[1] B. only.
[2] B. les abreuements.
[3] B. only.
[4] The full stop is given here in B.
[5] B. only.
[6] B. biens.
[7] B. parmye.

ou maladez, preigne pour liuere j dare de pain, demi piche de vin, demi galoun de seruois, j messe grose de la cuissine, j messe de rost; et hors de court pur purueantz faire iiij d. ob. pur sa bouche all rolle de la cuissine.

*Deux Sargeants Keus pour la bouche le Roy* [1]

2 Serieants Cookes for the mouthe. Item deux sergeantz kus pur la bouche le roi, dount quaunt lun trauaille ov le roi cheuaugera deuaunt pur soun graunt mangier apparailler, et lautre demura derer pur soun dyner. Et chescun de eux prendra pur soun coche j galoun de seruoise, iij chaundelx; vij d. ob. pur gagez; ij robez par an, ou xlvj s. viij d. en deniers. Et seigne ou maladez, preigne pur liuere j dare de pain, demi piche de vin, demi galoun de seruoise, j messe gros de la cuissine, j messe de rost.

5 [2] groomes. Item v vallettz de mestier de la cuissine le roi, desoubz les sergeantz auauntditz, dount lun serra vssher, et querra, par lez commaundementz de sez mestrez, au graunde lardere et a lestable, tou, la chare et la pissoun qi serra despendu en la chambre le roi, paint vin et seruois de la pantrie et butillerie, et espicez de la spicerie pur la dit cuissine par lez commaundementz et lordenauncez de sez mestrez. Et vn autre vallet serra ewer, qi receiuere le vesselle de la dit cuissine par endenture de lesquillere,[3] et la gardera auxibien en trauaill come en soiourne. Et quira la grosse chare, et apparaillera le primer cours, auxibien de pissoun come de chare. Et vn autre vallet sera potager, qi fera lez potagez pur la chambre le roi, et toutz lez sewes qi serrount pur sa table. Et deux autres vallettz ferrount lez rostez et lez autres cours pur la dit chambre solonque lordnaunce lours mestres. Et chescune de eux vallettz prendra j robe par an en drap, ou j marc en deniers; et pur chauceure iiij s. viij d. par an. Et seigne ou maladez, preigne pour liueree j dare de pain, j galoun de seruois, j messe gros de la quissine. Dez queux v vallettz eient vn garson pour lour lite porter et eider en la quissine.

*Deux Seriantz Keuz de la mesnee* [4]

Cookes for the meyny. f. 57v. Item deux sergeantz keus pour la mesne, lez queux ferrount apparailler la viaunde pur la mesne de la sale solonqe ceo qi commande | lour serra par seneschall et tresorer ou lour lieux tenauntz. Et lun seruira et lun mangera a lauter a lauter. Dount chescune prendra pur coche j galoun de seruoise, iij chaundelx; vij d. ob. pur gagez; ij robez par an en drap, ou xlvj s. viij d. en deniers. Et seigne ou maladez, pur liueree j dare de pain, demi piche de vin, demi galoun de seruoise, j messe gros de la cuissine, j messe de rost.

5 groomes of the kitchyn. Item v vallettz de mestier pur la cuissine la mesnee desoubz lez ditz sergeantz. Et [un de eux] [5] fera toutz maners de potagez qi serrount serui en la sale. Et vn auter vallet sera quisour du gros chescun iour qi sera serui en la sale, auxibien de chare come de pissoun. Et iij autrez vallettz ferrount lez rostez et lez autres cours pur la dit sale solonqe lordinaunce de lor mestrez. Et chescun de eux v vallettz prendra j robe par an en drap, ou vn mars en deniers;

[1] B. only. [2] 2 in MS. [3] B. esquillier.
[4] B. only. [5] Words in brackets supplied from B.

pur chauceure iiij s. viij d. Et seigne ou maladez, preigne pur [liueree] [1] j dare de pain, j galoun de seruoise, j messe de gros de la cuissine. Et ij eient j garson pur lour lite porter et eider en la cuissine.

Item deux vallettz doffice, qi sount appelez akers, qi receiuerent la vessele de la cuissine de la mesnee par endenture del esquiller, et la mettrount et le garderount, auxibien en trauaille come en soiourne. Et chescun de ceux deux prendra vn robe par an, ou vn mars en deniers ; et pur chauceure iiij s. viij d. Et seigne ou maladez, pour liueree j dare de pain, vn galoun de seruoise, j messe gros de la quissine ; et entre eux deux j garson. 2 groomes, Akers.

*Le Sargeant du Larder* [2]

Item j sergeant lardere, qi receiuera la chare et la pissoun, qi lez achatours ferrount venir en lardere, ou qi viendra de present, et de la venisoun, qi y viendra dez venours le roi, ou qi ceo soit. Et liuera lez auauntditz chare et pissoun pur lez despensez del hostell le roi par parcell, et par lauisement de countreroller, lussher de la sale, chiualer, ou mareschall chiualer de la sale, clerc de la cuissine, lasseour de la table le roi, et les meistrez kus. Et gardera la viande au dressour, et rendra au dit clerc chescun iour as breuementz certeins parcelx de auauntditz chare et pissoun despenduz en la manere auauntdit. Et si par cas aueigne qil soit maunde hors de court par seneschall et tresorer de faire nul manere de purueance, adonques lez face il en la manere qi suis est dit dez achatours. Et prendra pur coche j galoun de seruoise, iij chaundelx, iiij d. ob. le iour pur gagez. Et auera soun lite cariez en la cariage de soun office. Et prendra ij robez par an en drap, ou xlvj s. en deniers. Et prendra pur soun office, quaunt mestier serra, iij chaundelx. Et seigne ou | maladez, preigne pour liueree j dare de pain, demi piche de vin, demi galoun de seruoise, vn messe gros de la cuissine et vn messe de rost. Serieant of the Larder. f. 58.

Item vn vallet de mester, vssher de larder, desouth le lardiner, qi portera lez cliefs de larder, quant le lardiner est hors de court. Et adonquez receiuera, liuera et respondra de toutz chosez appartenauntz al office de lardere en mesme la manere come sus est dit de lardiner. Et qaunt le lardiner est en court, il ferra mesme soun office. Et lussher gardera la graunt quissine de la mesne qi null veigne forsqe deiuent de droit faire le. Et respondra chescun iour as breuementz au clerc de la cuissine dez parcelx de la chare et de pissoun, et de toutz chosez appartenauntz a soun office qil auera receu en la cuissine auauntdit, auxibien de gros hors de la ville dez achatours de lardere, come de la pulletrie hors de la herbergagerie. Et qaunt le suthclerc de la cuissine est seigne hors de court, il fera lez liuereez de la quissine, et quirra pain et seruoise de la panetrie et butillerie et espicez de lespicerie pur la dit cuissine, par lez commaundementz et ordinauncez de lez meistrez keus. Et prendra j robe par an en drap, ou j mars en deniers ; et pur chauceure iiij s. viij d. par an. Et auera soun lite cariez en la cariage de lardere. Et seigne ou maladez, preigne pur liueree j dare de pain, j galoun de ceruoise, j messe gros de la quissine. Vsher of the Larder.

Item ij vallettz de mestier, portours de lordere,[3] qi receiuerount Porters in the slaughter house or Butchery.

[1] Word in brackets supplied from B.
[2] B. only.
[3] B. lardere.

la chare en la bucherie del achatour par certein accompt a certein nombre. Et mesme la chare sauement garderont tant qil veigne en la court, et illoeqes la liueront par mesme lacompte et nombre au lardiner ou al vssher de larfer ; et mesme la manere de pissoun. Et porteront la chare et la pissoun dez chariettz al vssher de la quissine, tanque al estable et tanque au lardere, et hors du lardere tanque al quissine, et hors de la cuissine, ov leide dez ewers de la quissine, tanque al dressour. Et lez remenauntz de chare et pissoun, remiz au dit dressour apres qi len auera mange, porterount arere au lardere. Et si lun dez achatours de le quissine soit mande hors du court par seneschal ou tresorer de faire purueance dez bestez viuez, ou de pissoun, il auera ov luy lun dez ij portours susditz, par auisement du clerc de la quissine, pur luy estre en eide de faire venir en court sa mesme [1] purueance, quaunt il auera fait. Et le dit pourtour prendra chescune iour, tant come il est hors de court entre la boisoigne susdit, ij d pur gagez en rolle de la cuissine. Et chescune de mesmez ceux deux portours j robe par an en drap, ou j mars en deniers ; et pur chauceure iiij s. viij d. Et entre ceux deux aueront j lite cariez | en la care de lardere.

f. 58v.

*Le Sargeant Pulter* [2]

Serieant Poulter.

Item vn sergeant pulter, qi ferra lez achatez et la purueance de toutz maners dez chosez appartenauntz a soun office. Et prendra chescun auisement del asseour de la table le roi, du clerc de la quissine, et de mestrez queux, ceo qil ferra venir en court pur lez despensez de la chambre et de lostell. Et solonqe ceux despensez respoundra chescun iour au dit clerk az breuementz, et en ferra nulle manere de liueree forsque par lauisement de clerc auauntdit. Et prendra le iour [vi d. ob.] [3] en deniers. Et auera soun lite carie en la cariage de soun office. Et seigne ou maladez, eit liuere j dare de pain, demi piche de vin, demi galoun de seruois, j messe gros de la quissine, j messe de rost.

Grome.

Item j vallett [de] [4] mestier de mesme loffice, qi ferra le certein price de pullaille. Et quaunt il va en pays entre purueance de la pullaille, auera ove luy lez turmentours, qi bosoignent destre en la dit office, ou partie de eux, lez nouns dez queux tournentours serrount entres en garderobe, a carier le purueance qil auera issint purveu. Et paiera sur longle pur le pullaille sur soun perille par la reasoun de certein qi en est certein assise. Et respondra deuaunt le seneschall et tresorer si nulle pleint y veigne dez outragez qi ou lez ditz tournentours aueront fait en pays, ou defaut de paiement. Et respondra a soun mestre sergeant pulter dez deniers qil auera receu de luy, ou de la garderobe. Et quaunt il est hors de court entre la bosoigne auauntdit, il prendra ijd. le iour pur gagez en la rolle de cuissine ; j robe par an en drap, ou j mars en deniers ; et pur chauceure iiij s. viij d. Et seigne ou maladez, pur liuere j dare de pain, j galoun de seruoise, vn messe gros de la quissine.

Garbagers of foule.

Item j sergeant garbagere de la quissine saunz gagez, qi receiuera la pulleil hors de la pullerie, et lez eschaudera et tout manere de la

[1] A. reads sa after meme sa purueance.
[2] B. only.
[3] Words in brackets supplied from B. A blank space in A.
[4] Word in brackets from B.

volatile par certein nombre. Et lez liuera par parcelx a lez quisinez pur lez despensez de chambre de roi et de lostell. Et dez liuereez et de mesme cels parcelx respondra chescune iour as breuementz au clerk de la quissine. Et prendra j robe par an, ou xx s. en deniers. Et prendra pur soun office, quaunt mestier serra, ij chaundelx. Et seigne ou maladez, preigne pur liueree j dare de pain, vn galoun de seruoise, j messe gros de la quissine, j messe de rost ; et pur soun feez, qi est appellez le petit ewe, entre le Pasque et le Pentecost, j mars par an.

Item vn vallett de mesme loffice, saunz robez et saunz gagez, qi seruira en loffice desouz soun mestre, et prendra rien de roi forsque mangier et boiure en la sale ; et, seigne ou maladez, pur liuere j dare de pain, j galoun de seruoise, j messe de gros de la quissine.

### *Le Sargeant Esquyller* [1]

| Item vn sergeant esquiller, qi achatera et puruera bouche, car- f. 59.
boun et toutz maners de vesselle darrein, fere, et de fust, qi parteignent a la cuissine, et potage et plusours autres chosez appartenauntz a soun office. Et lez despendra en due manere solonqe ceo qi affiert. Et ent respoundra chescune iour as breuementz au clerc de la cuissine. Et prendra le iour pur coche j galoun de seruois, iij chaundelx, et, quaunt mestier serra, pur soun office ij chaundelx ; iiij d. ob. le iour pur gagez, ij robez par an en drap, ou xl s. en deniers. Et auera soun lite cariez en le cariage de soun office. Et seigne ou maladez, preigne pur liueree j dare de payn, demi piche de vin, demi galoun de seruoise, j messe gros de la quissine, j messe de rost.

Serieant of the Scullery.

Item ij vallettz de mestier de esquillerie, qi trauailleront et feront quaunt qi lour sergeant lour comande par resoun es chosez touchauntz lez officez. Et lun seruira en la sale al vn mangier, et lautre a lautre. Et chescune de eux prendra j robe par an en drap, ou vn mars en deniers, pur chauceure iiij s. viij d. Et auerount entre eux deux j lite cariez en la cariage del office. Et seigne ou maladez, preigne pour liueree j dare de pain, j galoun de seruoise, j messe gros de la quissine.

2 Groomes.

Item j sergeant esquiller qi receiuera la vesselle dargent en garde[robe] par nombre et par pois, cestassauoir chargeours esquellez, et lez gardera et en respoundra en la dit garde[robe] al fyn del an de nombre et de pois. Et prendra ij chaundelx pur soun office ; iiij d. ob. le iour pur gagez ; ij robez par an en drap, ou xvj s. viij d. en deniers. Et seigne ou maladez, preigne pur liueree j dare de pain, j galoun de seruoise, j messe gros de la quissine, j messe de rost.[2]

An other Serieant Sculler.

### *Le Sargeant Sauser* [3]

Item j sergeaunt sauser, qi achatera et puruera floure pur toutz maners de sauses et autres chosez qi bosoigneront pur loffice de la sawcerie et lostell le roi ; et lez despendera en due manere solonqe ceo qi affert, et fournera come appent de soun office. Et respondra as breuementz al clerc de la cuissine. Et receiuera lez saucers dargent en garderobe, et lez gardera, et ent respoundra au le dit

Serieant of the Sawsery.

[1] B. only. [2] This paragraph is omitted in B. [3] B. only.

garderobe al fyne del an del nombre et de pois. Et prendra pour liuere j galoun de seruoise, iij chaundelx, vij d. ob. le iour pur gagez demi piche de vin, demi galoun de seruoise, j messe gros de la quissine, j messe de rost, et pur soun office, quaunt mestier serra, iij chaundelx.

2 Groomes. Item ij vallettz de mestier de la sauserie qi ferrount quauntque le sergeant lour comandera par reasoun ez chosez touchantz loffice. f. 59v. Et lun seruira | a lun mangier, et lautre a lautre. Et chescune deux prendra vn robe par an en drap, ou j marc en deniers, et pur chauceure iiij s. viij d. Et auerount entre eux deux j lite, cariez en la cariage del office. Et si nulle deux soit seigne ou maladez, preigne pur liueree j dare de pain, j galoun de seruois, j messe gros de la cuissine.

*Le Sargeant Porter de la chamber le Roy* [1]

Serieant Porter. Item vn sergeant porter, qi gardera la porte par la ou le roi gist, issint qe nulle y entre fors ceux qi le deuent faire de droit; ne qil suffre qe nulle ne port hors de la court pain, vin, ne seruois, viande, littre, ne busche, ne nul autres chosez, fors ceux qi deiuent faire; ne rien ne soit emportez saunz certeins liuereez et autres chosez qi deiuent estre porte de droit. Et si nulle ne face, qil ne [2] face arester, et celluy ensement qi la chose emporte; et qil le mottera [3] en la proschein accompt deuaunt seneschall et tresorer. Et qil neit desoutz luy en soun office fors ceux qi portent lez robez le roi. Et ne mangera pas en sale; mais prendra sa liueree, cestassauoir chescun iour j dare de pain, j galoun de seruois, j messe gros de la quissine, j mess de rost. Et seigne ou maladez, eit j piche de vin, si come autres sergeantz de lacompte. Et prendra pur coche j galoun de seruoise, iij chaundelx; et pur soun office iij chaundelx, quaunt mestier serra; vij d. ob. le iour pur gagez; ij robez par an en drap, ou xlvj s. viij d. en deniers.

2 Groomes. Item ij vallettz doffice desouth luy, qi li serrount en eide de iour et de noet, et quaunt ils poent, de faire toutez chosez appartenauntz au dit office.[4] Et ne mangerount poynt en sale, mais chescune de eux prendra le iour pour liuere j dare de pain, j galoun de seruoise, j mess de gros de la quissine, j robe par an en drap ou j mars en deniers, et pur chauceure iiij s. viij d. par an.

*Le chief Clerk de la Marechaucie* [5]

Chief Clarke of the Marshalsie. Item vn chief clerc de marechaucie, qi receiuera lez taillez dez purueancez, faitz par la clerc chief purueour del aueinere et par lez vallettz purueours de mesme loffice, ensemblement ov purueancez contenuz ez mesmez taillez. Et ferra lez abreuementz de feine, aueins, littere, et toutz autrez chosez qi apparteignent al office de marchaucie solonque la price et lez achatez dez ditz purueancez. Et receiuera auxi lez taillez dez harneys [et] charettez. Et acountra chescun semain ouesqe lez purueours dez toutz maners doffice de harneys; et receiuera de eux lez parcelx issint qil puis acounter chescun semayne vn fois deuaunt seneschall et tresorer de tout

[1] B. only. [2] B. qil luy face arrester. [3] B. mette.
[4] The punctuation adopted is suggested by B. [5] B. only.

maner de purueance de harneys. Et ferra allower chescun iour en rolle de soun office lez gagez dez clercs, sergeantz dez armez doffice, esquiers de lostell, qi serrount as gagez. Et prendra pur coche j piche de vin, deux chaundelx, j tortis, ij robez par an en drap, | ou f. 60. xlvj s. viij d. en deniers. Et seigne ou maladez, j dare de pain, demi piche de vin, demi galoun de seruoise, j messe de gros de la cuissine, j messe de rost. Et auera deux chiualx a liueree de fein et de auein, et j garcon as gagez j d. ob. le iour.

*Le chief Clerc purueour del aueyne* [1]

Item vn clerk chief purueour de aueine, qi ferra lez purueancez Purveior of de fein et de aueins, littere, herneis, et autres chosez qi couent pur the Avenrye. loffice de marchaucie. Et suruera lez purueans fait par lez vallettz purueours souz lui ; et receiuera de eux lez taillz dez purueans qi il aueront faitz. Et ferra enterrer [2] en roulle deuers lui lez nouns dez vendours, issint qil puis certefier la garderobe si pleint aueigne qi [3] fraude omissioun soit fait dez taillez ou dez purueans. Et suruera lez purueanz dez harneys qi appartient al office de marchaucie. Et eidra de faire liueree de fein et de auiens quaunt il est en court. Et prendra parcelx au chief clerc de tout lez liuerez qil ferra. Et quaunt il serra hors de court entre [4] lez purueancez par tesmoignance du dit chief clerc de la marchaucie, il prendra iiij d. ob. le iour pur sa bouche en rolle de la marchaucie.[5] Et prendra liueree pur vn chiuall, et gagez pur vn garceoun j d. ob. le iour ; ij robez par an, ou xl s. en deniers. Et soun lite carie serra en cariage de soun office Et seigne ou maladez, prendra j dare de payne, demi piche de vın, demi galoun de seruois, j messe gros de la quissine, j messe de rost.

Item vn sergeant herberiour de palfreis le roi, qi gardra et ferra Serieant garder lez palfreiez, destrers, cousers et autres chiualx de la stable Herbenger. le roi. Et chiuauchera en le compaigne le roi, et portera la houshez de chiualx qi roy serra montez. Et mesura au roi le chiuall qe il montera ; et luy receiuera a soun descendre. Et ferra purueance de tout manere de harneys qi apparteignent a soun office, et ceo par la veue de chief clerc de la marchaucie ou de clerc chief purueour del aueinerie. Et accountra chescune semayne vn foitz oue le dit clerc de marchaucie de toutz chosez qil auera purueu, issint qi la dit chefi clerc purra en acounter deuaunt le seneschal et tresorer chescun semayne. Et mangera en sale. Quaunt il serra hors du court entre lez bosoignez le roy par tesmoignaunce du dit chief clerc de la marchaucie, il prendra iiij d. ob. le iour pour gagez en rolle du marchaucie ; et liuere pur deux chiualx, et liueree pur j garceon ; ij robez par an en drap, ou xlvj s. viij. d. en deniers ; et pur coche j galoun de seruois, iij chaundelx. Et seigne ou maladez, j dare de pain, demi piche de vin, demi galoun de seruoise, j messe gros de la cuissine, j messe de rost. Groome

Item vn vallett herberiour desoutz luy, qi herbergera destrez,[6] herbenger. palfr | eyez, cousours, et autres chiualx de le stable le roi ; ferra f. 60v. mettre et redresser lez stablez, et mesner a lestable littere, fein et

[1] B. only. [2] B. entrer. [3] B. si pleinte y aueyne qe.
[4] B. entour. [5] The words il prendra . . . marchaucie omitted in B.
[6] B. destrers.

aueine pur mesmez lez chiualz. Et trouera cresset chescun noet ardant en le stable, et prendra chescune iour pur la dit cresset ij d.; pur gagez ij d. le iour; j robe par an en drap, ou j mars en deniers; et pur chauceure iiij s. viij d. a ij soisons del an.

Item j sergeant herberiour de somers et de chiualx charettez. Et ferra redresser et ferra lez charettz qi serrount debrescez. Et puruera et achatera toutz maners de harneis qi couient pur lez somers et lez charettez par la vieue de chief clerc de marchaucie, ou chief clerc purueour del aueinere. Et doit liuerer lez taillez de toutz lez chosez qil ferra puruere, achate, faire redresser, au chief clerc de marchaucie; et accountera ove luy chescune semayn vn foitz de quaunt il auera purueux et achatez, issi qi la dit clerc puisse acounter chescun semayne en deuaunt le seneschall et tresorer. Et le dit herberiour face venir deuaunt la dit chief clerc lez charettz et harneis et [1] pluis longement ne purrount seruire, issint qe, par tesmoignance et surueue du dit clerc, puissent estre liuerez la ou le seneschal et tresorer ordeinerent. Et mangera en sale. [Et quaunt il serra entour soun office par quoy il ne poet manger en sale] [2] par tesmoignaunce du dit chief clerc et [3] prendra pur sa bouche iiij d. ob. le iour en rolle de marchaucie, liueree pur j chiuall, et gagez pur soun gars j d. mail [4] le iour; ij robez par an en drap, ou xl s. en deniers; et soun lite cariez en le cariage de soun office. Lt seigne ou maladez, preigne j dare de pain, j galoun de seruoise, et messe de gros de la cuissine, et vn messe rost.

2 Groomes. Item j vallett herberiour desouz luy, qi herbergera lez ditz chiualx, someres et charettz, et suruera qi lez ditz chiualx soient seruez couenablement; et eidra de faire toutz lez chosez del celle office solonque le comaundement et lordinaunce du dit sergeant. Et prendra pur gagez ij d. le iour; j robe par an en drap, ou j mars en deniers; et pur chauceure iiij s. viij d. en deniers a deux seisons par an.

*Le Sargeant Mareschall pur lez chiuaulx* [5]

Serieant mareshal of the Stable. Item vn sergeant mareschall, qi prendra garde qi lez chiualx soient bien gardez, ferra marchaus et medicines, et receiuera deners la garderobe [6] pur chosez medicinalx de soun office, solonque ceo qil auera affaire, et mestrier serra. Et rendra accomptez au chief clerc de la marchaucie del issue dez ditz deners, et prendra le mette de fee de ferrure, issint qil troue la mette dez coustagez de la dit ferure. Et mangera en sale. Et quaunt il serra entour soun office par quoy il ne purra manger en sale par la tesmoignaunce du dit
f. 61. chief clerc de la marchaucie, prendra iiij d. | ob. le iour pur sa bouche en roulle de marchaucie, et liueree du fein et dauein chescun iour pur ij chiualx; gagez pur vn garcon j d. ob. le iour; ij robez par an en drap, ou xlvj s. viij d. en deniers; et, seigne ou maladez, j dare de pain, j galoun de seruoise, j messe de gros de la cuissine, j messe de rost.

[1] B. qi. [2] Words in brackets omitted in B.
[3] This word seems superfluous.
[4] B. ob., clearly the better reading.
[5] B. only. [6] B. et receuera denyers de la garderobe.

Item ij vallettz, purueours del auein, qi ferrount lez purueanz de feins, aueins, littere, et autres chosez qi sount necessariez pur lez despenses de chiualx a greignour profit le roi et a mendre greuance du poeple, et ceo per auisement de lour soueraigns. Et ferrount taillez as vendours auaunt qi lez chosez passent hors de lour possessione, et lez foillez dez taillez lyueront au chief clerc purueour del auein, qi lez examinera et suruera lez achatez. Et puis soient lez ditz foils, ensemblement ov toutz vitailx et purueancez, liuerez au chief clerc de la marchaucie, qi lez ferra despender et allower en roulle de soun office. Et ferront la liueree de fein pur lez chiualx herbergez hors du court. Et liueront lez parcelx dez liuereez de iour en autre au dit clerc de marchaucie sur lez abreuementz. Et prendra chescun de eux gagez le iour ij d., j robe par an en drap, ou j mars en deniers ; et iiij s. viij d. pour chauceure. Purveiours of oates.

Item j valete porter de garner, qi portera lez sakez pleins au garner, quaunt lez purueauncez vendrount ; et mesure lez aueins en le garner a lentre et lissue ; et gardera lez sakez et lez mesurez a soun peril demesne. Et de ceo respondra au chief clerc de la marchaucie. Et gettera le fein par bracees a la liueree dez chiualx dedeins lostell. Et irra deuaunt a receyuer [1] lostell de liuere de mareschall herberiour. Et ferra herberiour [2] le gerner [3] chief de la marchaucie, le chief purueour, et lez autres de loffice. Et prendra ij d. le iour pur gagez ; j robe par an en drape, ou j mars en deniers ; iiij s. viij d. a deux soisouns del an. Et lez mesurez del officez deueins serrount accordantz a lestandard Dengleterre, issint qi lez aueins soient receux et liuerez par vn mesure de garner. Porter.

Item j vallett caruanere, qi sache machaucie [4] et ferrure, et gardera lez chiualx maladez et retreis [5] dez somers et charettz, tanque ils soient garniz et purrount trauailler solonque le chief clerc de marchaucie et dez sergeant marshall et ferrour. Et prendra ij d. pur gagez le iour ; vn robe par an en drap, ou x s. en deniers ; iiij s. viij d. pur chaucere a ij soisons del an. Groome for sick horses.

Item soient xx charrettz pur lez officez, chescun a v chiualx, qi serrount a liuere de fein et daueins et littere, et serrount frettez dez ferrours auaunt nomez. Et pur lez ditz charettz soient xx charetters, et chescune de eux eit vn auaunt cheuachour. Lez queux charetters et auauntditz chiuachours chacerount lez cha | rettz, et receiuerount charettz et toutz maners harneys, qi mestier serra pur lour officez, del sergeant herberiours del somers et charettz. Et chescun dez ditz charetters prendra pur sez gagez iij d. le iour ; j robe par an en drap, ou xx s. en deniers ; et pur soun auant cheuachour pur gagez j d. ob. le iour ; vn robe par an en drap, ou demi marc en deniers ; pur chauceure de soun auauntdit cheuachour iiij s. viij d. a ij seisouns. 20 Cartes eche of 5 horses. f. 61v.

Item xxxiiij somers, dez queux xvj pur la chambre le roi, et disoit [6] pur diuerse officez de lostell ; a la garde de queux soient assignez xxxiiij someters, qi garderount lez ditz somers ; et receyueront liuere de fein et daueins, et littere del office del aueinere. Et serrount fereitz de ferours auaunt nomez, et receiueront del 34 Somers.

[1] Or reteiner. B. reads retener, or receuer.
[2] B. herberger. [3] B. ganer.
[4] B. marchaucie. [5] B. retrens.
[6] B. misunderstands text and omits " disoit " (dixhuit).

sergeant herberiour soles, freins, cheuesters, et autres harneis qi mestier serra pur lez ditz somers.[1] Chescun de eux prendra pur gagez ij d. le iour, j robe par an en drap ou x s. en deniers, et pur chauceure iiij s. viij d. a ij seisons del an.

Groomes of the stable. Item [j][2] en lestable le roy soientz tanqe de vallettz come il y auera del chiualx. Et [ceux chiualx][2] ceux vallettz garderount destres, palfreys, coursours, et autres chiualx le roi par lordinaunce de chief herberiour et gardein de palfreis. Et chescun deux prendra pur gagez ij d. le iour, j robe par an en drap, ou x s. en deniers, et pur chauceure iiij s. viij d. a ij seisons del an.

Hakneyman. Item en mesme le stable soit j hakeneyman qi gardera le hakene de house, et querra chescun iour a suruer la liuere dez aueins pur lez chiaulx de lestable, et carira lez housez dez chiualx qi trauaillerent en la companye le roi pur le dit hakeney. Et prendra pur gagez j d. le iour, j robe par an en drap ou demi marc en deniers, et pur chauceure iiij s. viij d.

*Un Sargeant Mareschall pur lez graunts chiueoux* [3]

Great horses. Item j sergeant sufficeant mareschall gardein dez graunt chiualx, soiournantz hors du court, qi ferra achater et puruer fein et auein, littere et toutz autrez chosez qi serrount necessariez pur lez ditz chiualx, issint qi lez ditz purueancez et achatez soient faitz a greignour profit le roi, et a mendre greuaunce de peple ; et qil face gree par paiement ou par couenable taille de toutz chosez issint purueux. Et ceo face par tesmoignaunce et surueu de vicontes de pays, ou il serrount soiournantz, issint qi la dit visconte par sa lettre purra tesmoigner et certefier le garderobe le roi de ceux purueanz, achatez et paiement fait par le dit sergeant gardein, issint qi fraude, malice, nautre greuance soient faitz a gentz de pays par la dit sergeant gardein, ne par autre qi soit en cele soiourne. Et prendra liuere de
f. 62. fein | et auein pur deux chiualx ; j garcon a gagez de j d. ob. le iour ; ij robez per an en drap, ou xl s. en deniers par an ; j vallett de mestier, qi soit ferrour, pur seruir lez ditz cheualx de ferrour, et prendra ij d. pur gagez le iour, j robe par an en drap, ou x s. en deniers, et pur chauceure iiij s. viij d. a ij soisons del an. Et la dit sergeant auera tantz de vallettz pur garder lez ditz chiualx come il auera nombre dez chiualx en sa garde, et nient pluis. Et chescune dez ditz vallettz prendra ij d. le iour pur gagez, j robe par an en drap, ou x s. en deniers.

*Un Sargeant Mareschall pur lez joenes chiualx* [4]

Young horses. Item vn sergeant, qi soit sufficeant marescall gardein dez joenes chiualx, qi soient traiez hors de haras le roi, dez autres chiualx auxint, qi serrount liuerez a luy garder ascun foitz par comaundementz le roi ; qi gardera lez ditz joenez chiualx bien et couenablement, tant qils soient de poer a trauailler, et qi le roi auera ordeigne

[1] B. Et serront ferrez dez ferres auante nomez, et receueront del sargeaunt herbergour soles, freyns, cheuestres et autres harnoys qe mestier serra pur les ditz somers.

[2] B. omits words in brackets.

[3] B. only.

[4] B. only.

sa voluntee. Et mesme celi gardein puruera et achatera fein, auein, littere, et autres chosez qi sount necessariez pur lez ditz chiualx, issint qi lez ditz purueancez et achatez soient faitz a greignour profit de roy et a mendre greuaunce de poeple ; et qil face gree par paiement ou par taillez couenablez as vendours de toutz chosez issint purueux et achatez ; et cest face par tesmoignaunce de viconte de pays ou ils serrount soiournantz, issint qi le viconte purra par sa lettre tesmoigner et certefier la garderobe le roi de tieux purueaunz, achatez et paiementz faitz par la dit sergeant, issint qe fraude, malice, nautre greuaunce soient faitz az gentz de pays par le dit sergeant gardein, ne par autre qi soit en tiel soiourne. Et prendra liueree de fein et auein pur chiualx, j garcon a gagez j d. ob. le iour, et ij robez par an en drap, ou xl s. en deniers. Et auera tantz dez vallettz come il auera de chiualx, et nient pluis ; et chescun de eux vallettz ij d. le iour pur gagez, j robe par an en drap ou x s. en deniers, et pur chauceure iiij s. viij d.

Item Thomas de Borhount, qi tient de roy en chief j charue en Petit Weldone en counte de Norhamtone [1] del heritage Margarete, la file et heire Johanne Louelle, femme au dit Thomas, par certein seruice destre venour le roy dez dymers. Et auera en sa garde xxiiij chiens dymorez et vj leuerers dez chiens le roi. Et prendra pur sa puture de chescune chien j ob. le iour.[2] Et ij vallettz berners dount chescun prendra j d. ob. le iour pur gagez, et vn robe par an en drap, ou j marc en deniers, et chauceure ; j veutrer a ij d. le iour a gagez, j robe par an en drap ou j marc en deniers, et pur chauceure iiij s. viij d. en deniers. Lez queux chiens le dit Thomas doit sustener a sez coustagez demene xl iours | en quaresme, xv chiens deymers et lun berner, et le remenaunt de lan. Et le dit Thomas prendra en court vij d. ob. le iour pur gagez, et hors de court en bosoignez le roi xij d. pur gagez et despenses, ij robez per an en drap, ou xl s. en deniers. Et seigne ou maladez, preigne pur liuereez j dare de payn, j galoun de seruoise, j messe de gros de la cuissine, j messe de rost.

Office of the houndes. Weldon in Norfolke.

f. 62v.

Item j sterhont,[3] qi auera en sa garde xij chiens corantz pur loutre, et ij leuerers dez chiens le roi ; et ij gars pur la garde dez ditz chiens. Et prendra pur sez gages demene ij d. le iour ; et sil ne manguisse [4] en sale ove lez vallettz de mestrier, pur chescune garcon j d. ob. le iour, et pur chescune chein j d. ob. ; et pur luy mesmez j robe par an en drap, ou j mars en deniers, et pur chauceure iiij s. viij d.

Item j firetour qi auera ij firettz, et [5] j garcon en leide de luy pur prendra coyns [6] quaunt il serra chargez par seneschall ou tresorer. Et prendra pur sez gagez demene ij d. le iour, et pur soun garcon j d. ob., et pur la porture dez firretz j d., et vn robe par an en drap, ou j marc en deniers, et pur chauceure iiij s. viij d.

Fyrreter.

Item j perdrigour, qauera en sa garde ij cheins cochours pur

Partriger.

[1] B. North'. Little Weldon is in Northamptonshire, so that the gloss to MS. A. is in error. [*Cf. Cal. Inq. p.m.*, vi, no. 30, p. 10.]

[2] B. jd. ob. le iour.

[3] [The late Dr. W. A Craigie was of opinion that this was an error for oterhunt. There was a "kynges otyr hunter" at the beginning of the fifteenth century. Tate (1601) translated this passage as "an otter-hunt, who shall have in his custody twelve dogs running at the ottre."]

[4] B. mange. [5] B. only. [6] couyens.

perdriz, deux faucouns. Et prendra pur la puteur de chescun dez ditz cheins ob. et pur ij faucouns ob. ; pur sez gagez demene ij d., et pur vn garcon j d. ob. le iour, vn robe par an en drap, ou j marc en deniers, et pur chauceure iiij s. viij d. par an.

Fowler. Item j oisellour qi prendra ij d. pur gagez le iour, sil ne manguisse en sale entre valettz de mestrier, j robe par an, ou vn marc en deniers, et pur chauceure iiij s. viij d. par an.

Fisher. Item vn peschour qi prendra ij d. pur gagez le iour, sil ne manguisse en sale entre vallettz de mestrier, j robe par an, ou j marc en deniers, et pur chauceure iiij s. viij d. par an.

Trompeters, with musiciens. Item ij trompers soient, et ij autres ministralx soient, al fois pluis, al foitz meins, qi ferrount lour minstraucie deuaunt le roi a toutz lez foitz qi luy plerra. Et mangerount en chambre ou en la sale solonqe qils serrount comaundez. Et serrount a gagez et a robez, chescun solonqe soun estate al discrecoun seneschall et tresorer.

f. 63. Messengers. | Item xij messagers qi mangeront en sale, et ne aillont nulle part hors del hostell, sils nessoient en messagez, et eient conge de seneschall et de tresorer ; et sils le facent, soient oustrez hors de lostell. Et quaunt ils serrount enuoiez en messagez, serrount lour iournez limitez en certein. Et prendrount pur gagez iij d. le iour ; et pur lez temps sils ne remaignent au iour assignez, et ne se purrount escuser par resonable enchesoun, eient la pein deuaunt. Et chescune de eux prendra par an j robe dune seute, ou j marc en deniers, et pur chauceure iiij s. viij d.

24 Yeoman del Garde. Item xxiiij archers a pee, garde corps le roi, qirrount deuaunt le roi en cheminant par pays, dount chescune prendra pur gagez iij d. le iour, j robe par an en drap dune seute [a par eux],[1] ou x s. en deniers, et pur chauceure iiij s. viij d.

A chappeler. Item j chapellere, qi ferra lez chapeux pur lez [chapeux et] [1] esquier de lostell. Et mangera en sale a par lui [2] de sa propre nape ; et portera hors de la sale le relief de la viande dount il serra seruiz saunz autres chosez du roy.

Chief Butler. Item ordeignez est et expressement comandez qi la chief botiller nostre seignour le roy face desore en auaunt si bien si couenablement le purueance et lez achatez de vins pur la sustenaunce de soun hostell, qil et lez bouns gentz qi sount pres de luy puissent estre si honourablement serui de celle office come affiert, qi soun hostell soit couenablement serui de mesme cel office pur lonour le seignour meintenir ; issint qi ceux del ostell ne null autre puissent auer enchesoun desclaunder le dit hostell al deshonour le seignour par le defaut de dit botiller, ceo qi lez purueancez et lez achatez soient fait a mender damage et destourbance dez marchantz, qi la dit botiller sauera amender ou purra, ensi toutz foitz qi nostre seignour le roi eit sez ancienz pris, et toutz autres auauntage qi de droit doit auer par la reasoun de sa seignourie ; et apres ceo qi le botiller auera sez vins en celle maner achatez et fait gree as marchauntz, face tantost mesmez cez vins de pris achate carier et herberger par ou il serra assignez de par le seneschall et tresorer de lostell, et illeosqes face deliuerer lez ditz vins par bone endenture a sergeaunt botiller de lostell en lostell ou lez eschancelons de tonez souz les eux dez

[1] Words in brackets omitted in B. [2] B. apres lui.

marchauntz vendours, fesante mencion dez pecez du vins et du price et de nouns dez marchauntz dez queux ils serrount achatez ensemblement ou toutz autrez costagez; et mesme qil auera fait entre [1] le cariage de eux, ou en auter resonable maner aprez le primer achate iusques a cel heure qils soient ensi liuerez en lostell. Et soit mesme lendenture fait en trois partiez, | dount lune partie demurrat deuers f. 63v. le dit botiller purueour, lautre partie deuers le botiller sergeant en lostell, e la tierce partie deuers le clerc de la botellerie, par la quelle endenture le dit clerc accountra ove le chief botiller purueour de pris et de costagez, et ov le butiller de lostell del issue dez ditz vins. Et puis, quaunt lez ditz vins serrount couchez et reposez, soient vieux et assogez [2] par le countreroller vssher, ou mareschall cheualer de la sale, et clerc de la botillerie, si soient bouns et couenablez come estre deiuent, solonque le price contenuz en la dit endenture. Et sils soient trouez et acceptez pur bouns et couenablez, adonqes soient toutz lez foreins costagez, compris en la dit endenture, proportionez par ou lez parcelx, solonqe le nombre de toneux, dez queux costagez soient alloez en la rolle de la butillerie, solonqe la quantite de vin qi serra liuere et despenduz a la iournee. Et si lez ditz vins nessoient trouez si couenablez come estre dussent, solonque le price qils soient achatez, tantost soit la defaut monstrez a seneschall et tresorer,qils metteront tiel amendement qi le roi nessoit perdant en lostell male seruiz.[3] Et si par auenture lez ditz vins, ou partie de eux, nessoient despenduz auaunt qi le roy se depart de lieu ou ils serrount herbergez, adonqes soient rebaillez au chief purueour pur carier ou garder, solonqe ceo qil en auera eu comaundement de seneschall et tresorer. Et lez despensez qil mentra [4] de nouelle entour lez ditz vins, issint romiz,[5] li serrount de nouel allowez, si tost come ils serrount autres foitz resceiu al oeps le roy. Auxint lautre purueour soit chargez qil face venir en lostell pur la bouche le roi, si auaunt come il poet, toutz lez vinz qi achatera au le roi dez anciens price. Et si ceo ne puis faire bonement au profit du roi pur la lonce de lieu, adonqes lez face mettre a vent [6] issint qil respoigne au roi sur soun accompte de pluis haut price qi la vente dez vins qil auera purueu dachate.

[7] Item ordeigne est par nostre seignour le roi et soun counseill, pur Herberging, lesement de soun peple, qi la mesne de soun hostell, qi ne purra estre or Lodgyng. herbergez dedeinz lostell en la ville ou le roy, serra herbergez par lez herberiours deinz le verge, solonqe soun estate, cestassauoir chiualer ov iiij chiualx, clerc, sergeant, esquier, chescun solonqe lez agagez qil prendra de roy, cestassauoir a iiij d. ob. j chiuall, a vij d. ob.ij chiualx, a xij d. iij chiualx, a xv d. iij chiualx, auxibien en soiourne come en trauelle, issint qi le pays entour le roy ne soit encherri par tiel surkarke saunz reasoun. Et qi lez officers dostell soient herbergez a pluis apres la court [8] qils purrount estre prestez affaire lour office toutz lez foitz qi bosoigne serra; toutz lez autrez de la dit mesnee a pluis pres qi la pays purra bonement suffrer. Et soit la

[1] B. ouster. [2] B. veus et assaies.
[3] B. qe le roy ne soit perdant et lostell male seruye.
[4] B. mettra. [5] B. aynsi remuez.
[6] B. toutz les vyns qil achetera au roy pur la lonce de lieu, adonqes lez face mettre a vente. [7] This paragraph is repeated on p. 277.
[8] B. a plus pres de la court.

f. 64. liuere fait a chescun en tiel manere qi le | seignour del hostel eit pur luy, sa meigne et sez biens sufficeant esement de meisouns.[1] Et defendu est qi null de la meisne le roy, apres qil soit herbergez, preigne deinz soun hostell vitailx pur luy, ou sez chiualx, encountre la volunte de seignour de lostell, tant come il lez puisse trouer a vender par aillours. Et si ce ne puisse, adonqes lez preigne dedeinz soun hostell en la pluis curtesie et pluis plesante manere qil purra ; [2] issint qil paie lez deniers al value dez darrez.[3] Et qi chescun de la dit mesnee puisse, saunz empechement dautre, achat [4] lez vitailx qi luy couent par la ou ils serrount a vendre, auxibien en autre liueree come la sue propre. Et defendu est qi null dostell le roi nautre destourbe lez bons gentz deinz lour liueree a doner ou vendre lour biens par la ou plerra, ou carier en marche pur faire en lour profit a lour volunte, issint soit franche dordener et faire de sez biens demene ceo qi luy plerra ; qar la voluntee le roy nest mye de abaundener autres biens a distresse de sa mesne par colour de lour herbergage. Et pur ceo qi nostre seignour le roy doit estre serui partout [ou] [5] il vendra,[6] come appent a sa seigneurie, ordene et comaundez est qi null soit si hardie a destourber sez ministrez affaire sa purueance et sez achatez pur sez deniers la ou ils lez purrount melour faire au profit et honour de luy, et ceo auxi bien de toutz lez liuereez assignez az autres come aillours saunz null destourbancez. Et voet le roy qe lofficers lui facent en si couenable manere come appent pur soun honour sauir.[7]

The Accompt. Item ordeigne est qi le seneschall et le tresorer eient en garderobe chescun iour la counte de lostell [8] soiorne. Et sils passent la tierce iour dacounte, qils aquitent lez costagez de lostell en tel iour. Et si le roy trauaille, et homme ne poet acounter pur le trauaille, qi a proschein soiourne soit la counte si dez arreragez. Et si ensi ne soit fait, qils acquitent la moite de lez despensez dune iournee.

Item ordeigne est qi toutz lez sergeantz doffice qi sount de la countee, auxi bien ceux deuers la chambre come ceux deuers la sale, veignent chescun iour a la compte fait en garderobe de lostell, a respondre dez parcelx de lour office, et sils ne purrount excuser par boun et resonable enchesoun. Issint qi lez liuerez de pain, de vin et dez autres mestiers, qi apparteignent a la counte, soit chescun iour, quaunt homme purra, oiez et amendez, solonqe ceo qi reasoun serra, par la discrecion du seneschall et tresorer. Et toutz lez officez facent ceo qi appartient a lour office, si come pluis pleinement, sount a la primer foitz garnu [9] en bele maners par le seneschall et tresorer, qil
f. 64v. samende ; et si autre foiz soit troue | ou [10] mesme la defaute, et soit a gagez, perde dez gagez dun moys ; et al tierce foitz perde sez gagez ; et soit adeprimez garoun [11] en bele manere, et a la seconde foitz perde sa chauceure, et a la tierce foitz perde sa robe, et a la quart foitz perde lostell le roy saunz reuenu.[12]

[1] B. sufficeant esement dedeinz ses meysons.
[2] B. en la plus curtoise et plus pleysante manere qil purra. Compare p. 277.
[3] B. danrez.
[4] B. achater.
[5] Word in brackets supplied from B.
[6] viendra.
[7] B. sauuer.
[8] The last two words repeated in A.
[9] B. garniz.
[10] B. en.
[11] B. garny.
[12] B. reuenir.

Le rechief [1] ordeignez est qil ostell ne soit ostendit [2] a null chiualer mez cestuy neit esquier,[3] si soun estate nel demande; et qil ne demurge outre iij iours, sil ne soit par commaundement du roy.

For suche as be not of the household.

Derrechief ordinez est qi lez ordinementz, qi furent faitz a Wodestoke de lostiel le roi,[4] se teignent en le manere qils furont ordinez: cestassauoir qi mareschalx ne vssher de la sale suffrent qi null homme qi soit de la mesnee le roi, qi ne doit manger en la sale, solonqe lordeinement qi est deuisez, ne manguisse, ne rien ne preigne hors de lostell, fors ceux as robez le roi. Et de ceux null preigne gagez pur manger ou la liuerez, sauuie [5] toutz foitz quaunt lez estraungez serrount receiuez et honourez solonqe ceo qi deiuent estre. Et sil aueigne qi null del hostell, qi ne deiue manger en sale, y manguisse, saunz conge de ceux qil le purrount doner, eit la peyne desuis ordeinez, et lussher qi ne [6] soeffre entrer auxint.

Enterteignement of strangers.

Dautre part ordeigne est qi null demurge en nul dez office, come de panterie, butillerie, cuissine, esquillerie, salserie, et naperie et herbegerie, larderie, pullerie, marchaucie, aueinerie, chaundelerie,[7] ne en nul autre office de lostell, fors ceux qi ount certein office, et prenant lez robez de roi et de la royne. Et null tiel soit trouez, qil soit mayntenaunt pris et myz en prisone, iusque qil soit deliuere par le seneschall et tresorer en pleint [8] acounte. Et celi qi eit eu loffice a garde,[9] et lui et ensuit soeffert, eit la pein auauntdit. Et si lussher soit trouez en mesme coupe,[10] de mesme la coupe eit la peine auauntdit.

None but officers to abyde in any place of office.

Derrechief ordeigne est qi lez garsouns qi sount doffice, et qi prenent robez, et qi deiuent manger en sale, si come de panterie, butillerie, cuissine, et dez autres officez et de lostell, et garsouns, Gallez, archers, messagers, ou autres, qi nul nemport laumoisei [11] le roi. Et si null le face, qi le principal aumonier le monstre al countee deuaunt seneschall et tresorer, si come il est auauntdit; et qils ne deiuent lour volunteez [12] de la pein auauntdit.

Boys and chyldren.

The Alms.

Derrechief ordeigne est qi null vallett de mestrier eit desormez chiualx en la court, sil ne preigne certein gagez pur lui et pur soun chiualx de roy. Et si nul soit trouez qi eit chiualx, qi le chiualx soit priz de luy et | liuerez al aumosne; et qi laumosner lui done pur Dieu. Et cest ordeinement soit gardez a tant de foitz come le chiualx purra estre trouez ou lui.

No horses for gromes yeomen or pages.

f. 65.

Derrechief ordeinez est qi null sergeant, vallet, ne autre del hostell, manguisse en autre lieu qi en sale, sil ne soit seignez par conge le seneschall et tresorer, ou dautres qi teignont lour lieu, ou qil soit maladez, par quoy il deiue auer sa liuere hors de lostell. Et comaunde est ensement qi null estraunge ne manguisse [13] en null de officez ne lieux soit reccettez par ceux del office ne par autres del hostell. Et si nul ne face qi soit del hostell, eit peine auaunt dit;

Eating in the Halle.

[1] B. Item derechief.
[2] B. estendit.
[3] B. mes sil neit escuyer.
[4] [For contents see *Chapters*, ii, 248-9.]
[5] B. saue.
[6] B. le.
[7] The spellings adopted for these offices have been based on a comparison of A. and B.
[8] B. pleyn.
[9] B. eit loffice en garde.
[10] B. en la mesme coulpe, de mesme la coulpe eit le payne.
[11] B. qe null nen porte laumoisne.
[12] B. et quil ne dient leurs voluntez.
[13] B. mange.

et le paneter, botiller, et le keu, ou lez autres qi le seruent, eyent mesme la peyne qi est auaunt au comaundement ordeignez.

Groomes with pages.

Derrechief ordeignez [est] [1] qi null vallett eit page, fors ceux de la cuissine, et qi ceux deux et deux j page, et nient pluis. Et si nul autrement le face eit mesme la peine, et mesme cestuy qi le fait et celluy qi le soeffre a qi la garde appent.

No gyving away without leave.

Derrechief ordeignez est qi null vallett de mestrier de la cuissine, ne dautre office de lostell, rien ne doinent [2] ne facent lour curtesiez saunz cunge de ceux qi [ount] [3] la poair. Et qi null le face eit la pein auauntdit et cestuy auxi [a] [3] qi la garde appent.

Carying of meate.

Derrechief ordeigne est qi null esquier nautre ne ceo entremetent de porter cea ne la en lostell pain, vin, ne viande, puis qil est myz a la table, fors par droit seruice horz priz a qi le seruice appent par reasoun de lour officez. Et si null ne face et soit do [4] lostell eit la peine tiel come est suisdit.

Liverye.

Derrechief ordeignez [est] [5] qi null chiualer de lostell preigne liuerez, sil ne soit doffice forsque de lostell soulement.

Dogs.

Item ordeignez est qi le seneschall le roi et la royne examinent chescune semayn a meins vn foitz come dez chiens de roi et de la royne deiuent prendre liuere, [et] [5] sur ceo facent comaundement a clerc de la panterie [qi][5] respoigne a la compte.

Sick persons to have Livery.

Item ordeignez est qi a lez esquiers maladez, qi soit az gagez, [et] [5] a lez vallettz de mestrier maladez, soit donez liuereez solonqe lour estate par lordinaunce du seneschall et du tresorer.

Lyveries to Chambers.

f. 65d.

Ordeignez est qi lez gentz seignours, qi ount lour chambre de liueree deinz | le close ou le gist, preignent vin et chaundell et liueree pur lour chamberlayn solonqe lordinaunce du seneschall et tresorer.

The Quene.

Le seneschall madame la royne et soun tresorer soient toutz foitz a la compte pur faire examiner lez messes, et lez gentz de mestrier qi sount deuers madame et sa mesnee, et de faire amendre lez outragez ; et toutz lez sergeantz soient a la compte pur respoigner de lour faitz.

Foure courses of meate.

Item ordeignez est qi le roy soit serui de iiij bouns cours saunz pluis pur lui et pur lez autrez seignours qi mangent a la sale, et a madame auxint ; et qi eillours en soun hostell toutz bouns gentz soient seruiz de iij cours, et lez garsons de deux.

Palfreyours.

Ordeignez est qi toutz lez palfreours et toutz lez sometters de lostell le roy, queux ils soient, preigne ij d. le iour. Lez nompuissantz de lostell le roy, qi ne purrount mez trauailler, come de vallettz de mestrier, charetters, sometters, messagers, et toutz autres, soient enuoiez a diuers hospiteux et abbeys qi teignent du roy, qi ne sount mye chargez, et qi eient leinez [6] lour viure solonqe lour estate.

Livery.

Nulle liuere soit fait, quite ne crue, en nul part de lostell deuers le roy ne la royne, sinoun a lez graunt panterie, butillerie, cuissine, larderie de la grant hostell deuers la mesnee leez [7] liuereez de lostell deiuent estre ceux.

Guiftes or presents.

Est ordeignez qi toutz lez presentz, qi a nostre seignour le roi en auaunt serrount enuoiez, qi entierment saunz delay et auisement soient liuerees as sergeauntz dez officez de soun hostell, solonqe ceo qi

[1] Word in brackets supplied from B. [2] B. donent.
[3] Words in brackets supplied from B. [4] B. de.
[5] Word in brackets from B. [6] B. leynz. [7] B. lez.

lez presentz sount diuers ; issint qi hors de lour garde eient ceux lour fee, qi auoïr le deiuent, apres qil aueront dereigne deuaunt seneschall et tresorer et lez sergeant de la compte queu chose il deiuent auoir de fee de tieu manere de present. Et qi nul si face countre cest ordeinement, et tieu manere de fee preigne tout foiz le fee deregne, auxi come est auauntdit, si ne soit hors de la garde dez sergeantz dez officez de lostell. Qi qil soit, qi tieu chose fait, qil aquite tantost la value de tout la present qi au roi a cele heure serra demande. Et qi la tresorer de garderobe, tantost come il seuera [1] de tieux chosez soient prisez autrement qi hors la garde dez sergeantz de officez, soit chiualer, clerc, sergeant, ou vallett, qi preigne fee ou gagez ou robez de roi, qil tantost tant de value qi tout la present amontera, qi a cele hure serra au roi presentz, saunz autre reigement ou triement attender, face | mettre sur celi qi tieu chose auera prise. Et cel value recure ou de fee ou de gagez ou de robez solonqe ceo qil verra qi milx [2] et pluis tost et purra approcher a celle value alouer. f. 66.

Harbenging or lodgyng of the officers, etc.

Ordeignez est par notre seignour le roi et soun counsell, pur lesement de soun peple, qi la mesnee de soun hostell, qi ne purra estre herbege deinz soun hostiell et la vile ou le roi serra herbege, soient herbergez par lez herberiours deinz la verge, chescun solonqe soun estate, cestassauoir chiualer ov iiij chiualx, clerc, esquier, sergeant, chescun solonqe lez gagez qil prendra du roi, cestassauoir a iiij d. ob. vn chiuall, a vij d. ob. ij chiualx, a xij d. iij chiualx, a xv d. iiij chiualx, auxibien en soiourn come en trauelle, issint qi le pays entour le roy [ne] soit encherry par tiel sourcark saunz reisoun. Et lez officers del hostell soient herbergez a pluis pres la court, come ils purrount estre prestez affaire lour officez toutz foitz qi boisoigne serra. Et toutz lez autres de la dit mesnee a pluis pres qi la pays purra bonement soeffrer. Et soit [a] [3] liueree fait a chescun en tieu manere qi le seignour de lostell eit pur luy et pur sa mesnee et sez biens sufficeantz esement de mesouns.[4] Et defendu est qi null de mesnee le roi, apres qil soit herbege, preigne deinz soun hostell vitailx, pur luy et pur sez chiualx, encountre la voluntee de seignour de lostell, tant come il puisse le trouer a vendre par aillours. Et si ce ne puisse, adonqes lez preigne deinz soun hostel en la pluis courtousie et pluis plesante manere [5] qil purra ; issint qil paie lez deniers al value de darrez.[6] Et qi chescun de la dit mesnee puis, saunz empechement dautre achate, achater lez vitailx qi lui couent, par la ou ils serrount a vendre, auxibien autri come en sa sue propre. Et est defenduz qi null de lostell le roi, ne autre, destourbe lez bouns gentz deinz lour liueree a doner ou vendre lour biens par la ou il purra, ou carier a marche pur faire en lour profit a lour voluntee, issint qi chescun soit franche de ordiner et faire de sez biens demeigne ceo qi luy plerra ; gar la voluntee le roi neste mye de aboundoner autribiens a la distresse de sa mesnee par colour de lour herbegage. Et pur ceo qi nostre seignour le roy doit estre serui par tout ou [il] [7] viendra, come apent a sa seignourie, ordeigne et comaunde est qi null soit si hardi a destourber lez ministres affaire sa purueance, et sez

[1] B. sauera.
[2] B. myeux.
[3] Word in brackets omitted in B.
[4] B. en sa meison.
[5] B. en la pluis curtoise et pluis pleisant manere.
[6] B. danrees.
[7] Word in brackets supplied from B.

achatez, pur sez deniers, la ou il lez purrount meltz [1] faire a honour et profit de luy, et ceo auxibien deinz toutz liuerez assignez as autrez, come aillours, saunz nul autre destourbance. Et voet le roi qi mesmez lez officers lez facent en si couenable manere, come apent a soun honour sauoier.[2] Et ordeigne et comaunde est par nostre seignour le roi qi nul auantalour soit en lostell de notre dit seignour le roy
f. 66v. en la fourme souscrit. Et ceux qi serrount auaunt | alours, par queux il voillent respoundre a lour nouns, soient deliuerez as mareschalx. Et si nul auter soit troue mayntenaunt, soit pris en prisone, et noun pas deliuerez saunz especial comaundement le roy. Et qi nul soit auauntalour qi eit forsuire la court.[3]

| | |
|---|---|
| Pur la garderobe et pur toutz lez clercs dicele, | vn herbeiour nomez. |
| Et pur la priuee seale et toutz lez clercs, - | vn herbeiour nomez. |
| Pur ceux qi trenchent deuaunt le roy, - - | vn herbeiour nomez. |
| Pur le butiller de la bouche le roi et celi qi siert del hanaper, - - - - - - | vn herbeiour nomez. |
| Pur lez ij meistrez paneter et lez vallettz de mestier desouz eux, - - - - | vn herbeiour nomez. |
| Pur lez chapeleins et lez clercs de la chapelle, | vn herbeiour nomez. |
| Pur chiualers dez officers, chescun soun herbeiour, - - - - - - - | vn herbeiour nomez. |
| Pur le countrerollour, - - - - - | vn herbeiour nomez. |
| Pur le coeffre, - - - - - - | vn herbeiour nomez. |
| Pur toutz lez chiualers qi gisent ensemble, - | vn herbeiour nomez. |
| Pur toutz lez enfantz de garde, - - - | vn herbeiour nomez. |
| Pur lez vsshers de la chambre, - - - | vn herbeiour nomez. |
| Pur le fruter, et naper, ewarer, et lour vallettz de mestrier, - - - - - - | vn herbeiour nomez. |
| Pur lez esquiers qi sount entendantz deuers le roi, - - - - - - - - | vn herbeiour nomez. |
| Pur autres esquiers qi sount entendantz, - | vn herbeiour nomez. |
| Pur le chief butiller et soun compaignoun et lour vallettz, - - - - - - | vn herbeiour nomez. |
| Pur le clerc de la panetrie, butterie et ceux desouz lui, - - - - - - | vn herbeiour nomez. |
| Pur le clerc de la cuissine et lachatours, - | vn herbeiour nomez. |
| Pur le chaundeler et sez vallettz de mestrier, | vn herbeiour nomez. |
| Pur le aueinere et toutz ceux desouz lui, - | vn herbeiour nomez. |
| Pur le meistre esquiller et j compaignoun, - | vn herbeiour nomez. |
| Pur le aumosner et toutz ceux desouz lui, - | vn herbeiour nomez. |

[1] B. myeutx. [2] B. sauver.
[3] B. quy eit forsqe vire la court.

Pur le sauserie et toutz ceux desouz lui de loffice, - - - - - - - - vn herbeiour nomez.
Pur le pullerie, le herberger et lours vallettz, vn herbeiour nomez.
Pur deux ficisiens, - - - - - - vn herbeiour nomez.
Pur le confessour de roy, - - - - vn herbeiour nomez.
Pur le sirigien le roy, - - - - - vn herbeiour nomez.
Pur toutz lez ministraux, - - - - vn herbeiour nomez.
Pur toutz lez vallettz de la chambre, - - vn herbeiour nomez.
Pur toutz les mareschaulx de la sale, lez vsshers, et lour vallettz, - - - vn herbeiour nomez.
Pur le portour et lez vallettz, - - - vn herbeiour nomez.
Pur lez fauconers, - - - - - - vn herbeiour nomez.
Pur lez ij vaytez et wafrer, - - - - vn herbeiour nomez.
Pur lez venours, veutrez, et lez chiens toutz [1] et leuerers, - - - - - - - vn herbeiour nomez.

| Pur lez palfreis et coursours, - - - vn herbeiour nomez. f. 67.
Pur lez somtiers et charettz - - - vn herbeiour nomez.
Pur Adam Bowyer, John Haberiour, Robert Gynour, Huge Dungeye,[2] - - - vn herbeiour nomez.

Pur le clerc seneschall et coroner - - - vn herbeiour nomez.
Pur le pistour et lour vallettz, - - - vn herbeiour nomez.

Bribours {William Plane, Amice[3] Maure} lauendrers {Cristiane Scot pur la garderobe. dame Gonnore pur la chambre.

la femme Simon le Gawer pur la naperie.
Annote la Walisshe pur la commune de lostell.}

Et fait a remembrer qi nostre seignour le roi ad comaunde a sez mareschaux qil serchount de semeyne en autre si nul estraunge soit troue, suynt [4] la court, qi soit hors de auowerie, qi maintenaunt soit priz et puniz, solonqe ceo qi est ordeignez auaunt sez hures. Et nostre seignour voet qi la place de la marche de soun hostell ne soit charge dez autrez ministrez qi ne deyuent estre de droit: cestassauoir dune coronner et soun clerc de par le roy, et vn chiualer et vn clerc, vn sergeant, vn vallett de mestrier, pur garder la prisoun par le count mareschall. Et lez auauntditz ministres ne pensent pur faire lez comaundementz le roy et lez execucîouns dez billez de la dite place. Nostre seignour le roi voet qi lez viscountez et baillifs iureez de pays, ou le roi vendra, soient chargez en eide de sez marchalls de seruir lez billez de la place, et faire lez comandementz le roy, solonqe ceo qils furont chargez, par la ou notre seignour le roy vendra.

Knight marshal to arrest followers of the Court, that bee not avowable.

Pur ceo qi hidous pleintez et criez sount venuz a la cour de iour en autre, et dez grauntz affraiez et malueisteez, faitz en pays par tout ou le roi sen est ale, par gentz suyant la court, saunz estre avowe, et par ascun [5] femes de fole vie, come dez omicidez, roberiez,

The countrie to ayde the marshals.

[1] B. et toutz lez chiens, et lyuerers.
[2] B. Dungere.
[3] Both A. and B. read Amite or Annte.
[4] suyent.
[5] B. ascuns.

Followers of the court without masters, etc.

brusours [1] de mesouns, et torcenoisez [2] faitz par eux, le iour de seint Nicholas, lan du reigne nostre seignour le roy Edward xij$^{me}$, en citee Deuerwyk, pur la commune profit de pays et pur la court voider de tout manere de tielx gentz, [et] [3] comande est de par le roy qi toutz lez suytours couenablement voidassent la court, forspris ceux qi sount en rolle de corouner en la mareschalcie entrez, et receux par boun maynprise. Et si null auter soit troue, dedeinz la court ou dehors, null part dedeinz la verge, suyant le court, apres ceo qi le roi soit remoue hors de la dit citee, qil soit priz et mene a la prisoun et nom pas deliuere saunz le seneschall. Et qi null homme suwist la court, saunz ceo qil ne eust seignour ou maistre, | qi auower lui poet. Et qi null de la mesnee le roy, de quele condicioun qil soit, tenust sa femme a la court, ne nulle part dehors suyant la court, chiualer ou clerc, sergeant, esquier, charetter ou somere, garceouns ou page, ne null suide, fore tels femmez qi sount en chief ov le roi, ou ceux qi sount entitellez en le rolle de corouner en la mareschaucie as certeins officez saue. Et si null autre y sount troue, aprez la crie faire de ceux ordinancez, qi ceux, qi le tenissent, vodassant [4] hostell le roy, sil ne puissent quere [5] grace du roy. Et qi null de la court ne menast ouesque luy nulle femme de fole vie. Et si nulle tiel soit troue, qi celluy, par qi ele se auouwast, fuist priz, et lun et lautre mytz en boun prisoun, et noun pas deliueree saunz [le] [6] seneschall. Et ensement ordeigne est, et certein payne sur touz ceux qi soient trouez contre ceux ordenement. En droit dez hommez qi serrount trouez apres la crye fait, primez fortuirent hostell [7] et autre foitz soient priz et mytz en bouns ferrez, et la demoerent par xl iours, [et] [8] soient lour corps a la volunte le roi. En droit dez femmez de folie vie suyantz la court, qi primerment forzuirent la court, et autres foitz sils soient trouez, soient merche ou front dunse sechange ; [9] et la tierce foitz soient mytz en prisone par xl iours, come auaunt est dit. Et de toutz pointz auauntditz soit la crie fate en hostell nostre seignour le roy, al comencement pur iij iours, issi qi ceux toutz qi cuyent le hostell puissent couenablement est gaiens, et puit chescun dymenge en lan aprez.[10]

f. 67$^{v}$.

Single women.

Proclamation.

Market with counte.

Ensement pur ceo qi ascuns pleintz sount monstrez al seneschall auaunt dit de la grant charge dez gentz, qi suyent la place de la marche, ou le roi sen vaa, autres et pluis qi ne solent ou deyuent estre de droit, sur quoy le dit counsell ad ordeigne qi launcien custume, qi fuist vsee en temps le roy qi mort est, et en le temps lez countes mareschaulx, qi furent, ensoient desormez pleynement tenuz et vsee ;—cestassauoir par le countee soient en la dit place vn chiualer, lieutenaunt le dit countee, et vn clerc auxi, qi serra desouz luy, vn autre pur escriuer sez rollez. Et auxi vn sergeant par la dit countee affaire lez attachmentz, et herberger, qi auera vn homme

[1] B. brisours.
[2] B. extorcions.
[3] Et in both A. and B., but unnecessary for the sense.
[4] B. voidassent.
[5] B. aver.
[6] Word in brackets supplied from B.
[7] B. fortiurement lostell.
[8] Word in brackets supplied from B.
[9] B. marche ou front dun serge chaut.
[10] B. aynsi qe ceux, et toutz qui suyent lostel, puissent estre garniz, saunz enchesoun dymenge en lan apres.

a pee desouz luy affaire execucione de billes. Et auxint par le dit countee vn vallet prisoner.[1]

## B. The Household Ordinance of York, June 1323.

Lordenaunce de lestate de la garderobe et del acounte de lostell, fait et assentuz, en la presence nostre seignour le roy, par lez honourablez peres William de Melton, ercheuesque Deuerwik, Wauter de Stapiltone, euesque Dexeter, tresorer, Wauter de Norwici, Roger de Bellers, et autres barouns | del eschequer, et autres de counsell le roy, a Euerwyk en le moys de Juyn, lan de reigne le roy Edward, fitz le roy Edward, xvj^me^. Accompte. f. 68.

Pur ceo qi lez acountez de garderobe se delaient trop par diuers enchesouns, ordeigne est qi nul denier ne soit paie nassigne desore a purueance faire pur lostell le roy, ou pur autres chosez dount la gardein de la garderobe doit accounter, si ceo ne soit par sa mayn, ou par sez lettrez a ceo faire, ordine est qil eit toutz iours deniers suffisamment en garderobe. Accomptes severally of sundry officers.

Item de la conte de despensez de lostell soit ay [2] chescune iour en soiorne, ou chescun autre iour, si le seneschall et tresorer ne soient occupiez oue autres grossez bosoignez. Et voet le statuit de lostell qil, sil passent iij iours saunz acounter en soiourne, qi lez ditz seneschall et tresorer paient lez dispensez dune iourne de lour bourse, et semblable penaunce facent eux a mendrez officers, sil ne soient prestez chescun iour daccountrer.

Item le graunt butiller face veuwe de tout soun office en garderobe lendemayn de la seint Hillar, et vn autre veuwe en le seint John, ov final acounte a la seint Martyn, sur la payne desouth escript.

Item qi le clerc purueour de la graunde garderobe face vn vewe a la seint Andre de soun office, et vn autre veue a la Trinite, et final acounte a seint Michel suyant, sur payn desouz dit.

Item qi toutz lez autres ministres foreins, qi deuyent acountir en garderobe, facent especial vewe dacounte, chescun quartier ou demye an, solonqe la discrecione de gardein de la garderobe ; issint qi lez acountez de la garderobe de tele quartier puissent finalment estre ordinez en la quarter suyant, et qi par tant lez acountez de la garderobe puissant finalment estre renduz a lescheqer apres lan lendemayn de la chaundelure en temps de peas, et issint auaunt de an en an, saunz pluis delay ou excusacioun.

Item toutz lez ministrez qi deiuent acounter en garderobe, [qi] quaunt ils soient garniz par le gardin de la garderobe solonqe lez ditz sermez,[3] ne voignent mye de veuwe faire ou dacounter ou quauntqe a lour acount apent, soient adonqes oustez de seruice le roy pur toutz iours et greuement punitz, et lez nouns de tiels et lour targe liuerez as tresorer | , et barons del eschequer a prendre lour biens et chateux et corps, et suyer vers eux pur le roi, come deuers ceux qi duement [nont] [4] acompte solonqe la ley et la custume del eschequer. f. 68^v^.

Item qi lez clercz del officez acountent de lour somez par mois ou

[1] B. Pur le prison.
[2] B. ey.
[3] B. termes.
[4] Word in brackets supplied by B.

par quarter, solonqe la discrecion du dit gardein de garderobe, sur la peyne auauntdit.

Item qi celluy qi acounte en garderobe et demoert en arreragez, soit liueree a la mareschaucie, et illeoqes deteni [1] iesqes atant qil eit fait gree de sez arreragez.

Item pur ceo qi lacounte de la passe est molt diffius, et demande graunt delay qil soit bien araie pur lez purueancez dez vitailx et paiementz dez gagez pur la temps de guerre, et molt dautres resoun chargeantz, ordine est qi le coffrer, qi ad fait lez issuez et lez paymentz, preigne eide a lui, si mester soit, et soit tout attendant de arraier tel acounte ; et comande soit par le roy de ceo faire peniblementz et hastement, et qi vn autre soit myz en soun lieu coffrer al commaundement [2] del an xvij pur le meane temps, qi pluis chastier lez acomptz del appasse, qar par auenture il ne poet faire lun et lautre, si ceo ne fuist par trope grant delay. Et oiez primez par luy lez acomptz del hostell en mesme lostell. Apres la seint Michel, sil semble au tresorer de la garderobe, demoerge a Loundrez pur oier lez foreins accomptz, issi qil puis certefier lescheqer de ceux qi ne veignount pur faire lez venir al count deuaunt luy. Et celluy coffrer qi serra issi ordine de nouell pur le meane temps, teigne le cours auaunt ordine pur lez dispensez de la garderobe.

Rascalles. Item quaunt al hostell mesme soit ordeigne mesne couenable, et lez nouns liuerez en certein au dit gardein et le clerc de le marchaucie.

Item qi lez ministrez de lostell soient couenablez et suffissantz, et raskell soit remue de chescune office.

Pay for purveiances. Item qi lez paymentz pur lez chosez purueux pur lostell pur lez iourneez communez, sauuez lez grossez purueancez et la pullerie, soient faitz en garderobe en la presence dez clercz dez officez, qar donqes purra le tresorer de garderobe melour veer et examiner lez achatez au profit de notre seignour le roy.

f. 69. Oxen to be viewed. | Item quaunt a graunde purueance faire en feirs de grossez dez beastez countre parlement ou graunde fest, soient lez beastez vieux, quaunt ils serrount venuz en court, par seneschall et tresorer del hostell, sils puissent entendre, ou par le countroullour, le chief vssher de la sale, chiualer, et le clerc de la cuissine, et as queux appent proprement a veer tieux achatez. Et sils veient lez achatez couenablez, adonqes, quaunt ils verrount qi soit affaire, purrount faire tuer iij beastez de tel achate entre autres :—cestassauoir vn dez pluis haut price, j dautre de mesne price, et la tierce de la pluis bas price. Et doit le countrollour ou soun clerc estre au coper de tels beastez, et mettre en escripte combien dez meez rendra la melour beaste, comebien la meene, et comebien le pluis feble, et lez tesmoigne en garderobe a la count. Et si par auenture il y eit beastez qi ne vaillent mye le price a qei ils sount achatez, ils lez purront rentrer sur lachatour,[3] issint qi, sil eit folyment achate, la damage chete sur luy.

Hering and great fyshe. Item en droit de purueance de haryng et de grosse pissoun, soit ordine qi ele ce face en seisoun due, et la quantite de la purueance et le price soit tantost certefie en garderobe, et la harying et le pissoun vieu par le controllour, chief vssher de la sale, le clerc de la cuissine,

[1] B. detenue. [2] The reading of both A. and B.
[3] B. reentrer sur le achatour.

sicome desuis est dit de purueaunce dez charez.[1] Et fait assauoir qi dascun manere de pissoun contient la centeyne vj$^{xx}$, et dascun manere ix$^{xx}$.

Item quant a grosse purueance de vin contre parlementz en[2] solempnez festez, soit la purueance surueue, si come desuis est dit; —cestassauoir chescun clerc ou lez vinz serrount herbergez, comebien dez toneux soit en chescune celer, et qi null tonell soit plaine[3] et taste par le countrollour, chief vssher de la sale, clerc de la butillerie, issint qi si nul tonel soit troue purre eu autrement corumpu,[4] issint qil ne soit seyne pur corps de homme a boiuer, soit le fenuz[5] de tonell ouste et le vin expande,[6] et le damage gette sur le butiller, qi tieu vin achate. Et le nombre dez toneux et la price soit tesmoigne par la countrollour en garderobe, et apres ceo parlement ou fest, au partir le roi de ceo lieu, autrefoitz veu par le countrollour, et lez toneux demurrantz enoillez; et donqes soit examine si la loance de vin fait en lostell sacorde ov recete et remenaunt dez vinz auauntditz. Wyne.

Item en loffice de la marchaucie deuyent estre ij clercz et ij vallettz de mestrier, dount lun est nome clerc de la marchaucie, et lautre clerc de laueinere. Et clerc de laueinere et lun dez vallettz de mester vont par pays affaire purueance de fein et dauein, et de lenueer al hostell. Et le clerc de la marchaucie et lautres vallettz de mester deiuent demorrer a lostell et | receiure la dit purueance, et en faire la liueree pur lez cheuaux le roy. Et celi clerc de la marchaucie doit getter et enbreuer de iour en autre clercz, vallettz, sergeantz, qi sount as gagez en soun rolle, quaunt il vakent, et quaunt il veignent, et de ceo faire lez billez de sa mayn demeigne, de demye an en demye an, a liuerer en garderobe pur lour acountz a lez paymentz. Et sil ne face, soit chastie par discrecione de seneschall et gardein de garderobe. Clerks and others of the marshaucie. f. 69$^{v}$.

Item fait a remembrer de pistour et sez gentz, qi sount a dispensez le roi, qi ne rendent pluis de payn qi vn pistour estrange. Baker.

Fait a remembrer qi le roy doit offrer chescun iour vn graunt denier, qi peisera vij d.; quel denier le tresorer de la garderobe mandra au roi [a][7] quater festez de lan;—cestassauoir a la fest de tout Seintz, de Nowell, et Pasque, et de la Pentecost. Et cels iiij festez doit de tresorer et le coffrer porter c s., portez en deux basins dargent, dount ils deiuent profrer a chescun j d., qi voet offrer en la dit chapelle, qi en chose ils sount auxint communement as seruicez dez mortz, qi sount faitz par especialte deuaunt le roi en sa chapelle ou en auter esglise. Offeryngs by the Kyng.

Item le roi doit offrere en certein le iour de la Thesaigne vn florein a par soi, en remembrance de iij rois; quele offrande lui serra baille per la tresorer.

Item le roi doit chescun fest de seint Thomas de Canterbury offrer a la fertre de seint Thomas de Canterbury, ou enuoier illoquez a offrer, pur loy en la dit fest iij floreins en floreine en noun de cheuage. Saint Thomas of Canterbyry.

Item le roi doit offrer de certein le iour de graunde venderdy a crouce v s., queux il est acustumez receiura dieurs lui a le mene[8] le chapeleyn, a faire ent anulx a doner pur medicine as diuers gentz, et Offeryngs to heale the kyng's evel.

[1] B. bestez. [2] B. ou. [3] B. pleyn.
[4] B. purry on autrement corrumpy. [5] B. fod.
[6] expendee. [7] Supplied from B. [8] B. mayn.

a rementre autre v s. ; si le spine Dieu y soit, il doit offrer a le spine iij s.

Item a la crouce a la rasureccioun le iour de Pasque v s.

Item le roy est acustume a offrer a doner par especiale deuocione vn floreine de Florence, le iour de seint John le Euangeliste en Nowell ; et v floreins de Florence le iour de la Purificacione de Nostre Dame.

Item quant le roy doit offrer deniers a reliques, ou a autrez en esglisez, il doit offrer vij s. de custumez.

Almonee. f. 70. | Item dauncien custume lalmoner le roi receiura en la garderobe a chescune dez auauntz quater festez xxv s. pur la pouder de cc poudres en lonour dez ditz festez.

*Finis de hospicio regis.*[1]

[1] B. only.

# APPENDIX II

## LISTS OF OFFICIALS UNDER EDWARD II[1]

### A.—OFFICERS OF THE CHANCERY

Materials exist in the chancery rolls, and still more completely in the hanaper accounts, for compiling very full lists of chancery officials of this reign. A complete catalogue would be well worth making, but for the present I have limited myself to the chancellors and their deputies, and to the keepers of the chancery rolls, the next important chancery officers outside the head of the department. This latter involved, however, a list of the keepers of the *domus conversorum*, who were getting to be identical with the keepers of the rolls. Moreover, the list of temporary keepers of the seal includes some, though not all, of the most notable chancery clerks. Some personages of importance, as for instance Adam of Brome, are, however, excluded from notice.

#### (1) Chancellors and Keepers of the Great Seal

Except at the very beginning of the reign, the appointments of chancellors and of temporary keepers of the great seal are recorded in memoranda annexed to the close rolls, from which accordingly the following list is compiled. The temporary keeperships of the seal, when the normal keeper, the chancellor, was either engaged on other affairs or non-existent, are not perhaps of the greatest importance. It has, however, been thought worth while to give them, because they show very clearly the large extent to which the actual chancellor's work was at various times delegated to chancery clerks. This was notably the case with Walter Reynolds, who was seldom actually "keeping" the seal of which, as chancellor, he was the official custodian.

Reynolds is generally regarded as remaining chancellor until the late summer of 1314. However, his relations to the chancery

[1] [Mr. J. H. Johnson, M.A., is preparing for publication the results of many years' research on the official personnel of the reign. This may add some details in the case of the chief officials here listed and will supply for the first time exhaustive information, statistical and other, as to the lesser, including the household staff and the bailiffs of hundreds and liberties.]

became in the latter part of this time of such an ambiguous character as to demand special notice. For the first part of his term of office, though he seldom did the work, Reynolds was always described as chancellor. After the early part of 1312, however, his normal designation became that of "keeper of the great seal."[1] Occasionally he was still styled chancellor, but very much by way of exception. Once he was even spoken of as "keeper of the great seal by reason of his office of chancellor."[2] On 4 October 1312 the exchequer was informed that he had been appointed lieutenant (*locum tenens*) of the chancellor, just as on the same day Sandall was appointed lieutenant of the treasurer.[3] After this, Sandall and he are often mentioned together in their similar capacities.[4] His designation as keeper seems limited to the periods when he actually held the seal. When, on 6 October 1312, the seal, after being for some time kept by chancery clerks, was restored to him, it is perhaps significant that he is only restored to the "custody of the seal."[5]

On 1 October 1313 Reynolds was appointed archbishop of Canterbury by papal provision; he was enthroned on 17 February 1314. At first this increased dignity made no difference, and up to 30 March 1314 he was still "keeper of our great seal."[6] However, on 31 March, three chancery clerks received the seal from him, and directions were issued that the seal was not to go with the king against the Scots but to remain under Airmyn's charge in the Tower.[7] Accordingly, from 3 April the privy seal warrants for the chancery were sent to the "keepers of our great seal."[8] A privy seal of 20 April, is, however, addressed to Reynolds as archbishop, informing him that the keepers of the seal are to make writs "with the counsel and advice" of the archbishop.[9] After this a usual

1 The instances are too numerous to specify. An early one is 17 April 1312 (*C.C.R. 1307-13*, p. 581).

2 *C.P.R. 1307-13*, p. 592. This was on 3 June 1313.

3 Conway Davies, pp. 332-3, from K.R.M.R. no. 86, m. 73. [*Cf. Chapters*, ii, 215, n. 1.]

4 For instance on 29 Mar. 1313 (*C.P.R. 1307-13*, p. 562); on 27 Feb. he is "lieutenant" (*Foedera*, ii, 203) and on 7 April chancellor (*C.P.R. 1307-13*, p. 560). A papal nuncio called him chancellor on 15 Oct. (*Reg. Reynolds*, Worc. Hist. Soc., p. 75).

5 *Foedera*, ii, 181. The king writes to him, "E le gardez bien et sauvement, fesant coe q'apent a mesme la garde."

6 Thus in Chanc. Warr., file 87, the writs addressed to him, from 22 Feb. to 30 March 1314 call him "Walter, archbishop of Canterbury, keeper of our great seal."

7 *C.C.R. 1313-18*, p. 96. The three keepers were to "faithfully execute what pertained to the office of the great seal," that is, I imagine, seal writs. The order was probably revoked, as writs were sealed in the north, notably at York and Berwick, both before and after Bannockburn.

8 See Chanc. Warr., files 87 and 88, *passim*.

9 Chanc. Warr., file 87. "Auoms mandez as gardeins de nostre grant seal quil par le consail et lauisement de vous facent faire briefs de nostre dite seal."

form of address in chancery warrants became "to the archbishop *and* to the keepers of the great seal." [1] The inference, then, is that after 3 April Reynolds ceased to be official keeper, and I find nothing in the chancery warrants to suggest that he ever resumed this office. Nevertheless, even when the privy seals distinguish him from the keepers, he continued to receive mandates to make writs, receive petitions, and do other things that concerned the chancery.[2] Moreover, occasionally the chancery itself still called him chancellor, so late as 13 July for instance, and possibly even later.[3] He still retained a vague directive or advisory authority over the working clerks who used the seal. This authority continued the longer since the scheme devised in April for the deposit of the seal in the Tower, while the king went on the Scottish campaign, was not carried out. When Reynolds left the south with the king for the Bannockburn campaign early in June, Osgodby and his fellows took the seal north with them. Essentially Osgodby and his colleagues were independent keepers from 4 April onwards. Ordinary categories cannot, however, apply, as Reynolds was still sometimes consulted on chancery matters. This state of things continued until Sandall was made chancellor on 26 September, as part of the policy of forcing on the vanquished king the literal acceptance of the ordinances.

These details are formal enough, and we can only guess at their inner meaning. It is clear that the chancellor's title was not generally withheld because the men of this period still accepted the view of St. Thomas of Canterbury that an archbishop could not continue to act as the king's chief minister. The title is infrequent even when Reynolds was still simple bishop of Worcester. I should rather suggest that it was impolitic to parade the name, because Reynolds had never been accepted as chancellor by the baronage in parliament according to the ordinances. It is perhaps significant that the seal was seldom in his active charge during the crisis of the ordinances. Again, it was easier for Edward to drop the name than to deprive his friend of the thing. Perhaps also contemporary French usage suggested the simpler title of keeper. The obvious explanation that Reynolds was not called chancellor because he hardly ever did chancellor's work is too simple. And records show that he took an active part in the council and in the vouching for administrative acts. Nevertheless when the need

[1] Chanc. Warr., file 87. "Al honurable pere en Dieu W. erceuesqe de Canterbiry . . . et as gardeins de nostre grant seal," 9 May and 1 June.

[2] *Ibid.*, file 88, nos. 3015, 3021, 3033 and 3037, gives examples under the dates 1, 3, 6, and 9 June.

[3] *C.P.R. 1313-17*, p. 157 (13 July). The later reference in *ibid.*, p. 183, dated 25 Sept., means, I suspect, Sandall, who officially became chancellor on 26 Sept. The contrast of style between the privy seal documents emanating from the household and those from the chancery is interesting. I imagine that Northburgh, the keeper of the privy seal, was more under baronial influence than Reynolds.

arose for placating the barons, in order to get them to fight the Scots, Edward withheld from his ally even the name of keeper. After Bannockburn Reynolds ceased to be allowed even an advisory relation to the chancery. It mattered the less as permanent chancery clerks did all the work.

Reynolds' style as keeper suggests a new permanent type of keepership, similar in essence to the office of the chancellor, but less formal. Of such an office later history affords many examples. A more continuous feature of Edward II's reign is the oft-recurring but temporary deposit of the seal in the hands of a group of chancery clerks. The use of the seal was entrusted generally to one clerk, normally to the keeper of the rolls of chancery, while it was to be "kept" for safe custody under the seals of two or three of his colleagues, who were therefore in a fashion "controllers" to the acting keeper, since without their cognisance he could not obtain possession of the seal. As both these classes of officers are called keepers in the writs, I have mentioned them all in my list.

Of a different type of "keepers" are those with whom the seal was simply deposited for custody. The normal place of custody for this purpose was the wardrobe, and the treasurer of the wardrobe, or the steward of the household, was the usual keeper. Thus during Edward II's flight from the earls, before the fall of Gaveston, the seal was "kept" by Mauley the steward. The disturbances of 1321 to 1322, like those of 1311 to 1314, led to abnormal and revolutionary methods of keeping the seal. In those days the ill-health of the chancellor gave a good excuse for keeping a baronial partisan aloof from the seal. As a result we have such anomalous custodians as queen Isabella, at the time before and after the siege of Leeds in 1321, and king Edward in person, during his campaign against the marcher barons in the Severn valley, in the winter of 1321-2. On none of these occasions was the seal used. As in the earlier crisis, the only real keepers of the seal, that is keepers who sealed with it, were chancery clerks. Two of these, Osgodby, from 1310 to 1314, and William Airmyn from 1314 to 1323, are the "working chancellors" of the period. Henry Cliff, Robert Bardelby, and Richard Airmyn, once or twice replace the inevitable William Airmyn. In particular during bishop Salmon's chancellorship, the seal was constantly in William Airmyn's hands, largely through the ill-health of the aged chancellor. Baldock, alone of the chancellors of the reign, habitually discharged in person the characteristic function of his office. He only temporarily resigned its custody when he crossed the border to negotiate in 1324 the long truce with the Scots. After his flight from London the rebels, who used the name of the duke of Aquitaine, once more made revolutionary experiments in seal keeping, which continued until a regular chancellor was chosen immediately after the accession of Edward III.

## NOTE

[Substantial alterations in dates and references have been made in the following list. The reason is explained in each case. In deference to the wishes of some readers who found the former combined list inconvenient to use, chancellors have now been listed separately from keepers. In the list of keepers, the names of those who acted independently, while the chancellorship was vacant, are printed in italics. In other cases it must be understood that either unusual arrangements were in force, because the king was absent on campaign or otherwise, or else the chancellor had leave of absence on his own or the king's business.[1] Where groups of clerks were in charge of the seal, Mr. Tout in the first edition printed first and in capitals the name of " the person who has most right to be regarded as the actual keeper of the seal," leaving in lower case those of his colleagues " under whose seals the great seal was safeguarded." [2] Later, however, he spoke of " the only real keepers of the seal, that is, keepers who sealed with it." [3] On this definition many who appeared in lower case in his list deserved promotion to capitals,. for though the royal writs appointing keepers usually describe the seal as " in the custody " of one man and " under the seals " of others, memoranda on the Close Roll in many cases show that all alike took part in the sealing of writs. In the present list, the name of the person to whom custody is committed is printed first and asterisked, but the notes following include any information available as to those who shared in the use of the seal.]

H. J.

### (*a*) CHANCELLORS

Mr. RALPH OF BALDOCK, bp. of London. Apptd. 21 Ap. 1307 (Madox, i, 74). Res. seal, 2 Aug. 1307 (*C.F.R.*, i, 559).

JOHN OF LANGTON, bp. of Chichester. Acting 18 Aug. 1307 (Chanc. Warr. 58/1*a*). Res. seal 11 May 1310 (*C.C.R. 1307-13*, p. 258), but took fee to 13 May (E.A. 211/6).

WALTER REYNOLDS, bp. of Worcester and from 1314 archbp. of Canterbury. Apptd. 6 July, first sealed writs 7 July 1310 (*Foedera*, ii, 110). From early in 1312 usually called keeper, though occasionally chancellor, and on 4 Oct. 1312 apptd. *locum tenens* of the chancellor (*v. supra*, p. 286). Not in charge after 31 March 1314 (*C.C.R. 1313-18*, p. 96), but styled chancellor as late as 13 July 1314 (*v. supra*, p. 287, n. 3).

[1] [Sandall, for instance, between 1315 and 1318 was often called away by ecclesiastical affairs. He had as a prebendary of Lincoln to go to share in the election of a dean (*C.C.R. 1313-18*, p. 314), his own election as bishop of Winchester caused one visit to London and another to his diocese (*ibid.*, pp. 430, 576), and he visited Canterbury twice, once for the consecration of a bishop of London and once on pilgrimage (*ibid.*, pp. 469, 592). Once he went to Leicester " on the king's business " (*ibid.*, p. 603).]

[2] 1st edn., p. 322.

[3] *Ibid.*, p. 323.

JOHN OF SANDALL, kg.'s clk.,[1] and from 1316 bp. of Winchester. Apptd. 26 Sept. 1314 (*C.C.R. 1313-18*, pp. 197-8). Res. seal 9 June 1318 (*ibid.*, p. 619).

JOHN OF HOTHAM, bp. of Ely. Apptd. 11 June 1318 (*ibid.*, p. 619). Res. seal 23 Jan. 1320 (*C.C.R. 1318-23*, p. 219).

JOHN SALMON, bp. of Norwich. On 26 Jan. 1320 kg. delivered seal to Jo. "whom he had nominated his chancellor in full parliament" (*ibid.*, p. 219). Res. through ill-health 5 June 1323 (*ibid.*, p. 714).

Mr. ROB. OF BALDOCK, archd. of Middlesex. Rec. seal 20 Aug. 1323 (*C.C.R. 1323-27*, p. 134). Retained office till after appointment of Edw. duke of Aquitaine as keeper of the realm on 26 Oct. 1326 (*ibid.*, p. 655).

(*b*) KEEPERS

*WILL. OF MELTON*,* controller[2] of the wardrobe, *ROB. OF BARDELBY*, *MR. JO. FRANCIS*. 12 May 1310 (*C.C.R. 1307-13*, p. 258, and *Parl. Writs*, II, ii, App., p. 29). All sealed writs and seal was then deposited in wardrobe.

*AD. OF OSGODBY*,* *ROB. OF BARDELBY*, *MR. JO. FRANCIS*. May to 7 July 1310 (*Foed.*, ii, 110; *Ann. Paul.*, pp. 268-9). Seal in Ad.'s custody, under seals of Rob. and Jo.[3]

AD. OF OSGODBY,* ROB. OF BARDELBY, WILL OF AIRMYN.

*a*. 27 Aug. to 28 Sept. 1311 (*C.C.R. 1307-13*, pp. 435, 438). Seal in Ad.'s custody, under seals Rob. and Will.

*b*. 9 Dec. 1311 (*ibid.*, p. 443). All sealed writs, and seal under their seals was deposited daily in wardrobe.

*c*. 19 Dec. 1311 to 4 May 1312[4] (*ibid.*, pp. 447, 459). Conditions as in period *b*.

*d*. 17 May to 6 Oct. 1312 (*ibid.*, pp. 460, 552-3). Conditions as in period *b*.

*e*. 17 to 22 Ap. 1313 (*ibid.*, p. 581). Great seal placed under the seals of the three, while Reynolds took it with him[5] while on pilgrimage to Canterbury.

*f*. 23 May[6] to 16 July 1313 (*ibid.*, p. 583, and *C.C.R. 1313-18*, p. 66). Seal in custody of Reynolds, under seals of Ad., Rob. and Will., while king abroad.

[1] He had been a clerk in the service of the earl of Lincoln and was one of his executors (*Reg. Sandale*, Hampshire Rec. Soc., p. xxv).

[2] [Not keeper, as stated in 1st edn. and in *Chapters*, vi, 7.]

[3] [For the sake of brevity, clerks are here and later referred to, as in the Chancery enrolments, by Christian names instead of surnames.]

[4] [After writs had been sealed on morning of 4 May, Mauley, steward of the household, received the seal and started with it to the king at Tynemouth. It was not restored to the keepers till 17 May, at York. This interval is not noted in 1st edn.]

[5] [So that statement in 1st edn., p. 324, that they "received" and "surrendered" the seal conveys a slightly false impression.]

[6] [Date 13 June given in 1st edn. was due to miscalculation of "Wed. after St. Dunstan, to wit the eve of the Ascension."]

WILL. OF AIRMYN,* AD. OF OSGODBY, ROB. OF BARDELBY.
*a.* 31 March to 26 Sept. 1314 (*C.C.R. 1307-13*, pp. 96, 197-8).[1]
*b.* 2 June 1315 (*ibid.*, p. 233). Seal was left in custody of Will., under seals of Ad. and Rob., and all three "opened the seal . . . and caused writs to be sealed therewith."

AD. OF OSGODBY,* ROB. OF BARDELBY, ROB. OF ASKEBY. 14 to 23 Nov. 1315[2] (*ibid.*, p. 314). Seal was in custody of Ad., under seals of the two Robs., but all three or any two might "execute what pertains to the office of the seal." Ad. and Rob. of Askeby sealed writs on 14 Nov.

WILL. OF AIRMYN,* ROB. OF BARDELBY, HUGH OF BURGH (till 16 Sept.), ROB. OF ASKEBY (after 16 Sept.). 26 Aug. to at least 19 Oct. 1316 (*ibid.*, p. 430, and Chanc. Warr. 95/3739). Seal in custody of Will., under seals of the other two, but all three sealed writs.

WILL. OF AIRMYN,* ROB. OF BARDELBY. 11 to 18 May 1317 (*C.C.R. 1313-18*, p. 469). Will. and Rob. sealed writs. King's writ of privy seal, 8 May, ordered chancellor to "leave the chancery at London and the great seal in the custody of" Will. and Rob. "as has been usual hitherto." Chancellor left London on 11 May. Seal was then in custody of Henry of Cliff, under seals of Will. and Rob., who opened it and sealed writs.

WILL. OF AIRMYN,* ROB. OF BARDELBY, ROB. OF ASKEBY. 9[3] to at least 20 Nov. 1317 (*ibid.*, pp. 576, 577). Seal in custody of Will. under seals of other two. All three sealed writs.

Mr. HEN. OF CLIFF,* WILL. OF AIRMYN, ROB. OF BARDELBY, ROB. OF ASKEBY. 13[4] to 19 Feb. 1318 (*ibid.*, pp. 592-3). Seal in custody of Hen. under seals of other three. Will. and Rob. of Askeby sealed writs.

Mr. HEN. OF CLIFF,* WILL. OF AIRMYN, ROB. OF ASKEBY. 29 Mar. 1318 (*ibid.*, p. 603). Seal in custody of Hen. under seals of Will. and Rob. All sealed writs.

[1] [In 1st edn. Osgodby was capitalised as chief keeper, and a distinction was made between conditions up to 4 Ap. and from 5 Ap., after which date the three were described as "independent keepers." The Close Rolls state that on 31 March Reynolds, in whose custody the seal then was under the seals of Ad., Rob. and Will., willed that while the king was at the war against Scotland the seal should remain at the Tower of London under the seals of Ad. and Rob., and that Will. should "dwell in the Tower . . . for the custody of the seal." Reynolds did not leave London till 5 Ap., and till then the seal remained in his custody though under the seals of the three keepers. When the seal was delivered to the king at York on 26 Sept. it was "under the seals of Ad. and Rob." but all three were described as keepers. If any one of the three can be distinguished from the others, it is Airmyn.]

[2] [Date 25 Nov. given in 1st edn. was due to slip as to date of Sun. after octave of St. Martin.]

[3] [Date 20 Oct. given in 1st edn. was misprint for 26 Oct., date of letters to the keepers, which did not reach them till 9 Nov., when the seal was handed over to their charge.]

[4] [Date 6 Feb. given in 1st edn. was that of the letters of appointment.]

*WILL. OF AIRMYN,* ROB. OF BARDELBY, MR. HEN. OF CLIFF.* 9 [1] to 11 June 1318 (*C.C.R. 1313-18*, pp. 619-20), between resignation of Sandall and appointment of Hotham as chancellor. Seal in custody of Will., under seals of Rob. and Hen. All three sealed writs.

WILL. OF AIRMYN,* ROB. OF BARDELBY, MR. HEN. OF CLIFF, ROB. OF ASKEBY.

*a.* 12 June [2] to 2 July 1318 (*ibid.*, pp. 619-20). Seal was in custody of Will. under seals of the other three. Will. sealed writs, and on 2 July handed over seal under seals of the two Roberts.

*b.* 4 to 16 July 1318 (*ibid.*, p. 620). All four sealed writs. Will. handed over seal on 16 July under seals of the other three.

*c.* 20 to 29 July 1318 [3] (*ibid.*, p. 620). Same conditions, but Askeby was given licence to return home.

*d.* 1 to 4 Aug. 1318 (*ibid.*, p. 620). Same conditions, but Hen. fell ill, so seal was in Will.'s custody under Rob.'s seal.

WILL. OF AIRMYN,* GEOFF. OF WELFORD, WILL. OF HERLASTON. From 11 Oct. 1318 (*C.C.R. 1318-23*, p. 103). Seal in custody of Airmyn, under seals of the other two. Airmyn sealed writs.

ROB. OF BARDELBY,* MR. HEN. OF CLIFF, GEOFF. OF WELFORD, WILL. OF CLIFF. From 2 Dec. 1319 [4] (*ibid.*, p. 216). Seal in Rob.'s custody under seals of the other three. All sealed writs.

WILL. OF AIRMYN,* ROB. OF BARDELBY, HEN. OF CLIFF. 23 to 26 Jan. 1320 (*ibid.*, p. 219). Seal in custody of Will. under seals of Rob. and Hen. All sealed writs.

WILL. OF AIRMYN,* ROB. OF BARDELBY, WILL. OF CLIFF. 9 June to 23 July [5] 1320 (*ibid.*, pp. 237-8, 317). Small "seal of absence" in custody of Will., under seals of the other two, while king abroad. All sealed writs.

WILL. OF AIRMYN,* MR. HEN. and WILL. OF CLIFF. 6 Aug. to 27 Sept. 1320 (*ibid.*, p. 323). Seal was to be kept by Airmyn "jointly with" the other two, and under their seals, and all sealed writs. It was Airmyn who handed over the seal on 27 Sept., under the seals of Hen. of Cliff and Geoff. of Welford, as Will. of Cliff had been absent.

ROG. OF NORTHBURGH,* keeper of the wardrobe, MR. HEN. OF CLIFF, WILL. OF HERLASTON. 16 to 24 Ap. 1321 (*ibid.*, p. 366). Seal in custody of Rog. under seals of Hen. and Will. On 18 Ap. all sealed writs, and after that seal was to remain in wardrobe in Rog.'s custody, and Hen. and Will. were "to do daily what pertained to the office of the seal."

[1] [Translation of St. Edmund. Not 10 June, as in 1st edn.]

[2] [Not 13 June as in 1st edn. Letters of appointment were dated 12 June, and Will. "received the seal from the chancellor on the same day, and opened it immediately after dinner."]

[3] [This period was omitted in 1st edn.]

[4] [Letters of appointment were dated 1 Dec.]

[5] [Date 22 July in 1st edn. is that of letters ordering seal to be used no more. Airmyn received these on 23 July "and from that hour nothing was done by the aforesaid seal," though it was not restored to the chancellor till 29 July.]

The same, with WILL. OF AIRMYN.[1] 24 Ap. to 3 May[2] 1321 (*C.C.R. 1318-23*, pp. 366-7).

WILL. OF AIRMYN,* ROB. OF BARDELBY, Mr. HEN. OF CLIFF. 20 May to 24 July 1321 (*ibid.*, pp. 367, 477).

WILL. OF AIRMYN,* with seal in safe keeping, first of Queen Isabella[3] and later of Rog. of Northburgh. 24 July to 24 Aug. 1321 (*ibid.*, pp. 477-8).

WILL. OF AIRMYN,* ROB. OF BARDELBY, Mr. HEN. OF CLIFF.

*a.* 24 Aug. to 23 Oct. 1321 (*ibid.*, p. 478). Seal was in Will.'s custody under seals of Rob. and Hen. All sealed writs.

*b.* 23 Oct. to 3 Nov. 1321 (*ibid.*). William[4] sealed, but afterwards gave seal into custody of Queen Isabella.

*c.* 5[5] to 14 Nov. 1321 (*ibid.*). All sealed, but seal remained in king's custody under their seals.

WILL. OF AIRMYN,* Mr. HEN. OF CLIFF. 14 Nov. to 14 Dec. 1321 (*ibid.*). Seal in king's custody under seals of Will. and Hen.

WILL. OF AIRMYN,* WILL. OF CLIFF, WILL. OF HERLASTON. 15 Dec. 1321 up to and after 3 March 1322 (*ibid.*). Between 5 Nov. 1321 and 24 Jan. 1322, and again after 3 March 1322 the seal was in the king's custody when not being used for sealing.[6]

WILL. OF AIRMYN,* Mr. HEN. OF CLIFF, WILL. OF HERLASTON and after 28 Oct. WILL. OF CLIFF. 12 Sept.[7] to 17 Nov. 1322 (*ibid.*, pp. 676-7).

WILL. OF AIRMYN,* Mr. HEN. and WILL. OF CLIFF, WILL. OF HERLASTON. 10 Jan.[8] to 2 May 1323 (*ibid.*, p. 689).

*WILL. OF AIRMYN,* Mr. HEN. OF CLIFF, WILL. OF HERLASTON.* 5 June[9] to 20 Aug. 1323 (*ibid.*, p. 714 and *C.C.R. 1323-27*, pp. 134-5), during vacancy between resignation of Salmon and apptt. of Baldock as chancellor. The three received the seal "to keep it as they have done heretofore" and all sealed writs, seal afterwards remaining in Airmyn's custody.

[1] ["With the aforesaid Master Henry" not "substituted for" him, as stated in 1st edn., p. 326.]

[2] [On 3 May, at Wallingford, the king gave Airmyn the great seal to take to London, where on 6 May the chancellor received and used it.]

[3] ["The queen to keep the seal in her possession and to deliver the seal to the said Will. daily when he should go to her for the seal to seal therewith."]

[4] [Mr. Tout omitted the names of Rob. and Hen. as Will.'s colleagues during this period. But the record states that when Will. needed the seal he sought it from the queen, and after sealing carried it back to her "under the aforesaid seals" (*C.C.R. 1318-23*, p. 478).]

[5] [Not 4 Nov. as in 1st edn.]

[6] [The statement in 1st edn., p. 327, that while the seal was in the king's custody it was not used is belied by the closing phrases of the incomplete Close Roll memorandum. "From 3 March the seal remained in the king's possession under the seals of the said Will., Will. and Will. and [writs] were sealed therewith, etc., as above until ——."]

[7] [Date 24 Sept. in 1st edn. is a slip. Airmyn and the two Cliffs were appointed by letters of privy seal dated 2 Sept. On 12 Sept. the chancellor gave the seal to Airmyn, to be kept under the seals of Hen. of Cliff and Herlaston till Will. of Cliff, then absent, should arrive. He did so on 28 Oct., but after that Herlaston still acted on occasion.]

[8] [Letters appointing these keepers were dated 30 Dec. 1322.]

[9] [Letters bidding them to receive the seal were dated 4 June.]

RICH. OF AIRMYN,* Mr. HEN. OF CLIFF, WILL. OF HERLASTON. 16 Nov. to 12 Dec. 1324 (*C.C.R. 1323-27*, p. 328). Seal in Rich.'s custody under seals of Hen. and Will.

*Arrangements during Period of Revolution*

*ROB. OF WYVILL.*[1] 26 Oct. to 20 Nov. 1326, in charge of privy seal to be used by Edw. duke of Aquitaine as keeper of the realm "because he had no other seal for the rule at that time" (*C.C.R. 1323-27*, p. 655).

*WILL. BLOUNT*, knight. Carried great seal from king at Monmouth to queen and duke at Marcle, which he reached on 26 Nov. 1326 (*ibid.*).[2]

*WILL. OF AIRMYN*, bp. of Norwich. 30 Nov. 1326 (*ibid.*). He presumably remained in charge till Hotham was apptd. chancellor by Edw. III on 28 Jan. 1327 (*C.C.R. 1327-30*, p. 98). Till 4 Dec. 1326 he kept the seal under his own privy seal (*C.C.R. 1323-27*, p. 655), but after that restored the seal under his own seal to the queen and duke for custody after each sealing. After 17 Dec. Hen. of Cliff's seal was also affixed when it was thus restored (*ibid.*, p. 656).

## (2) THE KEEPERS OF THE CHANCERY ROLLS AND THE HOUSE OF CONVERTS

The keeper of the rolls of chancery was always a leading chancery clerk. He often "kept the household of the chancery," and normally acted as a keeper of the great seal in a temporary vacancy or during the chancellor's absence from duty. This was notably the case in Edward II's reign.

The custom now arose of appointing the keeper of the rolls of chancery as keeper also of the *domus conversorum*, the house for the reception of the Jewish converts and their chaplains in Chancery Lane, on the site of the modern Public Record Office. The last keeper of the house of converts under Edward I had been the royal chaplain and almoner, Henry of Bluntesdon.[3] Early in the new reign Adam Osgodby, already keeper of the rolls, became warden of the converts also. The two offices were, however, still distinct, as the appointment of Robert Holden, who was not even a chancery clerk, to the keepership of the house of converts shows. Robert was, at the time of his nomination, controller of the wardrobe, and the entrusting of this office to a *garderobarius* is characteristic of the deliberate confusion of chancery and wardrobe under Robert

[1] [Described as clerk of Edw., duke of Aquitaine, though long in the service of Queen Isabella (*Chapters*, ii, 309-10; v, 285), for at this date the queen and her son were pooling resources and staff.]

[2] [Date 20 Nov. given in 1st edn. for opening of Blount's custody seems too early. The bp. of Hereford had started on 20 Nov. as envoy to the king, and it was only as the result of his embassy, after deliberation, that Edw. surrendered the seal to Blount.]

[3] *C.P.R. 1292-1301*, p. 341. He was appointed on 10 April 1298.

Baldock. The two offices were formally united under Richard II, and after 1381 the old house of converts became mainly the office of the rolls of chancery.[1] The keepers of the rolls became known later as masters of the rolls, and by modern legislation their authority has been extended from the chancery rolls to the custody of all the records of the crown.

Even under Edward II, the combination of the two offices had the advantage of securing adequate London quarters for the chancery records, which were less liable to loss when not exposed to the hazards of being carried about by a peripatetic court.[2] The house of converts also afforded accommodation upon occasion to the "household of the chancery." Osgodby used the *domus conversorum* so freely for these purposes that the chaplains and converts complained in 1315 that he had made them all houseless, and had harboured the chancery clerks there, and even leased some of the tenements to strangers. Naturally the chancellor decided against the converts, and in favour of his own subordinate.[3]

The large extent to which the great seal was in the keeping of such men as Osgodby and William Airmyn makes the position of the keeper of the rolls of some practical importance for Edward II's reign. Here, as elsewhere, the office increases in importance, and the official head recedes somewhat into the background. The keeper of the chancery rolls is now keeper of the seal almost as often as the chancellor.

### (*a*) Keepers of the Rolls of Chancery

AD. OF OSGODBY, kg.'s clk. Apptd. 1 Oct. 1295 (*C.C.R. 1288-96*, p. 454); acting 17 Ap. 1316 (*ibid.*, *1313-18*, p. 333); dead by 1 Sept. 1316 (*C.F.R.*, ii, 299).

WILL. OF AIRMYN, kg.'s clk. Acting 26 Aug. 1316 (*C.C.R. 1313-18*, p. 430); gave up keys 26 May 1324 (*C.C.R. 1323-27*, p. 186).

RICH. OF AIRMYN, kg.'s clk. Apptd. 26 May 1324 (*ibid.*); gave up keys 4 July, 1325 (*ibid.*, p. 386).

Mr. HEN. OF CLIFF, kg.'s clk. Apptd. 4 July 1325 (*ibid.*); acting 17 Dec. 1326 (*ibid.*, p. 656).

### (*b*) Keepers of the *Domus Conversorum*

AD. OF OSGODBY, kg.'s clerk, keeper of chancery rolls. Apptd. 7 Nov. 1307, during pleasure (*C.P.R. 1307-13*, p. 15); died 1316 (*v. supra*).

WILL. OF AIRMYN, kg.'s clk., keeper of chancery rolls. Apptd. 20 Aug. 1316 for life (*C.P.R. 1313-17*, p. 534).

ROB. OF HOLDEN, kg.'s clk., controller of the wardrobe. Apptd. 4 Oct. 1325 (*C.P.R. 1324-27*, p. 176); acting to [11 Aug.] 1326 (I.R. [218, m. 14)].

[1] *C.P.R.* [1374-77, p. 451 ;] *ibid.*, *1381-85*, pp. 41, 269.

[2] [But see Wilkinson, pp. 58-9].

[3] *C.C.R. 1313-18*, pp. 228-9. There is an interesting history of the "Rolls chapel" by Sir H. Maxwell-Lyte, in *D.K. 57th Rep.*, pp. 19-47, and notices of the House of Converts by Mr. W. J. Hardy are in *Middlesex and Hertfordshire Notes and Queries*.

## B.—OFFICERS OF THE EXCHEQUER

Modern writers tend to stress the distinction between the exchequer of receipt and the exchequer of account. The distinction is a real one, but the fourteenth century professed to emphasise the unity rather than the division of the great financial office, so that it was regarded as a presumptuous act for the ambitious baron Bellers to strive to split into two divisions an office which from the beginning had always been indivisible.[1] Similarly there has been a tendency to distinguish unduly between the judicial, financial, and executive sides of the exchequer, and to classify its staff according as its work is thought to fall mainly into one of these three categories.[2] Thus the "barons," being judges in more modern times, are regarded as exercising primarily judicial functions; the "upper exchequer" is regarded as mainly engaged in accounting and drawing up rolls, while officers of the "receipt" are absorbed in paying out and receiving money and in making tallies. But the barons were financial even more than judicial officers, and the "lower exchequer" now had, in the issue and receipt rolls, rolls and accounts of its own as elaborate as those of the "exchequer of account." Even in so highly organised an office as the exchequer there was in the fourteenth century no clear differentiation of functions, but every officer was employed in judicial, executive, or financial work, according to the needs of the moment. This becomes still more evident when we take into account the extra-official work, the extraordinary judicial and executive commissions, which were assigned to all prominent officers of the exchequer, as to every other minister of state in those days.

The lists of exchequer officers now given might easily have been enlarged. For instance, the issue rolls alone would enable us to give an absolutely exhaustive list of all the officers of the receipt. But I have thought it enough to limit myself to those ministers who shared the chief responsibilities, though some prominent persons in my list began their work as minor exchequer clerks. I may add further that the officers of the exchequer seem to have lived a corporate life, like that of the clerks of the chancery, or, in later times, the clerks of the privy seal. The details of this collegiate existence are much less closely illustrated by the records than is the case with the two chief administrative offices. Yet there is evidence, notably in the case of the barons, that "residence at the exchequer" involved much more than attendance during office hours, and included living there in common with their colleagues of the same rank. This residence must have been very

[1] *Flores Hist.*, iii, 232. "Scaccarium domini regis apud Westmonasterium prima sua institutione semper indivisum."

[2] For instance, Mr. H. Hall, Preface to *Red Book of Exchequer*, III, cccxxxi-iii, makes this separation even in 1290, when there was less differentiation than in our period.

loosely interpreted in the case of the increasing number of lay dignitaries, who had manors and estates as well as houses of their own. Perhaps it was already becoming obsolete.

## (1) Treasurers

Enough has been said in the text as to the duties and responsibilities of the treasurer of the exchequer. It need only now be added that in this list the keepers of the treasury and the lieutenants of the treasurer are alike printed in italics. [When the officer is acting, not on behalf of another treasurer, but independently, his name is asterisked.] Sometimes, as in 1322 and 1325, the division of the exchequer into two branches necessitated a principal and a lieutenant acting at the same time. Such an acting treasurer was generally a baron, and continued to discharge his duties as a baron, as, for instance, Norwich, Everdon and Bellers.

Walter of Langton, bp. of Lichfield. Apptd. 28 Sept. 1295 (*C.P.R. 1292-1301*, p. 149) ; office ended 22 Aug. 1307 (*C.P.R. 1307-13*, p. 1).

Walter Reynolds, kg.'s clk., later bp. of Worc. Apptd. 22 Aug. 1307 (*ibid.*) ; office ended 6 July 1310 (*ibid.*, p. 234, and *Ann. Paul.*, p. 269).

*John of Sandall*,, kg.'s clk. [30 Dec. 1307 (Madox, i, 314)] [1] to 6 July 1310.

John of Sandall, kg.'s clk. Apptd. 6 July 1310 (*C.P.R. 1307-13*, p. 234, and *Ann. Paul.*, *ut supra*) ; office ended 23 Oct. 1311 (*C.P.R. 1307-13*, p. 396).

*Walter of Norwich*,* baron of exch. Apptd. 23 Oct. 1311 (*ibid.*) ; ordered to give up keys on 23 Jan. 1312, when Walter of Langton, bp. of Lichfield, apptd. "till next parliament" (*ibid.*, p. 413) ; ordered on 17 May to continue to act, as Langton has been prevented "for divers reasons" from entering office (*ibid.*, p. 459) ; [2] office ended on 4 Oct. 1312 (*ibid.*, p. 501).

[1] [For date 6 May 1308 (1st edn., p. 332, and *Chapters*, vi, 20) no authority was given (but *cf. Dict. Nat. Biog. s.v.* Sandale). For instances in Jan. 1308 and June 1309 see Madox, i, 380, ii, 279.]

[2] [As the patent of 23 Jan. 1312 was] ignored in the south, it was "vacated because surrendered and cancelled," and another was issued from York to the same effect on 14 Mar. (*C.P.R. 1307-13*, p. 440). On 12 Ap., from Newcastle-on-Tyne, the king commanded the barons "sicut alias" to obey Langton as treasurer ; "et hoc sicut indignationem regis vitare voluerint nullatenus omittant" (Madox, ii, 38). Langton, too, had been afraid to act, and on 13 April the king sternly ordered him to do his duty (*Foedera*, ii, 164). Excommunicated by Winchelsea and threatened by the barons, Langton was, on 1 May, allowed to go to Avignon to appeal (*ibid.*, p. 167). Thus the second treasurership of the great treasurer of Edward I's declining years proved a purely nominal one. I imagine Norwich, the baronial nominee, acted continuously as keeper of the treasury from Oct. 1311 to May 1312. [*Cf. Chapters*, ii, 187 and n. The full text of the writs addressed to the exchequer, calendared in *C.P.R.*, may be read in K.R.M.R. no. 85 or L.T.R.M.R. no. 82.]

*JOHN OF SANDALL,** kg.'s clk. Apptd. 4 Oct. 1312 (*C.P.R. 1307-13*, p. 501) ; office ended 26 Sept. 1314 (*C.P.R. 1313-17*, p. 178).

WALTER OF NORWICH. Apptd. 26 Sept. 1314 (*ibid.*) ; office ended 27 May 1317 (*ibid.*, p. 657).

JOHN OF HOTHAM, bp. of Ely. Apptd. 27 May 1317 (*ibid.*) ; office ended 10 June 1318 (*C.P.R. 1317-21*, p. 155).

Mr. JOHN WALWAYN, kg.'s clk. Apptd. 10 June 1318 (*ibid.*) ; office ended 16 Nov. 1318 (*ibid.*, p. 227, I.R. 186, m. 1).

JOHN OF SANDALL, bp. of Winchester. Apptd. 16 Nov. 1318 (*C.P.R.*, *ut sup.*) ; died 2 Nov. 1319.

*WALTER OF NORWICH.** [Was paid fee as keeper from 29 Sept. 1319 to 23 Feb. 1320 (I.R. 189, m. 9) ; office ended 18 Feb. 1320 (*C.P.R. 1317-21*, p. 417) ; ceased acting 20 Feb. (R.R. 230).] [1]

WALTER OF STAPELDON, bp. of Exeter. Apptd. 18 Feb. 1320 (*C.P.R.*, *ut sup.*) ; office ended 25 Aug. 1321 (R.R. 235, *C.P.R. 1321-24*, p. 14).

*WALTER OF NORWICH.** Apptd. 25 Aug. 1321 (*ibid.*) ; office ended 9 May 1322 (*ibid.*, p. 112).

WALTER OF STAPELDON. Again apptd. 9 May 1322 (*ibid.*) ; took up office 10 May (R.R. 240) ; office ended 3 July 1325 (*C.P.R. 1324-27*, p. 128).

*WALTER OF NORWICH.** Apptd. (*a*) 3 Nov. 1322 (*C.C.R. 1318-23*, p. 613) ; (*b*) 2 July 1324 (*C.C.R. 1323-27*, p. 116).[2]

*WILL. OF EVERDON*, baron of exchequer. Acting as deputy for Norwich, 6 [3] July to 20 Aug. 1324 (R.R. 251).[4]

WILL. OF MELTON, archbp. of York. Apptd. 3 July 1325 (*C.P.R. 1324-27*, p. 128, Malmesb. p. 283) ; in office till 14 Nov. 1326 (I.R. 219).

*ROGER BELLERS*, baron of exch. Apptd. 9 Aug. 1325 (*C.P.R.*, *ut sup.*, p. 159).

*WALTER OF NORWICH*, chief baron of exch. Apptd. [4 Aug. 1326 (*ibid.*, p. 306)] ; office ended 6 Nov. 1326 (K.R.M.R. 103, m. 130).

JOHN OF STRATFORD, bp. of Winchester. Apptd. 6 Nov. 1326 (*ibid.*) ; began to act 14 Nov. (I.R. 219, m. 1d.). Acted till 28 Jan. 1327 (*Chapters*, vi, 21).

## (2) BARONS

Under Henry II " baron of the exchequer " was a descriptive title of the greater ministers of state—the *maiores*—who had seats in the exchequer. It included not only the treasurer, the chamberlains and other definitely financial officers, but all the dignitaries of state, from the chancellor downwards, in their relations to the exchequer. In the fourteenth century, however, " baron of the

[1] [I can find no authority for appointment on 6 Nov., as in 1st edn., and no reference in I.R. 187 there cited. It seems certain that Walter was acting before Sandall's death.]

[2] [This appointment, not included in the 1st edn. or in *Chapters*, is added from note in Mr. Tout's own copy.]

[3] [Not 2 July as in *Chapters*, vi, 21.]

[4] [I have not been able to find this fact in R.R. 251.]

exchequer" was the name of a definite class of exchequer officers, who were so far contrasted with the ancient *maiores de scaccario* that, as the case of Walter of Norwich shows, a baron on becoming treasurer ceased to be a baron, though a baron might hold temporary office as *locum tenens thesaurarii*.

The process by which the meaning of the term baron became entirely changed has not yet been worked out in detail, but the most essential stages of it took place during the reign of Henry III. Late in the reign of John,[1] and again in the early years of Henry III,[2] the phrase "baron of the exchequer" was still used in the same sense as in the days of the *Dialogus*. So late as 1230 the treasurer is still one of the barons.[3] The later sense of baron only begins when barons of the exchequer were first appointed *ad hoc* and the first recorded instance of this is in 1234, immediately after the fall of Peter des Roches, when William of Beauchamp, Alexander of Swerford and Richard of Montfichet were formally assigned as fellows of the other barons to be resident at the exchequer.[4] Yet even after this the term baron remains so vague that Swerford is officially described in 1235, not as baron, but as a resident at the exchequer in the king's service.[5] In 1245 Alexander le Seculer was appointed *baro et socius*.[6] No other appointment of a baron of the exchequer is recorded until 16 June 1253, when that of Peter of Rivaux, then nearing the end of his long career, is enrolled on the close roll.[7] But from that time references to official barons in close and liberate rolls become not uncommon, and on 1 November 1263 Roger de la Ley, remembrancer of the exchequer, was appointed baron "because the king at present has not a baron in the same exchequer,"[8] apparently as the result of civil disturbances.

[1] See, for instance, *Rot. Lit. Claus. 1204-24*, p. 132, where John, in 1212, tells the bishop of Norwich that he has sent "nuncios vestros . . . ad fideles nostros G. filium Petri, justiciarium nostrum, S. comitem Wintonie, W. Briwerre, magistrum R. de Marisco, tunc ad scaccarium nostrum residentes, et ad *ceteros barones de scaccario nostro*." Here we have the justiciar, Geoffrey FitzPeter, Richard Marsh, the powerful clerk of the chamber, who soon became chancellor, and two other magnates called barons of the exchequer, while they were attending the exchequer session, in quite the twelfth-century fashion.

[2] Madox, i, 675, from Pipe Roll, 5 Hen. III, mentions "H. de Burgo, justiciarium, W. Briewerre, *et alios barones de scaccario*." Brewer and other magnates are called in 10 Richard I, "barones ad scaccarium" (*ibid.*, ii, 228), a formula which precisely expresses the situation. Again in 9 Hen. III a long list of magnates and officials are called barons of the exchequer (Madox, ii, 27).

[3] *Ibid.*, ii, 28.

[4] *Close Rolls 1231-34*, pp. 569-70. Compare *ibid.*, pp. 467-8. Swerford was already an exchequer clerk of great experience, and had compiled the *Red Book* four years previously, when already "residens in regis scaccario" (*Red Bk. Exch.*, i, 4).

[5] *Close Rolls 1234-37*, p. 80, "qui residet ad scaccarium regis in servitio domini regis."

[6] *Ibid.*, p. 302.

[7] Madox, ii, 55; *Close Rolls 1251-53*, p. 371.

[8] *Ibid.*, p. 21; Madox, ii, 55.

Clearly, however, by this date it was abnormal that there should be no official baron in residence, and we may safely infer that "baron" had now definitely ceased to be a descriptive term and had become an official title. Under Edward I the office became regularised, and henceforth there generally seem to have been at least three barons of the exchequer acting at once.[1] Towards the end of the reign the custom arose of appointing barons by letters patent, so that henceforth their succession is easy to trace.[2]

Under Edward II twenty-five persons acted as barons of the exchequer, each of whom received his appointment by patent. The number serving at once was still not quite determined, being never less than three, and once at least as high as six. This latter number occurs in 1318-19,[3] and was regarded as excessive by the reformers of the York parliament of October 1318. Accordingly orders were issued to the new treasurer, bishop Sandall, on 2 January 1319, to deliberate, "if you see that the office be overfilled, which of the said barons can be most easily dispensed with." [4] The result was that the number was cut down by 1323 to four,[5] a number already regarded at the beginning of the reign as a normal one. This is suggested by the fact that while five barons were appointed in 1307, yet two were old and infirm, one of whom died almost immediately, while another virtually retired in a few months. Anyhow only one appointment was made in place of these two vacancies, so that the office was considered sufficiently equipped with four barons in 1308. As the result of the reforming ordinance of 1323, the normal number of barons was raised to five.[6] In 1324-26 there were seven, as the result of Bellers' division of the exchequer, but after 1327 only four again.

[1] For instance, in 1278, when a stipend of twenty marks each is ordered to be paid to three barons, Roger Northwood, John Cobham, and Philip of Willoughby (*C.P.R. 1272-81*, p. 295); compare *ibid.*, p. 311. Again, in the parliament of 1305, three barons appeared among the members of the council summoned to attend parliament, namely William Carlton, John de Lisle and Roger Hegham (Maitland, *Memoranda de Parliamento*, pp. cvii-viii).

[2] The first appointment of a baron by patent was that [of Richard of Saham in place] of Mr. Elias of Winchester to the Dublin exchequer on 1 Sept. 1295 (*C.P.R. 1292-1301*, p. 145). The earliest English examples are those of Mr. Richard of Abingdon, appointed on 23 Sept., and John de Lisle, appointed on 17 Oct. 1299 (*ibid.*, pp. 438, 442). The other instances under Edward I are Roger Hegham, appointed 1 April 1300 (*ibid.*, p. 503), and Humphrey of Walden, appointed 19 Oct. 1306 (*C.P.R. 1301-7*, p. 467).

[3] In 12 Edw. II (1318-19) six barons were acting, namely, Walter of Norwich, John Abel, Robert Wodehouse, John Ockham, John Foxley, and John Everdon, but wages for four only are recorded in the Issue Roll for Michaelmas term (I.R. 186, m. 3).

[4] Madox, ii, 61. Two barons, Wodehouse and Ockham, were declared to be "suffisaunz et necessaires," and were "to remain in peace in their posts." For the other barons see previous note.

[5] *Red Bk. Exch.*, iii, 903.

[6] *Ibid.*

The position of baron was traditionally one of great dignity and importance. When the official barons came in, it was thought worth while, in 1255, to extend to them all the liberties and privileges which had belonged to barons of the exchequer in the original sense.[1] The salary assigned to Swerford, the first official baron, in 1234, was 40 marks a year,[2] and in 1278 this salary was assigned to each of three barons.[3] Thus long before Edward II's reign the stipend of 40 marks which each still received had already become the accustomed fee.[4]

The lay and clerical barons under Edward II were almost equally balanced.[5] Fourteen of the twenty-five were clerks when appointed, but as Norwich soon renounced his clergy, the permanent proportion is thirteen clerks to twelve laymen, at least eight of the latter being knights. Of the clerks, at least three were professional exchequer clerks. Of these Norwich reached still higher dignities, but like the more obscure William of Everdon and William of Fulbourn was treasurer's remembrancer before he became a baron. Three other king's clerks, Warley, Ockham and Wodehouse, were wardrobe clerks, who had held high office in that department. Of close affinity to these is Humphrey of Walden, a knight, who had been chief steward of chamber manors. Other barons like Threckingham, Staunton, and Friskney, this latter a layman, had been regular justices of one or both of the two benches; while others had had judicial experience in eyres and similar temporary commissions, among them Bakewell, Lisle and Gloucester. Bakewell's position as a veteran alderman of London raised to be baron is worth special emphasis.[6]

Three of the lay barons, Scotter, Friskney and Passelewe, had been advocates in large practice in the common law courts, or, in contemporary language, "narratores," "counters" or "sergeants assigned to the king's pleas." This class, Mr. Turner tells us, was

[1] Madox, ii, 13, from Memoranda Roll, 39 Hen. III.

[2] *C.P.R. 1232-47*, p. 75.

[3] *C.P.R. 1272-81*, pp. 295, 311. Is it possible that "year" on p. 295 should there be read "term"? Otherwise the entries are contradictory. [The original (Pat. roll 98, m. 26) of the entry on p. 295 reads: "unicuique xx marcas super feodum suum de anno presenti," i.e. an instalment only of the total annual fee.]

[4] Madox, ii, 326; Issue Rolls, *passim*.

[5] [On view taken by author of *Mirror of Justices* see *Chapters*, ii, 193 n.]

[6] The identity of the baron with the alderman seems almost established by the will of Cecilia of Baukwell, dated 29 Dec. 1323, and calendared in *Cal. of Wills in Court of Husting*, i, 342. She speaks of her husband as Sir John of Bauquell, and their son and heir's name is Thomas. Thomas' own will is in *ibid.*, i, 390. Thomas, son and heir of John Baukwell, is already acting in that capacity on 10 March 1308, soon after the baron's death (*C.C.R. 1307-13*, p. 53). See also below, p. 306, n. 1.

already limited to laymen under Edward II,[1] so that the development of the lay element among the barons resulted from the increase in the number of barons trained in the practice of the common law, where their clerical brethren were seldom advocates though often judges. The departmental exchequer and wardrobe officials had a more purely financial training. All barons were, however, put on so many commissions to hear and determine, to hold assizes and eyres, that every one could not but acquire plenty of judicial experience, even outside revenue cases. The election of Scotter, who apparently was a distinguished advocate, straight from the bar to the first place among the barons, is the most striking instance of the promotion of a pure lawyer to a high exchequer post during the reign. The clerical barons do not seem in some cases to have profited much by their clergy. The highest church promotion obtained by them in the reign was the deanery of St. Paul's, which went to John of Everdon. Perhaps the exchequer clerks were now so remote from the court that they had not the chances of advancement by royal favour enjoyed by wardrobe and even chancery clerks. However, the clerical element persisted longer among the barons of the exchequer than on the two benches of common law justices. It was not until the anti-clerical days of 1371 that parliament included the office of baron of the exchequer among those to which they prayed the crown to appoint no " men of holy church." [2] Even later than this, knowledge of the common law was not regarded as indispensable for a baron, if he were otherwise well-informed in the laws, course and ways of the exchequer.[3] Let us not then think of fourteenth-century barons as lawyers and judges so much as superior treasury clerks with many opportunities for varied administrative and judicial experience.

The corporate life of the exchequer as an office is negatively illustrated by the licences given to more than one baron of long service to " retire from court and dwell in his own house as often and as long as he thinks fit, and to return to the exchequer when he pleases." Such permission was granted by Edward I to the barons John Cobham in 1300, and Peter of Leicester in 1301.[4] Similar permission was given to the veteran William Carlton in 1308 by Edward II.[5] As Carlton continued to act when so minded, the favour must be regarded as exemption from compulsory " living

[1] *Year Books,* IV, xv-xxi. The passage in the *Mirror of Justices,* p. 47, on which Mr. Turner partly relies, does not, however, fully bear out this statement. There is nothing in the exclusion from the office of " contour " of " homme de religion," and those " dedenz seinz ordre de subdeacone en amont, ne clerk benefice de cure des almes," to prevent a clerk either in minor orders, or simply admitted to the first tonsure, who had no cure of souls, from being a pleader.

[2] *Rot. Parl.*, ii, 304.

[3] *Ibid.*, iii, 119. Commons' petition of 1381. The list included also the remembrancers and other chief men of the exchequer.

[4] *C.P.R. 1292-1301*, pp. 485-6 and 615.

[5] *Ibid., 1307-13*, p. 139.

in college," rather than as involving complete retirement. I have lighted upon no later orders to the same effect, and it is permissible to wonder whether the silence of the records suggests a relaxation of the corporate life of the exchequer at a time when the "household of the chancery" was becoming so strong, and the humbler household of the privy seal was already having its beginnings.

Each baron had his allotted place in the exchequer, and in many cases a new baron was put into the position vacated by the outgoing officer. All barons had the same salary and status, but there is already evidence that the office of chief baron was now established, and that, soon after the end of the reign, there was also a secondary baron to hold the next place to the head of the society.[1] Thus already, under Edward I, William Carlton, the most senior baron, is described as "capitalis baro," [2] and it is clear that he continued to hold this rank during our reign, though both he and his successors are very occasionally so described in the records. Nevertheless the ordainers of 1311 mention the chief baron of the exchequer as one of the high functionaries who are always to be nominated by the baronage in parliament. This may have tended towards emphasising the distinction already existing between the chief baron and his junior colleagues. Already Carlton had been succeeded by Thomas Cambridge in 1308, and Cambridge by Roger Scotter in 1310. It is clear that the chief post was no longer a question of seniority, for Cambridge had only served a few months and Scotter, an advocate in large practice, had never had any relation to the exchequer at all. In all these cases, however, though the appointment was to the office of Carlton's successor as chief baron, the patent makes no distinction of paramountcy between that post and the other baronships. However, within a few months of the ordinances, Walter Norwich, already a baron since August 1311, was, on 3 March 1312, appointed by patent as baron in place of Scotter,[3] and on 8 March was specifically described as chief baron.[4] We need not hesitate, therefore, to construct, as I have done, a separate list of chief barons for the reign, though until Norwich's second period of service, beginning in 1317, it is a long one. Nor need we be afraid to assume that Norwich's first appointment was one of the important changes brought about in 1312 by the ordinances. A stipend of £50 was soon assigned to him as deputy treasurer,[5] so that the chief baron for the first time had a higher salary than his colleagues.

[1] Robert Wodehouse, already a baron in part of this reign, was, on 16 April 1329, appointed "second baron of the exchequer" (*C.P.R. 1327-30*, p. 383). But so early as 1308 Thomas Cambridge was appointed "to sit next" the chief baron (*C.P.R. 1307-13*, p. 141). This was during Carlton's partial retirement. Tho. was "to take the latter's place in the exchequer and to sit next him when present."

[2] Dugdale, *Chron. Ser.*, 32, from Liberate Roll, 31 Edw. I, m. 2.

[3] *C.P.R. 1307-13*, p. 433.

[4] *Ibid.*, p. 437.

[5] Madox, ii, 326, from Liberate Roll, 6 Edw. II (22 July 1312).

In 1314 Norwich became treasurer and gave up his position as chief baron. Hervey of Staunton may be regarded as in high favour with the ordainers, since in the time of drastic change, after Bannockburn, he succeeded to Norwich's post. Two years later the reaction had gathered force, and Staunton was made chancellor of the exchequer, a place of not greater emolument and hardly equal dignity. Ingelard of Warley, expelled from court by the ordinances, stepped into the vacant post, but after eighteen months was reduced to a junior barony in favour of Norwich. In the patent of Norwich's reappointment the office of chief baron is described as one of "moderate labour," and as a natural relief to a useful and faithful veteran after the excessive cares of the treasurership.[1] His special duty was to "supervise the business of the exchequer with the treasurer and attend the king's councils."[2] So little was the chief baron considered at this time to be a judge! Norwich's whole record is a striking example of the continuity of administrative office under Edward II.

It is less easy to trace the succession of the junior barons of the exchequer to each other. We know that Hegham, Foxley and Bellers represent one baronial post, held by them in succession, and we can guess that Redeswell was Bellers' successor. We can probably assume that Cambridge was succeeded by Gloucester, and know that Gloucester had as his successors Norwich and Abel. As Cambridge was second in dignity to the chief, these barons may also be regarded as holding the second post, one after the other. Other probable successions can be suggested by the list, but they are uncertain and not very profitable to work out. The fluctuation of the number of barons baffles any theory of fixed succession, but we may believe that Fulbourn is the fifth, or new baron, of 1323, though his patent is a fortnight earlier in date than the final issue of the ordinance which authorised his existence.

I should add that I have in the lists identified the Walden made baron in 1324 with the Walden who acted from 1306-7, and the Lisle made baron in 1313 with his namesake, baron between 1295 and 1299. I am, however, by no means certain of either of these identifications. [The Walden identification was proved incorrect by a writ which Mr. Tout printed in 1916.[3] In his own copy, however, he notes, "Which was the Walden called in Muniments of Westminster Abbey 29179, on 19 January 1305, *custode auri et receptore firmarum et exituum terrarum domine Margarete regine Anglie?*"][4]

[1] *C.P.R. 1313-17*, p. 655. [2] *Ibid.*, p. 657.

[3] From K.R.M.R. no. 97 (*Coll. Papers*, ii, 303 and n.).

[4] [In 1918 his attention was drawn to this entry by Canon Pearce, afterwards bp. of Worcester. Later I noticed Walden in the train of Queen Margaret in Dec. 1307 (*C.P.R. 1307-13*, p. 25) and still in her service in 1314 (K.R.M.R. no. 89, m. 81). As many persons formerly in the service of Eleanor of Castile passed into that of Margaret after the king's

## (*a*) Chief Barons

William of Carlton, kg.'s clk. Acting justice of Jews, 1290 (*Red Bk. Exch.*, iii, cccxxxi); apptd. chief baron 26 July 1303 (Lib. Roll. 31 Edw. I, m. 3, in *Chron. Ser.* 32); reapptd. chief baron 16 Sept. 1307 (*C.P.R. 1307-13*, p. 7); partial retirement allowed 24 Oct. 1308 (*ibid.*, p. 139).

Thomas of Cambridge, kg.'s clk. Apptd. baron 16 Sept. 1307 (*ibid.*, p. 7); apptd. chief in Carlton's absence and second in his presence, 24 Oct. 1308 (*ibid.*, p. 141); replaced by Scotter 17 July 1310 (*ibid.*, p. 265); sent to Gascony with Benstead 2 Aug. 1315 (G.R. 30, m. 20).

Roger of Scotter, layman, narrator in the common bench. Apptd. to succeed Cambridge 17 July 1310 (*C.P.R. 1307-13*, p. 265); dead before 24 Jan. 1311 (*Cal. Inq. p.m.*, v, no. 349).

Walter of Norwich. Desc. as clk. of exch. 24 Nov. 1308 (*C.C.R. 1307-13*, p. 131), kg.'s clk. 18 Aug. 1311 (*ibid.*, p. 183), and knight 21 Sept. 1312 (*ibid.*, p. 551). Apptd. baron 29 Aug. 1311 (*C.P.R. 1307-13*, p. 385); apptd. to succeed Scotter 3 Mar. 1312 and called chief baron 8 Mar. 1312 (*ibid.*, pp. 433, 437); apptd. treasurer 26 Sept. 1314 (*C.P.R., 1313-17*, p. 178); succeeded by Staunton 28 Sept. 1314 (*ibid.*, p. 179).

Hervey of Staunton, kg.'s clk., justice of common bench. Apptd. to succeed Norwich 28 Sept. 1314 (*ibid.*); apptd. chancellor of exch. 22 June 1316 (*ibid.*, p. 479); succeeded by Warley 29 Dec. 1316 (*ibid.*, p. 606).

Ingelard of Warley, kg.'s clk., formerly keeper of wardrobe. Apptd. to succeed Staunton 29 Dec. 1316 (*ibid.*); succeeded as chief baron by Norwich 30 May 1317 (*ibid.*, p. 655).

Walter of Norwich, knt., formerly treasurer. Again apptd. chief baron 30 May 1317 (*ibid.*) and acted for rest of reign, but from 1324 to Jan. 1326 for North only. Roger Bellers acted 18 June 1324 to 19 Jan. 1326 for South.[1] Reapptd. chief baron 2 Feb. 1327 (*C.P.R. 1327-30*, p. 2).

## (*b*) Barons

### (*In order of appointment under Edw. II*)

William of Carlton, kg.'s clk. First apptd. 5 Feb. 1291 (L.T.R.M.R. no. 62, m. 10 d.);[2] apptd. 16 Sept. 1307 (*C.P.R. 1307-13*, p. 7). (See list of chief barons.)

Roger of Hegham,[3] knt. First apptd. 1 Ap. 1300 (*C.P.R. 1292-1301*, p. 503); apptd. 16 Sept. 1307 (*C.P.R. 1307-13*, p. 7); dead and succeeded by Foxley 28 Feb. 1309 (*ibid.*, p. 100).

second marriage, this may be the same Humphrey de Walden who, as one of Queen Eleanor's bailiffs, appeared with other of her ministers to answer complaints before a special commission of enquiry appointed after her death (Assize Rolls, 542, 836, 1014).]

[1] [See *Eng. Hist. Rev.*, xxxi (1916), p. 483.]

[2] I owe this reference to Miss Mabel H. Mills.

[3] "An advocate of distinction" (G. J. Turner, *Year Books*, iv, xxii).

20

THOMAS OF CAMBRIDGE, kg.'s clk. Apptd. 16 Sept. 1307 (*C.P.R. 1307-13*, p. 7); conditionally apptd. to succeed Carlton 24 Oct. 1308 (*ibid.*, p. 141). (See list of chief barons.)

JOHN OF BAKEWELL,[1] knt., alderman of London 1286-98, seneschal of Ponthieu 1299-1305. Apptd. 10 Nov. 1307 (*ibid.*, p. 16); killed 25 Feb. 1308 (*Ann. Lond.*, p. 153, *Ann. Paul.*, p. 261).

Mr. JOHN OF EVERDON, kg.'s clk. Apptd. 28 Nov. 1307 (*C.P.R. 1307-13*, p. 22); admitted dean of St. Paul's 25 Sept. 1323 (*Ann. Paul.*, p. 306).

Mr. RICHARD OF ABINGDON, kg.'s clk. First apptd. in place of Lisle 23 Sept. 1299 (*C.P.R. 1292-1301*, p. 438); reapptd. to place held under late king 20 Jan. 1308 (*C.P.R. 1307-13*, p. 44); replaced by Jo. of Ockham 18 June 1317 (*C.P.R. 1313-17*, p. 671); dead by 3 Ap. 1322 (*C.F.R.*, iii, 115).

ROGER OF SCOTTER, *narrator*. Apptd. 17 July 1310 (*C.P.R. 1307-13*, p. 265). (See list of chief barons.)

JOHN OF FOXLEY, knt. by 29 Sept. 1307 (*Chapters*, ii, 180 n.); apptd. in place of Hegham 28 Feb. 1309 (*ibid.*, p. 100); succeeded by Bellers 20 July 1322 (*C.P.R. 1321-24*, p. 182); dead by 28 Nov. 1324 (*Cal. Inq. p.m.*, vi, no. 571).

WALTER OF GLOUCESTER, layman, formerly escheator south of Trent. Apptd. 15 May 1311 (*C.P.R. 1307-13*, p. 348); acting 5 July 1311 (*ibid.*, p. 360); dead by 29 Aug. 1311 (*ibid.*, p. 385).

WALTER OF NORWICH, clk., afterwards knt. Apptd. to succeed Gloucester 29 Aug. 1311 (*ibid.*); apptd. chief baron 3 Mar. 1312 (*ibid.*, p. 433). (See list of chief barons.)

JOHN ABEL, knt., formerly "bachelor" of Queen Margaret (Anct. Corr., xxxv, 70). Apptd. to succeed Norwich 8 Mar. 1312 (*C.P.R. 1307-13*, p. 437); apptd. escheator south of Trent 30 Dec. 1312 (*C.F.R.*, ii, 158); again apptd. baron 4 May 1315 (*C.P.R. 1313-17*, p. 279); possibly removed 1320-21 (Foss, *Biog. Jur.*, p. 3); dead by 13 Sept. 1322 (*Cal. Inq. p.m.*, vi, no. 398).

JOHN DE LISLE,[2] ? knt. Admitted 20 Oct. 1295 (Madox, ii, 56-7); superseded because engaged on other business 20 Sept. 1299 (*C.P.R. 1292-1301*, p. 438); apptd. (? to succeed Abel) 30 Jan, 1313 (*C.P.R. 1307-13*, p. 526); ? acting till 1318-19 (Foss, p. 369); dead by 5 June 1320 (*C.C.R., 1318-23*, p. 240).

HERVEY OF STAUNTON, kg.'s clk. Acting from 28 Sept. 1314 to 29 June 1316. (See list of chief barons.)

INGELARD OF WARLEY, kg.'s clk., formerly keeper of wardrobe. Acting as chief baron from 29 Dec. 1316; succeeded by Norwich 30 May 1317. (See list of chief barons.) Continued as baron after 30 May 1317; succeeded by Wodehouse 24 July 1318 (*C.P.R. 1317-21*, p. 193); dead by 14 Oct. 1318 (Madox, ii, 60).

[1] For this rendering of "Bauquel" or "Banquel," see Beaven, *Aldermen of London*, ii, lxxi, and Stow, *Survey of London*, ii, 336-7, ed. Kingsford. Mr. Kingsford, however, inclines to Backwell as the form; but John's London house was later called "Bakewell" or "Blackwell" Hall. I owe the dates of his seneschalship to Miss H. Johnstone, who will give further details in her forthcoming article on Ponthieu [" The County of Ponthieu, 1279-1307," *Eng. Hist. Rev.*, xxix (1914). Biographical notes, pp. 450-1.]

[2] "An advocate of distinction" (G. J. Turner, *Year Books*, iv, xxii).

JOHN OF OCKHAM, kg.'s clk., formerly cofferer of wardrobe. Apptd. to succeed Abingdon 18 June 1317 (*C.P.R. 1313-17*, p. 671); declared sufficient and necessary 2 Jan. 1319 (Madox, ii, 61).

ROBERT OF WODEHOUSE, kg.'s clk., formerly controller of wardrobe. Apptd. to succeed Warley 24 July 1318 (*C.P.R. 1317-21*, p. 193); barons told to admit him 14 Oct. 1318 (Madox, ii, 60); declared sufficient and necessary 2 Jan. 1319 (*ibid.*, p. 61); acting until reapptd. controller of the wardrobe 8 July 1323 (I.R. 203, mm. 4 and 5, Enr. Acc. (W. and H.) no. 2, m. 1); keeper of wardrobe 1323-28; apptd. second baron 16 Ap. 1329 (*C.P.R. 1327-30*, p. 383) and treasurer of exch. 16 Sept. 1329 (*ibid.*, p. 440).[1]

LAMBERT OF THRECKINGHAM, clk., formerly justice of common bench (1299) and king's bench (1316). Apptd. 6 Aug. 1320 (*C.P.R. 1317-21*, p. 504);[2] acting ? to end of reign.

WALTER OF FRISKNEY, *narrator*, knt. by 8 March 1321 (*C.C.R. 1318-23*, p. 362). Apptd. 6 Aug. 1320 (*C.P.R. 1317-21*, p. 504); apptd. justice of bench 9 July 1323 (*C.P.R. 1321-24*, p. 322); succeeded as baron by Passelewe 20 Sept. 1323 (*ibid.*, p. 338).

ROGER BELLERS, knt. Apptd. to succeed Foxley 20 July 1322 (*ibid.*, p. 182); acted till death 19 Jan. 1326 (*Ann. Paul.*, p. 310).

WILLIAM OF FULBOURN, clk., treasurer's remembrancer, 1321-23. Apptd. 1 June 1323 (*C.P.R. 1321-24*, p. 303); acting till at least 6 Nov. 1326 (I.R. 219, m. 2).

EDMUND OF PASSELEWE, *narrator*, knt. in 1321 (*Ann. Paul.*, p. 291). Apptd. to succeed Friskney 20 Sept. 1323 (*C.P.R. 1321-24*, p. 338); acted to end of reign. Dead by 27 Mar. 1327 (*Cal. Inq. p.m.*, vii, no. 32).

Mr. ROBERT OF AYLESTON, kg.'s clk., formerly keeper of privy seal. Apptd. 21 May 1324 (*C.P.R. 1321-24*, p. 415); acted till after Easter 1326 (I.R. 218); apptd. chancellor of exch. 18 July 1326.

WILLIAM OF EVERDON, exch. clk., treasurer's remembrancer 1311-18. Apptd. 18 June 1324 (*C.P.R. 1321-24*, p. 429); acted to end of reign.

HUMPHREY OF WALDEN, knt., formerly steward of chamber manors, 1320. Apptd. 18 June 1324[3] (*ibid.*, p. 429).

Mr. JOHN OF REDESWELL, clk. Apptd. 1 Sept. 1326 (*C.P.R. 1324-27*, p. 313); admitted same day (K.R.M.R. no. 103, mm. 19, 115).

## (3) CHANCELLORS OF THE EXCHEQUER

The chancellor of the exchequer was keeper of the exchequer seal and therefore responsible for the secretarial department of that office. He received the stipend of a baron, viz., 40 marks a year, and in the records of Edward I's reign his name often precedes those of the barons. It was natural then that the chancellor should often be confused with the barons, as when *Ann. Paul.*, p. 285, calls

[1] [This reference was supplied by Miss D. M. Broome.]

[2] G. J. Turner (*Year Books*, iv, xx) says he "never took his seat"; but he received his fee for Easter term 1321 (I.R. 195, m. 8) and Michaelmas term 1321-22 (I.R. 196, m. 7).

[3] [The appointment of his namesake on 19 Oct. 1306 is omitted for reason given above, p. 304.]

Staunton a baron in 1319. Like all keepers of seals, the chancellor of the exchequer was almost invariably a clerk, though one holder of the office, Benstead, some years later abandoned his clergy for knighthood. Except Markenfield, all Edward II's chancellors of the exchequer were men of mark; four became bishops, three treasurers, two chancellors, and two keepers of the wardrobe. Droxford seems to have combined the office with the keepership of the wardrobe, and Stapeldon, when already treasurer, also became chancellor of the exchequer, being "appointed at the usual fee to keep the exchequer seal." This interesting combination was occasioned by Staunton's appointment as chief justice of the king's bench. He resumed the exchequer chancellorship on resigning the office of chief justice, and abandoned it to become chief justice of common pleas. It seems then that this post was as dignified as a baronship of the exchequer or the chief justiceship of either bench. Under the Tudors its scope was considerably enlarged, but its modern position, as the acting head of the ministry of finance, only begins after the treasurership was permanently put into commission.

JOHN OF BENSTEAD, kg.'s clk., formerly controller of wardrobe. Apptd. 25 Sept. 1305 (*C.P.R. 1301-7*, p. 378).
JOHN OF SANDALL, kg.'s clk. Apptd. 7 Aug. 1307 (*C.P.R. 1307-13*, p. 6).
JOHN OF DROXFORD, kg.'s clk., keeper of wardrobe. Apptd. 20 May 1308 (*ibid.*, p. 72).
JOHN OF MARKENFIELD, kg.'s clk. Apptd. 5 July 1310 (*ibid.*, p. 235).
JOHN OF HOTHAM, kg.'s clk. Apptd. 13 Dec. 1312 (*ibid.*, p. 515).
HERVEY OF STAUNTON, clk., baron of exch. Apptd. 22 June 1316 (*C.P.R. 1313-17*, p. 479).
WALTER OF STAPELDON, bp. of Exeter, treasurer. Apptd. 27 Sept. 1323 (*C.P.R. 1321-24*, pp. 339, 353).
HERVEY OF STAUNTON. Apptd. again 26 Mar. 1324 (*ibid.*, p. 400).
Mr. ROBERT OF AYLESTON, kg.'s clk., formerly baron of exch. Apptd. 18 July 1326 (*C.P.R. 1324-27*, p. 299).

## (4) REMEMBRANCERS OF THE EXCHEQUER

Already, under Edward I, the two remembrancers of the exchequer are sometimes distinguished as the king's and treasurer's remembrancers respectively.[1] Under Edward II the distinction is more often made, though it remained the exception.[2] The normal description of either remembrancer was still *unus rememoratorum de scaccario*. There is no doubt whatever as to the separation of the two offices, and as to the persons designated to each. The king's

[1] Madox, ii, 266.
[2] Madox, ii, 267, quotes the admission, on 11 Oct. 1311, of Everdon, "ad officium rememoratoris thesaurarii in scaccario"; Hall, *Antiquities of Exchequer*, p. 86, quotes a good instance later in the reign.

remembrancers were appointed by patent, so that their succession can be easily established by the enrolments in the patent roll. As in each case but one [1] the name of the outgoing as well as of the ingoing officer is mentioned in the patent, there is a double security for the order of appointments to this post. The treasurer's remembrancer seems, as was natural, to have been [usually] the treasurer's own nominee. By exception, however, the appointment of one treasurer's remembrancer, Hugh of Nottingham, is recorded on the close roll soon after Edward II's accession.[2] This personage never seems to have acted, for Walter Reynolds preferred to keep on Walter of Norwich, the remembrancer of his predecessor Langton. The treasurer's remembrancer was, however, paid by the crown. Accordingly we can trace the succession of these officers by the enrolments of the payments of their wages in the issue rolls.

The comparative dignity of the two remembrancers is not clear. Their " fee " was different, for the king's remembrancer had, as a normal wage, £20 a year,[3] while his colleague took 40 marks, that is £26 13s. 4d. Apparently, however, the former sum was a personal wage, while the latter was *ad sustentacionem suam et clericorum suorum secum in officio illo existencium.*[4] As one of the treasurer's remembrancers had five clerks acting under him at the same time,[5] it is unlikely that the post was really so good a one as the king's remembrancership. This is also suggested by the promotion of

[1] The one exception is that of William of Brocklesby, whose patent does not mention his predecessor, Robert of Nottingham. But Brocklesby had been Nottingham's personal clerk (I.R. 218, m. 9), and the holder of the other remembrancership still continued in office, so that there is no doubt as to the succession.

[2] *C.C.R. 1307-13*, p. 2, records this, along with the reappointment of John of Kirkby, king's remembrancer under Edward I. As Walter of Norwich was Kirkby's colleague under the old king, it looks as if Edward II made an attempt to claim for himself the appointment of treasurer's remembrancer, and preferred not to continue in office a man who had clearly been Walter Langton's confidential subordinate. A little earlier, on 20 Sept., the king had issued an order, preserved on the memoranda roll (Madox, ii, 270), directing Hugh of Nottingham to go at once to the exchequer, " omnibus aliis rebus praetermissis," as the king wished him to have the custody of the great rolls of the exchequer during pleasure. During the first years of Edward II Nottingham regularly received wages as one of the three scribes of the exchequer (I.R. 142, 144, 146, etc.). Compare his position with that held later by William of Everdon, who, after being a remembrancer for some years, became a simple scribe, and was styled " engrosser and keeper of the great roll." Norwich was restored 19 Nov. 1307, when the king ordered Reynolds to receive him. [See *Chapters*, ii, 220, based on Conway Davies, p. 223.]

[3] This could be supplemented. See, for instance, *C.P.R. 1313-17*, p. 632, an additional grant of £20 to Everdon for long service.

[4] I.R. 187, m. 4, is one of innumerable instances.

[5] I.R. 195, m. 3, records the payment of Robert of Nottingham's fee in 1321, to John of Norwich, and four other clerks of his, at a time when Robert was not at court.

Robert of Nottingham, treasurer's remembrancer from 1311 to 1321, to the king's remembrancership in 1322. Perhaps the additional allowance of £5 a term, always given to the treasurer's remembrancer for writing the summonses of the exchequer, was by way of a set-off to the burden imposed upon him of sustaining a large staff of subordinates. It clearly suggests, however, that harder work, perhaps more mechanical duties, fell to the lot of the treasurer's remembrancer. The ultimate differentiation of the two offices, a result of Stapeldon's exchequer ordinances, had not yet been worked out in our reign.

Both remembrancers were always clerks, and few holders of the office attained a high position. Walter of Norwich is the chief exception in this reign. Of the rest, Adam Limber is the best known. Some wardrobe officers became remembrancers, as, for instance, Walter Bedwyn, the cofferer of Edward I's later years. The fortunate remembrancer often became a baron of the exchequer. It is a further suggestion of the more responsible duties of the treasurer's remembrancer at this period, that the holders of this office obtained their promotion to be a baron more often and more quickly than did the king's remembrancers. Thus three treasurer's remembrancers—Norwich, Everdon and Fulbourn—became barons under Edward II, while of the three remembrancers who had to wait until the next reign for promotion—Nottingham, Coshall, and Lymbergh—only one, Coshall, was treasurer's remembrancer. Another treasurer's remembrancer, John Travers, was directly promoted at this time to be constable of Bordeaux, the chief financial minister of Gascony. On the other hand, the treasurer's remembrancer, William of Everdon, went back to be a simple exchequer clerk, possibly as a result of the political changes in the autumn of 1318. He was later engrosser and keeper of the great roll, that is, one of the three scribes. He was, however, once more baron in 1324, and was *locum tenens* of the treasurer in 1324. Hugh of Nottingham, temporarily nominated to the treasurer's remembrancership in 1307, also fell back on this office of keeper and engrosser of the pipe roll. It hardly looks as if the remembrancers were much higher in dignity than the ordinary exchequer clerks.

### (*a*) King's Remembrancers

John of Kirkby, kg.'s clk. Admitted 11 Nov. 1293 (Madox, ii, 266); reapptd. 26 Sept. 1307 (*C.C.R. 1307-13*, p. 2); dead by 1 Mar. 1308 (Madox, ii, 267).

Walter of Bedwyn, kg.'s clk., formerly cofferer of wardrobe. Apptd. 1 Mar. 1308 (*ibid.*).

John of Markenfield, kg.'s clk. Apptd. 1 Mar. 1310 (*C.P.R. 1307-13*, p. 220).

John of Cockermouth, kg.'s clk. Apptd. 2 Aug. 1310 (*ibid.*, p. 273).

ADAM LIMBER (LYMBERGH), kg.'s clk. Apptd. 8 Oct. 1311 (*C.P.R. 1307-13*, p. 392).

ROBERT OF NOTTINGHAM,[1] kg.'s clk. Apptd. 21 June 1322 (*C.P.R. 1321-24*, p. 137).

WILLIAM OF BROCKLESBY, kg.'s clk. Apptd. 2 Oct. 1326 (*C.P.R. 1324-27*, p. 322).

(*b*) TREASURER'S REMEMBRANCERS

HUGH OF NOTTINGHAM. Apptd. 26 Sept. 1307 (*C.C.R. 1307-13*, p. 2).

WALTER OF NORWICH, kg.'s clk. Acting under Edw. I (I.R. 146, m. 2); reapptd. 19 Nov. 1307 (K.R.M.R. 81, m. 38d.); acting till 29 Sept. 1311 (I.R. 157, m. 3).

WILLIAM OF EVERDON, kg.'s clk. Acting from 11 Oct. 1311 (I.R. 159, m. 2) to 29 Sept. 1318 (I.R. 184, m. 2); *cf.* Madox, ii, 269.

ROBERT OF NOTTINGHAM, kg.'s clk. Acting from 30 Sept. 1318 (I.R. 186, m. 3) to 29 Sept. 1321 (*ibid.*, 195, m. 8).

WILLIAM OF FULBOURN, kg.'s clk. Acting from 30 Sept. 1321 (*ibid.*, 196, m. 4) to 1 June 1323 (*ibid.*, 205, m. 5).

JOHN TRAVERS, kg.'s clk. Acting from 1 June 1323 (*ibid.*) to 29 Sept. 1324 (*ibid.*, 213).

WILLIAM OF STOWE, kg.'s clk. Acting from 3 Ap. to 29 Sept. 1324 (*ibid.*, 207, m. 9).[2]

WILLIAM OF COSHALL, kg.'s clk. Acting from 30 Sept. 1324 (*ibid.*, 213, m. 7) to at least 18 Aug. 1327 (*C.C.R. 1327-30*, pp. 160-1);[3] apptd. baron 5 Nov. 1329 (*C.P.R. 1327-30*, p. 456).

(5) CHAMBERLAINS OF THE RECEIPT

The two chamberlains of the exchequer were hereditary magnates who held the office in fee. In the twelfth century these posts were in the hands of the families of Fitzgerald and Malduit. The Fitzgerald chamberlainship passed by marriage to the earls of Devon of the house of Redvers, and finally lapsed to the crown with the great Fors-Redvers inheritance in 1293, on the death of the countess Isabella. The other chamberlainship was still held under Edward II in fee by the Beauchamp earls of Warwick, the heirs of the Malduits. Dignitaries so great as the hereditary chamberlains naturally appointed deputies to discharge the duties of their office. In the thirteenth century, separate deputy chamberlains for the receipt and for the exchequer of accounts seem to have been regularly nominated by the chamberlains in fee. Under Edward II, however, I find little trace of the chamberlains of the upper exchequer. The only conspicuous officers of the exchequer now bearing this name are the deputy chamberlains of the receipt.

[1] Gervase of Clifton was *locum tenens* for Nottingham between 14 Aug. and 27 Sept. 1325 (I.R. 218, m. 19).

[2] [This reference was kindly supplied by Miss D. M. Broome.]

[3] Neither Coshall nor any successor appear on Stratford's Issue Roll (220), which begins on 20 Nov. 1326.

They are often described as "chamberlains of the exchequer," and sometimes even as "the king's chamberlains," though that was precisely the title of the chamberlain, such as Despenser, who was at the head of the king's chamber.

Under Edward II the deputies to the sometime Fitzgerald chamberlainship were appointed by the crown by patent, and their succession is easy to establish from the patent roll. Up to 1315 earl Guy of Warwick continued to nominate the second chamberlain, and memoranda prefixed to the issue rolls testify to his admission to office. Moreover, the wages of both chamberlains were paid by the crown and recorded in the issue rolls, so that not only the date of appointment, but the duration of each term of office, can be easily ascertained. When earl Guy died in 1315, his son was a minor, and the custody of the Warwick estates remained in the king's hands for the rest of our reign. It follows that for the last eleven years of the reign both chamberlains were appointed by patent.

The early chamberlains of the exchequer were knights, who kept their accounts in tallies. From the early thirteenth century, the elaboration of the enrolments, and of the system of accounting in the receipt, made it necessary that the chamberlains should have an education such as knights then seldom enjoyed. Accordingly, so early as 1240-1, it had been found desirable to admit to the office suitable persons who were not knights.[1] By the time of Edward II, the original conception of the office had become so utterly changed that every chamberlain of the reign was a clerk and engaged upon strictly clerical duties. The special function of the chamberlain now was to act as controller to the receipt and issue of the exchequer.[2] Accordingly, three copies were made of each issue and receipt roll, for which the treasurer and each of the two chamberlains were severally responsible. Writs addressed to the receipt were normally addressed to the treasurer and chamberlains, just as writs to the upper exchequer were generally addressed to the treasurer and barons. The chamberlains then were jointly second in command over the receipt, ranking immediately after the treasurer.

### (*a*) The Former Fitzgerald-Redvers Chamberlainship

William of Brickhill, kg.'s clk. Apptd. 1298 (Madox, ii, 301).

Henry of Ludgershall, kg.'s clk. Apptd. 23 Aug. 1307 (*C.P.R. 1307-13*, p. 7); retired sick 28 Feb. 1312 (Madox, ii, 301).

Mr. John of Percy, kg.'s clk. Apptd. 16 Mar. 1312 (*C.P.R. 1307-13*, p. 442); ordered to abandon office 27 March 1312 (*ibid.*, p. 447).

[1] Madox, ii, 295.

[2] This position is well brought out by the phrase in I.R. 203, m. 1, recording the admission to office of John Langton as chamberlain in 1323, "et die lune proximo sequente, videlicet secundo die mensis Maii, incepit primo idem Johannes contrarotulare receptam et exitum scaccarii."

RICHARD OF CROMWELL, kg.'s clk. Apptd. 27 Mar. 1312 (*C.P.R. 1307-13*, p. 447).

Mr. JAMES OF SPAIN, clk. and kg.'s kinsman. Apptd. 30 Jan. 1317 (*C.P.R. 1313-17*, p. 614).

JOHN OF LANGTON, kg.'s clk. and clk. of Walt. of Langton (Exch. Plea Roll 31, m. 34). Apptd. at London 6 Ap. 1323 (*C.P.R. 1321-24*, p. 269); admitted at York 29 Ap. and began to act 2 May 1323 (I.R. 203, m. 1).

(*b*) THE FORMER MALDUIT-BEAUCHAMP CHAMBERLAINSHIP

WILLIAM OF PERSHORE, clk. Dead by 7 Ap. 1309 (I.R. 146, m. 1).

PETER LE BLUNT, clk. Admitted 7 Ap. 1309 (*ibid.*); ceased to act 17 May 1315 (*ibid.*, 174).

Mr. JOHN GOLAFRE. Apptd. by earl and began to act 18 May 1315 (*ibid.*).

Mr. WILLIAM OF MALDON, kg.'s clk. Apptd. by kg. 1 Sept. 1315 (*C.P.R. 1313-17*, p. 345).

JOHN WARIN, kg.'s clk. Apptd. by kg. 20 Jan. 1326 (*C.P.R. 1324-27*, p. 212).

## C.—OFFICERS OF THE WARDROBE AND HOUSEHOLD

Officers of the wardrobe and household were generally appointed by the king by word of mouth (*oretenus*). It is therefore exceptional to find any record of their appointment or removal from office. The only household place of any dignity habitually filled up by letters patent was the keepership of the great wardrobe, the least important post of all. There is, therefore, no difficulty in determining the list of holders of this office. It is also fairly easy to ascertain the succession of the keepers and controllers of the wardrobe, since the periods of accounts for which they were severally responsible are always exactly recorded in their wardrobe accounts. In other cases all that can be done is to ascertain the dates at which each officer acts for the first and the last time. By Edward II's reign the custom had fortunately grown up of describing such officers by their official title in records. The task is therefore less impossible than in the thirteenth century, when official designations are only exceptionally mentioned. Such mentions may occur in almost any record, but the most useful are the wardrobe accounts, where entries constantly occur of payments made to the household staff, notably for fees and robes. Unfortunately, there are not for a large part of this reign wardrobe accounts which enter enough into particularities to afford such precise information. Nevertheless, there is sufficient detail to enable us to present here a rough list of cofferers of the wardrobe and keepers of the privy seal. It would not be impossible also to collect most of the names of the subordinate clerks of the wardrobe and privy seal.

On the whole the difficulty of drawing up lists of knightly officers of the household is greater than is the case with the clerks of the wardrobe. I have therefore only attempted to do so in the case of the stewards of the household and the king's chamberlains. The latter case is particularly troublesome, since the chamberlains, important though they were, are very seldom designated by their official titles.[1] From this follows the difficulty already discussed in determining whether Gaveston was ever chamberlain, and the great uncertainty when Charlton entered upon that office. Later, difficulties are lessened by the fact that Charlton and the younger Despenser held the charge in succession for nearly the whole of Edward II's reign.

It was otherwise in the case of the stewardship of the household, which was held by eleven different knights within twenty years. There is fortunately a fairly easy way of obtaining a rough list of stewards by working through the list of witnesses to charters recorded in the charter rolls. By the fourteenth century it had become usual for a large proportion of the royal charters issued from the chancery to be attested by the steward of the household. Unluckily the published calendar of charter rolls has up to the present excluded all lists of witnesses, so that the enquirer has to have recourse to the charter rolls themselves. From these, however, a good working list can be obtained. Even when supplemented from other sources, there remain occasional gaps and in more than one case the stewards seem to overlap each other. These overlappings are of no great moment, and are probably due to carelessness and especially to a habit of the chancery clerks of putting down names without much regard as to whether their bearers were actually present or not. In many cases they are probably due to the few days' delay between appointment and entering on office.

The most difficult case in the reign is that of Hugh Audley. His appointment was due to the circumstance that Sir Edmund Mauley was compelled to answer in the steward's court an accusation of complicity in a forgery of the privy seal. As Mauley could not preside as steward over his own trial, it was necessary to remove him from office, pending these proceedings. Accordingly we find Audley presiding as steward over the court, which first met on 27 October 1312, and concluded its proceedings before 8 February 1313.[2] Audley never attested a charter as steward, and as Mauley attested one on 2 November, after Audley's appointment, it looks as if Audley had simply been appointed steward to preside over the tribunal which tried his predecessor. Mauley, on his acquittal, at once resumed his functions as steward.

[1] This was the case continuously from early Norman times (Davis, *Regesta Regum Anglo-Normannorum*, I, xxv).

[2] *Foedera*, ii, 200-1 ; *Ann. Paul.*, p. 273, states wrongly that the trial took place *coram justitiariis domini regis sedentibus in magna aula Westmonasterii*.

## (1) Lay Officers of the Household

### (a) Stewards of the Household

[The dates given from Charter Rolls are the earliest and latest at which each steward appears as a witness.]

Miles of Stapleton. 29 Aug. 1307 (Ch. R. 94, m. 10, no. 32); 22 Nov. 1307 (*ibid.*, m. 8, no. 21).

Robert Fitzpayn. 11 Mar. 1308 (*ibid.*, m. 8, no. 15); 14 Dec. 1310 (Ch. R. 97, m. 15, no. 50).

Edmund of Mauley. 28 Dec. 1310 (*ibid.*, m. 15, no. 49); 4 Oct. 1312 (Ch. R. 99, mm. 24, 25, nos. 55, 56); 2 Nov. 1312[1] (*ibid.*, m. 24, no. 54).

Hugh of Audley, senr. Acting 27 Oct. 1312 (*Foed.*, ii, 200).

Edmund of Mauley. 12 Feb. 1313 (Ch. R. 99, m. 14, no. 28).[2] Killed 24 June 1314 (Bridl., p. 46, *Ann. Lond.*, p. 231).

John Cromwell. 17 July 1314[3] (Ch. R. 101, m. 22, no. 58); 20 Nov. 1316 (Ch. R. 103, m. 15, no. 41).

William of Montagu. 18 Nov. 1316 (*C.C.R. 1313-18*, p. 441); 3 Nov. 1318 (Ch. R. 105, m. 16, no. 65).

Bartholomew of Badlesmere. Apptd. 20 Oct. 1318 (Cole, *Records*, p. 3); acting 14 June[4] 1321 (Ch. R. 107, m. 1, no. 2).

Gilbert Pecché.[5] 14 Jan. 1322 (Ch. R. 108, m. 8, no. 27); 30 Ap. 1322 (*ibid.*, m. 5, no. 14).

Simon of Dryby, senr. 8 May 1322 (*ibid.*, m. 4, no. 6); 14 July 1322[6] (Ch. R. 109, m. 7, no. 30).

Richard of Amory. 11 July 1322 (*ibid.*, m. 5, no. 18); 11 Ap. 1325 (Ch. R. 111, m. 2, no. 8); 5 May 1325 (*C.P.R. 1324-27*, p. 121).

Thomas le Blount. 14 May 1325 (Ch. R. 111, m. 2, no. 7); resigned 20 Jan. 1327 (Baker, p. 28).

### (b) King's Chamberlains

John of Charlton. Acting at least as early as 1310 (Cotton MS. Nero C viii, f. 36, I.R. 150, m. 11); barons petitioned for his removal Oct. 1311 (*Ann. Lond.*, p 200); received robes for year 1312-13 (E.A. 375/8, m. 33); acting Ap. 1313 (Cotton MS. *ut sup.* ff. 91d, 93), 25 Jan. 1314 (*C.F.R.*, ii, p. 188) and 19 Ap. 1318 (*C.P.R. 1317-21*, p. 133); had ceased to act by 20 Oct. 1318.

[1] There are no attestations of charters by any person described as steward between this date and 12 Feb. 1313.

[2] [*Cal. Ch. Rolls*, iii, 206, is in error in dating charter 11 Feb.]

[3] No charters were issued between 7 June 1314, when Edward II entered Scotland, and 17 July 1314, when he had returned to York; the chancery did not accompany him on the Bannockburn campaign.

[4] *Chron. de Melsa*, ii, 339, says he was still steward at time of siege of Leeds in Oct. 1321, but *Flores*, iii, 199, states that Edw. hated Barth. at that date *eo quod ab officio senescalliae contra regis affectum recesserat.*

[5] On 2 Nov. 1315 he had been admitted to robes and fee as *baneretlus hospicii* (E.A. 376/7).

[6] At that date, at York, Dryby also witnessed a release as "the king's hospicer" (*C.C.R. 1318-22*, p. 576). This is plainly a synonym for steward, but his successor was already in office.

HUGH LE DESPENSER, jun. Appointment renewed in parliament, 20 Oct. 1318 (Cole, *Records*, p. 4); described as *banerettus hospicii* in 1323 (Stowe MS. 553, f. 65); acting, save during exile in 1321, till end of reign, 1326.

### (2) CHIEF CLERKS OF THE WARDROBE

The lists of keepers and controllers of the wardrobe, and that of the keepers of the great wardrobe, are, with some corrections, taken from lists published by me in the *English Historical Review*, xxiv, 499-505, where the authorities are given.[1] To these I have now added somewhat tentative lists of cofferers of the wardrobe and keepers of the privy seal. It would not be hard to supplement these by lists of the *ostiarii*, the *subostiarii*, and the other subordinate wardrobe clerks, including the four clerks who wrote for the privy seal.

#### (*a*) KEEPERS OR TREASURERS OF THE WARDROBE

JOHN OF BENSTEAD. 8 July 1307 to 7 July 1308.
JOHN OF DROXFORD. 8 July 1308 to 7 July 1309.
INGELARD OF WARLEY. 8 July 1309 to Dec. 1311.
PETER OF COLLINGBOURN. Before 2 Jan. 1312 to at least 4 Feb. 1312.
INGELARD OF WARLEY. Before 25 Feb. 1312 to 30 Nov. 1314.
WILLIAM OF MELTON. 1 Dec. 1314 to 31 Jan. 1316.
ROGER OF NORTHBURGH. 1 Feb. 1316 to 30 Ap. 1322.
ROGER OF WALTHAM. 1 May 1322 to 19 Oct. 1323.
ROBERT OF WODEHOUSE. 20 Oct. 1323 to 24 Jan. 1327.

#### (*b*) CONTROLLERS OF THE WARDROBE

WILLIAM OF MELTON. 8 July 1307 to 30 Nov. 1314.
ROBERT OF WODEHOUSE. 1 Dec. 1314 to 7 July 1316.
Mr. THOMAS OF CHARLTON. 7 July 1316 to 7 July 1318.
GILBERT OF WIGTON. 8 July 1318 to 2 July 1320.
Mr. ROBERT OF BALDOCK. 7 July 1320 to 8 July 1323.
ROBERT OF WODEHOUSE. 8 July to 19 Oct. 1323.
ROBERT OF HOLDEN. 20 Oct. 1323 to 1 Nov. 1326.
NICHOLAS OF HUGGATE. 1 Nov. 1326 to 24 Jan. 1327.

#### (*c*) COFFERERS

[The following list includes corrections made in *Chapters*, vi, 30-31, but omits from authorities there given those which merely show a cofferer at work on dates intermediate between the earliest and latest known. Information now printed for the first time is enclosed in square brackets.]

PETER OF COLLINGBOURN. 8 July 1307 (E.A. 373/19) to at least 12 Mar. 1308 (*ibid.*, 373/15, f. 3).

JOHN OF OCKHAM. [26 May 1308 or earlier (I.R. 142, m. 2)] to 7 July 1309 (E.A. 373/23, m. 1).

[1] [Three additions and some corrections are here made from *Chapters*, vi, 26, where the authorities are given.]

ROBERT OF WODEHOUSE. 8 July 1309 (*C.C.R. 1318-23*, p. 115) to 31 Jan. 1311 (Bodleian Lib., Tanner MS. 197, m. 63d.).

JOHN OF OCKHAM. 16 Feb. 1311 (E.A. 373/30) to [11 Nov. 1314 (I.R. 172, m. 3)].

NICHOLAS OF HUGGATE. [24 Dec. 1314 (I.R. 172, m. 5)] to 31 Oct. 1315 (E.A. 376/7).

HENRY OF HALE. 1 Jan. to at least 31 Dec. 1316 (*C.C.R. 1313-18*, p. 548, and *ibid.*, *1318-23*, p. 444).

ROBERT OF WODEHOUSE. 30 May 1317 or earlier (I.R. 180, m. 6) to [1 July] 1318 (I.R. 184, m. 6).

RICHARD OF FERRIBY. 19 Jan. 1320 (I.R. 189, m. 3) to 19 Oct. 1323 (Stowe MS. 553, f. 121).

The household ordinance of June, 1323 (p. 282 above), ordered that an additional cofferer should be appointed to act after 8 July, 1323, to lessen the delays caused by the diffuseness of the accounts of past years, which had not yet been passed by the exchequer. I have failed to discover the name of this officer.

## (*d*) KEEPERS OF THE PRIVY SEAL

[Abbreviations used in this list are w. = wardrobe and p.s. = privy seal.]

WILLIAM OF MELTON. 1 Oct. 1307 (*C.C.R. 1307-13*, p. 42). Melton, like his immediate predecessors, kept the privy seal as part of his work as controller, and therefore probably from 8 July 1307 to some time after October 1311, when the ordainers insisted upon the appointment of a separate keeper.

ROGER OF NORTHBURGH. Nov. 1312 [1] (E.A. 375/8, f. 8) to May 1313 (*ibid.*, f. 11 v°). Captured with seal at Bannockburn, 24 June 1314 (*Cont. Trivet*, p. 14). Acting 7 Jan. 1316 (E.A. 376/7, f. 11 v°) and presumably till apptd. keeper of w., 1 Feb. 1316.

Mr. THOMAS OF CHARLTON. Contrary to ordinances, held keepership p.s. while controller of w., 7 July 1316 to 7 July 1318. Acting as keeper p.s. 15 Nov. 1316 (*C.C.R. 1313-18*, p. 440) and 13 May 1318 (Chancery Warr., file 1328, no. 130,[2] with which *cf. C.C.R. 1313-18*, p. 610). Appointment renewed in parl., Oct. 1318 (Cole, p. 4).

Mr. ROBERT OF BALDOCK. Apptd. keeper p.s. 27 Jan. 1320 (Add. MS. 17362, f. 9 v°) ; as such, exercised office of controller of w. by deputy, 1 May 1322 to 8 July 1323 (K.R.M.R. 105, m. 153).

ROBERT OF WODEHOUSE. As keeper p.s., exercised office of controller of w. by deputy, 8 July to 19 Oct. 1323 (K.R.M.R. 105, m. 153).

[1] [I have failed to find evidence for date 18 Sept. 1312 given in *Chapters*, vi, 50, but] as the first independent keeper Roger may have been acting as early as March 1312.

[2] [Formerly numbered 4686 and misprinted as 4685 in 1st edn.]

Mr. Robert of Ayleston.[1] 3 Oct. 1323 (Chanc. Warr., file 124, no. 6699, printed by Conway Davies, App., p. 578, and *cf. Cal. Chanc. Warr.*, I, 543) to 15 May 1324 (*Reg. Cobham*, p. 170). Apptd. baron of the exch. 21 May 1324.

William of Airmyn. Probably became keeper after Ayleston's appointment to exch., for resigned custody of rolls of chancery on 26 May 1324 (*C.C.R. 1323-27*, p. 186); acting 8 Aug. 1324 (*ibid.*, p. 306); probably resigned Jan. or Feb. 1325 (*Chapters*, ii, 307).

Mr. Henry of Cliff. 2 April 1325 (*Chapters*, ii, 308);[2] 4 July 1325 made keeper of the rolls of chancery (*C.C.R. 1323-27*, p. 386); latest writ issued "on the information of Master Henry de Clif" dated 1 July 1325 (*C.P.R. 1324-27*, p. 134).

William of Herlaston. 12 Oct. 1325 (*C.C.R. 1323-27*, p. 413) to 1 Oct. 1326 (*ibid.*, p. 617); described as "late keeper" on 16 May 1328 (*C.C.R. 1327-30*, p. 291).

Robert of Wyvill. Acted as keeper of privy seal used from 26 Oct. 1326 by Edward, duke of Aquitaine, while governing the realm in his father's name, "because he had no other seal for the rule at that time" (*C.C.R. 1323-27*, p. 655, but *cf Chapters*, ii, 310).

### (*e*) Keepers of the Great Wardrobe

Ralph of Stokes. Apptd. 26 Aug. 1307[3] (*C.P.R. 1307-13*, p. 1); acting 28 March 1318 (*ibid.*, *1317-21*, p. 129).

William of Cusance. Apptd. 11 Sept. 1320 (*ibid.*, p. 504).

Gilbert of Wigton. Apptd. 20 Dec. 1321 (*ibid.*, *1321-24*, p. 41).

Thomas of Ousefleet. Apptd. 26 Aug. 1323 (*ibid.*, p. 337).

## D.—MISCELLANEOUS OFFICERS

### (1) Justices and Keepers of the Forest

Up to the early thirteenth century there was normally one chief forest official, the *capitalis forestarius* of the forest charter of 1217, cap. 16. In 1238, however, a permanent division of the control

[1] [Ill-fortune seems to have dogged dates and references used in connection with Ayleston with such persistency that it seems worth while to mention some instances here. In 1st edn., p. 357, Mr. Tout quoted *Parl. Writs*, II, ii, App., p. 248, as evidence that A. was keeper p.s. on 9 March 1324; in *Chapters*, ii, 305, n. 3, the page reference was rightly extended to pp. 244-8, but the date wrongly altered to 19 March. In the list of keepers given in *Chapters*, vi, 50, the references given for A.'s dates concern 1323 only, and the evidence for his still being in office in 1324 is found in *Corrigenda*, *ibid.*, 123, *viz.*, that A. "is mentioned as keeper of the p.s. on 16 May 1324 in Cobham's *Register*, x, 95." I cannot trace the x, but an entry on f. 95 of the register is calendared in Dr. Pearce's edition (p. 170) as describing A. as king's secretary, the further description of keeper of the p.s. being merely a justifiable editorial gloss within brackets. Also, the date is *xviij kal. Junii*, *i.e.*, not 16 but 15 May.]

[2] [The reference there given in n. 2 is inapplicable. Earliest writ issued on Henry's information is dated 12 April 1325 (*C.P.R. 1324-27*, p. 112).]

[3] [After acting already 15 April 1300 to 7 July 1307.]

into two was effected and separate justices were assigned to the forest north and south of Trent. They were rarely officially described in these terms, though there are in our period some instances of this being done, when, for example, Ralph of Monthermer is called, in the roll of the York parliament of 1318, *gardien de la forest de la Trente devers le south.*[1] The usual official practice was the perplexing one of describing the justices as acting *ultra* or *citra Trentam* according to the position of the place at which the king happened to be staying when he wrote the letter in which they were so described. Thus if the king or chancery were in Yorkshire, the justice *citra Trentam* would be the official in charge of the northern forests, while if the court were at London, *citra Trentam* would indicate the justice governing the southern forests.

The justice of the forest had more administrative than judicial functions, for though he was commonly included with other justices in judicial commissions for the forest, he was never prominent among them, and often did not act at all. It was not, however, the desire to make the name fit the office that caused the change in the official designation of these functionaries in 1311. It was rather the influence of the ordinances, which enumerated, among the ministers to be appointed by the counsel and consent of the baronage in parliament, *un chief gardein de ses forestes decea Trente et un autre dela Trente.*[2] The term " keeper " suggested a more modest and restricted function than that of justice, and found, perhaps, more favour in the barons' eyes by reason of their long-standing difficulties with Edward I, in reference to the delimitation and the administration of the forests. Even before the ordinances there was a tendency in this direction, for on 1 October 1310 Gaveston was appointed " to the keeping of the office of justice of the forest," and his subordinate, Hotham, is described after the ordinances as " acting keeper of the said forest." Similarly, Hugh le Despenser the elder, appointed to " the office of justice of the forest " in March 1308, is described at the time of his removal from office, on 2 December 1311, as " late keeper of the said forest." It should be noted that the two first definite appointments to keeperships, those in favour of Robert Fitzpayn and Henry Percy, both took place on the same day, 2 December 1311, a few weeks after the ordinances had been promulgated. The record of Percy's appointment makes it certain that this change was agreeable to the ordainers. The title of justice was only revived in 1397, by which period the office had become little more than formal. Even Hugh le Despenser, in 1312 and 1324, was called keeper only. See for complete list of forest justices south of Trent, and valuable remarks on the office, Mr. G. J. Turner's paper in *Eng. Hist. Rev.*, xviii, 112-16. I must also refer to Mr. Turner's important

[1] Cole's *Records*, p. 3. [2] *Rot. Parl.*, i, 282.

*Select Pleas of the Forest* (Selden Soc., 1901), and especially to his introduction, pp. xiv-xvi.

The justice or keeper of the forest had great authority. The tyrannical proceedings of Hugh le Despenser when charged with the office excited bitter complaints. The office was always held by laymen of position, knights, barons, and even earls. The acting deputy might be a clerk, as the case of Hotham shows, but William of Claydon, deputy for earls Aymer and Hugh in succession, was a knight.[1] Only a few of the accounts of the keepers of the forest are extant for this period. Among them are those of keepers Cromwell and Scrope for the northern forests for the whole period of their office. None have been printed. The wage of the keeper of the southern forest was the large one of £100 per annum; his northern colleague only received 100 marks.

### (*a*) Justices and Keepers of the Forest North of Trent

Robert of Clifford. Apptd. 22 Aug. 1297 (*C.P.R. 1292-1301*, p. 306); reapptd. 28 Aug. 1307 (*C.F.R.*, ii, 2); surrendered 12 Mar. 1308 (*ibid.*, p. 17).

John of Seagrave, senr. Apptd. 12 Mar. 1308 (*ibid.*); surrendered 1 Oct. 1310 (*ibid.*, p. 73).

Peter of Gaveston, earl of Cornwall. Apptd. for life 1 Oct. 1310 (*ibid.*).

*John of Hotham*, kg.'s clk., acting keeper. Surrendered 2 Dec. 1311 (*ibid.*, p. 117).

Henry of Percy. Apptd. keeper 2 Dec. 1311 (*ibid.*, p. 116). "And afterwards the ordainers consented to the aforesaid."

John of Seagrave, senr. Apptd. 4 Sept. 1312 (*ibid.*, p. 144); surrendered 19 Feb. 1315 (*ibid.*, p. 230).

Robert of Umfraville, earl of Angus. Apptd. 19 Feb. 1315 (*ibid.*); surrendered 23 Nov. 1316 (*ibid.*, p. 311).

John of Cromwell. Apptd. 23 Nov. 1316 (*ibid.*); apptd. for life 25 Sept. 1317 (*ibid.*, p. 341); surrendered 10 Sept. 1323 (*C.F.R.*, iii, 238).

Henry le Scrope. Apptd. 10 Sept. 1323 (*ibid.*); acting 7 Ap. 1326 (*C.P.R. 1324-27*, p. 256).

John of Cromwell. Again acting, 10 Dec. 1326 (*C.C.R. 1323-27*, p. 622).

### (*b*) Justices and Keepers of the Forest South of Trent

Hugh le Despenser, senr. Apptd. 12 Feb. 1297 (*C.F.R.*, i, 382); surrendered 18 Aug. 1307 (*C.F.R.*, ii, 1).

Payn Tibotot. Apptd. 18 Aug. 1307 (*ibid.*); surrendered 16 Mar. 1308 (*ibid.*, p. 19).

Hugh le Despenser. Again apptd., as justice, 16 Mar. 1308 (*ibid.*, p. 18); surrendered, as keeper, 2 Dec. 1311 (*ibid.*, p. 116); king resumed office "in compliance with the ordinances" (*C.P.R. 1307-13*, p. 464).

[1] *C.C.R. 1327-30*, p. 518.

Robert Fitzpayn. Apptd. keeper 2 Dec. 1311 (*C.F.R.*, ii, 116); surrendered 14 June 1312 (*C.P.R. 1307-13*, p. 464).

Hugh le Despenser. Again apptd., as keeper, 14 June 1312 (*ibid.*); surrendered 19 Feb. 1315 (*C.F.R.*, ii, 230).

Ralph of Monthermer. Apptd. 19 Feb. 1315 (*ibid.*); surrendered 18 May 1320 (*C.F.R.*, iii, 23).

Aymer de Valence, earl of Pembroke. Apptd. 18 May 1320 "to keep till next parl." (*ibid.*); apptd. 13 Oct. 1320 "by kg. in full parl. by assent of the magnates there" (*ibid.*, pp. 34-5); died in office 23 June 1324.

*William of Claydon.* Lieutenant for Aymer; surrendered 27 June 1324 (*ibid.*, p. 387).

Hugh le Despenser, earl of Winchester. Again apptd., for life, 27 June 1324 (*ibid.*).

*William of Claydon.* Lieutenant keeper. Surrendered 10 Nov. 1326 (*ibid.*, p. 423).

Thomas Wake, kg.'s kinsman. Apptd. 10 Nov. 1326 (*ibid.*).

## (2) Escheators

The escheators, like the justices of the forest, were officially designated as acting *citra* or *ultra Trentam*, according to the place at which the chancery or court was sitting at the time of the letter in which they were so described. The control exercised by the escheators over the sheriffs made them in a sense representatives of the central power in the various local districts. Though not strictly officers of the exchequer, they necessarily stood, like the sheriffs, in a specially close relation to it. The authority of the escheators was at all times looked upon with great suspicion by the baronage, since their office of safeguarding the interests of the crown, as supreme lord, could easily be diverted into claiming as escheats land for which there was a natural heir, and in many other ways. Accordingly, from the provisions of Oxford onwards,[1] the barons took great pains to secure the appointment of good escheators. The ordinances of 1311, therefore, provided that the two escheators should be appointed in parliament. The earliest escheators' accounts surviving begin in Henry III's reign.[2] Those for the reign of Edward II are tolerably complete.[3]

In 1258 the system of two escheators, one for the north and one for the south, was already in existence and it was recognised by the ordinances in 1311. It was therefore, perhaps, part of the revolt of the Despensers from baronial tradition that in 1323 the two escheators were superseded by eight escheators, appointed to various groups of counties. The crucial date for this change is

[1] *Select Charters* (1913), p. 382; "bons eschaeturs seient mis."

[2] Those north of Trent in 1237-38, those south of Trent in 1260-61. In 1246 there seem to have been county escheators (*Close rolls, 1242-47*, pp. 455-6).

[3] *P.R.O. Lists and Indexes, Foreign Enrolled Accounts*, p. 265.

29 November 1323, when the then escheators, Burgh and Walwayn, surrendered a large number of the counties entrusted to them and remained in office as escheators for a portion of their earlier spheres. Walwayn resigned all save four counties and Burgh three of his seven shires. Six new escheators were then appointed in addition to the two old ones. The old escheators soon disappeared altogether from office, for Walwayn gave up what was left to him on 10 January 1324 and Burgh surrendered his remaining shires in June 1324, so that by the summer of 1324 the new system was worked by entirely new hands. In the new arrangements the old dividing line of the Trent was ignored. One of the new escheatries took from the northern province Nottingham, Derby and Lancaster, and from the southern, Warwick and Leicester.[1] It is curious that this rearrangement should seem to have been made so as to include shires in which the estates of the house of Lancaster, then in the king's hands, were specially important. The fees assigned to three of the new escheators, the first three groups in our list, were fixed at 20 marks a year. The other five new escheators each received £10.

### (*a*) Escheators North of Trent, 1307-23

Richard Oysel, merchant, bailiff of Holderness. Apptd. 19 Ap. 1305 (*C.F.R.*, i, 515); dead by [26 June] 1308 (*C.C.R. 1307-13*, p. 72).

Roger le Savage, knt. Apptd. 24 Nov. 1307 (*C.P.R. 1307-13*, p. 19); surr. 23 May 1308 (*C.F.R.*, ii, 23).

Gerard Salvayn,[2] knt., of Harswell, Yorks. Apptd. 23 May 1308 (*ibid.*, p. 22); surr. 10 Dec. 1309 (*ibid.*, p. 52).

John of Hotham, kg.'s clk., later bp. of Ely. Apptd. 10 Dec. 1309 (*ibid.*, p. 52); surr. 2 Feb. 1311 (*ibid.*, p. 77).

Robert of Wodehouse,[3] kg.'s clk., formerly clk. of kitchen. Apptd. 30 Dec. 1310 to act from 2 Feb. 1311 (*ibid.*); surr. 3 Feb. 1313 (*ibid.*, p. 162).

John of Evre,[4] knt. of Cleveland. Apptd. 3 Feb. 1313 (*ibid.*); surr. 19 Feb. 1315 (*ibid.*, p. 232).

Robert of Clitheroe, chancery clk., parson of Wigan, Lancastrian partisan (*V.C.H. Lancs.*, ii, 31, and *Hist. Ch. Wigan*, Chetham Soc., pp. 38-45). Apptd. 19 Feb. 1315 (*C.F.R.*, ii, 232); surr. 27 Sept. 1316 (*ibid.*, p. 301).

Robert of Sapey, kg.'s yeoman in 1308 (*C.P.R. 1307-13*, p. 52), lord of Huntley, Glos., in 1326 (*Cal. Inq. p.m.*, vi, p. 466). Apptd. 27 Sept. 1316 (*C.F.R.*, ii, 301); surr. 25 Nov. 1318 (*ibid.*, p. 381).

Mr. Ralph of Crophill, clk. Apptd. 25 Nov. 1318 (*ibid.*, p. 380); surr. 29 Jan. 1320 (*C.F.R.*, iii, 15).

[1] *C.F.R.*, iii, 251-2.

[2] In 1311 the ordainers petitioned that Salvayn should be deprived of all office and removed from court (*Ann. Lond.*, p. 200).

[3] [*Cf. Chapters*, ii, 271-2, for his career. Mr. Tout there calls attention to his own omission of Robert's name from list of escheators in 1st edn.]

[4] Evre is Iver, Bucks.

GILBERT OF STAPLETON, kg.'s clk. Apptd. 29 Jan. 1320 *C.F.R.*, iii. 15); died in office before 7 Aug. 1321 (*ibid.*, p. 66).
THOMAS OF BURGH, kg.'s clk. Apptd. 25 Aug. 1321 (*ibid.*, p. 69); surr. Notts., Derbys., Lancs., 29 Nov. 1323 (*ibid.*, p. 252); surr. Yorks., Northumberland, Cumberland, Westmorland, 13 June 1324 (*ibid.*, p. 283).

## (*b*) ESCHEATORS SOUTH OF TRENT, 1307-23

WALTER OF GLOUCESTER. Apptd. 26 May 1298 (*C.F.R.*, i, 400); reapptd. 8 Nov. 1307 (*C.F.R.*, ii, 7); surr. 26 Ap. 1311 (*ibid.*, p. 89).
ROGER OF WELLESWORTH, steward of household of Edw. of Carnarvon in 1303 (*Chapters*, ii, 171), kg.'s clk. Apptd. 26 Ap. 1311 (*C.F.R.*, ii, 89); surr. 30 Dec. 1312 (*ibid.*, p. 158).
JOHN ABEL, once "bachelor" of Margt., queen of Edw. I (A.C. xxxv, 70) and steward of her household (*Chapters*, v, 240).[1] Apptd. 30 Dec. 1312 (*C.F.R.*, ii, 158); surr. 19 Feb. 1315 (*ibid.*, p. 232).
Mr. JOHN WALWAYN, kg.'s clk., also clk. of earl of Hereford (Conway Davies, pp. 355-6, and *Chapters*, ii, 214). Apptd. 19 Feb. 1315 (*C.F.R.*, ii, 252); surr. 6 July 1318 (*ibid.*, p. 365).
Mr. RICHARD OF CLARE, kg.'s clk. Apptd. 6 July 1318 (*ibid.*); surr. 22 Feb. 1320 (*C.F.R.*, iii, 16).
RICHARD OF RODNEY. Apptd. 22 Feb. 1320 (*ibid.*); surr. 14 Nov. 1321 (*ibid.*, p. 78).
Mr. JOHN WALWAYN,[2] clk., formerly treasurer of exch. Apptd. 14 Nov. 1321 (*ibid.*); surr. most of counties 29 Nov. [and 8 Dec.] 1323 (*ibid.*, pp. 251, 252); surr. Surrey, Sussex, Kent, Middlesex, London, 10 Jan. 1324 (*ibid.*, p. 252).

## (*c*) LOCAL ESCHEATORS, 1323-27

Wilts, Hants, Oxon, Beds, Bucks, Berks.
RICHARD LE WAYTE. Apptd. 29 Nov. 1323 (*C.F.R.*, iii, 252); surr. 29 June 1326 (*ibid.*, p. 393).
THOMAS OF HARPDEN. Apptd. 29 June 1326 (*ibid.*); acting 10 Jan. 1327 (*ibid.*, p. 432).

Norfolk, Suffolk, Cambs, Hunts, Essex, Herts.
JOHN OF BLOMVILLE. Apptd. 29 Nov. 1323 (*ibid.*, p. 252); acting 16 Jan. 1327 (*ibid.*, p. 432).

Yorkshire, Northumberland, Cumberland, Westmorland.
THO. OF BURGH, kg.'s clk. Limited to these shires, 29 Nov. 1323 (*ibid.*, p. 252); surr. 13 June 1324 (*ibid.*, p. 283).
SIMON OF GRIMSBY. Apptd. 13 June 1324 (*ibid.*, p. 283); acting 6 Jan. 1327 (*ibid.*, p. 431).

[1] [For his activities *cf.* E.A. 366/25.]

[2] [Mr. Tout noted in his own copy: "He was D.C.L. and deceased by 3 Edw. III (*Cal. Inq. p.m.*, vii, 184) though alive 1 Edw. III and writing to chancellor about attacks on Berkeley." An undated entry on the Close roll for 1 Edw. III, adjacent to entries dated 15 March 1327 (*C.C.R. 1327-30*, p. 104) speaks of the executor of the will of Master John Walwayn, deceased.]

Cornwall, Devon, Somerset, Dorset.

JOHN EVERARD. Apptd. 29 Nov. 1323 (*C.F.R.* iii, p. 252); surr. 10 Dec. 1325 (*ibid.*, p. 370).

ROB. OF BILKEMORE. Apptd. 10 Dec. 1325 (*ibid.*, p. 369); acting 6 Jan. 1327 (*ibid.*, p. 431).

Hereford, Gloucester, Worcester, Salop, Stafford, Welsh March.

JOHN OF HAMPTON. Apptd. [8 Dec.] 1323 (*ibid.*, p. 252); acting 18 Jan. 1327 (*ibid.*, p. 432).

Surrey, Sussex, Kent, Middlesex, city of London.

Mr. JOHN WALWAYN, kg.'s clk. Limited to these shires 29 Nov. and [8 Dec.] 1323 (*ibid.*, p. 252); surr. 10 Jan. 1324 (*ibid.*).

WILL. OF WESTON. Apptd. 10 Jan. 1324 (*ibid.*); acting 10 Jan. 1327 (*ibid.*, p. 432).

Warwick, Leicester, Nottingham, Derby, Lancashire.

JOHN OF BOLINGBROKE. Apptd. 29 Nov. 1323 (*ibid.*, p. 251); acting [16] Jan. 1327 (*ibid.*, p. 432).

Lincoln, Northampton, Rutland.

MATTHEW BROWN. Apptd. 29 Nov. 1323 (*ibid.*, p. 252); acting 13 Jan. 1327 (*ibid.*, p. 432).

North Wales.

ROBERT POWER, kg.'s clk., chamberlain of N. Wales. Apptd. 19 July 1323 (*ibid.*, p. 230); acting 27 Jan. 1325 (*ibid.*, p. 327).

### (3) KEEPERS OF THE EXCHANGES OF LONDON AND CANTERBURY

These officers were known later as wardens of the mint,[1] but it seems safer to describe them here by their proper contemporary designation, especially as the actual coining operations were performed by moneyers in various mints, out of strict relation to the keepers of the exchanges. The appointments of the keepers are in every case, save those of [John of Everdon and] William Trent, recorded in the fine roll. The duration of each term of office is clear from the keepers' accounts preserved in the pipe rolls. These accounts are, with a few exceptions, complete for this period. The first important exception is that of Amerigo dei Frescobaldi, who was exiled by the lords ordainers in 1311; the next is that of the last year of Hawstead, also a period of political confusion; and the last the last three years of Haselshaw, including the revolutionary end of the reign. The alternation of clerical and mercantile keepers is interesting. In compiling these lists, I have availed myself of the summary of these "mint" accounts in Messrs. C. G. Crump and C. Johnson's valuable "Tables of Bullion coined under Edward I, II, and III," reprinted from the *Numismatic Chronicle*, Fourth Series, vol. xiii (1913). Special references to these sources have not therefore been thought necessary, but I have noted in each case the dates for which *extant* accounts survive.

[1] [On this title and that of *magister monete* see *Chapters, Addenda*, vi, 130.]

In each case the exchanges of London and Canterbury had the same keeper. Operations at Canterbury, though smaller than at London, were on a large scale. Pence only were coined there, and the archbishop had a share of the seignorage.

JOHN OF EVERDON, kg.'s clk. Acctd. from 1 May 1305 to 18 Sept. 1307.

AMERIGO DEI FRESCOBALDI, kg.'s merchant. Apptd. 20 Aug. 1307 (*C.F.R.*, ii, 2); acctd. from 19 Sept. 1307 to 29 Sept. 1309.

JOHN OF COCKERMOUTH, kg.'s clk. Apptd. 9 Oct. 1311 (*ibid.*, p. 104).

JOHN OF LINCOLN, citizen and alderman of London. Apptd. 20 Oct. 1311 (*ibid.*, p. 105); acctd. from 23 Oct. 1311 to 24 Feb. 1315.

WILL. TRENT, citizen and alderman of London. Acctd. from 25 Feb. 1315 to 20 June 1316; died 1316; will enrolled 25 Oct.

JOHN OF COCKERMOUTH, kg.'s clk. Apptd. 21 June 1316 (*ibid.*, p. 284); acctd. from 21 June 1316 to 11 Ap. 1317.

AUGUSTINE LE WALEYS, of Uxbridge, kg.'s clk. Apptd. 28 Jan. 1318 (*ibid.*, p. 351); also 12 June 1318 (*ibid.*, p. 363); surr. 12 Aug. 1320 (*C.F.R.*, iii, p. 31); acctd. from 11 Ap. 1317 to 13 Aug. 1320.

WILL. OF HAWSTEAD, kg.'s clk. Apptd. 12 Aug. 1320 (*ibid.*, p. 31); surr. 6 Oct. 1322 (*ibid.*, p. 180); acctd. from 14 Aug. 1320 to 30 Sept. 1321.

ROB. OF HAZELSHAW, kg.'s clk. Apptd. 6 Oct. 1322 (*ibid.*, p. 180); still in office at end of reign; acctd. from 7 Oct. 1322 to 30 Sept. 1323.

### (4) MAYORS OF THE MERCHANTS OF THE STAPLE

For the functions of these officers, see above, pp. 220, 222, 223, 226-37. The subjoined, very incomplete, list is only offered as a first attempt.

[The dates, except in the last entry, are the earliest and latest at which evidence has been found of the mayor at work. Mr. Tout adds in his copy "Who was the 'mayor of merchants of the king's realm' at Antwerp on 29 Jan. 1317 (*C.C.R. 1313-18*, p. 392)?"]

RICHARD STURY, burgess of Shrewsbury. [Sent to treat with count of Flanders] 26 Nov. 1312 (*Foedera*, ii, 188); acting as "mayor of the merchants of our realm" 15 Feb. 1313 (*ibid.*, p. 202), acting as "mayor of the wool staple" 22 Aug. 1313 (*C.P.R. 1313-17*, p. 15).

JOHN OF CHARLTON, mercer of London. 22 Nov. 1318 (*Foedera*, ii, 378); 22 July 1323 (*C.C.R. 1323-27*, p. 9).

WILL. OF MEREWELL. 13 Aug. 1324 (*C.P.R. 1324-27*, p. 13).

RICH. OF BETHUNE, pepperer of London, alderman 1322-33,[1] 2 May 1325 (*C.C.R. 1323-27*, p. 378); 27 Nov. 1325 (*ibid.*, p. 527).

JOHN OF CHARLTON, again. Elected by merchants 12 June 1326 (*ibid.*, p. 564); apptd. by patent 30 July 1326 (*C.P.R. 1324-27*, p. 301).

[1] See Beaven, *Aldermen of London*, i, 382, and Sharpe, *Wills in Husting*, i, 445. He is generally described as a goldsmith. He is called "Betoyne" in contemporary documents, but I feel fairly confident that this means Béthune in Artois.

## E.—OFFICERS OF THE TWO BENCHES

### (1) Chief Justices, Justices and Chief Clerks of the Bench for Common Pleas

In the first commission appointing justices of the common bench for this reign, six judges were empowered, of whom Ralph of Hingham, or, as he is more often called, Hengham, the first mentioned, was continued chief justice. Of the rest, Peter Mallory was old, and never seems to have acted, while William Howard, the founder of the great family of Howards, only sat in Trinity term 1307.[1] Both these judges died in 1308, and Hingham, whose judicial career went back to Henry III's reign, also ceased to act early in 1309.[2] In place of the two former justices, only one appointment, that of Henry le Scrope, was made. Bereford was, however, made chief justice in 1309 in succession to Hingham, and kept that post for the next seventeen years, being replaced on 18 July 1328 by Hervey of Staunton. The provision of the ordinances of 1311 that the chief justice must be appointed in parliament made no difference to his position. Probably he was deemed "sufficient," as was certainly the case in 1318, when the York parliament of October expressly agreed to his remaining in office.[3]

In 1307 and 1308 the number of working judges for common pleas had never been more than five, and for the greater part of 1309 only four. On the 18 September of that year, an ordinance of the king and council raised the number to six, "as it is necessary to have two places, owing to the number of pleas, now greater than ever."[4] This suggests that two courts, each with three judges, were to sit simultaneously. Two new judges were immediately appointed. One, John Benstead, a prominent minister of Edward I, had relinquished, in July, 1308, the great post of keeper of the wardrobe, which was not assuredly, as Mr. G. J. Turner suggests, but a "stepping stone" in his career. Benstead took a less important post, one imagines, because he wished to marry, and

[1] For the judicial officers of the early years of Edward's reign see the admirable "legal calendars" compiled by Mr. G. J. Turner for the *Year Books of Edward II*, Selden Soc. I have also had the advantage of using a manuscript article on the changes of ministers after Edward II's accession by Miss Mabel H. Mills, to whom I am indebted for several points, especially as to judicial offices.

[2] [The fullest and most recent biography of Hingham is that prefixed by Dr. W. H. Dunham, Jr., to his edition of the *Summae*, 1932. See also "Ralph of Hengham as chief justice of the common pleas," by Sir Paul Vinogradoff, in *Essays presented to T. F. Tout*, pp. 189-96.]

[3] Cole's *Records*, p. 3.

[4] *C.C.R. 1307-13*, p. 231. *Cf.* Turner, *Year Books of Edward II*, IV, xxv-xxvi, where the working of the two divisions of the court is indicated.

abandon the clerical state, and his previous appointments at the wardrobe and the exchequer were only open to clerks.[1] Whether he was well qualified for his new duties is perhaps problematical. It is certain that a career hitherto purely political, financial, and administrative seems to modern eyes a curious preparation for a common law judgeship. But the line between lawyer and layman was loosely drawn in the fourteenth century, and the bench at least secured in Benstead a distinguished personality. William of Bourn, the other new justice of 1309, apparently never acted,[2] so that despite the royal ordinance there remained only five justices of common pleas.

Two points of interest are suggested by the lists. These are, first, the proportion of laymen to clerks among the justices, and secondly, how far judgeships were filled by men of little forensic or judicial experience, and how far they had become the natural reward of distinguished advocates. With regard to the former point, it is noteworthy that of the nineteen justices of the common bench of the reign, eight or nine were clerks ; [3] and that the clerical element was already on the decrease is suggested by the fact that no fresh clerical justice was appointed after 1316. Moreover, one of the proved clerks, Benstead, promptly gave up his clergy, so that the laymen were in a substantial majority in the latter part of the reign, though at the beginning there were three clerical and three lay justices. But the clerk Hingham still represented that order ; [4] Threckingham and Staunton, and still more Bacon and Roubury, kept up the clerical tradition, while the end of the reign saw in Staunton a new clerical chief justice. These details should make us hesitate to accept suggestions as to the natural antagonism of clerk and lawyer, such as F. W. Maitland was delighted to stress, and, I think, to stress unduly, anyhow for this period. When we realise how a substantial proportion of common lawyers was still clerical, the antagonism disappears of itself. But the differentiation of the clerical profession from that of the common lawyer had already made large strides.

As regards the antecedent qualification of the justices for judicial work, we are still struck by the way in which men like Benstead became judges without ever having been "at the bar."

[1] *Year Books of Edward II*, IV, xx. Mr. Turner brings out very clearly, though but in outline, the special interest of Benstead's remarkable career.

[2] *Ibid.*, II, xxiv.

[3] I am uncertain as to the status of William Bourn, but he may be identical with William Burne, clerk, who in 1305 and 1306 was a benefactor of St. John's Hospital, Bristol, and Glastonbury abbey (*C.P.R. 1301-7*, pp. 408, 481). Bourn's clergy is also suggested by his description in the writ of appointment (*C.C.R. 1307-13*, p. 231). If this be so, the defection of Benstead from his clergy is compensated for.

[4] [On the way in which "the Church . . . assumed the burden of Hengham's maintenance in a social position becoming England's Chief Justice" *cf.* Dunham, *op. cit.*, pp. xlviii-l.]

Staunton's case points in the same direction. He began life as a "king's clerk," and certainly had no experience as an advocate. Yet he lived to become chief justice of both benches, chief baron of the exchequer, and chancellor of the exchequer. Unlike Benstead, however, he had plenty of judicial experience. Staunton's alternation between the two benches and the exchequer suggests that the various branches of the royal service were in no ways closed departments, and that administrative experience was still regarded as a qualification for judicial work. He is one of the numerous examples of a similar tendency. Against these we may set the long career of Bereford at the common bench, where he sat as judge for more than thirty years. Maitland has made us realise his strongly marked character, his shrewd sayings, his power of getting to the point, his jests and his oaths.

Herle, Geoffrey le Scrope, Mablethorp (see king's bench list), and Stonor, are the best examples of men raised to the bench in this reign by reason of their distinction as advocates. Besides these there were Scotter, Friskney, and Passelewe, eminent "counsel" who had their reward in the administrative work of a baron of the exchequer. Of these, however, Friskney soon went from the exchequer to the common bench.

Our conclusions, then, are that judicial office was still freely open to clerks and other persons who were not professional lawyers. The increasing tendency was, however, to appoint as judges laymen who had made their mark as advocates.

Among the offices specified in the ordinances of 1311 as henceforth to be filled up with the counsel and assent of the magnates in parliament was that of the chief clerk of the king in the common bench.[1] It must be assumed, therefore, that it was an office of some political importance, or, at least, a post which in the hands of an irresponsible courtier might do serious harm to the interests of litigants. References to this office occur very occasionally in the records, but the chancery rolls enable us to make out a fairly complete list of keepers of the rolls and writs of the common bench, and there is sufficient indication that the keeper of the rolls of the bench was also its chief clerk. Thus John Bacon, king's clerk, who had been keeper of the rolls of the bench since 1292,[2] is spoken of in an ordinance enrolled in the close roll of 1309 as chief clerk of the bench. Bacon is, moreover, charged to keep a counter roll of all the pleas and essoins in bench.[3] Moreover, in the York parliament of October 1318, when for the first time a systematic review of all the posts to which parliament was to nominate was made, the person who we know was then acting as keeper of the rolls of the bench, Adam of Herwington, was formally confirmed by parliament

[1] *Rot. Parl.*, i, 282. [2] *C.P.R. 1281-92*, p. 485.
[3] *C.C.R. 1307-13*, p. 231.

in the office of chief clerk of the bench.[1] With these facts before us, it is hardly rash to conclude that the two offices in question were always combined during our period. We may, then, complete our catalogue of all the officers of state and household which the ordainers claimed to nominate, by adding this list to our collection.

### (*a*) Chief Justices

Ralph of Hingham or Hengham, clk. Acting 19 Sept. 1301 (*C.P.R. 1301-7*, p. 606) to 15 Mar. 1309[2] (*C.P.R. 1307-13*, p. 109); reapptd. 6 Sept. 1307 (*ibid.*, p. 2).

Will. of Bereford, knt. Apptd. 15 March 1309 (*ibid.*, p. 109); acting till 18 July 1326 (*C.P.R. 1324-27*, p. 297); dead by 19 Jan. 1327 (*ibid.*, p. 346).

Hervey of Staunton, clk. Apptd. 18 July 1326 (*ibid.*, p. 297).

### (*b*) Justices

Ralph of Hingham, clk. First appointment [1269] to 1274 (Dunham, *op. cit.*); for appts. as chief justice *v. supra*; also acted as justice and chief justice of kg.'s bench; retired 1309.

Will. of Bereford, knt. Apptd. 22 Aug. 1294 (*C.P.R. 1292-1301*, p. 115); reapptd. 6 Sept. 1307 (*C.P.R. 1307-13*, p. 2) and 18 Sept. 1309 (*C.C.R. 1307-13*, p. 231); apptd. chief justice 15 Mar. 1309 (*v. supra*); acted till July 1326.

Peter Mallory, knt.[3] Apptd. 28 Aug. 1292 (*C.P.R. 1281-92*, p. 507); reapptd. 6 Sept. 1307 (*C.P.R. 1307-13*, p. 2); ceased to act in 1308.

Lambert of Threckingham, clk. First apptd. 1300; reapptd. 6 Sept. 1307 (*ibid.*) and 18 Sept. 1309 (*C.C.R. 1307-13*, p. 231); made justice of kg.'s bench 6 Aug. 1316 (*C.C.R. 1313-18*, p. 358).

Hervey of Staunton, kg.'s clk. First apptd. 20 Ap. 1306 (*C.P.R. 1301-7*, p. 428); reapptd. 6 Sept. 1307 (*C.P.R. 1307-13*, p. 2) and 18 Sept. 1309 (*C.C.R. 1307-13*, p. 231); apptd. baron of exch. 28 Sept. 1314 (*C.P.R. 1313-17*, p. 179); chancellor of exch. 1316-23, 1324-26; justice of kg.'s bench Sept. 1323 to 1324; apptd. chief justice of cmn. pleas 18 July 1326 (*C.P.R. 1324-27*, p. 297).

Will. Howard, knt. First apptd. 8 Oct. 1297 (*C.P.R. 1292-1301*, p. 319); reapptd. 6 Sept. 1307 (*C.P.R. 1307-13*, p. 2); ceased to act Trinity term, 1308 (*Y.B.* I, xciii).

[1] "Mestre Richard de . . . Sire Adam de Herwynton, Chef Clerk du commun Bank: Vis est as toutz . . . demorrount en cels offices. Et le seigneur le roi se acord aussint par assent deux toutz qil te . . . as offices come avant" (Cole's *Records*, p. 4).

[2] [His successor was appointed on this date and Hingham was not among the justices summoned to the Stamford parliament by writs dated 11 June. Yet he is named with three colleagues on a commission of oyer and terminer by letters patent dated 29 June (*C.P.R. 1307-13*, p. 173, cited by Dunham, *op. cit.*, p. lviii).]

[3] Thus described in *C.C.R. 1302-7*, p. 337.

HENRY LE SCROPE, of Bolton, knt. Apptd. 27 Nov. 1308 (*C.P.R. 1307-13*, p. 147); reapptd. 18 Sept. 1309 (*C.C.R. 1307-13*, p. 231); apptd. chief justice kg.'s bench 15 June 1317 (*C.C.R. 1313-18*, p. 419).

JOHN OF BENSTEAD, clk. as late as 16 Mar. 1309 (Cole, p. 164), knt. by 12 Feb. 1311 (*C.C.R. 1307-13*, p. 340). Apptd. 18 Sept. 1309 (*ibid.*, p. 231) or 6 Oct. (*C.P.R. 1307-13*, p. 193); acted till 16 Oct. 1320 (*C.P.R. 1317-21*, p. 508).

WILLIAM OF BOURN, ? clerk. Apptd. 18 Sept. 1309 (*C.C.R. 1307-13*, p. 231) or 6 Oct. (*C.P.R. 1307-13*, p. 193); never acted (*Y.B.*, IV, xxiv-v).

JOHN BACON, kg.'s clk., keeper of rolls of cmn. pleas since 1288. Apptd. 19 Feb. 1313 (*C.P.R. 1307-13*, p. 552); succeeded by Stonor 16 Oct. 1320 (*C.P.R. 1317-21*, p. 508).

WILLIAM INGE, knt. Apptd. in place of Staunton, 28 Sept. 1314 (*C.P.R. 1313-17*, p. 181); succeeded by Roubury, 10 Mar. 1316 (*ibid.*, p. 435).

GILBERT OF ROUBURY, clk.[1] Justice of kg.'s bench 1295-1316; apptd. in place of Inge 10 Mar. 1316 (*ibid.*, p. 435).

JOHN OF MUTFORD, *narrator*.[2] Apptd. 20 Ap. 1316 (*ibid.*, p. 450); acted till 1329.

JOHN OF DONCASTER, layman. Apptd. 5 June 1319 (*C.P.R. 1317-21*, p. 344); did not act after 1320.

WILL. OF HERLE, kg.'s sergeant, knt. Apptd. in place of Benstead, 16 Oct. 1320 (*ibid.*, p. 508); acted for rest of reign (I.R. 220, m. 4).

JOHN OF STONOR, kg.'s sergeant, knt. Apptd. in place of Bacon, 16 Oct. 1320 (*ibid.*, p. 508); reapptd. 3 May 1324 (*C.P.R. 1321-1324*, p. 412); acted for rest of reign.

JOHN OF BOURCHIER, knt. Apptd. in place of Roubury, 31 May 1321 (*C.P.R. 1317-24*, p. 593); acted for rest of reign (I.R. 219, m. 3).

WALTER OF FRISKNEY, knt., baron of exch. Apptd. 9 July 1323 (*C.P.R. 1321-24*, p. 322); acted for rest of reign.

GEOFFREY LE SCROPE, of Bolton, kg.'s sergeant, knt. Apptd. 27 Sept. 1323 (*ibid.*, p. 340); apptd. chief justice of kg.'s bench 21 Mar. 1324.

### (*c*) CHIEF CLERKS AND KEEPERS OF THE ROLLS AND WRITS

JOHN BACON, kg.'s clk. Apptd. 17 Ap. 1292 (*C.P.R. 1281-92*, p. 485); reapptd. 6 Sept. 1307 (*C.P.R. 1307-13*, p. 2); entrusted with additional duties 18 Sept. 1309 (*C.C.R. 1307-13*, p. 231); apptd. justice of cmn. bench 19 Feb. 1313 (*C.P.R. 1307-13*, p. 552).

WILL. OF RASEN,[3] kg.'s clk. Apptd. to custody of writs and rolls of bench, 19 Feb. 1313 (*ibid.*).

[1] Thus described in *C.C.R. 1302-7*, p. 542.

[2] *Year Books*, I, xciv. Mr. G. J. Turner, *Y.B.*, IV, xv-xvii, identifies the "narrator" or "counter" with the "sergeants," who later had exclusive audience in the common bench. Some, but not all the class, are described as king's sergeants at this period, and received stipends in that capacity.

[3] [Not Raven, as in 1st edn. He may be the same Will. who was parson of West Rasen, Lincs., in July 1312 (*C.P.R. 1307-13*, p. 469). A Will. of Rasen was presented to another church in Lincoln diocese on 30 Jan. 1313 (*ibid.*, p. 526).]

ROB. OF HAUVILLE, kg.'s clk. Apptd. 21 Mar. 1314 (*C.P.R. 1313-17*, p. 94).

ADAM OF HERWINGTON, kg.'s clk. Apptd. [3] Oct. 1314 (*ibid.*, p. 185).; appointment confirmed in parl. Oct. 1318 (Cole, p. 4); mandate to surrender dated 11 June 1322 (*C.P.R. 1321-24*, p. 133).

Mr. WILL. OF AYLESTON, kg.'s clk. Apptd. 11 June 1322 (*ibid.*, p. 133).

Mr. JOHN OF SHOREDITCH, kg.'s clk. Apptd. 11 Sept. 1323 (*ibid.*, p. 340); acting June 1326 (I.R. 218, m. 7).[1]

### (2) CHIEF JUSTICES AND JUSTICES OF PLEAS *coram rege*, OR JUSTICES OF THE KING'S BENCH

There were never more than three justices acting at once to hear *placita coram rege*, and their history and succession is further simplified in this reign by their long continuance in office. The proportion of clerks to laymen was that of three to six, rather smaller than in the common bench. Moreover, only one of the five chief justices of the reign was a clerk. The habit of transferring officers from the one bench to the other has been already mentioned. There were also two cases of barons of the exchequer becoming justices of pleas *coram rege*. The chief justice of each bench was by the ordinances to be appointed in parliament, but Brabazon, like Bereford, was allowed to continue in office. In 1318 Henry le Scrope was similarly pronounced "sufficient" by the York parliament.

#### (*a*) CHIEF JUSTICES

ROGER LE BRABAZON, knt. First apptd. 1295; ordered 6 Sept. 1307 to continue in office [and to take oath on 4 Oct.] (*C.C.R. 1301-7*, p. 41); resignation accepted 23 Feb. 1316 (*C.P.R. 1313-17*, p. 437).

WILLIAM INGE, knt., formerly justice of cmn. bench. Apptd. after 23 Feb. 1316; ordered to surrender records, 15 June 1317 (*C.C.R. 1313-18*, pp. 415, 419).

HENRY LE SCROPE, knt., formerly justice of cmn. bench. Apptd. before 15 June 1317 (*ibid.*, pp. 415, 416, 419).

[1] Shoreditch was much engaged in diplomatic work in France and elsewhere, and it is difficult to believe that he remained effective keeper of the rolls of the bench for the rest of the reign. However, I find no fresh appointment to the office until 4 Feb. 1327, when Peter of Lodington was appointed (*C.P.R. 1327-30*, p. 17). Between 1323 and 1326 there are indications that chief justice Bereford, or a deputy appointed by his letters patent, was personally responsible for the records and rolls (*C.C.R. 1323-27*, pp. 42, 593). Under Edward III Shoreditch renounced his clergy and became a knight. [Mr. Tout discovered later the Issue Roll evidence quoted above.]

HERVEY OF STAUNTON, clk., already chancellor of exchequer.[1] Apptd. before 27 Sept. 1323 (*C.P.R. 1321-24*, p. 339).

GEOFFREY LE SCROPE, knt., formerly justice of cmn. bench. Apptd. before 21 Mar. 1324 (*ibid.*, p. 409); acted to end of reign.

(*b*) JUSTICES

GILBERT OF ROUBURY, clk. Apptd. 1295; ordered to continue, 6 Sept. 1307 (*C.C.R. 1307-13*, p. 41); apptd. justice of cmn. bench 10 Mar. 1316 (*C.P.R. 1313-17*, p. 435).

HENRY SPIGURNEL, knt. Apptd. ? 1300; ordered to continue, 6 Sept. 1307 (*C.C.R. 1307-13*, p. 41).

LAMBERT OF THRECKINGHAM, clk. Apptd. justice of cmn. bench 1299; apptd. to kg.'s bench 6 Aug. 1316 (*C.C.R. 1313-18*, p. 358); apptd. baron of exch. 6 Aug. 1320 (*C.P.R. 1317-21*, p. 504).

ROBERT OF MABLETHORP, *narrator*. Apptd. 1320; acted for rest of reign (I.R. 220, m. 5).

## F.—OFFICERS OF THE PRINCIPALITY OF WALES AND THE EARLDOM OF CHESTER

The administrative system of Wales and Cheshire remained, under Edward II, exactly as it had been settled by his father's statute of Wales of 1284. Edward of Carnarvon had entered upon the direct government of both the principality and the earldom in 1301. He retained the principality in his own hands for the whole of his life, never creating his eldest son prince of Wales. Edward of Windsor was, however, made earl of Chester when still a baby, so that after his creation he was supposed to appoint the officers of his palatinate personally.[2] The change was of course nominal, but it had this untoward result for historians, that the last appointment of a high Cheshire officer to be enrolled in the chancery rolls of Edward II was that of Robert of Holland, nominated in December 1311. Later appointments of justices, and all appointments of chamberlains of Chester, have accordingly to be sought out in the imperfect financial and the voluminous judicial records of Cheshire. On the other hand, the nomination and the removal of the justices and chamberlains of Wales are, with one or two exceptions, to be found enrolled on the fine rolls of Edward II for the whole of the reign. Accordingly the Cheshire lists are much more tentative than

[1] [Letters patent dated 27 Sept. 1323 gave custody of seal of exch. to Stapeldon, "as H. de Staunton, chancellor of exch., has been commanded to take the office of chief justice of pleas before the king." This conflicts oddly with Staunton's definite appointment as chancellor of exch. in 1324 (*v. supra*, p. 308).]

[2] So anxious were the Cheshire officers to act in the name of the infant earl that they paid twelve pence for a temporary copper seal, "pro breuibus cancellarie Cestrie sigillandis antequam sigillum comitis ibidem venit" (M.A., 771/7).

the Welsh lists, especially as the lists in Ormerod's *History of Cheshire*, though excellent so far as they go, do not always take us very far. I have, however, been greatly helped by the recently published calendars of the extant chamberlains' accounts of Cheshire under Edward II, by Mr. R. Stewart-Brown, and of Flintshire by my old pupil Mr. Arthur Jones.[1] [In the present edition these lists have been made more complete with the help of the list of justices prefixed by Prof. Tait to his *Chartulary of St. Werbergh Abbey* (Chetham Soc., 1920), and a list of chamberlains kindly supplied by Mrs. W. D. Sharp (see below, p. 340).]

The details of the administrative system of Wales and Cheshire after 1284 have not yet been fully worked out.[2] It is, however, I think, clear that Edward I extended to the principality a system of government very similar to that which he had inherited in Cheshire from Simon of Montfort and the Norman line of earls, and found existing in his lands in south-west Wales. The vicegerent of the earl or prince, and the acting head of the government, was the justice, who was nearly always a great baron. His chief subordinate was the chamberlain, who was the chief financial officer, "charged with the issues thereof," and required to answer for them at the exchequer at Westminster. By a survival of older usage the justices of Wales, the official superiors of the chamberlains, were also their controllers, and the chamberlain's accounts were tendered to the exchequer by the "view and testimony" of the justice as controller.[3] There was also a chancery at each of the three centres of government, but this was less prominent than the office of the chamberlain which, like the financial department of the English kings, was called an exchequer. Speaking roughly, the system was that of a great feudal barony rather than that of the English crown, and may be instructively compared with both the pre-Edwardian administration of the Scottish kings, and still more with the system which Edward I tried in vain to establish in Scotland. The analogies with the English administrative system are, however, very close, since the baronial court was always organised after the model of the royal court, though after a somewhat simpler fashion. It seems, however, that Edward I consciously supplemented what he found ready to his hands, by borrowing much from England, and notably by the establishment of something

[1] *Cheshire Chamberlains' Accounts, 1301-60*, Lancs. and Cheshire Record Soc., 1910; *Flintshire Ministers' Accounts, 1301-28*, Flintshire Hist. Soc., 1913. [To the Cheshire accounts must now be added item (*h*) in Wynnstay MS. 86, Nat. Lib. of Wales. This is Melton's account, 7 Feb. to 29 Sept. 1301, to be printed as appendix to a forthcoming vol. of Cheshire Pipe Rolls (Lancs. and Cheshire Record Soc.).]

[2] [For subsequent work on the subject see *Chapters*, ii, 170, n. 2.]

[3] The preface to the enrolment of any of the Welsh chamberlains' accounts illustrate this, for example, the prior of Carmarthen's accounts in Pipe roll 159, m. 37, rendered "per testimonium Rogeri de Mortuo Mari, iusticiarii parcium illarum, contrarotulatoris eiusdem camerarie."

very closely approaching the English shire system in all these districts.

Normally there were three centres of administration, each under a justice with its exchequer and chancery, and local capital. The justice of Cheshire ruled from Cheshire not only the old county palatine but also the newly established and subordinate county of Flint, which mainly consisted of the districts conquered from the Welsh, which Edward ventured to keep in his own hands.[1] Chester was the seat of the exchequer and chancery of the two shires, but each had its own sheriff, and the other apparatus of county self-government. The northern part of the ancient principality was the sphere of the justice of north Wales, whose residence was at Carnarvon, where the exchequer and chancery were established. The keeping of Carnarvon castle, his natural residence, was generally to be at the justice's own cost and risk, and occasionally, the justice himself acted as constable, and therefore also as mayor of the town. Under the justice were " the three old shires of Gwynedd," namely Anglesea, Carnarvon, and Merioneth. Similarly the southern portions of the principality were under the jurisdiction of the justice of south or west Wales, indifferently described as justice of either or of both those districts. Carmarthen and its castle stood to the justice of south Wales as Carnarvon stood to his northern colleague. His sphere of jurisdiction was divided between the counties of Carmarthen and Cardigan and the cantred of Cantrevmawr.[2] Marcher franchises, however, limited the authority of the justice of south Wales to regions much more limited than those of the modern Carmarthenshire and Cardiganshire. Cardiganshire yielded most of his revenue, but the receipts of the south Welsh administration were insignificant as compared with those of the government at Carnarvon.[3] However, the justice of south Wales was also appointed to act as justice in the lands of the bishopric of St. David's,[4] and sometimes also in the lands of the bishopric of Llandaff.[5] For a large part of Edward II's reign, namely from 1308 to 1315, and again from 1317 to 1326, the same

[1] See for this my paper on " Flintshire and its Records," *Flintshire Hist. Soc.*, 1911. [Reprinted in *Coll. Papers*, ii, 21-44.]

[2] In most of the accounts of the chamberlains of Carmarthen the receipts are grouped under these three heads, except, of course, during the years in which Hugh le Despenser the younger held Cantrev mawr independently of the Carmarthen exchequer. I can find no reference to the sheriff of Cardigan, though the " steward of Cardiganshire " occurs regularly. Rhys ap Gruffydd (see p. 336) held this post, 1310-17.

[3] Thus in 6 Edward II the receipts in south Wales were only £979 13s. 11¾d., of which £682 13s. 5¼d. came from Cardiganshire (Pipe roll 159, m. 37). In the same year the north Welsh receipt was £3,182 10s. 8¾d. (*ibid.*, m. 40) [but Mr. Tout notes in his copy, " not typical," and quotes Mr. W. H. Waters as giving the normal sum as £2,400-£2,500. For Mr. Waters' work see *Chapters*, vi, 58. His *Edwardian Settlement of North Wales* has now been published (1935).]

[4] *C.F.R.*, ii, 8, 13, 316, 402.

[5] *C.F.R.*, iii, 87.

individual held the office of justice in both districts of the principality. He was then described as the justice of Wales. The two exchequers and chanceries remained distinct, even when there was a single justice. Accordingly, there was for the whole of the reign a separate line of chamberlains of Carnarvon and Carmarthen, for thus the chamberlains of north and south Wales were often designated. I have spoken elsewhere of the significance of the great aggregations of power in this reign under marcher chieftains.[1]

With the one exception of Walter of Petherton, the justices of both north and south Wales were noblemen of high standing, generally with interests in Wales and the march. Mortimer and Arundel, the great justices, and ordinary governors such as Grey of Ruthin and Martin of Kemmes were heads of marcher lordships, and Audley and Berkeley had influence in the lands immediately adjacent to the march on its English side. The traditional fee of the justices of north and south Wales was 200 marks a year.[2] When they also "kept" the castle and town of Carnarvon or Carmarthen, they received an additional stipend of £100 on that account.[3] A larger stipend was given to the justice of all Wales. Thus Roger Mortimer received 350 marks, besides £100 for the custody of Carnarvon.[4] The justice of Chester's fee was £100, a sum which included the custody of his castles.[5] Both the Welsh and Cheshire offices were within the influence of general political tendencies in England: the alternating supremacy of Mortimer and Arundel shows this in Wales. In Cheshire Payn Tibotot represents the courtier element, and Robert Holland the Lancastrian. There was some difficulty in getting rid of Tibotot after the ordinances. Sapey represents the restoration of the courtier party to authority, and Ingham and Amory the royalist reaction of the end of the reign.

The chamberlains were always clerks. Each of the three chamberlains had a normal fee of £20 a year. They were seldom of much personal importance. The close connexion of the southern chamberlainship with the priory of Austin canons at Carmarthen is an interesting survival of the time when the "religious" often acted as finance ministers in England. Two priors in succession held the office for rather more than half the reign. They generally acted through attorneys, who were usually canons of their house. The only clearly Welsh officials were these attorneys to the southern chamberlains, notably John Goch, who is not described as a canon. The joint chamberlainship of the two priors with Thomas Doun or

[1] See above, pp. 124-29, 138-40.

[2] This was the sum received by Audley, and by his predecessor William of Sutton (Pipe roll 176, m. 55).

[3] *Ibid.* This was the sum received by Audley as keeper of Carnarvon.

[4] *Ibid.* The 350 marks were "tam pro Norwallia quam Suthwallia."

[5] M.A., 771/9.

Dwnn, who also may have been a Welshman, shows a curious wish to keep the office in the priory even at the risk of its unity and efficiency.

The hardest list to establish was that of the chamberlains of Chester, which remains even more imperfect than that of the justices. More careful examination of the Cheshire plea rolls and recognisance rolls than I have been able to give would probably produce a much more precise list. As it is, my list suggests a few small problems which others must be left to solve.[1] It includes in Richard of Bury one famous name. Incidentally it may be noticed that the employment of this famous clerk of Edward of Windsor's wardrobe in Cheshire destroys the widespread fiction that this illiterate but book-loving official was Edward III's tutor.

### (1) Justices of North and South Wales

Hugh of Audley, sen., knt. (N.). Acting 10 May 1306 (*C.C.R. 1302-7*, p. 385); ordered to surr. 15 Jan. 1308 (*C.F.R.*, ii, 13).

Walter of Petherton, kg.'s clk. (S.). First apptd. 24 Sept. 1298 (*C.F.R.*, i, 404); reapptd. 10 Nov. 1307 (*C.F.R.*, ii, 7); surr. 15 Jan. 1308 (*ibid.*, p. 12).

Roger Mortimer of Chirk,[2] baron (N. and S.). Apptd. 15 Jan. 1308 (*ibid.*); began to act 12 Feb. 1308 (Pipe roll 174, m. 55); surr. 19 Feb. 1315 (*C.F.R.*, ii, 232).

John Grey, lord of Ruthin, baron (N.). Apptd. 19 Feb. 1315 (*ibid.*); surr. 23 Nov. 1316 (*ibid.*, p. 312).

Will. Martin, lord of Kemmes, baron (W. and S.). Apptd. 19 Feb. 1315 (*ibid.*, p. 232); surr. 24 June 1316 (*ibid.*, p. 285).

Roger Mortimer[3] of Chirk (N.). Apptd. 23 Nov. 1316 (*ibid.*, p. 312).

Maurice of Berkeley, baron (W. and S.). Apptd. 24 June 1316 (*ibid.*, p. 285); surr. 7 Oct. 1317 (*ibid.*, p. 342).

Roger Mortimer of Chirk, baron (N. and S.). Apptd. for life 7 Oct. 1317 (*ibid.*); removed for rebellion before 5 Jan. 1322 (*C.F.R.*, iii, 86).

Edmund Fitzalan, earl of Arundel[4] (N. and S.). Apptd. 5 Jan. 1322 (*ibid.*); capt. and executed 17 Nov. 1326 (Bridl., p. 87).

[1] See below, p. 340.

[2] John Peacock was Mortimer's attorney in 1314-15 (Pipe roll 161, m. 53).

[3] William of Shalford was Mortimer's attorney in north Wales from Easter 1317 to Easter 1319; Robert Malleie in south Wales from 29 Sept. 1317 to 29 Sept. 1321; and William Meverel, clerk, in north Wales from 29 Sept. 1320 to 15 May 1322 (Pipe rolls 164, m. 35, 168, mm. 40, 46, and 169, m. 56). [N.B.—In this and later references to roll 169 Mr. Tout was misled in the 1st edn. by erroneous numbers pencilled on the roll itself. All such references have here been corrected.]

[4] Rob. of Hope, clk., was his attorney in N. Wales from 16 May 1322 (Pipe roll 168, m. 46), and Matthew Lestrange, clk., from Easter 1323 to 29 Sept. 1326 (*ibid.*, 169, m. 52), and also for Amory and Mortimer (*ibid.*, 173, m. 45). In S. Wales Rhys ap Gruffydd was Arundel's lieutenant in 1326 (*C.P.R. 1324-27*, p. 219).

RICHARD OF AMORY, knt. (N.). Apptd. 12 Dec. 1326 (*C.P.R. 1324-27*, p. 338); [superseded by Rog. Mortimer of Wigmore 20 Feb. 1327 (*C.F.R.*, iv, 19)].
RHYS AP HOWEL, knt. (S.). [Superseded by Rog. Mortimer 20 Feb. 1327 (*ibid.*).]

### (2) JUSTICES OF CHESTER [1]

[The non-committal phrase "appointed by" a certain date is used below because for these officers we have no definite writs of appointment, and must not assume that the writs *de intendendo*, informing those within their jurisdiction of their appointment, were always sent out as soon as the appointment was made. For example, in the case of Robert of Holland's first term of office, the writs *de intendendo* were dated 1 Oct. 1307; yet already letters dated 18 Aug. had informed his predecessor of the new appointment.

In this and the list of chamberlains, unprinted records are cited only where the same information is not accessible in print in *D.K., Reps.*, or elsewhere. The records formerly known as recognizance rolls are cited as Chester Enrolments (Ch. Enr.).]

WILL. OF ORMESBY, knt. Acting 10 May (Ch. Plea roll 19, m. 3) to 11 Sept. 1307 (*D.K., 36th Rep.*, App. ii, 35); ordered to surr. 18 Aug. 1307, but order did not reach him till 18 Sept. (Ch. Plea roll 19, m. 11 d).
ROB. OF HOLLAND, knt.[2] Apptd. by 18 Aug. 1307 (*ibid.*, and *cf. C.F.R.*, ii, 5); ordered to surr. 24 Oct. 1309 (*ibid.*, p. 50).
PAYN TIBOTOT, knt. Apptd. by 24 Oct. 1309 (*ibid.*); ordered to surr. 25 Jan. 1312, [having already "treated with contempt" a former mandate] (*C.P.R. 1307-13*, p. 427); [still refusing to surr.] 30 Jan. 1312 (*C.C.R. 1307-13*, p. 396).
ROB. of HOLLAND, knt. Apptd. by 26 Dec. 1311 (*C.F.R.*, ii, 122); acting 24 Nov. 1312 (*C. Chart. R.*, iii, 202); desc. as "late justice," 27 Nov. 1312 (*ibid.*).
HUGH OF AUDLEY, sen., knt.[3] Acting 7 Dec. 1312 (S-Brown, p. 78); from Easter to Mich., 1315 (M.A. 771/8); 31 Mar. 1316 (*C.P.R. 1313-17*, p. 476); 1 Nov. 1317 (*C.C.R. 1313-18*, p. 505); and 30 May 1318 (Ch. Plea roll 31, m. 13).
JOHN OF SAPEY, knt. Acting 11 July 1318 (Ch. Plea roll 31, m. 17d) and 23 Oct. 1318 (Eyre roll 2, m. 3).
ROB. OF HOLLAND, knt.[4] Acting 6 Feb. 1319 (Ch. Plea roll 32, m. 10d); and 26 Jan. 1322 (Ch. Plea roll 34, m. 6).
OLIVER OF INGHAM, knt. Acting 30 Mar. 1322 (*ibid.*, m. 8) to *c.* May, 1325 (Ch. Plea roll 37).

[1] [For list made by Prof. Tait see above, p. 333.]

[2] [Gilbert Singleton acted as his *locum tenens*, 28 May 1308 (*Arley Charters*, p. 35). This new fact is supplied by Mrs. Sharp.]

[3] David and Rob. Hemington acted for him in Apr. and May 1315 (Ormerod, i, 62; Ch. Enr. 7, m. 1 d).

[4] In 1320 and 1321 Rob. of Shirburn was *locum tenens* (*D.K., 36th Rep.* App. ii, p. 472; Jones, p. 80; Ch. Plea roll 33, mm. 3, 13d).

RICH. OF AMORY, knt.[1] Acting 4 June 1325 (Ch. Plea roll 37, m. 9); [2] and 16 Feb. 1328 (Ch. Plea roll 39, m. 10); desc. as "late justice" 28 Feb. 1328 (*C.P.R. 1327-30*, p. 242).

## (3) CHAMBERLAINS OF NORTH WALES

Mr. THO. OF ASTHALL, kg.'s clk.[3] Apptd. 29 Sept. 1302 (Pipe roll 176, m. 53); surr. 11 Oct. 1312 (*C.F.R.*, ii, 148); accounts extant 29 Sept. 1305 to 29 Sept. 1312 (Pipe roll 176, mm. 53-6).

THOMAS OF CHEDWORTH, kg.'s clk. Apptd. 11 Oct. 1312 (*C.F.R.*, ii, 148); surr. 9 Oct. 1315 (*ibid.*, p. 262); acctd. from Mich. 1312 (Pipe roll 159, m. 40) to Mich. 1315 (*ibid.*, 170, m. 55).

WILL. LE DUYN, clk. Apptd. 9 Oct. 1315 as from previous Mich. (*C.F.R.*, ii, 262); ordered 12 Jan. 1317 to surr. [to successor appointed from Easter next, i.e. 3 Ap. 1317] (*ibid.*, p. 315); [described on 17 Aug. 1317 as Master Will. le Hore, late chamberlain of N. Wales (*C.P.R. 1317-21*, p. 12)]; acctd. Mich. 1315 to 1 May 1317 (Pipe roll 163, m. 30).

EDM. OF DYNIETON, kg.'s clk.[4] Apptd. 12 Jan. 1317 from Easter next, i.e. 3 Ap. 1317 (*C.F.R.*, ii, 315); surr. 3 June 1319 (*ibid.*, p. 402); acctd. from 1 May or Easter 1317 to Easter 1319 (Pipe roll 164, m. 35).

HEN. OF SHIREOAKS, kg.'s clk.[5] Apptd. 3 June 1319 (*C.F.R.*, ii, 402) [from previous Easter, i.e. 8 Ap.]; surr. 8 Nov. 1320 (*C.F.R.*, iii, 38); acctd. Easter 1319 to Mich. 1320 (Pipe roll 166, m. 30).

[1] John Hegham and Rob. of Shirburn acted for him in 1326 (Ch. Plea roll 38, m. 8d; Ormerod, i, 62).

[2] [Stated in *D.K.*, *31st Rep.*, App., p. 189, to have been apptd. 31 July, but note in official copy states: "This is doubtful. It does not appear in recognizance roll."]

[3] This person is called "Esthalle" and "Estehalle" in the rolls, but these are also the spellings representing Asthall, Oxfordshire, a village between Witney and Burford. I have, therefore, ventured to describe him by the modern form of the place from which he in all probability derived his surname. On 24 May 1312 orders were issued to release Asthall, who was then imprisoned in the Fleet for not paying his chamberlain's account (*C.C.R. 1307-13*, p. 423). But he remained in prison till Nov. 1331, when he was pardoned on proof that his accounts as chamberlain had been burnt, through no fault of his own (Anct. Pet., file 271, no. 13545, and *C.P.R. 1330-34*, pp. 219, 222). His own property was seized, and it was not until 1332 that his accounts were passed. The delay was largely due to the confusion of the wardrobe accounts (see above, pp. 74-5, 160). Finally the executors of archbishop Reynolds were burdened with a large proportion of Asthall's deficit (Pipe roll 176, mm. 53-6).

[4] An exchequer clerk since 1311 (I.R. 157, m. 2), he is called "Dynyeton," "Dynieton," "Dinyeton," "Dymeton," and "Dynynton" (Pipe roll 163, m. 30), and Seebohm, *Tribal System in Wales*, App., pp. 22-3. *Cf.* Henry of Dynyeton, sheriff of Carnarvon in 1307 (Pipe roll 176, m. 55). The form Dynynton suggests Dennington, Suffolk, as the origin of this name; but it is never used in his own accounts.

[5] [Mr. Tout notes: "wardrobe clk. 1319-20 (Add. MS. 17362, m. 13 d) but never receives robes.]"

ADAM OF WETTENHALL, kg.'s clk. Apptd. 8 Nov. 1320 (*C.F.R.*, iii, 38); surr. 11 May 1323 (*ibid.*, p. 208); acctd. Mich. 1320 to Easter 1323 (Pipe roll 168, m. 46).

ROBERT POWER, kg.'s clk.[1] Apptd. 11 May 1323 (*C.F.R.*, iii, 208); acting 20 Oct. 1326 (*ibid.*, p. 421); acctd. Easter 1323 (Pipe roll 169, mm. 52, 53) to 31 Oct. 1327 (*ibid.*, 171, m. 40, 173, m. 45).

### (4) CHAMBERLAINS OF SOUTH WALES

WILL. OF ROGATE. Acting before Oct. 1307 (Pipe roll 159, m. 36).

Mr. WILL. LE HORE. Apptd. 4 Oct. 1307 (*C.F.R.*, ii, 9); surr. 25 Aug. 1312 (*ibid.*, p. 144); acctd. Mich. 1307 to 25 Aug. 1312 (Pipe roll 159, m. 36).

ROBERT, prior of Carmarthen.[2] Apptd. 25 Aug. 1312 (*C.F.R.*, ii, 144); surr. 5 May 1315 (*ibid.*, p. 246); acctd. 25 Aug. 1312 to 5 May 1315 (Pipe roll 159, m. 37, and 161, m. 53).

Mr. RICH. OF MUSTLEWICK, clk. Apptd. 5 May 1315 (*C.F.R.*, ii, 246); acctd. 5 May 1315 to Mich. 1317 (Pipe roll 162, m. 35d).

WALTER OF FULBOURN, clk. Apptd. before Mich. 1317; surr. 11 Sept. 1318 (*C.F.R.*, ii, 375); acctd. Mich. 1317 to Mich. 1318 (Pipe roll 168, m. 40).

ROBERT, prior *ut sup.*[3] Apptd. 11 Sept. 1318 (*C.F.R.*, ii, 375); acctd. 20 Sept. 1318 to 29 Sept. 1321 (Pipe roll 169, m. 56).

Mr. THOMAS DOUN,[4] clk., constable of Carmarthen. Apptd. to act with the prior from 29 Sept. 1321 (Pipe roll 171, m. 35); Rob. and Tho. acctd. jointly 29 Sept. 1321 to 29 Sept. 1325 (*ibid.*).

WILL. OF OTTERHAMPTON, kg.'s clk. Apptd. 12 Jan. 1324 (*C.F.R.*, iii, 253), but letters of appointment cancelled.

JOHN OF CHANDOS, prior of Carmarthen,[5] and Mr. THOMAS DOUN, clk. Acctd. jointly, 29 Sept. 1325 to 23 Oct. 1331 (Pipe roll 172, m. 47, and 178, m. 43).

[1] William de la Bataille was Power's attorney from 29 Sept. 1326 onwards (Pipe roll 173, m. 45; [*cf.* also *ibid.*, 176.] Power sent in a separate account as escheator (*ibid.*, 169, m. 53 d).

[2] From 29 Sept. 1314 to 5 May 1315, Henry of Somery, canon of Carmarthen, was the prior's attorney (Pipe roll 161, m. 53).

[3] Henry of Somery, canon of Carmarthen, was prior Robert's attorney from 20 Sept. 1318 to 29 Sept. 1325 (Pipe roll 169, m. 56, and 171, m. 35). Robert resigned his priorship before the end of his nominal tenure of office, for on 9 Oct. 1324 licence to elect his successor was issued (*C.P.R. 1324-27*, p. 33).

[4] Doun, also called Deyn and Doyn (? Dwnn, a well-known Welsh name) was "clericus assignatus eidem priori ad officium camerarie predicte una cum prefato priore exercendum." He is often called chamberlain, for instance in *C.F.R.*, iii, 342. Henry of Caerau was his attorney from 29 Sept. 1321 to 29 Sept. 1323 (Pipe roll 171, m. 35).

[5] His name comes from *C.P.R. 1324-27*, p. 45, the record of the confirmation of his election and the order for the restitution of his temporalities, dated 10 Nov. 1324. As canon of Carmarthen he had brought the king the news of his predecessor's resignation in October. John Winter, canon of Carmarthen, and Steph. Jacobs were attorneys for prior John up to 29 Sept. 1326 (Pipe roll 172, m. 47), after which his attorneys were John Goch and Will. Josephs (*ibid.*, 178, m. 43).

### (5) Chamberlains of Chester

[This revised list is based largely upon a list appended by Mrs. W. D. Sharp to her Ph.D. (Manchester) thesis on "Some aspects of the administration of Cheshire in the later middle ages."]

Hugh of Standish, clk. Acting 17 Dec. 1308 (Ch. Plea roll 21, m. 9 d); desc. as "late chamberlain" 11 Apr. 1309 (Ch. Enr. 2, m. 2).

John of Dalton, clk. Acting after 11 Apr. 1309 (*ibid.*) probably till Nov. 1309 (Ch. Plea roll 22, m. 8 d).

Will. Stonehall, clk. Acting 20 Nov. 1309 (Ch. Enr. 3, m. 1) till after Sept. 1311 (Ch. Plea roll 23, m. 47).

Hugh of Brichull. Acting from 22 Feb. 1312 (Ch. Enr. 5, m. 1).

Mr. Steph. of Cheshunt, clk. Acting 7 Dec. 1312 to 15 Sept. 1313 (S-Brown, p. 78); acting for part of year Mich. 1314 to Mich. 1315 (Ch. Enr. 7, m. 1).

Walter of Fulbourn, clk. Acting 9 June to 29 Sept. 1315 (S-Brown, p. 86).

Will. of Burstow, clk. Acting Mich. 1315 to Mich. 1316 (*D.K., 36th Rep.*, App. ii, p. 482); also *c.* 24 Ap. 1317 (*ibid.*, p. 191) and 30 Oct. 1317;[1] reapptd. 10 Dec. 1317 (Ormerod, i, 59); acting 28 May 1320 (*D.K., 36th Rep.*, App. ii, pp. 360-1).

Rich. of Bury, kg.'s clk.[2] Acctd. 26 May to 30 Sept. 1320 (Jones, p. 74 and S.-Brown, p. 89); acting 9 Ap. 1321 (*D.K., 36th Rep.*, App. ii, p. 361); acctd. Mich. 1322 to Mich. 1323 (K.R.M.R. 106, m. 130 d); descd. 18 July 1324 as late chamberlain (Ch. Enr. 13, m. 2).

Mr. Will. of Easington, clk. Acting Mich. 1324 to Mich. 1325 (Ch. Enr. 13, m. 1); acctd. 29 Sept. 1325 to 21 Dec. 1326 (Jones, p. 81).

John Paynel, parson of Rostherne. Apptd. 17 Dec. 1326 (Pipe roll 174, m. 44); acctd. 17 Dec. 1326 to 24 Jan. 1327 (Jones, p. 84) and till 13 Mar. 1328 (Pipe roll 174, m. 44).

## G.—OFFICERS OF IRELAND

The normal governor of Ireland was called the justice. He was appointed by letters patent issued from the English chancery, and was assigned a salary of £500 a year.[3] For this he was compelled to maintain at his own expense a corps of twenty men-at-arms with armoured horses.[4] Sometimes a higher dignitary was appointed,

[1] [Reference given in 1st edn., *viz.*, *Cl.* 178, cannot be traced; receipts from Will. as chamberlain are recorded in wardrobe receipts for 1317-18 (*Chapters*, ii, 363).]

[2] "Ricardus de sancto Edmundo," probably rightly identified with Richard of Bury, afterwards bishop of Durham, who was certainly clerk to the justice of Chester in 1319 (*D.K., 31st Rep.*, App., p. 181).

[3] *C.P.R. 1307-13*, p. 568.

[4] *Cf. ibid.*, *1317-21*, pp. 558 and 578, when the justice was himself reckoned as the twentieth man.

to whom wider powers were assigned, with the title of king's lieutenant and keeper of Ireland. The three cases of this under Edward II include the cancelled appointment of the earl of Ulster, the famous lieutenancy of Gaveston during his first exile, and the first period of office of Roger Mortimer of Wigmore, which covered the critical years of the invasion of Edward Bruce. Mortimer was, however, generally addressed as justice, even in official letters, and during his second term of office he was appointed by no other title. Both the justice and the lieutenant were frequently absentees, in which case they appointed a *locum tenens* or deputy. The justice could continue under a lieutenant and Wogan continued to act as justice all through the time of Gaveston's lieutenancy. In the subjoined lists justices are printed in roman capitals, king's lieutenants in italic capitals, and deputies of either in small italics asterisked. This latter method of printing has been also adopted in all later lists which include deputies and lieutenants.

Gaveston's position was unique. The majority of the other rulers of Ireland under Edward II[1] were either Irish magnates, such as the earls of Ulster, Carrick, Kildare, and Louth, or Irish ecclesiastics, such as archbishop Bicknor of Dublin, the only clerical justice of the reign, who, however, was a king's clerk in England before he went to Ireland with Wogan before 1305. Other governors, such as Theobald of Verdon and Roger Mortimer, had great territorial interests in Ireland, these two dividing between them the ancient Lacy palatinate of Meath. Three only had no connexions with the higher Norman-Irish aristocracy, namely Sir John Wogan, a Pembrokeshire vassal of the house of Valence, John Darcy, a Lincolnshire baron,[2] and Ralph Gorges, a Somerset landowner. Of these three all, except Wogan, were summoned as barons to the English parliament. Wogan established a branch of his house in Ireland, though not previously belonging to that country.

Under the justice was a system of administration which reproduced that of England with extreme fidelity. There was an Irish council, chancery, exchequer and two benches. I have contented myself here, however, with giving lists of the Irish chancellors and treasurers. It would be a simple matter to increase the number of

[1] [Mr. Tout notes, from an unpublished M.A. thesis by Dr. Arthur Redford, as follows: "Periods according to A.R. (1) The collapse of Wogan's policy 1307-14 = military reaction (Gaveston, Burgh, Butler) as of tradition; (2) Rule of baronial opposition, 1314-20 (Verdon, Butler, Mortimer); (3) Rule of new earls, 1320-23 (Kildare, Louth); (4) Administrative development and political decay (1323-27) = the Despensers' policy and radical revival of Wogan's officialism with stricter English control (John Darcy).]

[2] [*A Life of John Darcy, 1280-1347*, based mainly on the P.R.O. calendars and good secondary authorities, was published by Mr. R. F. D'Arcy in 1933.]

the lists of Irish officers, on the lines adopted here for the corresponding English offices, since the departments of Irish government were staffed on exactly the same lines as their English equivalents, and were so often filled up from England that the patent and other chancery rolls afford us ample material. I am inclined to believe that the study in detail of the administrative history of Ireland would be of value not only on its own account but as throwing considerable light on parallel developments in England. In any case the Irish equivalents in no wise lagged behind their English counterparts. Thus we have the record of a baron of the Dublin exchequer being appointed by patent before there is evidence of a similar appointment in England.[1] Similarly there was a chief baron, distinguished above his fellow barons, in Ireland almost as early as in England.[2]

The majority of the Dublin officials seem at this period to have been Englishmen; this is certainly the case with the chancellors and treasurers in our lists. Even the episcopal chancellors and treasurers were generally Englishmen; thus William Fitzjohn, successively bishop of Ossory and archbishop of Cashel, was emphatically English.[3] Alexander Bicknor, archbishop of Dublin after 1314, came from the southern march of Wales.[4] John Leek had been chaplain and almoner of Edward II, who had failed to establish him in the Scottish bishopric of Dunkeld.[5] As regards the lesser dignitaries, the majority of them seem to have had quite subordinate posts in England. They were not, however, raised to the highest Irish posts until they had done some preliminary work in subordinate offices. Adam of Herwington is the chief exception to this rule of official insignificance, as before he came to Ireland he acted, between 1314 and 1322, in the important office of keeper of the writs and rolls of the English common bench. With one exception, none of the Irish chancellors and treasurers took much share in Edward II's extra-Irish business. Archbishop Bicknor, however, played an important part in French and Gascon affairs

[1] *C.P.R. 1292-1301*, p. 145; the date is 1 Sept. 1295. See above, p. 300, n. 2.

[2] Walter of Islip was succeeded by William of Moenes as chief baron of the exchequer, Dublin, on 1 June, 1311 (*C.P.R. 1307-13*, p. 354).

[3] *C.P.R. 1317-21*, p. 137.

[4] Bicknor is the name of two villages in the forest of Dean. Alexander had, in 1311, licence to crenellate his house at Ruardean, Gloucestershire (*ibid.*, *1307-13*, p. 355).

[5] *Ibid.*, *1307-13*, p. 202. [He was in Edw. of Carnarvon's service as early as 1300 (E.A. 355/28, 360/17) and was his chaplain and almoner in 1303 (*ibid.*, 363/18, f. 2). By 1305 he was high in favour, and Edw. was urging the interests both of John himself and his relatives (*Letters of Edw.*, pp. 84, 90, 146, 157). His provision as archbishop of Dublin in 1311 provoked complaint in Ireland, for the Dublin chapter had elected Alex. Bicknor (*C. Chanc. Warrants, 1244-1326*, p. 360. My attention was drawn to this by my pupil Miss M. E. Lack, B.A., who is engaged on a study of the almoners of Edw. I and Edw. II).]

from 1324-25 and was a conspicuous supporter of Isabella and Mortimer in the rebellion of 1326. The archbishopric of Dublin was the chief reward within the scope of the king's clerks in Ireland. Not only did Leek and Bicknor hold this office, but Thornbury aspired to it in rivalry to Bicknor after Leek's death. However, Thornbury's own death avoided a prolonged contest. It is to be set down to the credit of these alien administrators that Leek and Bicknor were chiefly instrumental in procuring the foundation of the medieval university of Dublin. I have no information as to Roger Outlaw's origin. He probably owed his appointment as chancellor to the good service which he did in defending Ireland against Edward Bruce and the Scots.[1]

The subordination of Ireland was ensured by the Dublin treasurers being required, like the constables of Bordeaux, and the chamberlains of Chester and Wales, to account before the exchequer at Westminster. There is abundant evidence of the periodic crossing of the channel by Irish exchequer officials for the purposes of this account. Sometimes special officers were sent from England to enquire into or redress the state of affairs in Ireland. Thus the well-known John of Hotham was sent in August 1314 to "supervise the estate of the exchequer of Dublin."[2] The Dublin treasurer was expected to make large contributions towards the expenses of the war against Scotland, and surprisingly large sums were occasionally rendered.

### (1) Justices and Lieutenants of Ireland

John Wogan, knt. Apptd. 18 Oct. 1295 (*C.P.R. 1292-1301*, p. 155); ordered to surr. 30 Ap. 1313[3] (*C.P.R. 1307-13*, p. 568).

*Edmund Butler.** Desc. as late deputy of Wogan, 22 May 1313 (*ibid.*, p. 595).

*Richard de Burgh*, earl of Ulster. Apptd. kg.'s lieut. 15 June 1308 (*ibid.*, p. 83).

*Peter of Gaveston*, earl of Cornwall. Apptd kg.'s lieut. 16 June 1308 (*Foedera*, ii, 51); still acting 28 June 1309 (*C.P.R. 1307-13*, p. 122); called late lieut. 7 Oct. 1309 (*ibid.*, p. 194).

Theobald of Verdon, baron. Apptd. 30 Ap. 1313 (*ibid.*, p. 568); ordered to surr. 4 Jan. 1315 (*C.P.R. 1313-17*, p. 207).

Edmund Butler, earl of Carrick after 1 Sept. 1315. Apptd. 4 Jan. 1315 (*Foedera*, ii, 260); ordered to surr. 23 Nov. 1316 (*C.P.R. 1313-17*, p. 563).

*Roger Mortimer of Wigmore*, baron. Apptd. kg.'s lieut. 23 Nov. 1316 (*ibid.*).

[1] *C.P.R. 1317-21*, p. 197.

[2] *C.P.R. 1313-17*, p. 165. On 1 Sept. 1315 Hotham was empowered, jointly with the justice, to remove "insufficient officers in Ireland and appoint others" (*Foedera*, ii, 276).

[3] During the lieutenancy of Gaveston Wogan continued to act, even during the period when Gaveston was resident in Ireland.

Mr. *Will. Fitzjohn,** archbp. of Cashel, chancellor. Acting as Roger's deputy, 11 Aug. 1318 (*C.P.R. 1317-21,* p. 196).

Mr. Alex. Bicknor, archbp. of Dublin. Apptd. 11 Aug. 1318 (*ibid.*) ; ordered to surr. 15 Mar. 1319 (*ibid.*, p. 317).

Roger Mortimer of Wigmore, baron. Apptd. 15 Mar. 1319 (*ibid.*) ; ordered to surr. 1 Feb. 1321 (*ibid.*, p. 558).

Ralph of Gorges, baron. Apptd. 1 Feb. 1321 (*ibid.*) ; acting 30 Mar. 1321 (*C.C.R. 1318-23,* p. 295).

Tho. Fitzjohn (Fitzgerald), 2nd earl of Kildare. Apptd. 23 Ap. 1321 (*C.P.R. 1317-21,* p. 578) ; ordered to surr. 21 May 1321 (*ibid.*, p. 588).

John of Birmingham, 1st earl of Louth. Apptd. 21 May 1321 (*ibid.*) ; ordered to surr. 18 Nov. 1323 (*C.P.R. 1321-24,* p. 348).

John Darcy, baron. Apptd. 18 Nov. 1323 (*ibid.*) ; acting 31 Dec. 1326 (*C.P.R. 1324-27,* p. 344).

## (2) Chancellors of Ireland

Mr. Tho. Cantock, bp. of Emly after 1306. Apptd. 28 Oct. 1291 (*C.P.R. 1281-92,* p. 448) ; reapptd. 5 June 1308 (*C.P.R. 1307-13,* p. 76) ; died before 27 Feb. 1309 (*C.F.R.*, ii, 39).

Walt. of Thornbury, kg.'s clk., chan. of Dublin exch. since 1307. Apptd. 4 Mar. 1309 (*C.P.R. 1307-13,* p. 106) ; died before 28 Jan. 1314 (*C.F.R.*, ii, 188).

Rich. of Bereford, kg.'s clk. Apptd. 1 Ap. 1314 (*C.P.R. 1313-17,* p. 102) ; not chancellor by 29 June 1316 (*ibid.*, p. 486).

Mr. Will. Fitzjohn, bp. of Ossory since 1302. Apptd. 8 Aug. 1316 (*ibid.*, p. 524).

Nich. of Balscott, kg.'s clk., chief baron of Dublin exch. since 1313. Apptd. 2 June 1317 (*ibid.*, p. 658).

Mr. Will. Fitzjohn, archbp. elect of Cashel. Apptd. 4 Aug. 1317 (*C.P.R. 1317-21,* p. 10) ; ordered to surr. 4 Jan. 1322 (*C.P.R. 1321-24,* p. 46).

Roger Outlaw, prior of Hosp. of St. John of Jerusalem in Ireland. Apptd. 4 Jan. 1322 (*ibid.*) ; still acting 2 Oct. 1327 (*ibid.*, p. 175) [and as late as 22 Ap. 1328 (*C.C.R. 1327-30,* p. 275)].

## (3) Treasurers of the Exchequer at Dublin

Rich. of Bereford, kg.'s clk. Apptd. 8 June 1300 (*C.F.R.*, i, 429) ; ordered to surr. 28 Oct. 1307 (*C.P.R. 1307-13,* p. 13).

Alex. Bicknor, kg.'s clk., later archbp. of Dublin. Apptd. 28 Oct. 1307 (*ibid.*) ; ordered to surr. 20 May 1313 (*ibid.*, p. 585).

*Walter of Thornbury.** Apptd. 2 June 1311 as deputy while Bicknor attended the Council of Vienne (*ibid.*, p. 351).

John of Leek, archbp. of Dublin [since 1311]. Apptd. 20 May 1313 (*ibid.*. p. 585) ; died before 8 Aug. 1313 (*C.P.R. 1313-17,* p. 11).

Mr. Walter of Islip, kg.'s clk., baron of Dublin exch. since 1308. Apptd. 2 Feb. 1314 (*ibid.*, p. 82) ; [summoned to England] 4 Aug. 1317 (*C.C.R. 1313-18,* p. 561) ; addressed in Ireland 23 July 1318 (*C.C.R. 1318-23,* p. 5) and 28 June 1319 (*ibid.*, p. 90).

*Nicholas of Balscott*,* clk. Apptd. as deputy during Islip's absence, 4 Aug. 1317 (*C.C.R. 1313-18*, p. 561); removed from all offices 23 July 1318 (*C.C.R. 1318-23*, p. 5).

JOHN OF COGAN, kg.'s clk.[1] Apptd. 8 Aug. 1321 (*C.F.R.*, iii, 66); ordered to surr. 15 Mar. 1322 (*ibid.*, p. 109).

WALTER OF ISLIP. Apptd. 15 Mar. 1322 (*ibid.*); ordered to surr. 7 Dec. 1325 (*C.P.R.*, *1324-27*, p. 197).

AD. OF HERWINGTON, kg.'s clk., chief baron of Dublin exch. since 1323. Apptd. to "custody of the treasurership of the exch., Dublin" 7 Dec. 1325 (*ibid.*); ordered to surr. 23 July 1326 (*C.F.R.*, iii, 402).

JOHN OF COGAN, kg.'s clk. Apptd. 23 July 1326 (*ibid.*).

## H.—CHIEF OFFICERS OF SCOTLAND

The method of governing Scotland under its English king was first elaborated in 1305, after the conquest had apparently been definitively effected. It is elucidated in detail by a remarkable document on the Scottish king's household, originating in the English exchequer, but now among the manuscripts of Corpus Christi College, Cambridge, which has been published by the late Miss Bateson.[2] It belongs to the period between the conquest of Scotland and the dissolution of the order of the Temple, and if not perhaps descriptive of a system that ever got into real working order, is at least evidence of what a good many English officials, and a certain number of Scots of English sympathies, wished to establish. It shows a real desire to carry on the traditional Scottish offices and customs, with, however, certain conspicuous amendments suggested by English experience, notably in the case of the privy seal. Unluckily for the projectors of this system, it was destroyed by the success of Robert Bruce. After this there is something pathetic in the persistence with which ministers were appointed to carry out the government of Scotland on behalf of the English king. At their head was the king's justice or lieutenant of Scotland, who, as under Edward I, was an English nobleman of high rank. He received 10 marks a day as wages, but was required out of it to maintain the large number of sixty men-at-arms of his own private household.[3] Under him acted the chancellor and chamberlain of Scotland, both of these officials being promoted clerks of the English king. The controller, also a royal clerk, was

[1] Cogan was twice previously appointed in this year, on 1 Feb. and 31 May 1321, but the entries were cancelled in favour of the August one (*C.F.R.*, iii, 46, 59).

[2] *The Scottish King's Household and other Fragments* in Scottish Hist. Soc. Miscellany, 1904, ii, 1-43. Compare Miss Bateson's notice of the same document in the *Juridical Review*, Dec. 1901 and March 1902, Edinburgh. Compare M. R. James, *Catalogue of C.C.C. MSS.*, I, 73.

[3] *Foedera*, ii, 4, 6, 70.

the chief subordinate of and official check upon the chamberlain. Chamberlain was the traditional name of the first financial minister of Scotland, just as was the case in Wales and Chester. Generally the appointment was at this time made to the office of chamberlain and receiver. Except Hugh Cressingham, the unpopular English clerk appointed as treasurer in 1296, and slain at Stirling Bridge in 1297, there were no treasurers of Scotland before the fifteenth century. Sometimes, however, the chamberlains were informally described as treasurers by Englishmen.[1] None of the English officials contained in our lists could ever have exercised much power, and, after Bannockburn, their position was, outside Berwick, purely nominal. Nevertheless the farce was kept up till at least 1317. By that time the various offices were combined under the same person, and he was to seal "on the view of the receiver of stores at Berwick."[2] The chancellor and chamberlain of Berwick in later times[3] carried on the tradition, though limited to the administration of a single Scottish town, the sole permanent result of the Edwardian attack on Scotland.

### (1) Keepers and Lieutenants of Scotland

Aymer of Valence, earl of Pembroke. Reapptd. 30 Aug. 1307 (*Foedera*, ii, 4).

John of Brittany, earl of Richmond. Apptd. 13 Sept. 1307 (*ibid.*, p. 6), with payment to begin from Mich.; reapptd. 15 Jan. 1308 (*C.P.R. 1307-13*, p. 44).

*William of Ros*,* of Helmsley, baron. Apptd. lieut. of keeper, 20 May 1308 (*Parl. Writs*, II, ii, 372).

Rob. of Umfraville, earl of Angus, and Will. of Ros, of Helmsley, apptd. joint lieutenants and keepers, 21 June 1308 (*Foedera*, ii, 51).

John of Seagrave, baron. Apptd. keeper, 10 Mar. 1309 (*ibid.*, p. 70).

Rob. of Clifford, baron. Apptd. keeper, 15 Dec. (*ibid.*, p. 100).

John of Seagrave, baron. Apptd. keeper, 10 Ap. 1310 (*ibid.*, p. 106).

Aymer of Valence, earl of Pembroke. Apptd. keeper and lieut. till the kg.'s arrival, 24 Mar. 1314 (*ibid.*, p. 245).

### (2) Chancellors of Scotland

Mr. Will. of Bevercotes, kg.'s clk. Acting 8 Dec. 1304 (*C.C.R. 1302-7*, p. 229), acting 20 May 1308 (*C.C.R. 1307-13*, p. 66); acting 1 Nov. 1315 (*C.P.R. 1313-17*, p. 365); desc. as late chancellor 2 Feb. 1316 (*Cal. Doc. Scot.*, iii, 90).

James of Broughton, kg.'s clk., controller of chamberlain of Scotland after 1 July 1315. Apptd. 17 Jun. 1317 (*ibid.*, pp. 107-8).

[1] *C.P.R. 1307-13*, pp. 116, 464.

[2] *Cal. Doc. Scot.*, iii, 107-8. When Berwick was for a time captured he lost his indentures (*ibid.*, iii, 166).

[3] *Ibid.*, iii, 199, 208.

### (3) Chamberlains and Receivers of Scotland

John of Sandall, kg.'s clk. Acting 31 Mar. 1305 (*Hist. Doc. Scot.*, ii, 488) ; ordered on 10 Sept. 1307 to surr. at Mich. (*C.P.R. 1307-13*, p. 6).

Mr. Eustace of Cottesbach, clk. Apptd. 10 Sept. 1307, to act from Mich. (*ibid.*) ; ordered to surr. 14 Mar. 1309 (*ibid.*, p. 104).

*Rob. Heron*,* kg.'s clk., controller of Scotland. Apptd. his deputy 10 Sept. 1307 (*ibid.*, p. 6).

Mr. John of Weston, kg.'s clk. Apptd. 14 Mar. 1309 (*ibid.*, p. 104) ; ordered to surr. 4 June 1315 (*C.F.R.*, ii, 250 ; *Cal. Doc. Scot.*, iii, 82).

Stephen le Blunt, kg.'s clk. Apptd. 1 June 1315 (*Foedera*, ii, 268) ; ordered to surr. 1 July 1315 (*C.F.R.*, ii, 252).

Mr. John of Weston, kg.'s clk. Apptd. 1 July 1315 (*ibid.*) ; accused of fraud and peculation before the council, 4 June 1317 (*Cal. Doc. Scot.*, iii, 106-7) ; called " late chamberlain," 16 Oct. 1317 (*C.P.R. 1317-21*, p. 34).

James of Broughton, " chancellor of Scotland." Apptd. chamberlain, 17 June 1317 (*Cal. Doc. Scot.*, iii, 107).

### (4) Controllers of the Chamberlains of Scotland

Robert Heron, kg.'s clk. Acting 10 Sept. 1307 (*C.P.R. 1307-13*, p. 6).

Robert of Well, kg.'s clk. Apptd. 2 Aug. 1311 (*ibid.*, p. 381).

James of Broughton, kg.'s clk. Apptd. 1 July 1315 (*ibid.*, *1313-17*, p. 305).

## I.—OFFICERS OF THE DUCHY OF GASCONY

The two chief officers of the English king in his capacity of duke of Gascony were, first, the seneschal, whose position corresponded to that of the justices in Wales and Chester, and, secondly, the constable of Bordeaux, who, like the chamberlains in Wales and Chester, had the supreme responsibility for finance. As regards the reign of Edward I, full details of the holders of these offices and their functions are given in M. Bémont's admirable introduction to the *Rôles Gascons* of Edward I.[1] It is much to be regretted that we have no such help for the reign of Edward II, whose Gascon rolls remain unpublished and uncalendared. Some help is got, however, from the casual and unsatisfying, but generally accurate, excerpts in Carte's *Gascon Rolls*,[2] from the numerous extracts from the rolls in Rymer's *Foedera*, and also from the abbé Tauzin's *Les Seneschaux anglais en Guyenne*.[3] For the latter reign

[1] *R.G.*, III, xix-cii. [Mr. Tout notes in his copy : " The constable's office at the castle of L'Ombrière is sometimes called *scaccarium nostrum Burdegale*, as on 6 June 1276 (*R.G.*, ii, 16) "]

[2] Thomas Carte, *Catalogue des rolles gascons, normans, et françois*. 2 vols. London, 1743.

[3] *Revue de Gascogne*, t. xxxii, pp. 353 *et seq.* This list is unluckily not very accurate.

we have chiefly to notice the short duration of the various seneschalships, the long time which often ensued between the appointment and the actual taking up of office, and the frequent absence of the seneschals in attending the parliament of Paris or in going on missions to Avignon and elsewhere. Accordingly the duties were often discharged by lieutenants of the seneschal. The result was that the traditional seneschal's fee of 2000 " good small pounds of Tours," equivalent to £500 sterling,[1] was inadequate, the more so as he was expected to pay the wages of his deputies, which were usually ten shillings a day.[2] Accordingly, " reasonable expenses " were also allowed the seneschal, when absent on duty at the French court or elsewhere, and sometimes considerable gifts were made in addition.[3] The seneschal was sometimes required to provide a retinue, as, for instance, John of Hastings, who, when lieutenant of Edward I, received wages at the rate of £1095 per annum, " for himself and thirty men-at-arms staying on the king's service in the duchy." [4]

The authority of the seneschal is sometimes distinguished from that of the royal lieutenant. Normally the same person acted in both capacities, but sometimes, especially in critical periods, or when a very great personage was sent to Gascony, the seneschal's authority was subordinated to that of the king's lieutenant. On these occasions the latter was primarily the military commander, and the seneschal the administrator.[5] The chief instance in our period is that of Edmund of Kent, under whom the seneschal continued to discharge the routine duties of the government in his presence, or to represent him in his absence. On several occasions special commissions from England limited the authority of the seneschal, exploited Gascon revenues in English interests, aimed at promoting administrative reform in Gascony, or simply represented its duke in the unending negotiations with France. Allusion to these has been made elsewhere.

In all the Gascon lists the names of deputies of the various ministers are printed in italic capitals.

[1] G.R. 24, m. 5 : " duo millia librarum bonarum paruarum turonensium quarum quatuor valent unum sterlingum."

[2] *C.P.R. 1317-21*, p. 53, gives this as the sum received by Amanieu du Fossat, in 1309-10. The king paid Amanieu, but deducted the sum from the seneschal's wages. Compare *Foedera*, ii, 345, for the case of Anthony di Passano.

[3] For instances of these payments see G.R. 24, m. 5 ; *Foedera*, ii, 221, records a supplementary grant to Amaury de Craon of £5000 of Tours ; *cf. ibid.*, ii, 377, 404, for expenses and gift to W. Montagu.

[4] *C.P.R. 1317-21*, p. 53. These " wages " were still unpaid in 1317, as were those of Hastings as lieutenant of Edward II. The latter were at the more normal rate of £1 7s. 4¾d. a day, *i.e.* nearly, but not quite, £500 a year.

[5] Bémont, *R.G.*, III, lxxxiii.

## (1) SENESCHALS OF GASCONY

[*Note.*—A few details in this and the next list have been added from an unpublished Ph.D. (London) thesis, on the political and administrative history of Gascony, by Miss E. Pole Stuart. These are indicated by S.]

JOHN OF HAVERING, knt. Apptd. (for second time) 24 March 1305 (Bémont, *R.G.*, nos. 4685-4689); addressed as seneschal on 6 Oct. [1309] [1] (*Foedera*, ii, 95).

GUY FERRE, knt. Apptd. (for second time) 12 Mar. 1308 (G.R. 24, m. 24); ["late seneschal" on 8 May 1310 (Bémont, *R.G.*, III, lxxiv, n. 13)].

*AMANIEU DU FOSSAT*. Ferre's lieutenant on 15 May 1309 (G.R. 24).

JOHN OF HASTINGS, knt. Apptd. (for second time) "locum tenens regis et senescallus," 24 Oct. 1309 (*Foedera*, ii, 95); paid wages as seneschal 26 Oct. 1309 to 15 Apr. 1310 (*C.P.R. 1317-21*, p. 53).

*AMANIEU DU FOSSAT*. His lieutenant for same period (*ibid.*).

*ASSIEU DE GOULARD*. His lieutenant, 13 Aug. 1311 (G.R. 30, m. 8).

JOHN OF FERRERS, knt. Apptd. 24 Jan. 1312 (G.R. 25, m. 6); [summoned to England in Aug., died, perhaps by poison, Sept. 1312 (S. from *Foedera*, ii, 177 and *Flores Hist.*, iii, 153)].

*JORDAN MORANT*, clk. His lieut. 26 June 1312 (G.R. 25, m. 1).

STEPHEN DE FERREOL, lord of Tonneins, knt. Apptd. 28 Oct. 1312 (*Foedera*, ii, 185); Pembroke empowered to revoke his commission and appoint another, 3 Feb. 1313 (*ibid.*, p. 198).

AMAURY DE CRAON,[2] knt., kg.'s kinsman. Apptd. [5] July 1313 (G.R. 26, m. 3).

*GAUCELIN DE CAMPAGNE*. His lieut. 18 June 1316 (G.R. 30, m. 2).

GILBERT PECCHÉ,[3] knt., kg.'s kinsman. Apptd. 18 July 1316 (G.R. 31, m. 12); acting 12 Sept. 1317 (*C.C.R. 1313-18*, p. 567).

ANTONIO DI PASSANO, of Genoa, knt. Apptd. 3 Nov. 1317 (G.R. 32, m. 16, *Foedera*, ii, 345); summoned to England 17 Nov. 1318 (G.R. 32, m. 5).

[1] [Not 1308, as in 1st edn. This was probably during the absence of Guy Ferre at Avignon (Bémont, *R.G.*, III, lxxiv). The statement made in 1st edn. that John was acting as seneschal on 17 Oct. 1307 was based on an *inspeximus* cited by Bémont, *op. cit.*, p. lx, but this refers to an act of 24 Nov. 1306, before Guy Ferre's appointment (*C.P.R. 1307-13*, p. 9).]

[2] See for the Craon family, Bémont (*R.G.*, III, l-lii), who refers to B. de Broussillon, *La maison de Craon* (1893). Amaury's grandfather, Amaury IV de Craon, married Isabella de la Marche, half sister of Henry III. His father, son of this couple, Amaury V de Craon, was lieutenant of Gascony, 1289-92, and died in 1293. Edward II's officer was therefore Amaury VI of Craon. Créon is in Anjou, dep. Mayenne, arr. Chateau Gontier. The family also held Sablé in the same district.

[3] I do not know why Pecché is called king's kinsman. Perhaps his grandmother Eva, "de partibus transmarinis oriunda" (*Liber memorandorum ecclesie de Bernewell*, p. 48), the wife of an earlier Gilbert Pecché, was one of the Lusignan brood. This would perhaps help to account for their son, father of the seneschal, bequeathing the patronage of Barnwell priory and much of his property to Edward I and queen Eleanor (*ibid.*, p. 50.) The name, in Latin "Peccatum," Maitland boldly wrote as Pecché, modern form Peachey (*ibid.*, Introd., xlvi).

*Amanieu du Fossat.* 17 Nov. 1318 "regimen senescalcie custodiendum quousque prefatus senescallus noster redierit" (G.R. 32, m. 5).

William of Montagu, knt. Apptd. 20 Nov. 1318 (*ibid.* and *Foedera*, ii, 377); dead by 6 Nov. 1319 (*v. infra*).

*Amanieu du Fossat.* Apptd. keeper 6 Nov. 1319, after Montagu's death, "quousque aliud inde duxerimus demandandum" (G.R. 33, m. 16 and *Foedera*, ii, 406).

Maurice of Berkeley, knt., kg.'s kinsman. Apptd. 28 Feb. 1320 (*Foedera*, ii, 418).

Amaury de Craon. Again apptd. 22 July 1320 (G.R. 33, m. 7); acting 16 Feb. 1322 (*C.C.R. 1318-23*, p. 522); [resigned before 11 Ap. 1322 (S. from *Foedera*, ii, 483)].

Fulk Lestrange, knt. Apptd. 11 Ap. 1322 (G.R. 35, m. 15); [dead by 23 Jan. 1324 (S. from *Cal. Inq. p.m.*, V, no. 516)].

Ralph Basset of Drayton, knt. Apptd. 11 June 1323 (G.R. 35, m. 10); removed before 15 Mar. 1324 (*Foedera*, ii, 547).

*Rob. of Shirland*, mayor of Bordeaux. Apptd. keeper "quousque de senescallo ibidem ordinaverimus" (G.R. 35, m. 6).

Richard Grey, knt. Apptd. 1 Ap. 1324 (G.R. 35, m. 4); still acting, 10 July 1324 (*Foedera*, ii, 560).

Edmund of Woodstock, earl of Kent. Apptd. "locum tenentem . . . et capitaneum et ductorem," [1] 20 July 1324 (*Foedera*, ii, 562).

*Ralph Basset*, knt. Apptd. seneschal under Kent, 21 July 1324 (G.R. 36, m. 30).

*John of Wisham*,[2] knt. Apptd. 18 Nov. 1324 (*ibid.*, m. 21); Edw. of Windsor empowered to reappoint him, 14 Sept. 1325 (*C.P.R. 1324-27*, p. 174); surr. seal 2 Jan. 1327 (I.R. 217, m. 1).

*Edward*, earl of Chester.[3] Apptd. duke of Aquitaine, 10 Sept. 1325 (*Foedera*, ii, 607-8).

Oliver of Ingham, knt. Apptd. 10 Mar. 1326 (G.R. 38, m. 5).

## (2) Constables of Bordeaux

Mr. Rich. of Havering, kg.'s clk. Apptd. 28 Mar. 1305 (Bémont, *R.G.*, III, cii); entered office 22 Sept. 1305; ordered to surr. 15 Mar. 1308 (*Chapters*, vi, 67).

Mr. Jordan Morant, kg.'s clk. Apptd. 15 Mar. 1308 (G.R. 24, m. 22); entered office 11 May 1308 (*Chapters*, vi, 67); [4] ordered to surr. 6 and 8 Ap. 1309 (*ibid.*).

Amerigo dei Frescobaldi, kg.'s merchant. Apptd. 6 Ap. 1309 (G.R. 24, m. 12); his agents and property in Gascony seized 12 Oct. 1311 (*ibid.*, 25, m. 10).

[1] John of Warenne, earl of Surrey, was appointed captain of the army in Gascony until the arrival of the king's lieutenant (G.R. 36, m. 9).

[2] [John of Seagrave, sen., knt., also received letters of appointment to the post (G.R. 36, *loc. cit.*), but the appointments were alternative, and Wisham acted.]

[3] The administration was continued in the name of Edward II, who described himself on later writs as "Edwardi filii nostri primogeniti, Aquitanie ducis ac comitis Cestrie Pontiue et Montisstrolli, ac terrarum ac rerum ipsius, gubernator et administrator."

[4] [Delete reference there given to *C.P.R. 1307-13*, p. 2.]

*Ugolino Ugolini*. Apptd. his attorney 8 Ap. 1309 (G.R. 24, m. 11); in office from 29 Ap. 1309 to 9 Nov. 1311 (*Chapters*, vi, 67).

*Guelfo dei Frescobaldi*. Acting as lieut. 22 and 26 Feb. 1311 (Lubimenko, *Jean de Bretagne*, pp. 138, 140).

Mr. *John Guitard*, clk., controller of Bordeaux, and *Aubert Mège*, clk. Apptd. joint receivers, 12 Oct. 1311 (G.R. 24, m. 11).

Mr. Jordan Morant, kg.'s clk. Again apptd. constable, 1 Dec. 1311 (G.R. 25, m. 8); entered office 6 Feb. 1312 (*Chapters*, vi, 67).

Mr. *John Guitard*. Lieut. 1312-13;[1] and with Mr. *Aubert Mège* up to and after Easter 1313.

Mr. Aicard Barbe, kg.'s clk. Acctd. 4 Mar. 1314 to 1 June 1315 (Misc. Bks. Exch. T.R., 187, p. 191); still acting 2 Aug. (G.R. 30, m. 20) and 6 Oct. 1315 (*ibid.* m. 16).

Galhard de la Casa [canon of S. Sever, Bordeaux]. Const. while Passano was seneschal, i.e. 1317-18 (*C.C.R. 1330-33*, p. 513); [named as constable in a book of customs, 10 Nov. 1317 to 25 Feb. 1318 (S. from E.A. 164/12)].

Richard of Elsfield, kg.'s clk. Apptd. 6 Dec. 1318 (G.R. 32, m. 4); received protection as [staying in] Gascony, 20 July 1319 (*C.P.R. 1317-21*, p. 380); ordered to England to answer complaints, 27 July 1320 (Lehugeur, *Hist. de Philippe le Long*, p. 262).[2]

[John Hoquet. Acting during seneschalcy of Amaury de Craon, prob. soon after 15 July 1320 (S. from G.R. 35, m. 15); surr. office 9 June 1322 (Pipe roll 183, m. 58); granted 50 l. a year for service "quod impendit et impendet," 3 Feb. 1323 (S. from G.R. 35, m. 12d.)]

Adam Limber (or Lymbergh), kg.'s clk.[3] Apptd. 23 Ap. 1322 (G.R. 35, m. 15); [entered office 9 June 1322 (Pipe roll 183, m. 58); surr. office 17 July 1324 (*ibid.*)]

John Travers, kg.'s clk. Apptd. 1 Ap. 1324 (G.R. 35, m. 4); [entered office 17 July 1324 (Pipe roll 183, m. 58]; Edw. of Windsor empowered to reappt. him, 14 Sept. 1325 (*C.P.R. 1324-27*, p. 174); acting Easter term, 1326 (I.R. 218, m. 9).

Richard of Bury, kg.'s clk. Acting 19 Feb. to 16 Ap. 1326 (*C.P.R. 1330-34*, p. 383).

Mr. Aubert Mège, clk. Apptd. 12 Mar. 1326[4] (G.R. 38, m. 5); acting till John Weston, clk., apptd. 7 Feb. 1327.

[1] [The authority given for this in 1st edn. is *ibid.* (*i.e.* G.R. 4-5 Edw. II), m. 1; but I have failed to find the evidence there or in the next roll (no. 26, 6 Edw. II).]

[2] [A survey by Miss Pole Stuart and myself of Elsfield's career, with an analysis of the charges against him, has been accepted for publication by the *English Historical Review*.]

[3] [Limber's account, which gives also the dates of Hoquet's retirement and Travers' succession, is enrolled on the Pipe roll for 12 Edw. III, and was ascribed in the official printed lists of Foreign Accts. to that reign. This led Mr. Tout to omit Hoquet from his Edw. II list in 1st edn. and to insert all three in the list for Edw. III in *Chapters*, vi, 68-9. The correction has recently been made by Miss Helen M. Briggs.]

[4] [For explanation of seeming inconsistencies of dates in case of three last constables see *Chapters*, iii, 26, n. 1.]

## J.—SENESCHALS OF PONTHIEU AND MONTREUIL

RICHARD OF ROKESLE, knt. Apptd. 1 Nov. 1307 (*C.P.R. 1307-13*, p. 10); still acting 14 May 1308 (*ibid.*, p. 74).

JOHN DELAUNAY, knt. Apptd. 14 May 1309 (*ibid.*, p. 114).

JOHN LENFANT, knt. Appt. 5 Oct. 1312 (*ibid.*, p. 501); still acting 18 Sept. 1315 (*Foedera*, ii, 278).

ROBERT DE FIENNES, knt.[1] Apptd. 25 Aug. 1316 (*C.P.R. 1313-17*, p. 539); ordered to surr. 15 Aug. 1320 (*C.P.R. 1317-21*, p. 502).

JOHN DE CASTRE, knt. Apptd. 15 Aug. 1320 (*ibid.*, p. 501); still acting 30 Dec. 1322 (*C.P.R. 1321-24*, p. 231); ? deceased before 11 Aug. 1326 (*C.P.R. 1324-27*, p. 307).

Edward, earl of Chester. Made count of Ponthieu 2 Sept. 1325 (*ibid.*, p. 173); empowered to nominate a seneschal 14 Sept. 1325 (*ibid.*, p. 175).

[1] *Cf. Chapters*, v, 277-8.

# INDEX

C

## H

## I

J



K



L

Q



R

## Y